A TRAVELER'S GUIDE to the
GALAPAGOS ISLANDS

Second Edition

Barry Boyce

SAN JUAN BAUTISTA, CALIFORNIA

A TRAVELER'S GUIDE TO THE GALAPAGOS ISLANDS

Second Edition

Published by:

GALAPAGOS TRAVEL
P.O. Box 1220
San Juan Bautista
CA 95045
(800) 969-9014

Printing: **COLORCRAFT LTD.,** Hong Kong
Typesetting/Interior & Cover Design: **HOLMES TYPOGRAPHY,** San Jose, CA
Maps: **Kathleen Neault**
　　　Authorized use by the *Instituto Geografico Militar,* Quito, Ecuador
　　　(Permit #890509-IGM-g-62561, November 7, 1989).
Photos #16, #46, and Photo of Author on Back Cover: **Dr. Elaine Heron**
Photo #7: Original Artwork by **Edgar Vargas,** Naturalist Guide, Galápagos
All Uncredited Photos: **Barry Boyce**
Front Cover: A Giant Tortoise in Slow-Motion Pursuit
Back Cover: A Squadron of Frigatebirds in Piratical Pursuit

Library of Congress Catalog Number: 93-79633

ISBN: 1-55650-640-6

CONTENTS

ACKNOWLEDGEMENTS

This is the section of a book we tend to skip over. To the reader, it's a series of names and "thank yous." True enough, and yet it should be understood that many of the "acknowledged" are volunteers, giving their time and energy to help a stranger who's nosing around while "working on a book."

Many people have answered my questions and provided information. Others have gone beyond that. Among the Tour Operators, Sr. Patricio Suarez of CANODROS made it possible for me to experience the comforts of a Cruise Ship (the GALAPAGOS EXPLORER). Dolores & Eduardo Diez and Gonzalo Fernandez of QUASAR NAUTICA introduced me to Quito and provided continual assistance in solving the difficult logistics of getting around the Galápagos. Judy Carvalhal and Captain Martin Schreyer of ANGERMEYERS ENCHANTED EXCURSIONS helped me arrange a very special trip to the western islands of Fernandina and Isabela on-board the CACHALOTE.

Among the Guides who shared their time, thanks to Ernesto Vaca, Yvonne Mortola, and Edgar Vargas, whose drawings animated the daily briefing sessions (see Photo #7). The arranging of interviews in the Galápagos was aided tremendously by the efforts of Daniel Geller and Alexandra Bahamonde of the Hotel Galápagos in Puerto Ayora.

Finally, for background information, I want to thank Johannah Barry of the *Charles Darwin Foundation* and Dr. Chantal Blanton, Director of the *Charles Darwin Research Station*. A special thanks to Dr. Linda Cayot of the Darwin Station for the thorough background on the herpetology programs of the C.D.R.S.

This section would not be complete if I didn't say, "Thank you!" to my mother Evelyn Johnson, for understanding "why I didn't call or write" for 6 months.

To Garza

CHAPTER I

THE ENCHANTED ISLES

October 8th — The natural history of these islands is eminently curious, and well deserves attention. Most of the organic productions are aboriginal creations [endemic species] found nowhere else; there is even a difference between the inhabitants of the different islands; yet all show a marked relationship with those of [South] America, though separated from that continent by an open space of ocean, between 500 and 600 miles in length. Considering the small size of these islands, we feel the more astonished at the number of their aboriginal [endemic] beings, and at their confined range. Seeing every height crowned with its crater, and the boundaries of most of the lava streams still distinct, we are led to believe that within a period, geologically recent, the unbroken ocean was here spread out. Hence, both in space and time, we seem to be brought somewhat near to that great fact, that mystery of mysteries — the first appearance of new beings on this earth.

Charles Darwin, 1845

Darwin's astute observations were to set the stage for the development of the theory of evolution by natural selection as formulated in his famous publication, **THE ORIGIN OF SPECIES**. The ideas set forth in this work remain today as one of the major breakthroughs in scientific thought, and led the way for over 150 years of biological research. In the world of science, Charles Darwin and the Galápagos Islands share a prominent location!

There are several facts about Darwin's historic journey and findings that probably come as a surprise to many of us:

1. We picture Darwin in the Galápagos sitting under a tree, scratching his white beard and carefully observing the finches that would eventually bear his name. He may well have done just that, but his beard wasn't white; when Charles Darwin visited the Galápagos Islands, he was but 26 years old.

2. We think of Darwin as one of England's "big muckity-muck" scientists, sent by England to head up an important expedition. While Darwin was

destined to become a "very big muckity-muck," when he left England on board the H.M.S. BEAGLE in 1831 at the tender age of 22, his credentials to date were not overly impressive — a drop-out of the Medical School at Edinburgh University and a noticeably uninspired divinity student. His father, Dr. Robert Darwin, clearly underwhelmed by young Charles' progress, lashed out at him on one occasion, "You care for nothing but shooting, dogs and rat-catching, and you will be a disgrace to yourself and all your family." Darwin's capacity on the BEAGLE was that of an unpaid observer. At that, he was a second choice for the position that Captain FitzRoy described as available to someone who would simply "...profit by the opportunity of visiting different countries yet little known."

3. We envision Darwin making copious notes of his observations, conducting research studies, and spending a considerable period of time on each of the major islands. The notes were copious and some research was conducted, but Charles Darwin's length of stay on the Galápagos Islands was a very brief 5 weeks (September-October, 1835). Prior to visiting the Galápagos, the crew of the BEAGLE had already spent more than 3 years surveying the shores of South America and would spend another year asea after visiting the islands.

4. We tend to picture historic spots (such as the Galápagos) as just that — an empty stadium, a bare stage, the ruins that once flourished. "Close your eyes," we say to ourselves, "and imagine the way that it was, for it was right here that it all happened." The amazing thing about the Galápagos Islands is that it's still happening. You can still see what Darwin saw, for the Galápagos is quite young and is still in the early stages of formation; the western islands (Fernandina and Isabela) are a geologically brief 500,000 years old. This is indeed a very rare opportunity, containing an element of going back in time.

This is precisely the feeling you get while touring the Galápagos Islands, located on the equator and about 600 miles off the coast of Ecuador. It begins with the misty, volcanic land-and-seascapes. The Galápagos archipelago consists of thirteen major islands and six smaller islets; in addition, it has about fifty named minor islets and rock formations protruding from its waters. From the time when they first literally broke through the ocean floor, some 3-5 million years ago, the Galápagos Islands have remained a very active site of volcanic activity; as of this writing, the most recent eruption occurred in 1988 (on Fernandina Island). While touring the Galápagos and gazing at the rugged terrain from the bow of your ship, the term "moonscape" may seem more appropriate than "landscape." Indeed, with all the black, porous volcanic rock, jagged cliff formations, fragmented boulders, lava fields, spatter cones, pit craters, and columns of gas-driven steam, as you put your feet ashore your mind echoes, "That's one small step...." It was probably this somewhat surreal view that led the early Spanish explorers to give the islands their first name, *Las Islas Encantadas* — The Enchanted Islands.

It's not only the geology of these Enchanted Islands that is timeless, but the wildlife as well. You are immediately overwhelmed by the extraordinary nature and diversity of the animals — the same wildlife that so fascinated and inspired Darwin. In terms of the giant land tortoises, some as large as 500-600 lbs., there is a possibility (granted, a very small one) that you are looking at quite literally the same animal that Darwin saw; it is generally thought that these gentle giants live upwards of 125 years! With the facial features that were actually used to create the visage of **E.T.**, the giant tortoises themselves seem to be of another world. Watching their careful, slow motion crash-steps does little to diminish this feeling.

Another Galápagos creature seemingly of another time (some would say prehistoric) is the marine iguana. Often seen in a most curious (some would say bizarre) frozen pose atop lava rocks, the marine iguana is actually sunbathing to raise its body temperature after a dive in the Pacific Ocean. The marine iguana is a competent diver and swimmer, the only lizard to have achieved this ability. While warming itself, it will frequently spout forth or sneeze (some would say spit) brine out of efficient salt-excreting glands located in the nostrils.

The oddities of Galápagos wildlife are not limited to the reptiles; the birds have their share of interesting characters as well. Here you will see penguins on the equator and the flightless cormorants, who have traded their ability to fly for a streamlined body to assist their swimming prowess. You will see courting blue-footed boobies elaborately gather nesting materials only to apparently ignore such niceties, as the eggs are laid and incubated directly on the ground.

As you've gathered, things are a little different on the Galápagos. With isolation comes change, and on these islands, both the isolation and the adaptations have been extreme and therefore quite noticeable. This is what caught Darwin's eye so quickly and will catch yours as well.

Isolation has several interesting aspects to it, which will be discussed throughout this book. One truly fascinating aspect is the isolation from predators, including that noteworthy predator, man himself. As a result, the animals on the Galápagos have not learned or adapted themselves to flee or shy away when approached. One can get to within arms length distance of many of the Galápagos animals, and amazingly they will not dash or fly off. This experience is a constant source of pleasure and amazement, and it's one that is very difficult for many of us to get used to. We are very accustomed to slowly approaching an animal, camera in hand, using very powerful telephoto lenses to cut down the distance. It is not necessary to do this on the Galápagos, and the picture taking opportunities are unbelievable — to the point that you will shoot 2-3 times more than your usual daily quota (see Chapter V, PHOTOGRAPHING THE GALAPAGOS ISLANDS).

Some animals will not wait for you to approach them; they will approach you! I will never forget my first swim in the Galápagos, when I felt something zoom past me in the water. I quickly turned, and through my snorkel mask saw a huge black fin swerve and come back straight at me! After I audibly shuddered and took in a mouthful of water, I realized it was a sea lion. From that time on, I had my little yellow underwater camera ready, and the naturally playful Galápagos sea lions did not fail to perform; they would continuously be streaking by, sometimes two at a time (see Photo #15), almost but not quite touching me. This endless performance is awaiting your arrival.

Another animal that will approach, but not as predictably, is the bottle-nosed dolphin. Before describing this encounter, however, it would be worthwhile to point out how your Galápagos adventure will be spent. You will be touring the islands for 1-2 weeks on-board a boat with a full crew, including a Guide who has been trained at the *Charles Darwin Research Station* in the Galápagos. These boats will do the bulk of their travel at night, so your valuable daylight hours are actually spent on the islands with your Guide, exploring and photographing the wildlife. There is a wide range of boats to choose from — 4-6 passenger sailing yachts, 6-16 passenger motor yachts, and 34-90 passenger Cruise Ships (see Chapter IV, CHOOSING A TOUR).

You will often visit two islands (or two distinct parts of the same island) per day, so there is usually about a 1-2 hour cruise right after lunch. This time of day would usually find me lying on deck, up close to the bow, digesting lunch, reading up on the wildlife to be seen that afternoon, and catching a cool spray. On one such occasion, I became aware of a splashing sound close by. I turned my head, and there was a bottle-nosed dolphin leaping through the water right alongside the boat. Then I heard another splash, turned, and sure enough, there was another dolphin on the opposite side of the boat. When I stood up and looked around, there were dolphins in the distance in almost every direction, leaping towards the boat from a distance as if dashing homeward on the run after hearing the dinner bell. Eventually several of the dolphins would get alongside the boat and keep up with us, taking turns leaping (although there were several pairs that seemed to leap in tandem). If that wasn't enough excitement, I looked down right in front of the bow and there were two dolphins leading the way for our boat; I found out later that this activity is called "piloting" or "riding the bow wave."

The first time this happened, I didn't have my camera on deck; fortunately I had two other chances (see Photo #6). In fact, from that time on, I kept my camera handy, even when eating meals, and was rewarded for doing so. In the Galápagos, your curiosity is almost always rewarded!

If the cartographers on board the BEAGLE actually surveyed the archipelago, it was Charles Darwin that put the Galápagos Islands on the map! After Darwin's historic visit and his subsequent published observations, a great deal of scientific research has been conducted on the Galápagos. For the general public, however, the Galápagos was virtually inaccessible — difficult and expensive to get to, and (until the late 1960s) with no real facilities and means by which the tourist could comfortably see the islands. Also, the interest in the natural universe and issues such as wildlife conservation were not as widespread as they are today. Such issues were certainly not foremost in the minds of many of the early visitors to the Galápagos — the pirates and whalers; more about them later (in the History section of the next Chapter).

The Galápagos will inspire you in many of the same ways as it did Darwin, and your understanding of the natural world will take on a different perspective once you have visited these Enchanted Islands. When you get back home, you will be obliged to creatively express these thoughts and feelings. You will show your photos time and again, carefully explaining each shot. You may wind up writing songs (how about *The Sea Lion Serenade*), come up with new recipes (perhaps *Fettuccine Alcedo*), maybe even write a book! Whatever you do, your attitude about vacations and how to spend them will be forever changed.

CHAPTER II

ABOUT
THE GALAPAGOS ISLANDS

Before we begin a discussion of the climate, origin, and history of the Galápagos Islands, it would be worthwhile to point out a subject of some confusion — the names of the islands themselves. As we shall see when the history of the islands are discussed, the Galápagos were used as a haven of refuge by English buccaneers long before the islands were annexed by Ecuador in 1832. These nautical soldiers of fortune were patriotic and named the islands after British nobility — kings, dukes, earls, lords, admirals, captains, etc. In one case, Indefatigable (Santa Cruz), an island was named after a British ship. After the 1832 annexation, the islands were given Spanish names of like origin. Then in 1892, the islands were officially renamed in honor of the 400th anniversary of Columbus' first voyage and discovery of the Americas (he didn't just discover North America). To make matters worse, there have been other names given to the islands by the British, Spanish, and United States Navies. Some of these names have stuck. The result is that several of the islands have at least three names and some as many as eight!

Actually it's not that bad. For the purposes of touring the Galápagos, nine of the fifteen islands and islets you are likely to visit are commonly referred to by only one name. Of the remaining six, only two names are generally used. The confusion will come from reading some of the literature which tries to "help" the tourist by referring to the English-sounding names. Thus, you may read about Albemarle Island, even though it is almost always referred to as Isabela. I will attempt to use the most common name of an island throughout this book. This could be either a Spanish or English name. As an example, I will refer to Santa Cruz Island and not to the English name, Indefatigable. When two versions are commonly used, I will refer to the most common name first, occasionally followed by the second name in parenthesis. Thus, I will refer to Española (Hood) Island. If an island is mentioned several times in a particular section, the name in parenthesis will be omitted after the first reference.

CLIMATE

Considering that these islands are placed directly under the equator, the climate is far from being excessively hot; this seems chiefly caused by the singularly low temperature of the surrounding water, brought here by the great southern Polar current. Excepting during one short season, very little rain falls, and even then it is irregular; but the clouds generally hang low. Hence, whilst the lower parts of the islands are very sterile, the upper parts, at a height of a thousand feet and upwards, possess a damp climate and a tolerable luxuriant vegetation. This is especially the case on the windward sides of the islands, which first receive and condense the moisture from the atmosphere....

Charles Darwin, 1845

Darwin said it all. One of the keys to understanding the Galápagos is the climate. The islands are isolated (by several hundred miles of ocean), so the climate is determined almost entirely by the ocean currents, which in turn are influenced by the trade winds which push the currents. The Galápagos is a major intersection of several currents, which vary in intensity during the year as their driving trade winds blow and then weaken in a cycle that gives two distinct seasons to the islands. These currents also control the pattern and variety of Galápagos plant and animal life. Let's see how it works and fits together.

We'll start with the chain of food. Many of the Galápagos animals depend on the ocean for food. Several birds, the sea lions, and fur seals eat a variety of small fish and squid, which in turn, feed on plant life near the surface. The question is, "How do all these plants grow near the ocean surface, well out from shore?" The answer is that in most places in the world, they don't. For plants to grow, they of course need sunlight and nutrients (fertilizer material — phosphates and nitrates). In the natural state, these nutrients are produced by decomposition of organic materials (as in a compost pile or on a forest floor). The problem is that in the ocean, these organic materials sink to the bottom. So you have an ocean floor that is rich in nutrients, but where there is little or no light. On the surface, you have plenty of light but no nutrients. Consequently, there's not much plant growth, unless somehow the waters are churned up, effectively pumping the nutrients to the surface. As long as this pump was left on, there would be constant plant growth at the surface, providing the fish and squid with a continuous supply of food — plankton. There are actually a few places in the world where nature has engineered such a pumping system. This system is called the process of upwelling, and it occurs in the waters of the Galápagos for a good part of most years. Upwelling frequently occurs when two or more current systems converge in the proximity of land, thus agitating the waters and bringing the rich nutrients to the surface. There are many such current systems intersecting in the Galápagos, and a complete analysis is quite complex.

Let's simplify it a bit, starting with the Humboldt Current (sometimes referred to as the "Peru"). For most of the year, the cold Humboldt sweeps northward from the waters of the Antarctic, hugging the coast of South America. While the coastline changes contour at the northern tip of Peru, the

Humboldt (pushed by trade winds from the southeast) keeps on its original northwesterly course, arching its way across the Pacific, heading right for the Galápagos Islands, and washing the archipelago with cool water (about 68 Deg F).

The mass of cold water cools the air as well, and an inversion layer is formed. What's an inversion layer? Normally, the higher the elevation, the colder the air. But here you have this huge body of cold water that's going to cool the air directly above it. The result is that you have warm air sitting on top of the cooled surface air — an inversion. This process continues until an equilibrium is reached; on the Galápagos, this occurs at 1000-2000 ft above sea level, the height of the inversion layer where the warm air is trapped.

The inversion layer does a couple of things. First, it contains a heavy concentration of moisture droplets that have evaporated from the ocean. Some of the islands have highland areas that intercept the inversion layer and condense this moisture. A continuous mist is formed, called a *garúa*.

The inversion layer also upsets the usual weather pattern associated with the tropics — blue skies and afternoon showers. Thus, while the highland areas are kept lush and green by the *garúa* mist, the lowland areas of these islands (as well as entire low elevation islands) are bone dry. This then is the dry (or cool) season; oddly enough, it is called the *garúa* season, even though *garúa* itself is a form of precipitation.

The *garúa* season usually lasts from July to December; it is around December when the southeast trade winds slacken, no longer driving the Humboldt Current toward the Galápagos. This allows the warm waters of the Panama Current, flowing south and once again heading right at the Galápagos, to be dominant. Thus, the island waters are warmed (to about 78 Deg F), no longer cooling the air to a significant degree, and the inversion layer breaks up. The tropical weather pattern now asserts itself with rain cloud formation and daily shower activity. This is the rainy (or warm) season, typically lasting from January-June. The oddity here is that the highland areas receive more moisture from the *garúa* during the dry season than they do from rainfall during the wet season.

That's the way things usually work. Some years, however, the southeast trade winds are a "no show," causing the Panama Current to drastically warm the waters of the Galápagos. This phenomenon is called an *El Niño*, which is Spanish for "the child" because the condition begins around Christmas. The good news is that there is lots of rain, which the islands always need, and also lots of vegetation growth. The very bad news is that a very critical part of the food chain is broken, due to the lack of upwelling activity. In the extreme *El Niño* of 1982-83, when the water temperature rose to 84 Deg F, the food shortage had a serious impact on several Galápagos animals. The fur seals were hit very hard; almost all animals 1-4 years of age died off, and large male bulls were also killed (not being able to recover weight lost in territorial defense). The sea lions, able to dive deeper for their food, fared a bit better, but also recorded significant losses. Many sea birds of the Galápagos were adversely affected by the *El Niño* , especially the flightless cormorants and the Galápagos penguins, who could not attempt a winged escape from the food shortage. The marine iguanas switched to a diet of a different type of algae, but unfortunately the new food source had little digestible nutrient value. The result was that they literally starved on a full stomach of food. To us humans, nature does not always appear to be kind.

FORMATION

Seeing every height crowned with its crater, and the boundaries of most of the lava streams still distinct, we are led to believe that within a period, geologically recent, the unbroken ocean was here spread out.

Charles Darwin, 1845

The Galápagos Islands are volcanic in origin and appear to have been formed about 3-5 million years ago, geologically very recent. These volcanoes formed under the sea, broke through the ocean floor, grew in size, and eventually emerged, rising from the surface of the water and becoming islands. Each island formed from a single volcano with the exception of Isabela, a lava-welded union of six volcanoes. The eastern islands (the oldest is Española) seem to be significantly older than those on the west, with the rocks on Isabela and Fernandina Islands being less than 1 million years old. This is consistent with the "hot spot" theory of Galápagos Island formation.

In this case, the term "hot spot" doesn't refer to the popularity of the islands. Almost all the world's volcanic areas are over the boundary lines (called margins) between the relatively thin plates that make up the surface crust of the earth. Not so for the Galápagos, which instead seems to be directly over a "hot spot," a region of intense heat in the earth's mantle (the transition zone between the inner core and the outer crust), which is hot enough to burn through the crust, forming a volcano. As the plates are moving at a fixed rate (about 3 inches per year), a string of volcanoes is formed. Because of their underwater origin, the material forming the volcano builds and accumulates, spreading out like a sand hill. This gives rise to a gentle sloping shape with a central vent, which is characteristic (and the name origin) of what is called a *shield volcano.*

Today, the Galápagos are among the world's most active volcanic areas; there have been over fifty eruptions in the last 200 years, some quite recently. These events have been on the two westernmost islands, Isabela and Fernandina; their six active volcanoes are still being fed by the "hot spot" (only the Ecuador Volcano on Isabela Island is no longer active). That these are active volcanoes is evidenced by the columns of steam and gas (*fumaroles*) which the western island visitor can see rising from the Alcedo and Sierra Negra Volcanoes on Isabela.

Part of what makes visiting the islands so fascinating is that they are in the early phase of their development. Aside from the eruptions, the recent activity list is long and continues to grow. In 1954, almost 4 miles of the coastal seabed of Urvina Bay, Isabela Island were dramatically and suddenly uplifted about 15 ft. These *uplifts*, as they are called, occur frequently, but not as dramatically. Many of the islands themselves are uplifts, formed by the flow of molten rock inside the earth (*magma*) through a subsurface geological fissure (or fault). The magma exits the fissure as lava, hardening and gradually lifting the "land" mass through and past the ocean surface. Uplifts are typically associated with a previous or impending eruption. As the magma beneath the summit of a volcano cools and contracts, the entire peak may collapse inward to form a large, bowl-like depression called a *caldera*. In 1968, the Fernandina Island caldera collapsed, dropping about 1000 ft in 2 weeks, an event accompanied by hundreds of earthquakes.

The volcanic features are fascinating. On James (Santiago) Island, two distinct lava patterns can be seen — the smooth, rope-like *pahoehoe* (Hawaiian for "ropey" and pronounced pa-hoy-hoy), and the rough, broken *aa* (pronounced "ah-ah"). Also, across from James, on Bartolomé Island, is probably the most famous (and most photographed) landmark in the Galápagos, Pinnacle Rock, a remnant of what is known as a *tuff cone*. Tuff cones are interesting vertical rock formations of volcanic origin which are a consolidation of hardened ash particles (*tuff*). During an eruption, as the hot lava poured into the cold water, explosions would occur. Pockets and fragments would be sent flying in all directions and come spattering down to the ground, hardening into a cone shape. Not surprisingly, some of these formations are termed *cinder cones* and *spatter cones*.

Often, as the lava flowed, the exterior portion cooled and hardened even as the molten material continued to flow in the interior. When the lava flow abated, there was not enough liquid to fill the inner cavity, and a tunnel was formed (called a *lava tube* or *lava tunnel*). Several excellent examples exist in the Highlands of Santa Cruz Island, where a "climb down and walk through" tour is available; miner's lanterns are provided for these excursions (see the section on Santa Cruz Island in Chapter IX). When a lava flow subsides, the surface features that are directly over pockets of magma are somewhat unstable, causing depressions called *pit craters*; these are formed in the same fashion as a caldera, but are not located over a central vent. Most visitors to the Santa Cruz Highlands see the pair of giant pit craters called *Los Gemelos* (The Twins).

For a closer look at a volcano, special tours are offered (on 2 week Galápagos vacations) to the rim of the Alcedo Volcano, with spectacular views of the caldera (4 miles by 5 miles across) and the surrounding countryside, including the largest population of giant tortoises in the wild. Hikes to the Sierra Negra Volcano are also available (see the section on Isabela Island in Chapter IX).

As harsh and rough as this volcanic terrain may appear, it is also very fragile; the weight of a single tourist stepping off the trail to "get a better shot," can break apart the low density, crusty-looking rock. It is not a matter of administration and procedures that requires visitors to stay on the trails with their Guide; it's a matter of preservation.

THE ARRIVAL OF LIFE

As you tour the Galápagos, noting the richness of the wildlife, the question arises, "How did they get here?" Indeed, 600 miles is a long way to swim, fly, or even just to "hang on, baby!" Actually, some of these voyages may have been made from Central America, which puts the distance closer to 1000 miles. In either case, transportation was a formidable obstacle, and only a very small number of mainland plant and animal species were able to make this journey.

Initially there were only the bacteria, algae, and fungi, providing the beginnings of an organic base for the higher species. The next generation of flora consisted largely of plants with small, lightweight seeds and spores which could be wind-borne over long distances or digested intact and carried aloft by sea birds. Some seeds would actually stick to the feathers and wings of the sea birds. Having reached the Galápagos, the next problem was short-term survival. To be successful, the first plants had to have the ability to take root and grow without a lot of organic material. These *pioneers* or *colonizers*, as they are called, include lichens and mosses, followed by ferns and grasses — flora that not only would survive, but also provide the humus for future species of plant life in the Galápagos. On several islands, principally the more-recent Isabela and Fernandina, certain locations are still in the "pioneering" stage.

Some seedlings could be transported by the ocean, being steered to the archipelago by the currents. You may remember from our discussion of the climate that the currents are driven by trade winds in the direction of the Galápagos. Thus (as the recorded history well documents), unpowered vessels and their passengers, willing or not, are carried from the mainland to the Galápagos Islands, a voyage lasting about 2 weeks (4 weeks from Central America). Several such vessels were seedlings of the red mangrove, with the ability to float in the ocean, root in the mud, immediately take hold, and grow. In addition, the red mangrove has a root system that filters out salt, allowing the leaves to receive fresh water.

Other ocean passengers making the voyage from Central and South America to the Galápagos were animals. Reptiles, whose vessels were rafts of tangled vegetation, were able to survive the journey due to their ability to fast for long periods of time. No amphibians or land mammals, with the exception of a few species of rats, were able to survive the rigors of such an ocean passage; they are thus noticeably absent from the list of species indigenous (native) to the Galápagos.

There were those that could cross the ocean on their own power. Aside from the fish that swim the waters of the Galápagos, this group includes the sea turtles, penguins, and marine mammals — the sea lions, fur seals, and dolphins.

Not everyone had to take the ocean route; sea birds and shore birds had the ability to arrive by air. Land birds would either have to get caught up in a gust and be borne along by an exceptionally strong tail wind or take the ocean crossing, perched on a branch or perhaps in a tree hollow.

SHORT-TERM SURVIVAL

Now isolated, the struggle for survival began. For the early arrivals, it was a long shot. On islands comprised of volcanic rock, the odds certainly were not very high that a seed would land or be dropped in a crevice or other precise location in which there was a bit of soil and moisture sufficient for germination. And what if it were a flowering plant that depended on insects for pollination. Well, those insects weren't on the islands at that time (for the most part they still aren't), so that plant species wouldn't make it past the first generation.

It wasn't much easier for the animals, especially for the terrestrial species. If there wasn't any food to eat, they couldn't swim or fly away. Even if they were fortunate enough to find food, they still had to perpetuate their own kind for their species to survive in the islands. Remember, these animals didn't arrive on

Noah's Ark. There was no voluntary decision on their part to improve their lot in life, pack their bags, and head for the Galápagos. They were most likely caught up in a storm or flood; perhaps the piece of land beneath them broke off and fell into the waters. One second they were on land, and the next they were on an organic raft, just hanging on. Considering these circumstances, it's not too likely that a male and female of the same species would arrive together on such a raft, or even arrive at the same island during each other's fertile lifetime. There just aren't that many floods per lifetime. Rafts of tangled vegetation are rarely around when you really need them, and, in general, they tend not to be very seaworthy. Finally, the currents and prevailing trade winds are not anywhere near precise enough to get many rafts to the same island.

Even for the sea birds, who can fly where they will, conditions must be ideal for them to colonize a particular island — conditions such as vegetation, proximity to and abundance of food, availability of nesting materials, as well as climate. One island will be selected, and the neighboring islands avoided. Even today, almost all the red-footed booby colonies in the Galápagos are found on Tower (Genovesa) Island, and nearly the entire world population of waved albatrosses nest on Española (Hood) Island.

The odds weren't high for any particular plant or animal species surviving the first generation of arivees, but the factor of time enters into the equation. If the odds are one in a million, all you have to do is take a million chances. Drop a seed a day for a million days; eventually a seed is deposited in the perfect location, germinates, and grows. Land a tortoise a year on a given island for a million years; eventually, you'll get a mating pair, or a pregnant female will arrive. Future generations will eventually germinate, hatch, or be born. Sooner or later, the process of immediate survival is won. The process of long-term survival, however, is just beginning.

EVOLUTION AND NATURAL SELECTION

The long-term future outlook for a plant in the Galápagos is a lot brighter if the original seed happens to be that of a tolerant weed. A newly-arrived animal species is more likely to stay around for a few thousand years if it can stand the arid climatic conditions of the islands. Those plants and animals that were naturally well-suited for their new home had a greater chance of surviving, and those that survived the longest had more opportunities to reproduce their own kind. A look at the distribution of species in the Galápagos shows a high proportion of salt-tolerant plants and drought-resistant animals.

Some of these species had these desirable traits on arrival. Others, however, acquired these characteristics over many generations. This required a change or differentiation from the mainland parent population.

Some changes occurred quite rapidly. First, remember that we're talking about small numbers of arivees, which greatly increases the chances of a nonrepresentative population to begin with. The traits we're discussing are those such as strength, aggressiveness, fertility, pigmentation, intelligence, etc. Breeding will reproduce these traits, genetically transmitting the nonrepresentative characteristics to future generations, causing an immediate significant differentiation from the mainland population. Second, genetic mutations will also have a greater chance of impacting a small population, causing further differentiation. Finally, bear in mind that thus far we're talking about short-term random differences in that these traits may not necessarily be for better or for worse from a long term survival point of view.

Now here's where it begins to get interesting. If "survival of the fittest" was certainly true in terms of one species of plant or animal being more likely to survive versus another, wasn't it also true for individuals within a species? If a male lava lizard just happened to have the same coloration as the dark lava on which he lived, he probably would live longer and thus mate more often. As a result, his pigmentation gene would be transmitted more often. His progeny would multiply this effect, with those that had his protective coloring living longer, mating more often, etc. It seems basic to us now, but remember that in Darwin's day, the laws of Mendelian genetics had not been formally proposed to the scientific community. It wasn't until 1900, some 16 years after Gregor Mendel's death, that the relevance of his work was widely recognized.

Darwin's genius was in understanding that the variations he observed were non-random positive adaptations to the environment that could somehow be passed on through inheritance.

> *If variations useful to any being do occur, assuredly individuals thus characterised will have the best chance of being preserved in the struggle for life; and from the strong principle of inheritance, they will tend to produce offspring similarly characterised. This principle of preservation, I have called, for the sake of brevity, Natural Selection.*
>
> *Charles Darwin, 1859*

One species eventually becomes another; in evolutionary language, this is termed *descent with modification*. The marine iguana, once a land dweller, is now the world's only seagoing lizard, complete with specialized nasal glands that excrete (sneeze) salt. The flightless cormorants gradually exchanged their ability to fly for a streamlined body to assist their swimming prowess. These are not random changes of minimal importance that die out after a few generations; these are long-term adaptive modifications and can truly be termed as evolution at work.

Darwin called the Galápagos Islands a "living laboratory of evolution," a term often used today to describe the archipelago. What he meant was that the isolation, confined habitats, and the comparatively small number of species combine to give the observer a clear view of the adaptive processes. Our understanding of the laws of genetics, of the ways in which isolation statistically stuffs the genetic ballot box, makes Darwin's phrase all the more appropriate.

ADAPTIVE RADIATION

Darwin saw many examples in the Galápagos of one species eventually becoming another. What was especially surprising to him, and led him to the inescapable conclusion that adaptive processes were at work, was that one species eventually became several, based on their habitat. The term used to describe this phenomena is *adaptive radiation*, and the most famous example is the Galápagos finch. As a result of Darwin's work, these birds now bear his name and are called Darwin's finches. What Darwin saw were thirteen distinct finch species, each closely resembling each other in most ways, yet each had a characteristic beak structure well suited to a particular (specialized) food source. There were those with long, pointed beaks for feeding on cactus flowers (the cactus finch), stout beaks for breaking hard seeds (medium and large ground finches), parrot-shaped beaks for breaking up twigs to get at insect larvae (the large tree finch), and small sharp beaks for removing ticks from tortoises and iguanas (the small ground finch). The woodpecker and mangrove finches seemingly couldn't wait to develop a beak large and pointed enough to poke for grubs through decayed and dead wood; a beak extension was borrowed in the form of a twig or cactus spine. This is a very rare instance (except for primates) where tool-using skills have actually evolved.

It was the finches that clinched it for Darwin. They obviously were of the same parent population and yet they were distinct in a way that was inarguably purposeful and adaptive.

> *The most curious fact is the perfect gradation in the size of the beaks in the different species. One might really fancy that from an original paucity of birds in this archipelago, one species had been taken and modified for different ends.*
>
> *Charles Darwin, 1845*

What was remarkable was the relatively short time that these evolved changes took place. Equally remarkable to Darwin was the fact that many of the islands, though often within just a few miles of each other, had their own unique species of the same plant or animal.

> *The distribution of the tenants of this archipelago would not be nearly so wonderful, if for instance, one island had a mocking-thrush and a second island some other quite distinct species; — if one island had its genus of lizard and a second island another distinct genus, or none whatever. But it is the circumstance, that several of the islands possess their own species of the tortoise, mocking-thrush, finches, and numerous plants, these species having the same general habits, occupying analogous situations, and obviously filling the same place in the natural economy of this archipelago, that strikes me with wonder.*
>
> *Charles Darwin, 1845*

Thus, the finch is not the only example of adaptive radiation on the Galápagos. The giant tortoise had evolved into fourteen subspecies (of which eleven remain), many with differences in the shape of the shell (called a *carapace*). These differences were most useful and therefore adaptive in nature. The saddle-back tortoises have a carapace with an elevated front end;

this, combined with their long necks and ability to stand on their hind legs, enables them to reach for branches and cactus pads on the drier islands with no grasses — Española, for example. Other tortoises have dome-shaped carapaces, giving them a shorter profile and blunt front end, useful for pushing through the dense brush often found on islands with lush highlands, such as Santa Cruz and Isabela.

Other examples of adaptive radiation include the iguana (forming a land and marine species) and the fourteen species of prickly pear cactus (*opuntia*), with some actually evolving into tall trees to better compete for the sunlight and partially avoid being munched on by hungry tortoises and land iguanas.

ENDEMISM

Due to the serious transportation and short-term survival problems discussed earlier, there are relatively few species of plants and animals in the Galápagos. There are less than 600 species of plants on the islands, compared to the 20,000 or so on mainland Ecuador. There are but twenty-two species of reptiles, less than 100 bird species (including migrants), about 400 species of fish, and strikingly, only six *indigenous* (native or non-introduced) mammals (dolphins not included).

Not surprisingly, the evolutionary process has resulted in a large percentage of plant and animal species found nowhere else in the world, termed by the scientific community as a high rate of *endemism*. Thus, of the 600 species of plants, fully one-third are endemic to the islands. Of the fish, about 20 percent of the inshore species are endemic to the waters of the archipelago. Most noteworthy is that of all the land-based animals, including reptiles, mammals, and land birds, over 80 percent are endemic to the Galápagos Islands.

Not only are many of the plant and animal species endemic to the Galápagos, but many are only found on particular islands of the archipelago. This fact was not lost on Darwin:

> By far the most remarkable feature in the natural history of this archipelago... is, that the different islands to a considerable extent are inhabited by a different set of beings. I never dreamed that islands, about fifty or sixty miles apart, and most of them in sight of each other, formed of precisely the same rocks, placed under a quite similar climate, rising to a nearly equal height, would have been differently tenanted....

> Charles Darwin, 1845

An interesting concept in the evolutionary process is that of the *niche*, defined as a functional role in a bio-community. Since the Galápagos is species poor, certain roles are assumed by unlikely players. Take the case of the saddle-back tortoise. It is said that this reptilian species evolved to fill an available niche (an opportunity or open position) for a "reacher," as the usual niche-holders, tall mammals, did not exist in the Galápagos. In a similar fashion, the absence of a bonafide woodpecker left open a niche, which was filled rather quickly and interestingly by the woodpecker finch.

If the niche concept seems a bit anthropomorphic, think of it in genetic terms. The first trace of a saddle-back on a tortoise was most likely a mutation, a chance occurrence. The features were probably not very pronounced, although it did enable the tortoise to get at food that the others couldn't. Thus, the animal was more likely to survive, live longer, mate more often, and as a result, have a higher probability of transmitting this mutated trait. In the same manner, the saddle-back features would tend to become more enhanced in successive generations.

The key here was that the food was available. If the tall mammals were present, and/or an abundance of the particular food supply wasn't, the chance saddle-back feature would not have had the enhanced (statistical) opportunities of appearing in future generations.

HISTORY

Even a casual study of the history of the Galápagos archipelago reveals several dominant themes; as a point of orientation, they are worthy of mention.

1. Isolation. There are almost no other islands off the western coast of South America and no easy means of rapid communication with the outside world.

2. Strong currents. Many underpowered vessels (generally due to light wind conditions) were carried from the Central or South American coastal waters to the Galápagos.

3. Inaccessibility. Despite the natural tendency of a boat to drift in the direction of the Galápagos, access to the islands has been for the most part difficult due to their remote location.

4. Strategic location. The Galápagos Islands are an ideally-located supply port and lie directly in the entrance path of the Panama Canal. These facts were not lost on the major international powers.

5. Arid conditions. Many visitors arrived in search of water; most of the early arrivals failed in this quest. A seemingly disproportionate number came to Floreana Island, due to the known water supply.

6. Sanctuary. The Galápagos was thought of and used as a haven by many; most were disappointed with the reality of the harsh life.

7. Exploitation. The influence of man has brought several wildlife species, most notably the giant tortoise, sperm whale, and fur seal, to the point of extinction.

8. Unprofitability. Repeated attempts at commercial use of the islands have met with failure. Tourism is proving to be the sole exception.

9. Surrealistic image. The islands have always been perceived as a blend of the angelic and the demonic. Some have literally translated Las Islas Encantadas to mean "the Bewitched Islands."

The Galápagos Islands are often referred to as Darwin's "living laboratory of evolution." Thus, one is likely to imagine a history filled with scientific observation and experimentation with a little quiet contemplation thrown in. While this has been the recent emphasis, the history of the Galápagos reads more like a combined swashbuckling tale of the high seas, a story of men behind bars, and a murder mystery (unsolved to this very day). Let's take a look back in time and see how these seemingly disparate pieces fit together.

EARLY HISTORY

According to historians, the Galápagos Islands were probably first discovered by the Incas in the 1400s. Despite their refined culture, industrious nature, architectural knowledge, and craftsmanly skills, the Incas did not have a written language; documentation is therefore lacking. In terms of recorded history, the Galápagos were officially and accidentally discovered in 1535 by the Bishop of Panama, Fray Tomás de Berlanga. This was at the time of the Spanish conquest of South America, and word had gotten back to King Charles V of Spain that his conquistadors were, to be kind, overzealous in their behavior. Ruthless, barbarous, and brutal are words more commonly used to describe the actions of Francisco Pizarro and his men. At any rate, the Bishop was dispatched to Peru from Panama to look into the situation. Though a safe route was chosen, hugging the coast of South America, the ship began to drift out to sea when a calm descended. Almost out of drinking water, they finally sighted land. The crew dropped anchor and went ashore. Later, in a letter written to the King, Bishop Berlanga described in some detail the sea lions, iguanas, and, in particular, the vast quantity of giant tortoises that they came upon. But they didn't find what they were looking for — water. They finally gave up the search and, thinking they were within 100 miles of Peru, sailed back to the mainland, blending the remaining water into the supply of wine. Despite their thirst, they reached the mainland in not altogether bad spirits. The islands that they encountered were described as uninhabitable, incapable of sustaining life. In was in this manner then, that the Galápagos Islands were officially discovered.

The Bishop's report was relayed to a Flemish cartographer, Abraham Ortelius, who included the islands in his atlas, **ORBIS TERRARUM**, published in 1574. The islands were called *Insulae de los Galopegos*, the "Islands of the Tortoises." The Galápagos Islands could now be called as such.

The islands had another name as well. In 1546, a group of Spanish soldiers, at odds with Pizarro and his harsh ways, were forced to flee South America. Having no charts to guide them, they went with the currents which, of course, led them to the Galápagos. Several of their landing attempts were thwarted by the swirling currents, pushing them out of sight of the island. These soldiers had little, if any, scientific or nautical training; peering through the mist and losing sight of the eerie-looking volcanic land, they concluded that the island was drifting. Surely, they thought, the islands were bewitched (enchanted); these must be *Las Islas Encantadas*.

The Galápagos were eventually to receive a third name. In 1892, the 400th anniversary of the first voyage of Christopher Columbus (*Cristóbal Colón* in Spanish), the Galápagos Islands were officially renamed by the *National Assembly of Ecuador* as the *Archipelago de Colón*. The "official" name, for all practical purposes, is not used.

THE BUCCANEERS

Columbus' discovery had a more immediate effect. In 1493, influenced by the knowledge of the New World to the west, the Spanish Pope Alexander VI granted to Spain what amounted to the entire western hemisphere. This Papal Bull, as it was called, was understandably not met with overwhelming approval (and its name, therefore, had another interpretation) in Great Britain, the Netherlands, and France. While an act of war was not declared, the word was that these countries would not punish any of their citizens who took private action against Spain. At sea, such citizens were called buccaneers, sometimes referred to as pirates.

The difference between a buccaneer and a pirate is not all that obvious and depends on the circumstances. In times of cold war, as between Great

Britain and Spain during a good portion of the 1500s and 1600s, if you robbed a Spanish ship, the British said you were a buccaneer; if you captured a British ship, however, they accused you of being a pirate. During times of war, some of the buccaneers were pressed into service as privateers.

The western coast of South America was buccaneer territory. The prizes sought after were Spanish treasure ships carrying the vast sums of money (from Spain) required to purchase supplies and meet payroll for the forces and staff in South America. In between attacks, the buccaneers made for the haven of the Galápagos, recuperated, and fed on the giant tortoises. One of these British buccaneers, William Ambrose Cowley, drew the first navigational charts of the Galápagos. Cowley, the patriot that he was, also named several islands after British royalty at the time, including [King] Charles (Floreana), [King] James (Santiago), [the Duke of] Albemarle (Isabela), and [Admiral] Narborough (Fernandina).

This is not to say that the majority of the buccaneers were cartographers, quietly enjoying a cup of coffee while trying to decide which English duke or admiral should be honored with an island bearing his name. Many of these guys were pretty ruthless, and in general they were a tough lot. They didn't just seek out treasure ships either; many a port city, including Guayaquil on the coast of mainland Ecuador, was regularly sacked by this bunch.

When the buccaneers didn't have anyone else to fight, they fought each other. Many such battles, including mutinies, are well documented. The vanquished party, if still alive, was usually marooned. One such castaway was Alexander Selkirk, marooned for over 4 years on Juan Fernandez Island (off the coast of Chile). Upon his rescue by a British buccaneering ship, Selkirk took part in a raid on Guayaquil and retreated with the crew to the Galápagos. There he instructed his mates on the finer points of living off the land. The ship's captain, Woodes Rogers, was intrigued by the man, and included the story of Selkik's solitary existence in **A CRUISING VOYAGE ROUND THE WORLD**, published in 1712. Based on this account, Selkirk became the model for **ROBINSON CRUSOE**, written by Daniel Defoe.

THE WHALERS

As the nineteenth century began, Spain's world power was declining. South America began to trade with England and France; buccaneers were now considered pirates and no longer welcome. In their place, the waters were soon filled with boats of another kind — whaling ships.

This was the age of the Industrial Revolution, and oil was in short supply. The oil that was used at this time did not come from under the ground; it came from the ocean, courtesy of the whale. After hearing several buccaneers describe the vast quantity of sperm whales off the western coast of South America, the British sent a ship into these waters in 1792 to explore the whaling potential. The captain, James Colnett, spent a considerable time in the Galápagos, making up-to-date charts and naming several islands, including [Lord] Chatham (San Cristóbal), [Admiral] Hood (Española), [Admiral] Barrington (Santa Fe), and [Admiral] Jervis (Rábida). Floreana Island was described by Captain Colnett as a good resting spot for whaling crews, providing good anchorage, shelter, a known, dependable water supply, and a seemingly inexhaustible supply of fresh meat — the giant tortoises.

Colnett also started the first postal system in the Galápagos, a system that, although unofficial, is still in use today. It is the Barrel Post Office on Floreana Island, and it was used extensively by the whaling ships, which were often at sea for a year or two at a time. The crew of an outward-bound whaler, having rounded Cape Horn, would drop letters into the barrel; the letters would then be picked up by homeward-bound ships and ultimately delivered.

The main purpose of Captain Colnett's visit was to confirm that there was a sufficient supply of whales in the area to justify the development of the industry. Which he did, citing the upwelling activity of the currents that made these waters superb feeding grounds for the sperm whale.

Whaling, by the way, was not easy work. It required the small whaling hunt boats to get close enough to the whale so that the man in the bow, the whaling captain, could spear the chest. It took daring, skill, and a fair amount of luck to drive the harpoon between the ribs and pierce the lung, thereby mortally wounding the whale. And it didn't end there. Once killed, the whale was brought alongside the ship, whereupon the layer of blubber was stripped from the animal while it was pitching and rolling on the open seas. The blubber was hauled on-board, boiled, and the extracted oil was stored below in casks. Many of the ships sailed from New England and, as described above, were often gone for over a year before the casks were full.

As with most industries that tend to make men wealthy, whaling was poorly regulated. What transpired was short-sighted, even from a selfish whaling-oriented point of view. Things got out of hand, with the owners not willing or afraid to control the tough captains and crews required for such dangerous work. As a result, the sperm whales were killed to the point of near-extinction, also killing the very source of income upon which the industry depended. The whalers were soon gone from the archipelago.

The same scenario befell the sealers. The fur seals possess a two-layered coat, providing excellent insulation, and was therefore in great demand. Many thousands of fur seals were killed for their skins, and by 1900 the species was almost extinct.

The whalers and sealers not only decimated the very animal that supported their business, but the animal that fed them as well. Giant tortoises were easily caught, carted on board, and stacked upside-down in the ship's hold. They could be kept alive in this fashion without food or water for several months to a year. The crews thus had a supply of fresh meat, a delicacy in its own right and several times over when compared to the standard fare of salt pork and hardtack. Each ship would take between 500-600 tortoises at a time. When you consider that in the first half of the 1800s there were several hundred whaling ships operating in the general area, in addition to sealing vessels, the number of animals taken are astounding. Reports indicate that over 15,000 tortoises were taken from Floreana alone, resulting in the extinction of the subspecies found only on that island. A similar fate befell the subspecies on Santa Fe and Rábida (Jervis). In all, it is estimated that over 200,000 tortoises were taken.

The whalers and sealers also helped make life difficult for those animals that were left, as well as for future generations of tortoises. From their ships descended the black rat, an introduced mammal most effective at eating tortoise hatchlings. Too effective! Even today, the *Galápagos National Park Service* Wardens must hike through the brush and get to the tortoise eggs before the rats get to the hatchlings. The eggs are carried back to the *Charles Darwin Research Station* on Santa Cruz Island where they are incubated; the hatched tortoises are then raised in pens for about 5 years and then taken back to their native island. This is but one fight against many introduced animals, including feral dogs, cats, goats, pigs, and donkeys.

One whaler who left something good behind was Herman Melville. Melville spent several years on New England whaling ships, and the rich narrative expressed in **MOBY DICK** was acquired firsthand. Never one to hold back an opinion, Melville was decidedly underwhelmed by the Galápagos Islands. In a Melville anthology called the **PIAZZA TALES**, there is a short story set in the Galápagos entitled **THE ENCANTADAS**, which begins as follows:

> *Take five-and-twenty heaps of cinders dumped here and there in an outside city lot; imagine some of them magnified into mountains, and the vacant lot the sea; and you will have a fit idea of the general aspect of the Encantadas, or Enchanted Isles.*
>
> *Herman Melville, 1854*

THE SCIENTISTS

Melville may not have been very impressed by the Enchanted Isles, but there were a group that certainly was — the scientists. Darwin's publications, which voiced the theory of evolution and chronicled his visit to the Galápagos, were very timely. It was as if the world of science was waiting for someone to speak up. Several scientific expeditions soon made their way to the Galápagos to see the evidence first-hand.

The problem was that they took too much of the evidence back with them. In the midst of the whaling era, when the tortoise populations were hovering on the brink of extinction, the scientists took hundreds more. Many actually killed the animal first, so their museum would have a good specimen of the species "before it was too late."

THE STRATEGISTS

In 1859, the first commercial-scale petroleum was discovered beneath the ground in Pennsylvania, making available a less expensive source of oil, and whaling quickly declined throughout the world. During the rise and fall of the whaling industry, other ships were at sea in search of a different kind of prey. For most of the world, 1812 was a year of war. And England was in the thick of it, fighting Napoleon-led European forces on one hand and the United States on the other. While the hub of naval battle was in the Atlantic, there were some noteworthy exchanges in the waters off South America as well. U.S. Captain David Porter, in command of the warship U.S.S. ESSEX, created havoc among the scattered British ships in this area. Upon reaching the archipelago, Porter first headed for Floreana and inspected the letters in the Barrel Post Office. What he read helped him deduce the whereabouts of several British whalers, which he was able to intercept and capture. This was a time of war, in which commercial shipping plays a key part; in this case, it was a supply of much-needed oil.

In addition to his skills in naval battle, Captain Porter had the curious mind of the explorer, and wrote detailed accounts of the Galápagos. He noted the strategic importance (owing primarily to the location) as well as the notable absence of water on most of the islands. This written report would, over the years, stimulate serious U.S. interest in acquiring the Galápagos Islands.

With peace coming to much of the world in the 1820s, and the liberation of South America from Spanish rule in the 1830s, the strategic importance of the Galápagos was, for the time being, diminished. Ecuador's sovereignty, fully-achieved in 1830, was soon followed by their formal annexing of the Galápagos Islands in 1832. At that time Charles Island was renamed as Floreana (after General Flores, the first President of the Republic of Ecuador).

A settlement was soon started on Floreana under the direction of the first Governor General of the Galápagos, José Villamil. Owing to the desolate reputation of the islands, few of the original "settlers" actually volunteered for relocation; the "settlement" was more of a penal colony. Originally, it consisted of Ecuadorian soldiers who had been sentenced to death for mutiny and given a reprieve in return for deportation to the Galápagos. Soon they were joined by political prisoners and then by common criminals, including prostitutes.

The quality of the labor force, which numbered about 200-300 in the 1830s, did not deter the enterprising ambitions of Villamil, a man who today would be called an entrepreneur. Not content with the successful, if modest, farming achievements of the settlement (with the produce being sold to the whaling and sealing vessels), Villamil attempted to commercially harvest orchil, a lichen that grows freely on the island. At that time, orchil was used as a purple dye (mostly in the printing industry) and was commonly referred to as dyer's moss. As it turned out, the sale of orchil was not very profitable, and it was soon back to farming.

By 1840, the whalers and sealers had just about wiped out the tortoise population on Floreana, and the settlement disbanded, moving to other islands in the archipelago. Villamil's next enterprise was to mine coal on San Cristóbal Island. What possessed him to think there would be coal (formed from prehistoric plant life) on an island obviously of volcanic origin is difficult to imagine. Perhaps it was the black rocks, but at any rate, this attempt also failed. Undaunted and ever the optimist, he became convinced that there were vast (commercial-scale) amounts of guano in the Galápagos (from the sea birds, mostly the boobies). At that time, guano was the main source of nitrates (used in fertilizers and explosives), and the United States was interested, as the only guano available was from Peru and that at a very high price. The negotiations intensified when Villamil was appointed to a diplomatic position (to the U.S.). These talks soon broke off, however, when investigations showed that the vastness of the deposits were not in the Galápagos but in the mind of Villamil.

These negotiations did have the affect of once again stirring up foreign interest in gaining title to the Galápagos. The interest grew as plans were finalized for digging through the isthmus of Panama and building a canal. This would significantly open up trade between South America and Europe as well as with North America. The strategic location of the Galápagos with regard to Panama was recognized by all the world powers. Including the United States. Around the turn of the century, the U.S. made several offers for a long-term lease of San Cristóbal, which it intended to use as a refueling station. The negotiations went on for several years but, for one reason or another, stalemated.

1

Your Galápagos adventure will take you to Ecuador. Its beautiful capital Quito (#1), at 9300 feet, is located almost directly on the equator. If ''almost'' isn't good enough, you can be right on the equator by visiting the equatorial monument (#2), called **La Mitad del Mundo** (the Center of the World).

2

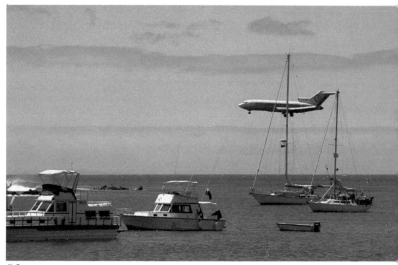

 # 3

Soon you'll be in the center of another world, as your plane lands in the Galápagos Islands (#3) and is met by a representative of the bio-community, a marine iguana (#4).

 # 4

#5

A few of the boats that cruise the waters of the Galápagos archipelago are seen anchored in Academy Bay, Santa Cruz Island (notice the port guardian in the foreground — #5). These waters are also cruised by the bottle-nosed dolphin (#6).

#6

SUNDAY 12   RABIDA   (JERVIS) 8:00
wet landing
short & easy trail - sandals

red beach, sea lions, flamingo lagoon,
pintail ducks, pelicans, galapagos doves

swimming & snorkelling

SOMBRERO CHINO 3:00 pm.
wet landing
short but rocky trail - good shoes
fresh lava flows, lava tubes
marine iguanas
swimming & snorkelling

 # 7

After a briefing from your Guide (often achieved with audio-visual aids — #7), you'll be off to Visitor Sites such as South Plaza Island (#8) and Kicker Rock (#9).

#8

 # 9

Entertainment will be provided on your Galápagos Island adventure, courtesy of the sea lions. These playful aquatic mammals will swim with you (#10) and serenade you in the morning (and the rest of the day for that matter — #11).

#11

#12

Barking (#12), playing (#13), sleeping (#14), and swimming (#15), the sea lions will provide you with an endless supply of photographic opportunities. Often they'll emerge from a quick cooling dip in the water, with the wet portion of their fur a shiny jet black and the dry portion a golden tan (#16).

#13

#14

#15

#16

E. Heron

#17

A resident bull will actively protect a territory of up to 70 feet of shoreline day and night against any and all challengers (see #12) and common enemies, such as the white-tipped shark (#17). In Photo #18, two bulls are seen ''defining'' the limits of their adjoining territories.

#18

This interest was based almost entirely on strategic location and was not at all influenced by the resource potential. Or the governmental management responsibility. After all, there had been several detailed reports in the world press describing the various revolts and uprisings by the workers in the Galápagos settlements. Apparently these were protests against the cruel working conditions. With a work population made up largely of criminals, and a decided lack of control from the remote mainland, these insurrections often got way out of hand, with murder being the rule rather than the exception.

One of the victims was a man named Manuel Cobos, probably the most successful, as well as the most ruthless, developers in the Galápagos. Cobos established a sugar plantation and milling operation around the turn of the century on San Cristóbal. The settlement he formed, called El Progreso, was tenanted and worked by convicts. They were treated harshly, basically as slave laborers. Eventually there was mass mutiny, and Cobos paid for his cruelty with his life. El Progreso is still the center of an agricultural community on San Cristóbal.

Not all developers were tyrants. In 1897, Antonio Gil formed two settlements on Isabela Island, one called Villamil on the coast and the other one a few miles inland called Santo Tomás. These settlements are now small towns, with a combined population of less than 1000 people. Santo Tomás was named after the volcano it adjoined (now generally called Sierra Negra), the oldest and widest volcano on the island. The town was founded to start a small-scale sulfur operation, mined from the crater. A coffee plantation was also established. On the coast at Villamil, lime was produced by burning coral. These ventures were somewhat successful, but on a small scale due to the very limited water supply.

Meanwhile back in Panama, after observing a long and gruelling but failed attempt to construct the canal, the United States intervened. The newly formed Republic of Panama was persuaded to sign a treaty creating an international Canal Zone under U.S. administration. A renewed construction effort was soon underway, and with what is considered a major engineering achievement, the canal was successfully completed.

The Panama Canal was opened in 1914. Just in time for World War I. As it turned out, the war was fought "Over There," with virtually no activity in the South Pacific. After the war, however, came the buildup of the Japanese presence in the Pacific, and now the full strategic role of the Galápagos was clearly seen. It guarded the entrance to the Panama Canal, which the Japanese Navy could either attack (to break an important supply line) or use to enter the Atlantic. The Galápagos was also an area to defend, lest the Japanese forces occupy the islands, from where an assault on the U.S. could be launched. As the build-up to war in the Pacific escalated, the U.S. Navy conducted several training exercises in the Galápagos.

Another transition period for the islands began in 1924 with the publication of Willaim Beebe's **GALAPAGOS: WORLD'S END**. Beebe, a renowned biologist and explorer, led a scientific expedition to the archipelago sponsored by the *New York Zoological Society*. His book paints a romantic account of this voyage; without sacrificing technical accuracy, Beebe expertly blended popular science and adventure travel. **GALAPAGOS: WORLD'S END** quickly became a best seller, inspiring many to follow in Beebe's footsteps.

Many of the early followers were wealthy and fancied themselves as amateur scientists. They traveled in their private luxury vessels, which were actually well-equipped floating laboratories, with a recruited team of professionals. The Galápagos was still inaccessible to most people, owing to the remote location, the limitations of the traveling possibilities, and the length of time required for such a trip.

Others who were likewise influenced by Beebe were visionaries, believing that the Galápagos would provide their particular "answer," be it health, wealth, or eternal peace. In 1927, a group of Norwegians, captivated by Beebe's book and by a slick promoter as well, put up their life savings for the opportunity to establish a profitable colony on Floreana. They tried everything from farming to a fish cannery operation, but as many others before them, their attempts ended in failure, disappointment, and for some, death. After 2 years, those that could, returned home. Others departed for the South American mainland. Only two Norwegians remained, making what money they could by selling dried fish. Finally, illness overtook them, and they abandoned their dwelling, their work, and their hopes for commercial success in the Galápagos. Today, the traveler can see the legacy of the community, including the remains of a corrugated-iron-and-wood structure near the beach at Post Office Bay, as well as bits and pieces of a narrow-gauge rail system (used for transport to and from shore).

FLOREANA — THE ISLE OF MYSTERY

> It tempts no wise man to pull off and see what's the matter, but bids him steer small and keep off shore — that is Charles' Island; brace up, Mr. Mate, and keep the light astern.
>
> Herman Melville, 1854

Another group of visionaries soon arrived that would forever shroud the island of Floreana in a real-life Agatha Christie mystery that could easily carry the title of "Death in Paradise." During your tour of the islands, you may visit the location of this fascinating tale and possibly get to meet a key player as well. Let's set the scene and follow the action.

The first set of characters are Dr. Friedrich Ritter and Dore Strauch who arrived in Floreana from Berlin in 1929. Dr. Ritter was very fond of wildlife, disliked hunting intensely, and was a vegetarian (although not a strict one — his dietary habits were to play a key part in the mystery that was to unfold). Although he was a medical doctor, Dr. Ritter strongly believed in the ability of the mind to control the body and to cure many physical ailments; he practiced what is now referred to as holistic medicine. Dore, one of his patients, was taken by the magnetic personality of Dr. Ritter, who was soon expounding that the powers of the mind were so great that they could even cure the multiple sclerosis that she was suffering from. The relationship expanded, and soon Dr. Ritter was sharing his dream for going off to a land of great solitude and freedom. Like many dreams however, there was the everyday realities of life that stood in the way, not the least of which was that they were both already married, although unhappily.

The plan they hit on was truly remarkable, mainly because, despite its absurdity, it worked. What they did was to bring their respective spouses together by convincing them that, to keep up appearances once they left, it would be best if Frau Ritter took over the household management for Herr

Koerwin (Dore's husband). Owing perhaps to a ready-made way of dealing with an embarrassing situation in a very proper bourgeois society, everyone went for the idea. Dr. Ritter and Dore were thus free to set off for their utopia.

Upon arrival in the Galápagos, they settled in Floreana, once again owing to the known, reliable source of water and its agricultural potential. Their home site, which they named Freido (a contraction of Friedrich and Dore), was located at an extinct volcanic crater. Aside from providing a great view, it formed a natural basin full of lush tropical vegetation and included a clear spring. Their vast gardening activities were extremely successful. Given the fact that the land which they worked was their psychic center, it was only natural that they eventually located their house at the center of the garden. The shape was octagonal, in the best geodesic dome tradition.

The solitude that Friedrich and Dore strived so desperately for would prove to be short-lived. Their journey was well-documented (ironically by Dr. Ritter's own letters), and they were now labeled by the world press as notorious lovers, an Adam and Eve in a real Garden of Eden. Soon they were playing hosts to an increasing number of curious visitors. A series of would-be inhabitants also arrived, looking for a new way of life. Most, however, were not up to the rigors of life on Floreana, and their visits were for the most part brief in duration.

Some would stay on, however. September of 1932 marked the arrival of the Wittmer family — Heinz, his pregnant wife Margret, and Heinz' 12 year old son Harry (via a previous marriage). The Wittmer's life in inflation-torn Germany had not been easy, and the romantic magazine article descriptions of the idyllic life of Friedrich and Dore gathered their interest, as did William Beebe's book.

The reception the Wittmer's received can be best described as cool. Margret and Heinz Wittmer were down-to-earth types, and the only purpose Dr. Ritter saw in socializing was an opportunity to preach his philosophic rhetoric, which was in his estimation above the level of these new arrivals. Thus, as it was apparent that the two couples did not have that much in common (aside from their common desire to be free of the problems of pre-World War II Germany) they basically kept to themselves.

While the Wittmer's and Friedrich & Dore were not fast friends, they were not enemies either, and helped each other out as common problems arose. Another group of settlers were to arrive in November, 1932, however, that would cause absolute mayhem. An Austrian woman, calling herself the "Baroness" landed with a retinue of three men; they established themselves in the abandoned Norwegian buildings on the shore at Post Office Bay. Her entourage consisted of two Germans, Rudolf Lorenz and Robert Philippson, as well as an Ecuadorian, Felipe Valdivieso. The Baroness claimed to be of Austrian royalty, using the formal name of Eloise Baroness Wagner de Bosquet. She was apparently quite the sight, with a get-up right out of an S&M magazine, complete with riding britches, black boots, whip, and revolver. The two Germans were apparently her love-slaves, while the Ecuadorian was under some sort of work contract to the group, but he took his orders directly from the Baroness . Her stated intentions were to build a grandiose luxury hotel, which she already had named Hacienda Paradiso.

Soon after the arrival of the Baroness and her party, trouble started brewing between the three groups of settlers. There were reports of theft, tampering with the mail, mostly leveled against the Baroness. Most of this was related to the increasing number of luxury yachts that were arriving at Floreana, with the visitors anxious to have a look at the bohemian existence of the by now well-known inhabitants. Often, on a prior visit, the owners of these yachts had promised to bring one or more of the settlers some longed-for items. On the return trip, these items were sometimes handed to a settler who promised and failed to deliver them to the intended recipient; this "settler" was usually the Baroness. One can imagine the frustration that built up from these situations and the hostile feelings that developed.

In January of 1933, the Island of Floreana was to have its first native; Margret Wittmer gave birth to a son, Rolf. Later on that year, the Governor of the Galápagos Islands arrived to look into the now-open dispute between the various inhabitants of the island. Also, by this time there were all sorts of rumors and reports about the "strange" behavior and goings on, and he felt compelled to investigate the situation. Probably not wanting to upset any of the inhabitants, an attempt was made to pacify everyone. The fact that the Baroness intended to build a luxury hotel was not lost on the Governor, who was no doubt intrigued by the prospect of a vast tourist trade and did not want to risk losing the expected revenues. This, combined with the allure that the Baroness was said to possess, resulted in the Governor actually offering her an invitation to his residence.

The relationship between Dore and Friedrich was beginning to take a turn for the worse. This is not surprising since Dr. Ritter was in the extreme sense a follower of Nietzsche; contempt for women is in keeping with this "higher" culture, whereby the noble man is devoid of sympathy and is seen as ruthless, cruel, and violent. Ritter went so far as to forbid Dore from planting flowers, condemning this activity as frivolous.

And then it all happened — a strange and bizarre sequence of events that to this day has no entirely clear explanation. Lots of interpretation and lots of theories. No doubt, after visiting Floreana, you'll have one too! Once again, we'll set the scene. It is March, 1934 and a severe drought has hit the Galápagos. Many of the springs have dried up, and water is generally scarce. The daily business of managing the land has become a major challenge. The tension level has increased, and hostility is beginning to surface.

For some time, the Baroness has paired off with Robert Philippson, with both of them treating the now-out-of-favor Rudolf Lorenz as a slave. He is reportedly over-worked, beaten, and starved. Photographs taken around this time show a very emaciated "holocaust-genre" portrait of Lorenz. The drought has made his situation desperate, and he becomes a frequent guest of the Wittmer's, seeking food, shelter, and perhaps a bit of sympathy. Often, he is just escaping from the harsh treatment. In somewhat of a daily ritual, the Baroness and Philippson would show up at the Wittmer's and take Lorenz back with them; for his part, Lorenz didn't seem to protest returning with his tormentors.

The domestic problems of Dr. Ritter and Dore Strauch have escalated and are now obvious to those around them. Ritter's treatment of Dore is described as very cruel, while she stoically defends him in public. Dore goes so far as to glorify his philosophy — the very same idealistic dogma that has led to his insensitive behavior and lack of respect for her.

With this emotional overtone and in the background of a severe drought, here's what happens next:

One afternoon, the Baroness shows up at the Wittmer's and announces (to Margret) that she and Philippson are leaving right away for Tahiti on a boat anchored in the bay and waiting for them. There is no evidence that there was any such boat. As it turns out, they are never seen or heard from again. Not a trace. They left behind almost all of their possessions, some of which would have been taken on even a short voyage.

Within a short time, Rudolf Lorenz finds passage out of Floreana on-board a vessel named the DINAMITA. Having sailed from Academy Bay on Santa Cruz Island, and ultimately bound for Guayaquil, the DINAMITA is reported missing. Several months later, Lorenz's mummified body is found on the beach of Marchena Island along with the body of the captain of the vessel. Both have died of thirst and starvation.

In December of the same year, Friedrich Ritter, the vegetarian, takes critically ill and dies from eating spoiled chicken. It is said by Margret Wittmer, who was at Ritter's bedside when he died, that he cursed Dore Strauch with his dying breath.

And that's the mystery of Floreana. Unsolved. A lot of speculation, but never anything conclusive. Soon after the death of Dr. Ritter, Dore Strauch returned to Germany. Margret Wittmer continues to live on Floreana with her daughter Floreanita and grandchildren. Rolf Wittmer, Margret's son and the first native of Floreana, is owner-operator and captain of a Galápagos touring yacht, the TIP TOP II (see the section, Boats of the Galápagos, in CHAPTER IV). When arranged in advance, tour groups visiting Floreana are taken to Margret's cafe, where one can sometimes have a taste of the family's orange-fermented wine, browse at the small assortment of souvenirs that are offered for sale, have post cards cancel-stamped with the official emblems of the Barrel Post Office, and generally let the mind wander back in time. After visiting the Wittmer Pension (rooms are actually let out), the after-dinner conversations on-board the boat are usually very stimulating; most of the Guides and Group Leaders will discuss the various theories pertaining to these mysterious events that transpired all those many years ago. Many questions are raised by the passengers, most of which are rhetorical in nature.

A few final comments. A complete and fascinating account of this who-done-it is offered in a book by John Treherne entitled **THE GALAPAGOS AFFAIR**. Unfortunately, this book is out of print, but is available at many libraries. Margret Wittmer has written her own version of the story as well as a complete chronicle of her near-60 years on Floreana Island; the name of the book, quite simply, is **FLOREANA** (see the Literature section for details on these books). A third account of these events is in the offing, as there is talk of a movie being made. ''That,'' says Margret, ''depends on the up-front money.'' Mrs. Wittmer will eternally be known and remembered as a survivor.

By the way, the story isn't quite over. Over the years, there have been other mysterious occurrences on Floreana. One event in the 1960s involved an elderly visitor who disappeared while hiking. An extensive search turned up nil. The solution and the body were found almost 20 years later; it was determined that the person apparently wandered off the trail, got lost, and was overcome by exposure to the elements. Two other situations directly involved the Wittmer family once again. The first was related to the drowning of Harry Wittmer in a 1951 boat accident. The second incident occurred in 1969 when the husband of Floreanita, Margret's daughter, also disappeared. In light of the events that transpired back in the 1930s, this last episode was investigated in some detail; while no formal conclusion was reached, some locals do offer their own "unofficial" version of the story.

GROWTH, TOURISM, AND CONSERVATION

Not all of the Galápagos settlers made the front pages of the international press. For most of them, it should be stated, notoriety is the last thing they wanted. Mostly, they wished to be left in peace while they provided for themselves. This includes some of the original Norwegian settlers who eventually relocated to Santa Cruz Island; there they began farming activities in the Highlands, a lush, fertile area owing to the garúa mist that blankets the high elevations for a considerable part of the year. These pioneers were joined by a few Americans and several Europeans, many from Germany. Probably the most famous of this group (again, not that they have sought fame, and somewhat resent the lack of privacy that tourism has brought) are the Angermeyers. As chronicled by Johanna Angermeyer in her beautifully written book, **MY FATHER'S ISLAND**, four Angermeyer brothers, Carl, Fritz, Gus, and Hans sailed for the Galápagos in 1935, leaving the politics of Germany behind them. The offspring of the Angermeyer family now rank among the best captains of the touring yachts that sail the waters of the Galápagos archipelago.

When World War II broke out, the Ecuadorian government agreed to let the United States construct an Air Force base on Baltra Island. The U.S. Sixth Air Force, stationed on Baltra as well as several other islands in the Galápagos, patrolled the approach to the Panama Canal and monitored enemy submarine activity in the South Pacific. The 29th Bomber Squadron, Sixth Air Force, still holds annual reunions, an event usually attended by noted Galápagos historian John Woram. John takes many authors to task for innacurately writing that the U.S. servicemen were responsible for the extinction of the land iguana on Baltra Island. Mr. Woram's statements, which cite the sensitivity of the soldiers to the local wildlife, are adamantly supported and seconded by scientists at the Darwin Station.

After the war, the air base was given to Ecuador and still serves as one of the two main airports in the Galápagos (the other is on San Cristóbal Island), the point of arrival for planeloads of tourists 6 days a week, every week of the year. Tourism is the latest and the only large-scale commercial endeavor in the history of the Galápagos. Some of the more contemporary break-even ventures include fishing and a salt mine operation on James (Santiago) Island. For tourism to succeed where other industries have failed, it is vitally important not to commit the same sins of greed perpetrated by the whalers and sealers, that is killing the proverbial goose that laid the golden egg. The Galápagos wildlife must be preserved!

Conservation of the Galápagos sounds logical to many of us, but it is also expensive. And for the third-world economy of Ecuador, it has been a luxury that, prior to tourism, it simply couldn't afford. Raising the standard of living for Ecuadorians by developing world trade has been the first priority, and rightfully so. Even adequate administration of the Galápagos has been more expensive than the country could afford. And difficult to achieve, especially with the remote location of, and lack of communications with, the islands. There is also politics to consider. For an administration to succeed, it must first survive, and through the years, "saving the Galápagos" was not high on the list of critical issues.

This is not to say that conservation has been overlooked. The legacy of Darwin's voyage and subsequent writings have generated international support for a Galápagos conservation effort. The year 1935 was the 100th anniversary of Darwin's visit. This was a noteworthy occasion in the scientific community. In anticipation thereof, the *National Assembly of Ecuador* had passed protective legislation in 1934, creating wildlife sanctuaries on some of the islands. However, this was largely a matter of form rather than substance. The need for effective controls as well as a nature preserve was made apparent as a result of a Darwin centennial event, the *Galápagos Memorial Expedition*, led by Dr. Victor von Hagen. The establishment of a research station was proposed by Dr. von Hagen. Unfortunately, before the practical considerations of this idea could be sorted out, the world went to war once again.

There was another Galápagos centennial in 1959, this one marking the publication of Darwin's **THE ORIGIN OF SPECIES**. This event formed the impetus to put in effect some of the conservation recommendations made as a result of a *UNESCO* expedition 2 years earlier. One of these recommendations was, once again, the establishment of a research station. This effort required international cooperation and funding, and in July, 1959 an organization of renowned scientists and Ecuadorian conservationists was formally established, the *Charles Darwin Foundation for the Galápagos Islands*.

Later that year, the Ecuadorian government passed legislation aimed at preserving the Galápagos. Through guidelines set by the Darwin Foundation, all land in the archipelago not already settled by man was declared a National Park, and strict regulations were enacted. This time the laws could be enforced, because plans were being formed to develop two administrative infrastructures — one scientific and the other regulatory.

First, the *Charles Darwin Research Station*, located on Academy Bay in the town of Puerto Ayora, was established in 1961 and officially opened in 1964. Four years later, the *Galápagos National Park Service* was formed. The role of the Research Station was to coordinate all scientific work in the islands, gather essential baseline data on endangered species, establish conservation goals based on the data, and recommend programs to support those goals (such as the eradication of certain introduced species — rats, feral pigs, etc). The role of the Park Service was to implement these programs.

The growing interest in the Galápagos as a tourist attraction was recognized as was the potential revenue this industry could produce. Owing partially to the location of the Darwin Station, the town of Puerto Ayora was selected as the "center of tourism." A road was built linking the town to the Baltra Airport, where the runway was also resurfaced. A Tour Operator based in Quito, METROPOLITAN TOURING, began offering island cruises in 1970. Soon, the industry and the number of boats began to grow. From a little over 4000 tourists per year in 1970 to about 60,000 per year in 1990.

This growth was somewhat unique. In accordance with the National Park regulations, facilities could not be constructed on over 90 percent of the land not already colonized, meaning zero development on all but four islands (not including Baltra, which is operated as a military base). Thus, the tour boat assumed the roles of both hotel and restaurant. As an added control, in 1986 the *Galápagos National Park* was extended to the waters surrounding the islands with the signing into law of the *Galápagos Marine Resources Reserve*. A 15 nautical mile boundary zone was established; now the waters and marine wildlife of the Galápagos could also be protected.

The problem is that the protection is only in writing; for the most part, it isn't enforced. There are virtually no patrol boats in the Galápagos. Illegal fishing boats (including large commercial vessels) are spotted on many tours, especially those that visit the western islands of Fernandina and Isabela. Here, the Humboldt and Cromwell Currents mingle and produce a double dose of upwelling, producing the coolest, nutrient-rich waters of the archipelago. The illegal fishing activities include the netting of sharks (for shark fin soup, an Asian delicacy), and inadvertently, sea lions, turtles, and bottle-nosed dolphins.

The latest fishery to "open" has been the taking of sea cucumbers (another Asian delight, richly coveted for the reputed aphrodisiac qualities). Starting in 1992 and continuing into 1994, literally hundreds of illegal sea cucumber fishermen (*pepineros,* as they are called) have been spotted (and occasionally apprehended) as they dive for and process (by boiling) the echinoderms. The sea cucumber requires a dense population to maintain its numbers (due to its method of external fertilization). They release their gametes (sperm and eggs) externally, and if a member of the opposite sex isn't close by, fertilization doesn't happen. As an analogy, you need a solid block of corn plants (not just a plant here and there) to ensure a good stand of corn. At any rate, the numbers of sea cucumbers are rapidly dwindling, and there's not a lot being done about it. Being slow movers, the sea cucumbers, cannot defend themselves. And it's not just the sea cucumbers. Most of us have finally learned that a broken food chain is just that. To make matters worse, the *pepineros* are introducing plants and animals in a very sensitive area. There are rumors to the effect that the once-pristine island of Fernandina now has introduced animals (perhaps including rats).

So the question is, "Why doesn't someone do something about it?" And the answer is — you guessed it, money! It talks loud everywhere, especially to a third-world economy and government. Is anyone fighting back? The *Charles Darwin Research Station* certainly wants to but their hands are tied. Basically the Darwin Station and current Director, Dr. Chantal Blanton, report to the *Charles Darwin Foundation for the Galápagos Islands,* an international organization created, in part, under the auspices of the Government of Ecuador. Since the responsibility of effectively patrolling the Galápagos falls squarely on the shoulders of the Ecuadorian government, it is very awkward politically for the *Darwin Station* to publicly complain about the very government that allows them to exist and function. Thus the tied hands and still lips. The result is no outcry forcing political action, and the word does not get out to the world press. Even when it does, very few people want to read (or write) that there are serious problems in the Land of Darwin.

It actually gets more complicated. As the tourist industry grows, so does the required support infrastructure and the population of the islands. In 1950, there were less than 1500 residents in the Galápagos. By 1974, the population was over 4000, with about 1000 residents on Santa Cruz Island. In 1990, the Galápagos population exceeded 12,000 people, with over 6000 living in the town of Puerto Ayora. The estimated growth rate is approximately 12 percent per year. This growth rate is exactly the heart of the problem. More and more people are moving to the islands because of the perceived opportunities. But not everyone is qualified for and/or able to find a job. One consequence is the beginning of "city problems," such as crime, drugs, etc. Another end product is the rising number of plants and animals that the residents are introducing to the Galápagos, an alarming situation that needs to be dealt with. Finally, getting back to the problem discussed earlier, there are a growing number of residents trying to earn a living through fishing — even illegal fishing, such as the taking of sharks and sea cucumbers. Unlike the Darwin Station (who they also dislike), this group is very vocal in their efforts to influence the government. "You let us move here," they say, "and now you have to let us earn a living here." the point is that many of them probably shouldn't have been allowed to move there in the first place. (Note: There is currently no restriction on an Ecuadorian moving to the Galápagos, one of the 21 Provinces of Ecuador). And they don't seem or want to understand that they are destroying the very resource that is bringing all the tourist dollars to the Galápagos.

As stated above, the burden is on the Ecuadorian government. This is the time for Ecuador to seriously begin patrolling the waters and planning a well-thought-out-and-enforced restricted Galápagos immigration policy.

On the positive side, the Darwin Station and the Park Service have worked together on several successful conservation programs. They have saved three species of land iguanas from extinction, raising several hundred animals in the Darwin Station and returning them to their native islands. In a similar fashion, eight tortoise subspecies were also saved; about 1000 tortoises have already been repatriated. Slowly, and one by one, battles against the introduced species of animals are being won. Goats have been eliminated from several of the smaller islands, wild dogs from Isabela, and rats from Bartolomé. Some battles are longer than others. The survival of the dark-rumped (Hawaiian) petrel, once on the verge of extinction due to rat predation, now looks promising, and the population of goats on James (Santiago) Island has been reduced from 100,000 to less than 60,000. But both of these programs have been tedious, have depended on dedication by a few as well as timely outside funding, and have taken 15 years to get this far.

Much more needs to be done, and money is the limiting factor. The Darwin Station has a very small budget which is used primarily on administrative matters (including the operation of a Visitor's Center which is an important part of every Galápagos tour), the wildlife conservation programs cited above, and gathering essential baseline data on endangered species. Thus, the operations are limited, and the scope of the programs undertaken must, by necessity, be quite narrow. The budget for basic research doesn't exist; thus, most scientific research in the Galápagos is conducted by visitng scientists (although the Darwin Station coordinates and gives logistical support to such research).

Aside from the Republic of Ecuador, funding is provided entirely by contributions — private donations, endowments, as well as a variety of foundations, institutions, and organizations. You (or your organization) are encouraged to make a personal (or corporate) contribution; use the following address:

Charles Darwin Foundation, Inc.
Dept. 0553
Washington, D.C., 20073-0053

Your contribution would be greatly appreciated and should typically meet tax-deductible guidelines; you may want to verify this with your tax accountant. Make your check payable to the **Charles Darwin Foundation, Inc.** All contributors of more than U.S.$25 will become members of the *Friends of the Galápagos* and receive a one year's subscription to **NOTICAS DE GALAPAGOS,** the journal containing articles on Galápagos science and conservation, and four issues of **GALAPAGOS BULLETIN,** a quarterly news publication from the *Charles Darwin Research Station.* Subsequent annual contributions will extend the subscription to both publications.

Donations often go towards immediate conservation projects. For long-term support, an endowment fund called the *Darwin Scientific Foundation* has been set up. If you, your organization, or corporation wish to contribute to this fund, send a check payable to the *Darwin Scientific Foundation* to the following address:

Darwin Scientific Foundation
100 N. Washington St., Ste 311
Falls Church, VA 22046

For those "high-techers" in the reading audience, the Darwin Station needs equipment — computers (desktop publishing systems) and electronic instrumentation, preferably with a battery-backup system, as the generating stations of the town and the Station are unreliable. All such "in kind contributions," as they are called, should be discussed with the office of:

Johannah Barry
Executive Director
CHARLES DARWIN FOUNDATION, INC.
100 N. Washington St., Ste. 311
Falls Church, VA 22046
PHONE: (703) 538-6833   **FAX:** 703-538-6835

Lastly, if this book serves its purpose, you will tour the Galápagos Islands. On your visit to the *Charles Darwin Research Station,* show your support and leave a donation.

In a sense, you will be making a donation by visiting the Galápagos and pumping money into the local economy. Hopefully, the revenue generated by the tourist industry may actually stimulate a perceived need by the Ecuadorian government to allocate more funds to wildlife conservation.

This brings us to a sensitive topic — the effect of tourism. "Surely," some say, "you cannot continue to increase tourism without an adverse impact." I tend to agree, but feel that the problem has a two-fold solution:

1. Responsible tourism — For the most part, those that tour the Galápagos are conservation-oriented and tend to follow the regulations of the National Park. As tourism increases, this responsibility will become greater. There is something to be said for keeping the number of "pleasure boats" with nightly live entertainment to a minimum. While the Cruise Ships have their place, especially for the elderly, it will be important for these boats to increase their orientation to a "natural history excursion." This criticism, by the way, is also leveled at some of the small yachts where a "party" atmosphere prevails at

night. The Galápagos should continue to be an adventure, not an "exotic cruise" destination. Have fun, but keep the orientation focused.

2. Controlled tourism — This is already in effect with the Guide program, the National Park regulations, the paperwork necessary for a tour boat to leave port (including a list of passengers, passport numbers, and a detailed itinerary), as well as the sanctions against private vessels entering the waters of the Galápagos. Enforcement is another matter. As stated above, this will require patrol boats operated by the *Galápagos National Park Service* and funded by the Ecuadorian government.

In conclusion, it's the quality more than the quantity that will make the difference. Those that are interested in seriously exploring the natural world of the Galápagos and have a healthy respect for conservation are, and will continue to be, a very valuable resource for the islands.

CHAPTER III

ABOUT
THE GALAPAGOS WILDLIFE

The fascinating wildlife of the Galápagos is extremely well documented in Michael Jackson's **GALAPAGOS: A NATURAL HISTORY GUIDE** (see the Literature section). It's not likely that you'll find this Michael Jackson moon-walking on MTV; Professor Jackson (a more appropriate designation) currently teaches at the *University of Calgary*. His **GUIDE** is most thorough in its discussions of the flora and fauna of the Galápagos, and it is strongly recommended that you take the book with you to the islands, where you will use it as a daily reference source. The Jackson **GUIDE** is available in mainland Ecuador, but my advice is to start looking for a a copy well before you depart for the islands. The **GUIDE** is becoming a little easier to find in the U.S., especially in travel-oriented bookstores, but there is still a chance that your local, friendly bookshop may have to order it for you; it is also available through GALAPAGOS TRAVEL, the publisher of the book you are reading.

The purpose of this Chapter is to augment the material found in the Jackson **GUIDE**, and to key in on certain anatomical, physiological, and more often, behavioral traits. In a sub-section called Photo Opportunities, a few suggestions for interesting shots will be briefly presented. As a point of reference, Spanish names for the animals will be cited; it may prove useful to learn them, as some of the Guides refer to certain animals by their Spanish name (*tintorera*, for example, the white-tipped shark).

Note: Terrestrial invertebrates will not be discussed.

REPTILES

As mentioned in Chapter II (in the section, "The Arrival of Life"), reptiles were able to survive the long ocean passage to the Galápagos due to their ability to tolerate arid conditions and a salt water environment; they can also fast for long periods of time.

An interesting point regarding the reptiles' arduous trip to the Galápagos was that it was a one-way voyage. The currents were not about to carry them back to the mainland! If they were going to survive, they had to adapt to the local conditions. Thus, it is not surprising that the number of reptile species is small (twenty-two in all), and of these twenty-two, twenty are endemic to the Galápagos.

The reptiles not only arrived, but they survived, reproduced, and assumed several of the niche roles typically filled by mammals. A key point is that land mammals were not able to make the ocean voyage on their own. It is for this reason that, along with amphibians, land mammals are noticeably absent from the list of indigenous species (with the exception of two species of rice rats). As evidenced by several introduced mammalian species proliferating to the point of detriment to native species, the Galápagos environment is fit for more than just prehistoric-looking reptiles. An "unfit environment" viewpoint was at one time held by many, including Herman Melville (in **THE ENCANTADAS**):

> *Another feature of these isles is their emphatic uninhabitableness. It is deemed fit [for] . . . the jackal itself; . . . but the Encantadas refuse to harbor even the outcasts of the beasts. Man and wolf alike disown them. Little but reptile life is here found; tortoises, lizards, . . . and that strangest anomaly of outlandish nature, the iguano. No voice, no low, no howl is heard; the chief sound of life here is a hiss.*
> *Herman Melville, 1854*

Being cold-blooded, the behavior cycle of the reptiles is governed by their body temperature, which they cannot control physiologically; they utilize sun and shade for this purpose. Even with such a strict limitation, they have managed to adapt (through evolution) in a remarkably efficient and most noticeable fashion to the harsh environment of the Galápagos as well as to the various microclimates of particular islands.

Note: Snakes and geckos will not be discussed.

GIANT TORTOISES — (*GALAPAGOS*)

> *I will describe the habits of the tortoise. Some grow to an immense size; the old males are the largest, the females rarely growing to so great a size: the male can be readily distinguished from the female by the greater length of its tail. They frequent in preference the high damp parts, but they likewise live in the lower and arid districts.*
>
> *The tortoise is very fond of water, drinking large quantities and wallowing in the mud. The larger islands alone possess springs, and these are always situated toward the central parts, and at a considerable height. The tortoises, therefore, which frequent the lower districts, when thirsty, are obliged to travel from a long distance. Hence broad and well-beaten paths branch off in every direction from the wells down to the sea-coast; and the Spaniards, by following them up, first discovered the watering-places. When the tortoise arrives at the spring, quite regardless of any spectator, he buries his head in the water above his eyes, and greedily swallows great mouthfuls, at the rate of about ten in a minute. I believe it is well ascertained that the bladder of the frog acts as a reservoir for the moisture necessary to its existence; such seems to be the case with the tortoise.*

> *The tortoises, when purposely moving towards any point, travel by night and day and arrive at their journey's end much sooner than would be expected. One large tortoise, which I watched, walked at the rate of sixty yards in ten minutes, that is . . . four miles a day — allowing a little time for it to eat on the road.*
>
> *During the breeding season, when the male and female are together, the male utters a hoarse roar or bellowing, which, it is said, can be heard at the distance of more than a hundred yards. The female never uses her voice, and the male only at these times; so that when the people hear this noise they can know that the two are together.*
>
> Charles Darwin, 1845

Of all the wildlife, it is the tortoise that most symbolizes the Galápagos Islands. The tortoise has given the Galápagos its name. It is the face of the tortoise that appears on the official insignia of the islands and stamped on the passport of the visitor.

The tortoise is a vegetarian, well known for its ability to fast for long periods of time. This ability proved to be a great asset, enabling the giant tortoise to make the long voyage to the Galápagos on rafts of tangled vegetation and to survive the arid conditions on many of the islands. This attribute became a liability as the buccaneers and whalers carted off over 200,000 tortoises, knowing the animals would stay alive in the ship's hold without food or water, thereby providing fresh meat to the crew for several months. Some, like Melville, thought the tortoise's fate was self-predestined.

> *Lasting sorrow and penal hopelessness are in no animal form so suppliantly expressed as in theirs. They are strangely self-condemned. Their crowning curse is their drudging impulse to straightforwardness in a belittered world.*
>
> Herman Melville, 1854

Indeed, Melville's shipmates believed that wicked sea officers were punished by being transformed into giant tortoises. The truth be known, the Galápagos giant tortoises have proven to be very adaptive, a fact not lost on Darwin (see the section in Chapter II on Adaptive Radiation). Starting as a single species, fourteen subspecies evolved (now reduced to eleven), each adapting to the vegetation of the particular island on which they settled. In the case of Isabela, five subspecies evolved (one for each major volcanic region). The method of adaptation is based on several variations in the shape of their carapace (shell). At one extreme is the saddle-back tortoise with an elevated, arched front end and long neck, able to reach for the tall vegetation on the drier islands. At the other extreme is the dome-shaped tortoise, with a shorter profile and blunt front end for pushing through the dense brush often found on islands with lush highlands.

By virtue of its great mass (up to 550 pounds), the giant tortoise is better equipped than most reptiles to keep an even body temperature. Actually, weight is another species variation. The saddle-back tortoises are smaller because they live on drier islands, which naturally have less food available. Thus, being a large saddle-back (and requiring more food than the island can provide) is not a great adaptive mechanism.

While longevity estimates are about 150 years (based on a few historical records), there is at present no precise method of determining the age of older tortoises. There are markings on the shell called growth rings, which occur between the plates (see Photos #27-28), but after about 10 years of age the growth slows and the rings are too close together to accurately count. Eventually the rings erode, and age determination becomes impossible. The tortoises reared at the Darwin Station are being tagged, so that future generations of scientists can keep score.

Photo Opportunities: The tortoise pens at the *Charles Darwin Research Station* present a great picture-taking opportunity. You definitely want to get a close up of the timeless face — an **E.T.** shot (see Photo #19). In fact, it was the facial features of the giant tortoise that were actually used to create the visage of **E.T.** Make sure you take a light meter reading off the face, so you don't lose the detail. If you're photographing the entire animal, there are often reflections bouncing off the age-worn, smooth carapace; use a polarizer to knock out the glare and get more definition.

You'll also be able to capture the aggressive male "posturing" behavior, two or three tortoises stretching their necks skyward and at each other, mouths agape, seeing who will back down and who will reign supreme — the umpire in a jaw-down with the wrinkled manager (see Photo #22). And if you want to "posture" with them, there are pens where you can pose right next to one of these friendly giants.

The best time to go tortoise shooting at the Darwin Station is early in the morning or in the evening, before and after the large Cruise Ships bring their passengers through. Once the tours start coming in, you can't really set up your shots, and someone's usually in the way. You can actually make two visits to the Darwin Station — once with your tour, when you can plan your shots, and once on your own, as most tours give you some "free time" in town. You **are** allowed to visit the Darwin Station without a Guide.

For those who see the tortoises in the wild, there may be good "water hole mud-wallowing" opportunities. The water holes are often dew ponds that form as a result of the *garúa* mist. In the Highlands of Santa Cruz Island, these ponds are often coated with duckweed, providing a beautiful green background (see Photo #25).

Where To See Them: For most visitors, the The Darwin Station presents the only opportunity to view the giant tortoise. Perhaps the breeding, incubation, rearing, and repatriating programs carried on at the Darwin Station will enable future generations of visitors to see the various species of tortoises on their native islands. But it won't happen quickly, especially when you consider that it takes 40 years for a tortoise to become sexually mature! So for now, most of us must be content with viewing the giant tortoises at the Darwin Station.

Actually, there are some alternatives. You can see giant tortoises in the wild by taking a trip to the Tortoise Reserve (or nearby farms) in the Highlands on Santa Cruz Island; several Galápagos tours provide such an opportunity (see the section on the Santa Cruz Highlands in Chapter IX). Also, those of you that make the hike to the rim of the Alcedo Volcano on Isabela Island will be rewarded with a view of a small "herd" of tortoises; this trip is typically offered as an option on 2 week Galápagos cruises (see the section on the Alcedo

Volcano, Isabela Island in Chapter IX). Of the 15,000 or so giant tortoises in the islands, the Alcedo region is home to the largest population, estimated at over 4000.

MARINE IGUANAS — (*IGUANAS MARINAS*)

The rocks on the coast abounded with great black lizards . . . a hideous looking creature, of a dirty black colour, stupid, and sluggish in its movements. The usual length of a full-grown one is about a yard, but there are some even four feet long; a large one weighed twenty pounds. Their tails are flattened sideways, and all four feet partially webbed. When in the water this lizard swims with perfect ease and quickness, by a serpentine movement of its body and flattened tail — the legs being motionless and closely collapsed on its sides. Their limbs and strong claws are admirably adapted for crawling over the rugged and fissured masses of lava which everywhere form the coast.

It is . . . most remarkable, because it is the only existing lizard which lives on marine vegetable productions. . . . We must admit that there is no other quarter of the world where this Order replaces the herbivorous mammalia in so extraordinary a manner.

Charles Darwin, 1845

Your introduction to the wildlife of the Galápagos will probably be the marine iguana. Your first encounter may be a bit shocking. It certainly was for me. My first evening in the islands, while lining up a sunset shot, I crouched down near a rock. Only after quite some time did I turn my head and become suddenly aware that I was eye-to-eye with a 3 ft long marine iguana. It takes a while to get past their prehistoric looks, especially meeting this way for the first time. Somehow you forget that these creatures are vegetarians, because your mind has somehow flashed-back to **GODZILLA** reruns. The crest of spines running down the back (of the male) and claw-like talons doesn't exactly ease these initial feelings. But, of course, they're harmless, and after a few days in the Galápagos, they start looking kind of cute. No, the sun isn't getting to you, and it's not closing time. You've simply gotten hooked on the Galápagos!

It's easy to walk right up to a few marine iguanas without noticing them at first. The dark coloring blends perfectly with the lava rocks, and they can keep their frozen pose for hours at a time. The coloring seems to serve a dual purpose. First, it offers a degree of protection to the juveniles from their only natural predator, the Galápagos hawk. Second, the dark color is better able to absorb the heat from the sun's rays. The marine iguana spends much of its day sunbathing in an elevated position, angling its body toward and facing the sun, as if searching the skies. When you encounter an entire colony in the same frozen pose, it seems as if they're worshiping the sun god, which in a way they are.

The marine iguana spends more time in the sun than other lizards, for it is the only seafaring member of the Order; it may lose as much as 20 Deg F during its daily excursion into the water, and it takes much of the day to restore its body temperature to normal (about 96 Deg F) as well as to repay its oxygen debt.

The marine iguana is not a casual surface swimmer; it is a strong diver, descending to depths of 35 ft. The dives are generally of brief duration (5-10 minutes) but if need be, the animal can slow its metabolism sufficiently to remain submerged for up to an hour. Typically, the divers are the larger males, possessing the swimming strength to make it through the breakers. The other members of the colony feed intertidally on the exposed lower portions of the rocks. Their diet consists almost exclusively of red or green algae-type seaweed.

The first impression of a marine iguana is not much improved when it appears to spit in your direction every so often. Actually, the animal is sneezing, expelling the excess salt from its system through a special gland connected to the nostrils. Yet another interesting adaptation, although for some people not a very pretty one to behold. Until they get hooked on the Galápagos!

Photo Opportunities: The frequent salt-sneezing gives the marine iguana a white-crusted forehead; it makes for a great close-up, especially early in the evening when there's less glare and a better chance of getting facial detail. Some are more white than others, giving the appearance of sneezing into the wind once or twice too often. You might want to document the blunt snout, useful for nibbling the thin layer of algae off the rocks. Remember to use your polarizing filter if you're shooting in bright sunlight. The same is true when you encounter a male in his bright breeding colors, which (in addition to animal size) varies from island to island. The males on Española (Hood) Island are colorful year-round; they are a very bright red and green (see Photos #32-33), and you will want to capture this image of "Beauty on the Beast."

The breeding season, which also varies between islands, presents the opportunity to witness the aggressive male territorial behavior. This "head-bobbing" activity goes on throughout the year but is intensified during the breeding months, as is actual conflict, which consists mostly of head-butting. All this makes for ideal footage for those with a video camera. For photographers, the action is a bit hard to capture, but a close-up of the scarred face of the vanquished iguana is very vivid.

You'll also want to get a few pictures of the entire body, making sure the focus is tight on the scales. Don't accidentally cut out the forelimb and talon from the foreground. An interesting shot is to have the iguana silhouetted against the sky and a breaking wave. Again, this is a great evening opportunity as they try to catch the last warm rays of sunlight.

Those with an underwater camera may be fortunate enough to get a shot of the marine iguana feeding on the algae beneath the surface. As the waters are not very clear (due to upwelling), for good results you may have to find a shooting opportunity in a pocket of sunlight; this is often easier said than done.

Where To See Them: While marine iguanas may seem to be everywhere, especially on the lava rock shores, their numbers (estimated at over 200,000) are in fact declining, and the distribution is patchy. In the extreme *El Niño* weather phenomenon of 1982-83, the cold Humboldt Current failed, thus reducing the upwelling of nutrients from the ocean floor. The marine iguanas were thus forced to feed on algae containing little nutrient value; many perished that year, actually starving on a full stomach of food.

The marine iguana can overcome natural disasters much easier than the ones that are manmade — specifically the hard-to-control feral cats that prey on young marine iguanas, as well as on the eggs and hatchlings.

LAND IGUANAS — (*IGUANAS TERRESTRES*)

> *The terrestrial species . . . is confined to the central part of the Archipelago. Like their brothers the sea-kind, they are ugly animals, of a yellowish-orange beneath, and of a brownish-red colour above: from their low facial angle they have a singularly stupid appearance. When not frightened, they slowly crawl along with their tails and bellies dragging on the ground. They often stop and doze for a minute or two, with closed eyes and hind legs spread out on the parched soil.*
>
> Charles Darwin, 1845

Just as its seafaring cousin, the land iguana is a vegetarian (although juveniles, with immature digestive systems, are known to eat insects as well). But the similarity in diet ends right there, for the land iguana dines mostly on prickly pear cactus. The pads as well as the fruit. Spines and all! It has been known to roll the cactus pads on the ground, thus knocking the tips off the spines, but the land iguana usually lies flat on the ground and munches away on the cactus with the tough spines intact.

The cactus provides both food and water to the land iguana, who, living in the drier parts of the archipelago, goes without fresh water for much of the year. Part of the adaptation to the drier environment is the conservation of energy. While capable of great speed, these 3 ft long creatures typically move quite slowly, and give the appearance of being lazy, as Darwin hinted at in his comments above.

Land iguanas are burrowing animals, and their shallow tunnels provide shelter at night, shade from the sun, a nesting place, and a temporary home for the hatchlings.

Photo Opportunities: The beautiful yellow coloring will really pop out if you can possibly shoot the land iguana in the shade of the cactus tree. It will also help to underexpose by a half to one stop. Watching the land iguana chomp away on a cactus pad will give you ample opportunity to snap off a good series. Every now and then while dining, the cute little beast will stick its tongue off to one side, as if licking its lips in exclamation of just how wonderful the meal really was. If you're using a telephoto, focus carefully on the intricate scales, which are similar in appearance to a knight's mail (see Photo #36). When you're facing the animal head-on, you won't be able to hold focus of both head and tail, so you'll have to make a decision. One answer is to shoot a bit slower and stop down as much as possible, giving a greater depth of field (which will work if you're using fast film). If you have time, and your camera is so equipped, use the depth of field preview button.

Land iguanas have the same sort of symbiotic relationship as the tortoises with the birds that remove ticks and other parasites. You may be fortunate enough to get a shot of this behavior. Also, on South Plaza Island, you may see male aggressive activity, with head-butting and all the rest.

Where To See Them: There are two endemic species of land iguanas living in the arid zones of six central and western islands. One species is found only on Santa Fe, and though there are few to be seen, the land tours ascend into the plateau area that they frequent. The other species will be viewed on your tour of

South Plaza Island as you pass through a small cactus forest; here, the quantities of land iguanas are much larger.

When Darwin visited the Galápagos, the land iguana was most plentiful, as evidenced by the following statement:

> I cannot give a more forceful proof of their numbers, than by stating that when we left at James Island, we could not for some time find a spot free from their burrows on which to pitch our single tent.
> Charles Darwin, 1845

Unfortunately, the land iguana has drastically declined in numbers since Darwin's day and is now an endangered species. Although the adults have no natural predators, they were reportedly considered quite tasty when roasted, and many have come to such a fate at the hands of man through the years. The greatest damage, however, has once again been caused by the introduced animals that have preyed on the young land iguanas and raided their nests. While the feral animal eradication programs have been started, it has become necessary to breed and raise land iguanas at the Darwin Station (where they are off-limits to visitors in order to maintain their naturally skittish behavior). Eventually the adults are repatriated to their home island. As with the giant tortoise program, the results will be long-term, for the land iguana, with a 60 year life span, takes about 10 years to sexually mature.

MARINE (PACIFIC GREEN) TURTLES — (*TORTUGAS MARINAS*)

I was on-deck as the yacht ORCA prepared to lay anchor when I heard the captain call out to the Guide, "¡Mire, mire, copulación!" This isn't exactly what you would expect to hear on a Galápagos Island tour. As curious as the next person, I walked over to the side of the boat they were on and looked down in the water where the captain was pointing. He was absolutely right! I started taking what turned out to be a great series of pictures — of mating sea turtles.

It's quite a show, a tiring one for the female, as there's often a second male onlooker waiting his chance. She's also does the swimming for both of them, as his flippers are busy just holding on.

The fascination of the marine turtle goes a lot further than their mating behavior. They can hold their breath for hours at a time, a process not well understood, but amazing nonetheless. Even more amazing is the growing evidence suggesting that the females return to the very beach on which they were hatched to nest and lay their eggs.

The marine turtle weighs 100-200 lbs and is a vegetarian, feeding on similar algae as the marine iguana, although the turtle's diet is not as narrowly restricted.

Photo Opportunities: If your tour occurs during the mating season, you'll get several shots of mating couples and threesomes. Your best photo opportunity will occur as you drift through the mangroves of Black Turtle Cove in the *panga*, the motor off to keep "tourist interruptus" to a minimum. The thick mangrove forest blocks out a lot of the sunlight, so you want to be shooting high speed film. In or out of mating season, marine turtles will swim past the *panga*, just under the surface of the water. Make sure your polarizing filter is on, and rotate the front filter until you can clearly see underwater with a minimum of reflection. This will also enable you to get some shots of the white-tipped shark (*tintorera*), which also swims these waters, as well as leopard rays.

As you're drifting along, keep alert in all directions. On shore, you will occasionally see a female resting between rounds. In the water, the head of a marine turtle will break the surface from time to time, mouth agape, to catch a breath of air, accompanied by a loud exhale. If you catch this shot just right, you can convince your friends you visited Loch Ness South when you show them the photos. The white-tipped sharks and leopard rays will suddenly come into view, and just as quickly be gone. You have to be ready and fast to catch the action here, but it's worth the effort.

Where To See Them: The marine turtle can be seen mating during the later part of the year in several beach locations just offshore and primarily in the secluded lagoons. Their favorite location is appropriately called Black Turtle Cove (Caleta Tortuga Negra) on the northern end of Santa Cruz Island; *tortuga negra*, by the way, is another local name for the Pacific green turtle.

Despite the extremely high mortality rate of the hatchlings, due to natural and introduced predators, the number of marine turtles continues to remain high in the Galápagos.

LAVA LIZARDS — (*LAGARTIJAS DE LAVA*)

These lizards, from four to eight inches in length, were marked with colours which I was beginning to expect in these islands, grey and black and scarlet-ash, and lava and flame — appropriate for a land where every hill was a volcano, every path a flow of lava, and with the plants growing from tufa beds and ash heaps. The male lizards were grey and brown above, mottled and banded with black, with the throat and underparts a mixture of pink, red and contrasting black. The females were usually more of a monochrome brown, with a brilliant slash of fiery scarlet over face, shoulders and sides.

They ran and frolicked about, running in and out of the lava crevices, with always a lookout for marauding birds. Of course they were absolutely tame and investigated all our luggage. When pursued, they would impudently pause until almost within reach, at the last moment going through a great show of intimidation, nodding the whole head and body violently up and down, and expanding the scarlet and black throat pouch to its fullest.

William Beebe, 1924

Beebe's accurate descriptions of the lava lizard appeared in the best-selling **GALAPAGOS: WORLD'S END** (see the Literature section at the end of this book). The narrative account of adaptive radiation is most graphic.

In all, the lava lizard has evolved to form seven endemic species in the Galápagos, with differences in size, color, and behavior. They all have many of the intriguing characteristics typical of lizards, such as the ability to regenerate a tail sacrificed in exchange for freedom and the change in color as a function of mood and/or temperature. What is unusual is the advanced development of color vision in the lava lizard, which is said to play a role in the courtship process, as the females have bright red throats during the mating season.

Lava lizards live up to 10 years, a relatively long time for such little beasts. They are omnivores, but dine mostly on insects.

Photo Opportunities: A close-up on the rocks is in order, especially a few shots of the red-throated female. For documentation, it would be great to shoot one while it was "tiptoeing" (to help regulate its body temperature by reducing the heat exchange potential).

Where To See Them: On most islands. While lava lizards are not the most exciting animals to watch, you may want to observe their territorial "push-up" behavior, which is said to vary from island to island.

SEA BIRDS

Of all the animals that call the Galápagos archipelago their home, only the aquatic birds (sea birds and shore birds) can come and go as they please. Thus, it is not surprising that the rate of endemism is low. Of the land-based animals, including reptiles, mammals, and land birds, over 80 percent are endemic to the Galápagos; of the nineteen species of sea birds, only five are endemic to the islands. Two of those five, the penguin and flightless cormorant, do not have the ability to leave via the air and are thus also captive endemic species.

While having the ability to leave, sea birds have obviously chosen to call the Galápagos their home. They were among the early settlers of the archipelago, as there were fish in the ocean well before there were plants and insects ashore to form the food supply for the land-based animals. In fact, it is the sea birds themselves who carried most of the pioneer plant seeds to the Galápagos, stuck to their wings and feet as well as in their digestive systems.

In the ocean-dominated environment of the archipelago, the sea birds play a most important role. Many of your hours in the Galápagos will be spent observing their behavior in flight, on the ground, along the surface of the ocean, and under the water. Their low rate of endemism does not take away from the fascination of observing these marvelous birds. For those of you that are non-birders or feel that our winged friends are "nice, but dull," you're in for a most pleasant surprise, for the members of the nesting sea bird community of the Galápagos Islands are most unusual, visually and behaviorally interesting, as well as extremely entertaining.

Note: Most all the sea birds feed on surface fish and squid who in turn depend on a continuous supply of algae for their food. For the algae to grow, nutrients are required. It is the current-generated upwelling activity that brings these nutrients to the surface. In the extreme *El Niño* of 1982-83, the Humboldt Current (responsible for upwelling) failed, and the food chain was broken. With most of the algae gone, there were significantly fewer fish that swam near the surface, thus drastically reducing the sea birds' food supply. Since many sea birds inhabit the Galápagos on a seasonal basis, for nesting and breeding purposes, and wander the oceans during the rest of the year, the adults were able to survive with little impact to the overall population. As we'll see later on, this wasn't true of the ground-based penguin and flightless cormorant. Also, in many cases the hatchling mortality rate was extremely high.

The brown noddy, Audubon's shearwater, sooty tern, and the petrels will not be discussed.

WAVED ALBATROSSES — (*ALBATROS DE GALAPAGOS*)

While most albatrosses are found in cool, southern waters, a species endemic to the Galápagos has evolved — the waved albatross. The largest bird in the islands, weighing about 10 lb with a wing span approaching 8 ft, the waved albatross is named for the wavy grey lines on its white undercarriage. Starting early in April, virtually the entire nation of waved albatross adults (over 10,000 couples) arrives at Española (Hood) Island to nest and breed, where they remain until the end of the year.

Upon arrival, the first order of business is breeding, followed by egg laying, hatching, and rearing. There is no time to waste, as the young albatross (or "bird of the year," in ornithologist talk) needs to be fledged by December, when the southern current slackens, significantly reducing the upwelling and the resultant food supply. That time, in fact, is short, is further understood when the 60 day incubation period and the 167 days to fledge are factored in.

That only a single egg is laid is understandable, given its weight of about 1/2 lb. That the parents roll the egg around each day, despite the obvious risk of it cracking, is less understandable. Some say this activity increases the hatching potential, but to date this has not been documented. After the 2 month incubation period, the chick is hatched and a unique feeding process begins. Many sea birds travel great distances to find food for their family, and on the return flights must guard their catch of fish and/or squid from the piratical frigatebirds. The waved albatross digests and stores its catch as an oily blend; it does not return to base until the supply room is full, thus ensuring much larger portions than it could carry otherwise as well as an incident-free journey.

The courtship behavior, at its peak in October, is quite the ritual, an elaborately choreographed set of moves. It is by no means a quiet celebration; as their long bills circle each other, they make loud, castanet-like clicking sounds and high-pitched vocalizations, most appropriate background music for the dance, which ornithologists have elaborately notated.

After the last dance is done, a strange thing happens — nothing! The marriage is not consumated; breeding behavior does not happen — at least not yet. For now, the couple have formed (or reformed, as these beautiful birds mate for life) what is termed a "pair bond." Breeding will wait for the following spring (as explained above), when the pair will return to Española.

The serious *El Niño* of 1982-83 resulted in a complete breeding failure; not a single egg hatched! Fortunately, for a couple of reasons, this doesn't seem to have affected the population. First is their relatively long life span, about 40-50 years; thus, one bad year has minimal effect. Second, the waved albatross tends to only breed about every other year on the average, so the *El Niño* seems to have altered the schedule rather than the overall population.

Photo Opportunities: The colors of the waved albatross are very rich and will provide you with some beautiful pictures. A telephoto lens is recommended. If you arrive in the fall, the courtship ritual is a must, which is said to be more pronounced towards evening. Great for video cameras too! The feeding behavior is somewhat humorous as the oversized, downy juveniles are the ultimate "Baby Huey" look-alikes (see Photo #41).

Where To See Them: On Española (Hood) Island. If you want to see the waved albatross, plan your visit to the Galápagos between April and the beginning of December.

BLUE-FOOTED BOOBIES — (PIQUEROS PATAS AZULES)

Of all the birds in the Galápagos, none is more famous than the blue-footed booby. Boobies are well represented in the islands, with three resident species. The derivation of their name most likely comes from Spanish sailors, who, between the birds' silly behavior and funny-colored feet, decided they truly were clowns (bobos). The birds would perch on raised hatches near the bow of British ships; this, as you can guess, is the origin of the term "booby hatch," which today has another uncomplimentary meaning, similar to "loony bin." There are, by the way, no loons in the Galápagos — none with wings at any rate.

While we're on the subject of names, the Spanish call boobies piqueros (lances), referring to the shape of their beaks. All three species dive steeply into the water, hitting the surface with tremendous force. Air sacs located in the skull serve as built-in shock absorbers, yet another interesting piece of evolutionary work. In addition, the blue-foots have proportionally longer tails than the other two species, which acts as a rudder and allows them to make bullet-like dives in less than 2 ft of water and thus feed closer to shore. The male has a somewhat longer tail, although the difference is not readily apparent to most visitors. And you can't tell he from she by who's sitting on the "pseudo-nest," because they share the brooding chore.

There are other ways in which male and female blue-footed boobies are easily distinguished — via sight and sound. The male's eye pupil appears to be smaller than the female's; in reality, the pupils are the same size, with the female's pupil surrounded by pigmentation. Also, in a bit of a role reversal, he is a whistling soprano while she is a honking tenor.

Aside from the color of their feet, it is their courtship dance for which the blue-footed boobies are so well known. After watching a few performances, I seriously wondered whether the choreographers of **OKLAHOMA** ever visited the Galápagos. It's easy to imagine a Broadway-style western dance while watching these little creatures looking up at the sky with wings behind their backs, tilting their heads to one side and then the other, while the feet are lifted in sequence, pointed out at a 45 degree angle.

The nest-building behavior of the blue-footed booby can be described as vestigial; twigs and other nesting material are dutifully gathered but are never used as the eggs are laid and incubated on the bare ground. This reminds me of a dog trying to bury a bone in the house by pawing at the carpet, going through the inbred motions.

During incubation, both parents take turns brooding, sitting out in the heat of the sun. At this time, a couple of interesting temperature-regulatory systems are put to work. The first, called gular fluttering, is characteristic of many sea birds, and it is an easily-observed behavior of the boobies. They look like they're gargling, while the function is closer to panting. What flutters and does the cooling is the gular sack, a loose flap of skin in the throat area. Another built-in temperature control device is the webbed foot, which, owing to its heavy vasculature, is an excellent heat exchanger. Thus, to provide warmth, blue-footed boobies gently place their webbed feet directly under the egg or chick.

An average of two chicks are hatched a few days apart. Rarely will more than one survive (the exceptions being in years of plentiful food). Typically the older chick, with its superior strength, will out-compete for the available food from the parents, eventually starving out the younger one. Another technique is for the older chick to force the younger one out of the nesting ring (a circle of guano), sort of a miniature *sumo* wrestling match, with the consequences here much more dire for the loser; once outside the ring, it is outside the family and no longer cared for. This kind of behavior seems cruel to us, especially when we see a dead or dying youngster lying just off the trail. This is a natural insurance policy, however; if something tragic were to happen to the older chick, the younger one would be raised. This guarantees a survival factor for each generation and guards against mass-starvation in the event of a major food shortage. Given the unpredictable nature of the environment, including the availability of food, this is a very practical system.

Photo Opportunities: Many of the blue-footed boobies choose a nesting site 1-2 ft off the trail, and as is the case with so many of the animals in the Galápagos, they do not move away when approached. Thus, you will have the chance at some great close-ups, especially of their pretty blue feet. The blue coloring will really jump out on a hazy day, early in the morning, or late in the afternoon. If you're shooting in direct sunlight, use a polarizing filter to get rid of the reflected glare coming off their feet, and you'll get deeper blue coloring. Also, if you're patient and look closely, you'll see one with the egg(s) and/or the chick(s) underneath. Occasionally, you'll see a recently-hatched chick and the broken shell, which together with the blue-footed background, makes for a great shot. This will often occur in the shade of the parent, so make sure your light meter isn't picking up ambient light. A spot meter would be useful in this tricky situation; if you increase the exposure to get the detail on the chick, you may wash out the blue coloring on the feet. The best is to bracket.

If you're lucky enough to see some landings, they come in with their feet up and forward, using them like flaps on an airplane. Its an excellent opportunity to get an outstanding blue-footed photo. The whole landing scene is great for video cameras as well.

The courtship dance is another wonderful opportunity, both for still and video photography. It's not a continuous dance, so you have to scan the colony carefully and anticipate the next likely dance partners.

Where To See Them: You are likely to see large colonies of blue-footed boobies on Española and Seymour Islands most times of the year. Another large colony exists on Daphne Major, an islet which is not included in most tours due to restrictions on the number of visitors set by the National Park.

The breeding cycle of the blue-footed booby is less than 1 year but is not related to any particular season. Thus, the colony size on a given island at a given time of the year may be forming, breaking up, or at its peak.

MASKED or WHITE BOOBIES — (*PIQUEROS ENMASCARADOS* or *PIQUEROS BLANCOS*)

Owing to their large size, masked boobies need a bit of takeoff assistance from the wind, and thus nest on high locations near the coast. They feed further out at sea but otherwise have many of the same behavioral patterns as the blue-foots, although less pronounced. This includes the somewhat vestigial nesting behavior, whereby twigs and other materials are offered to the mate as part of the courtship ritual (see Photo #45).

Photo Opportunities: Masked boobies are extremely photogenic, with brilliant white coloring and black face mask. They are frequently seen by the edge of a cliff, posed on a rock. A soft focus on the sea and sky adds to the dignity of this profile shot. The juveniles, with their downy, half-feathered appearance, are the ultimate boobs, and will no doubt provide you with some amusing photos.

Where To See Them: On the steep slopes of Tower (Genovesa) and Española (Hood) Islands. Unlike the other boobies, the masked has a fixed breeding cycle, although it varies from island to island. Thus, you are likely to see them on Tower from May to February, and on Española from September to May.

RED-FOOTED BOOBIES — (*PIQUEROS PATAS ROJAS*)

Feeding on flying fish far out at sea, the red-footed booby tends to nest on the outer islands of the archipelago. Unlike the other boobies, the red-foot nests in trees; it has little claws at the end of its webbed feet that are suitable for perching. It also builds real nests which, although nothing more than a fragile-looking arrangement of a few twigs, is a marked departure from the other boobies, who nest on the open ground.

Photo Opportunities: The photogenic qualities of the red-footed boobies were noted in detail by the famous zoologist, William Beebe, in the following vivid description; Beebe takes the opportunity to point out that these boobies truly were *bobos* (clowns):

> *When one of them looked down its long beak at me it reminded me more than anything else of a circus clown in full regalia. The bill was greenish-yellow shading into blue at the tip, the base of the bill and narrow forehead pink, set off by jet black pigment behind. The skin around the eye was bright blue grey, the eye itself cadmium-yellow, framed by eyelids of clear forget-me-not blue. When the bright red feet were added to this, the harlequin effect was most striking. And with it all, the bird wore an air of anxious sobriety which heightened the bizarreness of the colour scheme.*
>
> William Beebe, 1924

Where To See Them: While the red foot has the highest population of all the boobies in the Galápagos, it spends much of its time on the open seas and thus appears to be more scarce than the others. While scattered colonies exist on the outer fringes of the Galápagos, the red-footed booby can best be seen by visitors on Tower (Genovesa) Island, where well over 100,000 pairs come to nest. A colony also exists on Punta Pitt, San Cristóbal Island.

FLIGHTLESS CORMORANTS — (*CORMORANS NO VOLADOR*)

The flightless cormorant is endemic to the Galápagos Islands and is the only grounded cormorant species (out of about thirty species overall) in the world. This is yet another fascinating example of evolution to fill a niche. In this case, the niche was the lack of competition for an available food source (bottom-fish, eels, and octopuses) close to shore. At the same time, there was a lack of predators, thus reducing the need to flee on the wing. What took place was a slow, gradual evolution to a streamlined body (for swimming speed) and strong legs (for powerful diving ability), while the wings and supporting musculature atrophied through the generations. The sparsely-feathered wings are now considered vestigial.

Not only does the flightless cormorant swim as a means of hunting, but for romantic purposes as well. In a courtship display reminiscent of an Esther Williams movie, both male and female engage in an aquatic dance. Nesting takes place on the beaches of the western islands, just above the high water line; the nests are made of flotsam and jetsam, held together by seaweed.

In behavior uncharacteristic of Galápagos sea birds, flightless cormorants do not mate for life. In fact, after the eggs are hatched and the chicks partially raised, the female often takes up with another male, leaving dad to continue raising the young on his own.

Photo Opportunities: Although the wings are no longer used for flying pur- poses, the flightless cormorant still stretches its wings wide to dry them, which makes for a great photographic opportunity (see Photo #57). You may be lucky enough to get a chance at a sunrise or sunset shot, where the cormorant can be silhouetted against the golden twilight colors.

Where To See Them: Only on the western islands of Fernandina and Isabela, due to the high level of upwelling activity; there they can be found nesting on the beaches throughout the year.

The flightless cormorant is a vulnerable species. During a prolonged famine, it can not simply leave the islands in search of food elsewhere. Consequently, the already fragile number of 800 pairs was reduced by about 50 percent during the severe 1982-83 *El Niño*, from which there has fortunately been a recovery. A larger danger to survival is in attack from wild dogs. The flightless cormorant gave up its wings partially because there were no natural predators on land. Now, with introduced feral animals, the population could be threatened.

FRIGATEBIRDS — (*FRAGATAS*)

The frigates were war ships, commonly used by pirates; frigatebirds are the pirate ships of the air, a name earned by reputation and habit. They are built for and look the part. Adult frigatebirds are large, black birds with long wingspans and deeply forked tails, which combine to give them exceptional aerial maneu- verability. They have excellent vision and are fast, being extremely lightweight for their size. Their weapon is a long hooked-tip beak. They chase after other ocean birds returning home from fishing trips, harassing them in midair until the food is disgorged and dropped. The frigatebird then quickly and expertly swoops down and plucks the food out of the air. The most common victims of this aerial piracy are the boobies and red-billed tropicbird.

The outlaw ways of the frigatebird are described in several texts as cleptoparasitic feeding patterns! Despite the terminology, this is not an aberrant behavioral pattern which formed as a result of an underprivileged youth; it is an evolved trait, formed out of necessity. The frigatebird does not have a large enough preen gland to supply the amount of oil required to effectively waterproof its wings. Since it easily can become waterlogged, it cannot dive into the water after spotting a fish in the manner of the other sea birds. This is not to say, however, that it is incapable of directly catching its own food. On the contrary, it flies low over the water and uses the tip of its beak to expertly pluck a fish or squid from the surface. The limitation of this system is the availability of food near the surface, which is seasonal at best (due to the upwelling patterns), and not at all during a bad *El Niño* year. Thus, piracy evolved as a way of survival.

Frigatebirds nest in trees and bushes. When the single egg is hatched, the parental responsibilities have just begun; it takes the juveniles about 6 months to learn to fly and over a year to learn the world-class stunt flying skills required to survive on its own.

Photo Opportunities: One of the most sought-after photographs in the Galápagos is the bright red inflated balloon-like sac of the male frigatebird. During courtship, a group of males "on display" are seated in trees or shrubs, sacs inflated. When a female passes by overhead, they turn skyward, shake, and loudly call attention to themselves. Not very subtle, but an effective technique, as the female soon accepts an offer and lands nearby her chosen mate. Occasionally the males will take to the air with their sacs still inflated, which makes for a great photo opportunity. Telephoto lenses are required.

Part of your daily diet at sea will be fresh fish. Occasionally, while you're touring an island, one of the sailors (called a *marinero*) will take the *panga* out for a fishing trip, usually a successful one. When the cook (*cocinero*) cleans the fish, a squadron of frigatebirds will soon be overhead, seeming to glide without effort by moving their forked tails in and out. This makes for a wonderful opportunity for some great on-the-wing shots, and if you can convince the cook to do this towards late afternoon, you'll have excellent back lighting (see the front cover and Photo #37).

Where To See Them: There are two species of frigatebirds in the Galápagos — the "great" and the "magnificent" (sounds like a spaghetti western). While they can be distinguished from each other, we'll take the easy road and do it by geographic location. The "great" is more ocean going, and thus tends to be an outer island bird; a large colony can be seen displaying on Darwin Bay, Tower (Genovesa) Island during the first half of the year. There is also a colony on Punta Pitt, San Cristóbal Island. The "magnificent" are more central in their distribution, and just about all the tours visit their colony on Seymour Island, where they can be seen displaying throughout the year. Individuals from both species are distributed throughout the islands and everywhere at sea on their piratical journeys.

SWALLOW-TAILED GULLS — (*GAVIOTAS DE COLA BIFURCADA*)

Forming the night-shift of the working class sea birds, swallowed-tailed gulls are endemic to the Galápagos Islands. Every evening they fly out to sea, feeding on surface fish and squid. They are aided in their nocturnal hunting by extraordinary night vision as well as by the luminescent microorganisms that often "light up" these waters. Night hunting appears to be a form of adaptive behavior for the swallow-tailed gull, evolving from the necessity of bringing back food safely (as frigatebirds are not nocturnal) and/or the greater abundance of fish and squid on the surface at night. The latter is another form of adaptive survival behavior on the part of fish and squid — feeding on the surface at night and staying in deeper waters during daylight to avoid predators.

The swallow-tailed gull is noted for its vocal repertoire, including its alarm call, a "shake, rattle, and scream" alerting other members of the colony to the presence of an intruder.

Photo Opportunities: The swallow-tailed gull is a beautiful bird. It will be the first to greet you on dry landings along rocky shorelines, as you step out of the *panga* onto the steppingstone pier. Surprisingly, it won't fly off as you approach within a couple of feet. The coloring is so perfect, you can't pass up the shot. Its bright red eye-rings are set off against large dark eyes and a charcoal head, while the red feet are contrasted with its pink legs, grey and white body, and plumage.

Where To See Them: Along the sea cliffs of most of the central and northern islands, where excellent in-flight and landing shots can be taken. There are major colonies on South Plaza, Tower (Genovesa) and Seymour. In all, there are an estimated 10,000-15,000 pairs of swallow-tailed gulls in the Galápagos.

LAVA GULLS — (*GAVIOTAS DE LAVA*)

The lava gull, endemic to the Galápagos Islands, is somewhat enigmatic. Though it is quite scare, with only about 400 pairs, it doesn't seem to be in any danger of extinction. In fact, there's no evidence to suggest that the population was ever any greater. Considering their small numbers, lava gulls are quite casual in their nesting habits; the first nest wasn't found until the 1960s.

They may not have sound breeding patterns, but they are very protective when they do breed and are known for their dive-bombing attacks on intruders. From the rest of their habits, one can either classify lava gulls as lazy ne'er-do-wells or as filling the niche of the scavenger. They do scavenge, hanging around boat harbors and the fringes of coastal towns. They beg, permanently borrow, steal, and when they have to, hunt food. The loud laugh-like call supports their non-industrious image.

Photo Opportunities: Lava gulls, true to their name, blend in perfectly with the coastal lava rocks. You may want to get a close-up documentation shot; their white eye-ring makes a good focal point.

Where To See Them: Here and there, on the coastal areas of the central islands. The only significant numbers are found in the bays and lagoons of

Puerto Ayora on Santa Cruz Island, owing to the scavenging potential offered by the touring and fishing boats as well as the large human population.

BROWN PELICANS — (*PELICANOS*)

Often seen flying in formation, their wings alternately beating and gliding in synch, pelicans are one of the few familiar vacation landmarks that you'll see in the Galápagos — an old friend, and nice to have around.

Photo Opportunities: Here's a few more pelican scenes to add to your collection. If you're an early riser, go on-deck and check out the *panga* (towed behind the yacht). Once in a while, there will be a pelican seated at the helm, which makes for an interesting caption shot. This opportunity might also occur when the cook casts the dinner scraps overboard. A dramatic sequence of pictures can be taken at sunset, when one plunge-diving pelican after another is silhouetted against the glowing orange and red of the evening sky. During courtship, pelicans often intertwine their necks and bills in an interesting pattern, which makes for another good photo opportunity (see Photo #58).

Where To See Them: As in many parts of the world, brown pelicans are seen on just about every coast, dock, harbor, and anchorage in the Galápagos.

GALAPAGOS PENGUINS — (*PINGUINOS DE GALAPAGOS*)

What would possess a penguin to live on the equator? These flightless sea birds seem much more at home on an ice floe in the waters of the Antarctic. Once again the answer lies in the Humboldt Current, owing both to its direction and the cold waters it brings from the South Polar region.

This is not to say that the first penguins to arrive at the archipelago started their journey in the Antarctic Ocean; rather, the endemic Galápagos species originated in the extreme southern part of South America — the cold, stormy region known as Chilean Patagonia. One scenario is that they arrived during an Ice Age and were subsequently stranded as the earth warmed and the ice melted.

Penguins feed on small fish and crustaceans, using their swimming speed to advantage. As is true of many of the sea birds, they mate for life.

Photo Opportunities: If you are fortunate enough to visit the western islands, have your camera ready as you ride in the *panga*. Scan the bases of the rocky cliffs, where penguins are often seen standing outside the lava caves in which they nest. For most of you, this opportunity may occur on Bartolomé Island, but the colonies here are much smaller and the sightings are infrequent. When you do see them, notice how their arms are out at an angle, as if carrying a pair of invisible suitcases. This is a penguin heat exchange system, facing into the breeze and using the blood vessels in their wings as cooling fins. The photography is tricky, due to the dark background. While it may be necessary to underexpose the shot by a full stop (to negate the effect of the dark rocks and shadows on your light meter), the underexposure time may be significantly less than 1/60th of a second (especially if you have a telephoto lens on). The key is to use fast film (ASA 400) and to bracket the shot.

Snorkeling in these waters may give you the rare opportunity of getting a few underwater penguin photos. It's a real difficult shot, because of their blazing underwater speed; you actually have to pan underwater and hope you catch them.

Where To See Them: As pointed out above, the Galápagos penguin has a natural nesting and feeding preference for the cooler waters of the western islands, Fernandina, and Isabela. There is also a small colony on Bartolomé, near the famous Pinnacle Rock. Occasionally penguins are also seen off the coast of Floreana, swimming close to the beach.

The Galápagos penguin was severely affected by the 1982-83 *El Niño*, with losses estimated at over 75 percent! They are very slowly recovering, too slowly according to some. Population figures widely vary from a few thousand to less than a thousand individuals.

RED-BILLED TROPICBIRDS — (*PAJAROS TROPICALES* or *PILOTOS*)

The red-billed tropicbird is the most beautiful and graceful bird in the Galápagos. Hearing their piercing cries as they fly back and forth near the steep cliffs, your eyes are drawn upwards, riveted by the long, kite-like streaming tails (see Photos #26-27). Occasionally, one will swoop down and disappear from view; when you look down over the ledge, you can sometimes spot the white tail-feathers blowing in the strong off-shore winds, protruding out of a crevice in the lava rocks. This is the nest, ideally located for protection and takeoffs, but a most difficult landing target in the swirling winds.

Despite their beauty and grace, the red-billed tropicbirds seem to lead a somewhat dangerous life. The desired nesting locations are limited and frequently fought over. Once a site is settled and the single egg is laid and hatched, getting food back to the precarious nest isn't easy. It's a long journey, for they feed far out at sea. On the return flight, the frigatebirds are ever on the ready for mid-air piracy. Thus, there is an iffy food supply, and many hatchlings do not survive.

Photo Opportunities: Once again, a telephoto lens is required. Panning will produce several exciting shots, and often some surreal images as they are trying to land, their wings beating furiously against the wind in a stalemate (see Photo #28). They will sometimes remain suspended in the air less than 50 ft away, hovering close to their nest, their wings a blur. Another great opportunity for a video camera!

To get your best shots of the red-billed tropicbird requires patience, as they seem to be doing endless laps up and down the coast. Eventually they will make a landing attempt. Follow them in with your eyes, and eventually you'll find a nesting area on an overhanging ledge, where you can get some shots without danger of falling. These nesting shots can be beautiful, as you have a white streaming tail and scarlet red bill against the dark background of the crevice in which they dwell.

Where To See Them: Several locations throughout the Galápagos. Your best views will be on Española (Hood), Tower (Genovesa), and South Plaza Islands, where the trail follows the vertical cliffs. Afternoons are best, when they return from their fishing trips.

SHORE BIRDS

Shore birds are a fairly diverse group of wading or swimming birds. While they are capable of long distance flight and are often migratory, shore birds do not feed out at sea; instead they find their food on beaches, at tide edges, in coastal lagoons and salt ponds (*salinas*). In an isolated archipelago such as the Galápagos, with so much of the area being coastline, the shore birds play a very important role in the ecosystem.

Note: The egrets, night herons, striated heron, pintail duck, common stilt, and migrant species will not be discussed.

GREAT BLUE HERONS — (*GARZAS MORENAS*)

The name "great blue heron" is a bit of a misnomer. While it is certainly the largest heron in the Galápagos, the great blue is actually grey in appearance; this explains the adjectival portion of its Spanish name, *morena*, meaning dusky.

The great blue heron has the long legs and bill typical of wading birds. It feeds intertidally, primarily on small fish, waiting patiently and then suddenly stabbing the prey with a quick thrust of its beak.

Photo Opportunities: Always beautiful to photograph, great blue herons are often seen while you're *panga*-riding past rocky shores. With their overall size, long legs, head hunched on shoulders, and cowlick-looking head feathers, they are readily identifiable. Be watchful for an in-flight shot, as the great blue heron is most graceful in the air, with slow, smooth wing beats and its head drawn back on its shoulders.

Where To See Them: Usually seen alone on the coastal areas of all but the northern islands.

LAVA HERONS — (*GARZAS DE LAVA*)

The lava heron is the only endemic heron species in the Galápagos. With its dark coloring and small hunched appearance, it is hardly noticeable as it slinks along the lava rock background in search of food.

Photo Opportunities: Watching their patient, purposeful hunting behavior, you'll most likely be rewarded with a couple of interesting shots. When seen from the back, the dark plumage often resembles judicial robes.

Where To See Them: On the coastal areas of all the islands.

GREATER FLAMINGOS — (*FLAMENCOS*)

There are about 500 greater flamingos inhabiting the salty lagoons (called *salinas*) of the Galápagos. Their beautiful pink color is picked up from the pink shrimp which constitutes a major portion of their diet.

The greater flamingo is a filter feeder, stirring up the muddy lagoon bottoms by shaking its submerged head back and forth. The stirred material is then ingested and sifted through filter plates located in its bill. To facilitate this process, the flamingo gently curves its neck downward, thereby inverting the head underwater.

Photo Opportunities: With their rich pink coloring, flamingos are great subjects for a variety of photographs. On a calm day, you can capture shots of a single bird or group of flamingos as well as the reflection in the water. This is one time when you don't want to use a polarizer. Their running-flapping-splashing takeoffs are quite spectacular, both for still and video cameras. So are on-the-wing shots, with their long neck and legs completely outstretched in one plane. The use of a telephoto zoom allows you to get the whole flamingo in the picture without extraneous sky in the background.

The greater flamingos have not inhabited the islands for that long a time and are one of the more skittish animals in the Galápagos. They are easily disturbed and will fly off if approached or upset, even abandoning their nests (in which only a single egg is laid). Owing to their small population, it is important to be conservative when advancing to get a better shot; a telephoto lens is the best way to deal with this situation.

Where To See Them: Several locations. There is a large salty lagoon on Floreana that almost all tour groups visit. Other frequently-visited sites are the *salinas* located on James and Rábida (Jervis) Islands. For those who visit the western islands, there are a series of lagoons containing the greater flamingo on Punta Moreno and surrounding the small town of Villamil on Isabela Island.

AMERICAN OYSTERCATCHERS — (*OSTREROS*)

Usually seen in pairs along the rocky shores, the oystercatcher is unmistakable with its long red bill, orange eye-ring, black and white plumage, and flesh-colored feet.

Photo Opportunities: The oystercatcher is very striking, and shots of a pair feeding along the shore can be very dramatic, especially late in the afternoon when the red bill and eye coloring really jump out. They tend to keep their distance, and a telephoto lens is in order.

Where To See Them: Along the rocky shores, in isolated pairs. There are only 100-200 pairs in the Galápagos.

LAND BIRDS

Of land-birds, I obtained twenty-six kinds, all peculiar to the group and found nowhere else, with the exception of one lark-like finch from North America.

Charles Darwin, 1845

Most land birds are medium to small size perching birds with feet well adapted for this purpose — three toes in front and one long toe behind. Land birds do not have the ability of long distance flight. Thus, the only way they could have reached the Galápagos was by chance storms with extremely high winds, carrying the birds across 600 miles of ocean. Owing to the rarity of such conditions, there are very few species of land birds in the Galápagos. Also, those that did arrive and survive couldn't leave. Thus, it is not surprising that out of the twenty-nine species of land birds in the islands, twenty-two of them are endemic to the Galápagos. Darwin's count (see above) wasn't far off; not bad for a brief 5 week visit. Speaking of Darwin, the high rate of endemism of the land birds speaks very loudly for the process of evolution. This evidence was not lost on Darwin, as we'll see later on in this section.

The degree of endemism is related to the niche factor once again. Since land birds remain on one island, the degree of evolved specialization varies from island to island as a function of the number of Vegetation Zones. The greater the number of Vegetation Zones on a particular island, the greater the variety of food and the number of niches that are available to be filled, which in turn results in a greater number of specialized evolved land birds on that island.

The degree of specialization is thus ultimately related to food preference. Some of the land birds are vegetarians, relying on green vegetation for their food supply. Another group feeds on insects, while others are seed eaters. Each type has adapted itself, usually in bill structure, to its food preference. This is strikingly noticeable in the finch, a point that became central in Darwin's arguments for natural adaptation and evolutionary processes.

Colorful plumage does not play an important part in the courting habits of the Galápagos land birds. With notable exceptions, such as the vermillion flycatcher and yellow warbler, most are dull-colored. Some speculate that finding a mate is less competitive in isolated areas so the attractive coloring isn't necessary. The singing of "love songs" seems to play a more prominent role in land bird male courtship behavior.

As a group, land birds are surprisingly tame and can usually be approached for close-up photos.

Note: The paint-billed crake, dark-billed cuckoo, Galápagos flycatcher, common gallinule, Galápagos martin, the owls, and Galápagos rail will not be discussed.

GALAPAGOS DOVES — (PALOMAS)

Endemic to the islands, the Galápagos dove is the only resident member of the pigeon Family (the head-bobbers). It lives in the dry zones, feeding largely on prickly pear (opuntia) cactus seeds and pulp. During courtship, mating pairs occasionally bow to each other, Japanese-style.

Photo Opportunities: The Galápagos dove is a beautiful subject, with its spectacular blue eye-ring as the focal point. It is often half-hidden under shrubs, and your patience will be rewarded with an unobstructed shot.

Where To See Them: On the drier portions of several islands, including Española (Hood), Tower (Genovesa), James, Rábida (Jervis), and Santa Fe.

In the past, many Galápagos doves were hunted for food. Now protected, and not in immediate danger of extinction, there is still concern over their reduced numbers in areas with feral cat populations.

DARWIN'S FINCHES — (PINZONES DE DARWIN)

*A most singular group of finches, related to each other in the struc-
ture of their beaks, short tails, form of body, and plumage. There are*

> *13 species . . . peculiar to this archipelago. The most curious fact is the perfect gradation in the size of the beaks in the different species. One might really fancy that from an original paucity of birds in this archipelago, one species had been taken and modified for different ends.*
>
> Charles Darwin, 1845

Mighty important words and subject matter, especially when you consider the subject — a small, drab-colored, inconspicuous bird called the Galápagos finch. These birds were so central to Darwin's (r)evolutionary theory, that they were given the name "Darwin's finches" in the 1930s. Members of this group include four species of ground finches, two cactus finches, three tree finches, a vegetarian finch, woodpecker finch, mangrove finch, and warbler finch.

What fascinated Darwin was not only the diversity of what were inarguably thirteen unique species, but how quickly and purposefully they evolved from a common ancestor (see the section on Adaptive Radiation in Chapter II). The "purpose" was to adapt (which they did through modifications in beak structure) to the local food supply, which varied tremendously from island to island and even within an island, based on the Vegetation Zone(s). Thus, modifications in beak shape and size facilitated the specialized diets, including soft seeds, hard seeds, twigs, leaves, cacti, insects, ticks (removed from tortoises and iguanas), and even booby blood (in the case of the sharp-beaked "vampire" ground finch). There are two species (the woodpecker and mangrove finches) which actually use tools (twigs or cactus spines) to extract insect larvae from holes in the dead branches of trees.

These specialized adaptations are textbook examples of niche-filling, purposeful adaptation to exploit an available food source for which there is a minimum of competition. Unlike other animals in the Galápagos that have filled an available niche in the ecosystem, Darwin's finches have maintained a degree of generalization. Thus, while the flightless cormorant has lost the ability to fly, the Darwin's finches can and will change their diet in a time of shortage, such as during a drought. Perhaps this is a purposeful fallback, and some speculate that over-specialization never developed owing to all the bad years for a particular food supply. Such are the forces of survival and competition.

The competition among males during courtship is not quite as subtle but nonetheless socially interesting. The male builds several side-entrance nests which are used to help attract the female. It's easy to envision several rich men competing for the sweet young thing by impressing her with their accumulated land holdings. After selecting a mate, the female may want a house of their own, and yet another nest is built. To carry his devotion even further, the male feeds the female prior to egg laying and after incubation.

Photo Opportunities: Darwin's finches look very similar; it is the variations in beak structure which set them apart. As with the mockingbird, you may want to take a few finch pictures on several islands and compare them after you get back. In this case, you'll also want to take some shots in the different Vegetation Zones within the same island, specifically on Santa Cruz. Remember to note down the frame numbers and respective locations. For any kind of success, you'll need a telephoto lens.

Where To See Them: Just about everywhere. Very few casual and beginning birders can make positive identifications of all thirteen species, but you can narrow the possibilities based on the island and Vegetation Zone. Even here, there are annual variations based on the availability of a particular food source. Only the medium tree finch is endemic to a particular island — Floreana.

VERMILLION FLYCATCHERS — (*PAJAROS BRUJOS*)

True to their name, these birds feed on insects usually chased through the air and caught with a loud snap of the beak. While the Galápagos subspecies is endemic to the islands, it is not to be confused with the large-billed Galápagos flycatcher (an endemic species which is not discussed in this section).

Photo Opportunities: The male is a brilliant red, with black eye-stripe, wings, and tail. A telephoto lens will produce some beautiful close-ups. Try to photograph the bird against a dark background (such as a tree trunk) instead of the sky. Use a narrow depth of field to accentuate the subject.

Where To See Them: In the humid highland areas, in particular on Santa Cruz and Isabela (on the hike to the Alcedo Volcano).

GALAPAGOS HAWKS — (*GAVILANES DE GALAPAGOS*)

While birds of prey (raptors), Galápagos hawks are mostly scavengers, feeding on carrion and playing a useful role in the ecosystem. It has exceptional vision, which refines its skill as a hunter. An endemic species, the Galápagos hawk has an interesting social mating and breeding system in which two or more males mate with a single female and help raise the young. The texts refer to this as polyandric behavior.

Photo Opportunities: Soaring in wide circles above the coastlines, the Galápagos hawk is easy to spot in the air. With a telephoto lens, you can get some great back-lit shots, lighting up their outstretched rounded wings and broad, fanned tail. Owing to curiosity, a hawk will occasionally perch nearby, and by approaching slowly and carefully, some excellent close-ups can be had. Before approaching however, ask the Guide if it is safe, for if it is nesting (typically in the summer months), the protective instincts can result in aggressive behavior.

Where To See Them: In the outlying islands. You are most likely to encounter the Galápagos hawk on Española (Hood), Santa Fe, Isabela, Fernandina, and occasionally on James.

While the Galápagos hawk has no natural enemies, it has been hunted (as a varmint) by man to extinction on several islands, including Floreana, San Cristóbal, Seymour, Baltra, and Daphne. In all, there are just over 100 pairs remaining.

GALAPAGOS MOCKINGBIRDS — (*CUCUVES*)

The Galápagos mockingbirds are unusual in several respects. Belying their name (and differing from other mockingbird species), they do not mimic other birds. In many ways, they seem to fill the niche left vacant by the absence of small land mammals. The Galápagos mockingbirds feed on insects, small lizards, young finches, carrion, as well as unprotected food. They tend to get around more by running than by flying. Their breeding behavior is communal, with several generations staying with and defending the family territory as well as assisting in the care and feeding of the juveniles.

To classify this entire group as Galápagos mockingbirds is convenient, but at the same time a bit of a misnomer as there are actually several endemic species and subspecies. The endemic species include the Hood, Chatham, and Charles mockingbirds. The species actually called the Galápagos mockingbird is divided into several subspecies, each named for the island it inhabits. The island-to-island variations include overall size, length of leg, color, voice, and shape of bill. Collectively, they are another excellent example of adaptive radiation, and provided further evidence (in addition to the finches) to support Darwin's theory.

Photo Opportunities: The best opportunities are along the beaches. It might prove interesting to take a shot or two on several islands, making note of the frame numbers, and (with the aid of a field guide) compare the pictures to see if you can spot the variations between the species. The Hood mockingbird, a scavenger, has the longest bill, which you will probably see used to break open an abandoned booby egg; this is part of nature and makes for a good documentation shot and/or video sequence (see Photo #55).

Where To See Them: On most of the main islands. You will see the Hood mockingbird only on Española (Hood) and the Chatham mockingbird only on San Cristóbal (Chatham). The Charles mockingbird is extinct on Charles (Floreana) and is found only on the islets of Champion-near-Floreana and Gardner-near-Floreana, neither of which have Visitor Sites.

YELLOW WARBLERS — (*MARIAS* or *CANARIOS*)

The yellow warbler, true to its family name, is a brightly-colored songster, trilling a rapid series of clear, sweet notes. Its feeding habits are variable, from picking insects off trees, catching them in the air, or patrolling the intertidal zone.

Photo Opportunities: The yellow warbler is one of the prettiest and the only bright yellow bird in the Galápagos. The ideal pose is against a green foliage background. They tend not to sit still, so you have to be fast with the camera. A telephoto lens is recommended.

Where To See Them: On most of the main islands containing green vegetation, from the beaches to the highest hills. The yellow warbler is very common and abundant throughout the Galápagos.

MAMMALS

As discussed in Chapter II (see the sections on The Arrival of Life and Reptiles), mammals were generally not suited to the rigors of the long ocean voyage to the archipelago. Although understandable, it is still amazing to note that there are but six species of mammals that are indigenous to the Galápagos. It is even more amazing that, of these, there are only two land mammal species — both are rice rats! The balance of this under-represented Class were either carried through the air by storm-force winds (two bat species) or by long-distance swimming (the sea lions and fur seals).

While mammals were not readily able to make the journey to the Galápagos on their own, once transported there by man they survived all too well, usually at the expense of other wildlife members. Even the indigenous rats couldn't withstand the onslaught of the introduced black rat; of the seven species of native rice rats, all but two are now extinct, having been out-competed for the available food. Unfortunately, as we all know, the story doesn't end there. Introduced mammals are largely responsible for the long list of extinct and endangered Galápagos wildlife species. We are accountable and have the unpleasant, extremely difficult but necessary task of attempting to reset the balance of nature. Somehow, even though you know it's essential for the survival of the endangered species, it still sounds a bit incongruous to actively take steps to return things to their natural state. Especially when those steps are poisoning and hunting animals as well as stealing tortoise eggs for placement in incubators. I guess cleaning up a mess is a dirty job.

Note: While not considered indigenous to the Galápagos, bottle-nosed dolphins and whales are briefly discussed; the rice rats and bats are not.

GALAPAGOS SEA LIONS — (*LOBOS MARINOS*)

Entertainment will be provided on your Galápagos adventure, courtesy of the sea lions. These playful aquatic mammals will swim with you, serenade you in the morning (and the rest of the day for that matter), and play catch with a twig (or sometimes a marine iguana). As they lie on the beach, they will follow you with inquisitive eyes as you take your land tour of an island.

Sea lions, fur seals, true seals, and walruses are pinnipeds (meaning "finned feet"). They are all strong swimmers and divers. Unlike true seals, however, the sea lions and fur seals have external ears as well as highly-developed front flippers which enable them to be quite agile on land, even on very rocky terrain. The Galápagos sea lion is endemic to the islands and a subspecies of the larger California sea lion. Members of this extremely intelligent species are often trained as "performers," and after touring the Galápagos it's easy to see why.

The Galápagos sea lions may be smaller than their ancestors, but the bulls are pretty hefty and can weigh up to 600 pounds. Males are distinguished by a larger girth, thicker neck, and a noticeable bump on the forehead. Their large size is used to advantage in territorial defense.

A bull will actively protect a territory with boundary lines of up to 70 ft of shoreline. The territory extends into the shallow waters and encompasses all the beach-front real estate. All the females within the territory (numbering up to thirty) are claimed by the bull as mating partners, and along with the juveniles are diligently watched and protected (although females are free to leave one territory for another). The bull is constantly at work defending his territory, barking out his warning to would-be challengers as he swims from one end of the territory to the other. As there are many bulls and few herds, the dominance of the resident bull is often tested. Often, he can stare (and bark) down the challenger, but occasionally fierce, bloody battles erupt.

After no more than a few weeks of round-the-clock patrol duty, often going without food and sleep for extended periods, the beachmaster bull finally tires and is vanquished. There is a new champion, and the cycle repeats itself. Again and again. It's a curious process, and it's easy to think in terms of male vanity, chauvinism, etc. Perhaps, but I think it goes beyond that. The behavior is obviously useful or it would have evolved out. It doesn't seem related to family behavior, as there is no family unit per se. Could it be that, as with the terrestrial lion, territorial defense is an evolved mechanism to best defend and ensure the survival of the colony? Call it a designated guard, one that's always on the job.

The first order of protection is from the sharks that often lurk in the offshore waters. This involves lifeguard duty as well, and the bull is very good about keeping the playful pups confined to the shark-free shallow pools. Killer whales (orcas) are another concern, as they prey on sea lions in the western portion of the archipelago.

The sea lion pups require quite a bit of attention, as they nurse for up to 3 years, depending on the availability of food. In good times, a pup will be weaned within a year. In the event of a food shortage, however, the pup is fed quite a bit longer, while any new pups are not nursed and basically left to die. This is an extremely sad sight to see, but is necessary for the survival of the colony, as the older pup will generally make it through the tough year. The amount of milk would have been insufficient to feed both pups, and most likely neither of them would have survived. This would have also physiologically stressed the mother, making her susceptible to life-threatening diseases (such as the recently-prevalent sea lion pox). In an interpretation of nature, this is yet another example of a natural insurance policy often seen at work in the Galápagos (see the section on Blue-Footed Boobies).

This grim picture became all too vivid during the 1982-83 *El Niño* weather condition when the food supply of fish and squid was reduced, and successful hunting required a lot of work and deeper dives. Such food as was caught was not sufficient to feed the young pups, and most youngsters were lost that season. Stress-induced diseases took their toll as well.

These unfortunate facts of life fade from thought as you watch the sea lions frolic in the water. During adolescence, the playful aquabatics of the sea lion pups are excellent practice for the feeding skills required later in life. Owing to their large pressure-reinforced lungs and oxygen-rich blood, adult sea lions are capable of diving to depths of 500 feet and remaining underwater for up to a half hour.

The Galápagos sea lion has about a 20 year life span.

Photo Opportunities: Nursing, barking, playing, sleeping, and swimming, the sea lions will provide you with an endless supply of photographic opportunities. Every time you walk past them, you'll see a different expression or pose worth capturing on film.

Often they'll emerge from a quick cooling dip in the water, with the wet portion of their fur a shiny jet black and the dry portion a golden tan; the contrast is visually striking (see Photo #16). Galápagos sea lions will occasionally hop into and seemingly commandeer a *panga*, especially during the early morning hours. If you rise with the sun, bring your camera topside and you'll often be rewarded with great shots of sea lions or pelicans at the helm of the *panga*. I've seen as many as seven sea lions in a single *panga*; I wonder if there's a category in the **GUINNESS BOOK OF WORLD RECORDS**?

The Galápagos sea lions also make excellent subjects beneath the surface (see Photo #15). As the waters can be quite murky, depending on the amount of upwelling activity, you're going to have to shoot from close distance. The problem is compounded as the sea lions tend to zoom past you, resulting in a situation not unlike trying to photograph a speeding race car at close distance. Panning the camera is the only way to get good results. You may want to take several shots, as getting the whole sea lion in the frame isn't easy. An excellent underwater opportunity is offered on James Bay, James (Santiago) Island, in what is called the Fur Seal Grotto; here there are a series of rock-sheltered pools of clear sunlit water.

Where To See Them: All along the sandy beaches and rocky shores, where many of the 50,000 Galápagos sea lions can be seen and heard.

Older bulls that have fought and been defeated in one battle too many, live out their later years in exile, often in retirement communities. One such bachelor colony can be seen on the rocky cliffs of South Plaza Island. Here, several battle-scarred ex-champs lie around with a sad look in their eyes as they stare down at the shore.

Caution: Resident bulls will see you as invaders of their territory, and will occasionally charge right at you. Back away or move to the side at a steady pace. The basic rule is not to get between them and the beach they're defending. Do not taunt them; respect them and the situation. They can be on edge, guarding their territory day and night, often going without food to do so. The increase of tourism seems to have made them slightly more irritable, and occasionally people do get bit. When you sense an overly aggressive bull, take a safe detour; it's also best not to snorkel in this type of situation. In all cases, follow your Guide's instructions!

Females and juveniles are not dangerous; they are often on the trail and will usually move out of the way after a few moments. If in doubt about proceeding, the Guide will assist you.

GALAPAGOS FUR SEALS — (*LOBOS DE DOS PELOS* or *FOCAS PELETERAS*)

The fur seals seem as out of place on the equator as the penguin. Both originated in the cold waters off the southern coast of South America, made their way north along the Humboldt Current (probably during an Ice Age) to the Galápagos. Here they were isolated (after the waters warmed and the glaciers melted, according to the theory), and an endemic species developed.

Fur seals have a double coat for insulation (owing to their origin), which makes it more difficult for them to adapt to the warmer northern climates than the penguin or even the sea lion. Thus, when resting on land, they need more shade and must seek the shelter found only in the grottos formed on steep, rocky shores. The young pups have an even harder time of it as they cannot be cooled by the water; smaller than sea lions, they are in danger of being washed away by the powerful surf. Thus, until they are grown and their temperature-regulating mechanisms are developed, they have to be shuttled continuously between shade and sun.

The poor fur seal pups seem to have all sorts of survival problems, including each other. As with sea lions, fur seals nurse for up to 3 years (depending on the quantity of the food supply). The older pups fiercely compete for the highly nutritious milk (with four times the protein value of cow's milk), starving out the younger ones.

As the swallow-tailed gull, the Galápagos fur seal does its fishing at night, and quite possibly for the same reasons — to avoid predators as well as the greater number and variety of fish nearer the surface. In the case of the fur seal, the predators are sharks. Also, since fur seals cannot dive as deep as the sea lions, there is a greater dependance on fishing closer to the surface. The favored varieties of fish are more likely to surface-feed at night for the same reason as the fur seal — to avoid the majority of their predators.

The inability to dive as deep as the sea lion resulted in a much higher *El Niño* mortality rate among the fur seals. None of the pups survived, and there is a large age gap in the population. In addition, the fur seals suffer from the same seal pox that has inflicted the sea lions and reduced their numbers.

Photo Opportunities: It would be nice to get a few documentation shots, especially those that are useful for identification. Photographed head-on, the elongated flippers look like the prototype for the snorkeling variety that we use; a wide-angle lens will exaggerate this feature, making for a visually-interesting shot. The same picture will also show the pointed ears and rounded head, also helpful in distinguishing fur seals from sea lions. So too is their characteristic "sad" expression (see Photo #60).

Where To See Them: There are about 30,000-40,000 fur seals in the Galápagos, almost as many as sea lions but nowhere near as conspicuous to the visitor. We are fortunate to have the Galápagos fur seal still with us. It was thought that the sealers, seeking the valuable coat of the fur seal, had hunted the animal to extinction during the 1800s. A scientific expedition in 1906 reported finding only one fur seal during an extensive search throughout the Galápagos. It was their secluded locations that saved the fur seal.

The majority of Galápagos fur seals are found in the northern and western parts of the archipelago, where the waters are cooler and provide more upwelling activity. Thus, many fur seal colonies are established on Marchena and Pinta Islands (where there are presently no Visitor Sites), as well as on Fernandina and Isabela.

Such fur seals that are seen inhabit islands with sheltered caves. The best example is the Fur Seal Grotto on James Bay, James (Santiago) Island. The Galápagos fur seal can also be viewed on Tower (Genovesa) Island near the landing at Prince Philip's Steps.

DOLPHINS — (*DELFINES*)

While not indigenous to the Galápagos, the bottle-nosed dolphin is a frequent visitor to the islands. This highly-intelligent cetacean (a biological Order of aquatic mammals which includes the whales), brings much pleasure to other visitors (us two-legged types) and is certainly worthy of mention in this section.

Photo Opportunities: Dolphins (usually the bottle-nosed species) are likely to appear any time the boat is under way. While on-deck, keep your camera loaded and by your side. If you're lounging near the bow, protect the camera from the ocean spray by covering it with a plastic bag. The distance will vary, as some dolphins will be leaping alongside (see Photo #6), while others will "pilot" the boat, riding the bow wave. A 70-210mm zoom lens is ideal for this porpoise (who said that?) You might try bracketing the exposure, using slow shutter speeds for the dolphins off to the side, thus capturing the motion of the water while freezing the animal. To achieve this effect, use a shutter speed a little less than the numerical value of the focal length of the lens. Thus, with a 200mm lens, the shutter speed should be about 1/125th of a second.

Where To See Them: In front of and around your boat. If you're the first to spot them, call out to your shipmates. The dolphins are actually putting on a show for you, and will do encores after the 5 minute performance if you cheer them on and applaud. Seriously! Some captains will toot the horn, which sort of does the same thing.

WHALES — (*BALLENAS*) / SPERM WHALES — (*CACHALOTES*)

During the 1800s the sperm whale was hunted to the brink of extinction. Now protected, it frequently passes through the waters of the Galápagos, as does its enemy, the fatally-attractive orca or killer whale. Heralded as the great white whale in Melville's **MOBY DICK**, sperm whales are named for spermaceti organ which fills most of the upper portion of the massive forehead (called the case) and is used as a ballast tank, contolling buoyancy. As the whale dives, the colder water of the depths thickens the spermaceti fluid to a wax-like consistency, thus increasing the density of the head and enabling further descent. During ascension, the process is reversed and lift is provided.

Sperm whales spend much of their time commuting from the surface, where they breathe (for about 10 minutes, blowing every 30 seconds or so) to 1500 ft depths, where they feed (on large squid). Their deep-water hunting (achieved in total darkness) is assisted by sonar-like echolocation; scientists have frequently "tuned-in" to this once-per-second clicking sound with tracking instruments called hydrophones. Every couple of days, sperm whales spend some time socializing on the surface.

Photo Opportunities: Rare. Even when spotted, you usually won't see much more than a spout and part of their "back." On those occasions when they do feel social, and you have enough lens, go for it!

Where To See Them: Typically in the northern and western waters, with pods outside the 1000 fathom line; here there is a maximum of upwelling as the currents are forced to the surface by the land masses of Fernandina and Isabela. Individuals are often spotted in the narrow channel between Fernandina and Isabela. In addition to sperm whales, a variety of filter-feeding baleen whales are also seen in these waters, including the bryde's (pronounced "breedies"), humpback, minke, and sei. There are also "killer whales" (orcas) found in the Galápagos. True to their name, they hunt sea lions, dolphins, and occasionally other whales.

When they are in a breathing mode, whales swim just beneath the surface. Their great size is enough to break the ripple of the water, forming a whale "footprint" on the surface. So, if you're sailing the western islands, just look for their footprints. And keep looking! It's all worth it when you're the first on the boat to yell, "Thar she blows!"

MARINE LIFE

The subject of whale watching serves as an appropriate introduction to the underwater world of the Galápagos. Actually, many of the wildlife descriptions thus far would have served the same purpose. This shouldn't be very surprising given the pelagic setting, with the Galápagos surrounded by thousands of miles of open Pacific. For it is this very ocean that interconnects and affects all of the wildlife. Some in a direct basis, including the marine mammals, marine iguana, marine turtle, sea birds, and several shore birds. These animals depend on the ocean as a source of food. At this time, we will take a very brief look at the residents of the nutrient-rich waters of the Galápagos archipelago.

Note: Most visitors to the Galápagos spend very little time under the water, and at that, mostly to do some casual snorkeling. The vast majority of the marine life is therefore seen by very few tourists. Those species that are viewed will probably not be discussed at length with the Guide (with the notable exception of dive trips). The subject matter is somewhat specialized, and with this thought in mind, I have intended this section to be simply an overview. For those wanting more comprehensive information, several books are suggested including **A FIELD GUIDE TO THE FISHES OF GALAPAGOS** by Godfrey Merlin , **FISHES OF THE PACIFIC COAST** by Gar Goodson, **MARINE LIFE OF THE GALAPAGOS** by Pierre Constant, and **GALAPAGOS FISHES: A COMPREHENSIVE GUIDE TO THEIR IDENTIFICATION** by Jack Grove & Robert Lavenberg (see the Literature section).

Marine plant life, corals, and mollusks will not be discussed.

THE FISHES

Included here are the cartilaginous fishes (sharks and rays) and bony fishes. Recent literature estimates that there are just over 400 species (including pelagic fishes) in the archipelago, with over 10 percent being endemic to the islands. These numbers are quite interesting and are worth analyzing.

The species count is very high when compared to other Pacific Islands; Easter Island, for example, has little more than 100 species. Also, just as the land animals, many shore fishes would have had difficulty making the 600 mile ocean crossing. The large number of Galápagos fish species is related to the wide variety of habitats that the islands provide, such as mangroves, sandy bottoms, and rocky shores. The numbers would no doubt be higher with a fully-developed coral reef system, which the cool waters of the archipelago do not allow; such coral as does exist is sparse.

When reading these numbers, it is important to bear in mind that, as opposed to the study of land animals, the Galápagos marine life is still in the early stages of investigation; thus, the species count is ever on the increase. Also, the percentage of endemic species would be much higher (about 20 percent) if the pelagic fishes were excluded. This makes sense in that the open ocean fishes are not likely to become isolated and evolve unique characteristics.

BONY FISHES

These are vertebrates with a skeleton formed of true bone. Commonly seen bony fishes include the following:

White-banded Angelfish — One of the prettiest of all the fishes in the Galápagos and commonly seen while snorkeling near rocks. The black coloring with white vertical stripe beautifully contrasts against the orange-yellow tail; sharp heavy spines on their gill cover (cheeks) doesn't diminish their beauty.

Bonito — This open ocean fish will provide your boat with lots of tuna salad or *sushi*, depending on the cooking school your chef went to.

Creole Fish — These little (5-8 inch) grey fish form the largest schools to be found in the Galápagos and are commonly seen in reef areas, such as Devil's Crown. Locally, they are also called *gringo* fish, due to their red, sunburned-looking bellies.

Flying Fishes — You'll hear the splash more often than you'll see these "winged" fishes. The name "gliding fishes" is more accurate but has less PR image. What appear to be wings are actually greatly enlarged pectoral fins. They reach high speeds (about 30 mph) with the aid of the tail (which beats up to 50 times per second), enabling them to propel out of the water. Once airborne, flying fishes extend their fins and may glide for several seconds and over a hundred yards (the length of the field, as they say)! They "fly" to escape predators in the sea, but often leap into the waiting mouths of the frigatebirds.

Grouper — You're more likely to see them on the dinner table than in the water. The Ecuadorians call these fishes *bacalao*, and they are commercially caught and dried. Your cook will serve them as fillets. They are endemic to the Galápagos.

Yellow-tailed Grunts — They are usually seen in schools close to the bottom while snorkeling at Devil's Crown, off Floreana Island. Their name is derived for the sounds that (if disturbed) are produced by grinding teeth located in the pharynx (throat).

Hieroglyphic Hawkfish — One of the strangest-looking fish you'll see when snorkeling the Galápagos. A small predator fish, dressed in complete camouflage garb of stripes and bands (which look like "hieroglyphics"). It hides among the rocks where it waits for its dinner (other fish and crustaceans) to come by .

Moorish Idols — Another beauty, with a very tropical appearance (vertical black, white, and yellow bands) in addition to a long, streaming, white dorsal fin.

Moray Eels — The moray eel looks and acts more like a snake than a bony fish. They are fierce predators, waiting in caverns and crevices for their unwary prey (typically crabs) to come by. While morays are generally harmless to man unless provoked, caution must be taken while snorkeling, especially the urge to poke your face between rocks to see what fishes may be hiding on the other side. Their bites are not poisonous, but untreated wounds quickly become infected.

Blue Parrotfish — These reef-dwelling fishes feed on algae and are named for the male's bluish-green coloring (with pink definition lines) as well as for their teeth, which are fused into a "parrot-like" beak. The beak is used to bite off hunks of coral, which is then broken down by grinder teeth in the throat, separated from the food, and excreted as sand.

Concentric Pufferfish — These shallow water fishes are the ones you will see from your yacht and *panga*. They are not as good as they look, as their skin is covered with a very poisonous substance — quite an excellent defense mechanism. Their name is derived from another method used to deter predators (their ability to "puff up" by sucking in water or air) as well as from their concentric markings.

Yellow-tailed Surgeonfish — You will see these beautiful fishes traveling in schools quite often on your snorkeling adventures. With their grey body and brightly-colored tail, they are easy to identify. Found near reefs and rocks, yellow-tailed surgeonfish use their chisel-like teeth to scrape minute plant and animal food from the surface. Their name is derived from the scalpel-like spines located on both sides of the tail and used in defense (by waving the tail back and forth).

Yellow-bellied Triggerfish — These reef and rock fishes have striking black and yellow coloring. They are named for their ability to escape predators by swimming into a crevice and then cocking their first dorsal spine (like a "trigger") against the second spine, thus wedging themselves in.

Wahoo — You won't see this 6 ft long sport fish while snorkeling, but your crew may have some luck fishing and haul a wahoo on-board; related to the mackeral family, they are quite delicious.

CARTILAGINOUS FISHES

These are the sharks and rays, vertebrates with a skeleton formed of cartilage. Vertebrae are formed by layers of cartilage around a notochord. Commonly seen cartilaginous fishes include the following:

Cow-Nosed Rays — Also called yellow stingrays, these mustard-colored beauties really do have cow-like noses. With any luck, you will see a school of them swimming along the surface at Black Turtle Cove. If you're taking a picture, make sure your polarizer is on to minimize glare.

Manta Rays — The word *manta* in Spanish means "blanket," an appropriate name for these giants that measure 10-20 ft in diameter and weigh over 1000 lbs. They are vegetarians and open-ocean fishes.

Spotted Eagle Rays — Their name is derived from their swimming motion, in which they gracefully flap their strong, wing-like pectoral fins. They are often seen swimming (occasionally leaping) on the surface at Black Turtle Cove. With a keen eye, you will usually see one or more during your snorkeling sessions. For underwater photos, dive down to an area alongside them. If you swim easily and under control (stay about 4-6 feet away), you can usually get a great shot. If you try to dive at them, they will be gone in a flash-beat of their "wings." This goes for underwater fish photography in general.

Sting Rays — While snorkeling, you will see them on the bottom, partially buried in sand (for camouflage). Sting rays are often sighted just offshore from the white, sandy beach at Punta Cormorán, Floreana Island, where they are feeding on mollusks and crustaceans. While they are not aggressive to humans, and will generally not "sting" unless stepped on, their tail spines are poisonous. Keep your distance!

Caution: The following listings briefly discuss some of the sharks found in the Galápagos. You may encounter sharks when snorkeling; you certainly will if diving. These sharks are not aggressive, as your Guide and captain will be quick to point out, and snorkeling activities will be encouraged in several areas where there are known to be sharks present. The only reported attack that I am aware of occurred during very poor visibility conditions (toward nightfall) while the swimmer was hunting lobster. So my advice is not to be afraid, but be cautious; if you have cut yourself while scraping against some rocks, get out of the water.

The Spanish word for shark is *tiburón*.

Galápagos Sharks — To me they look like white-tipped sharks without the "white tip." So, if I can't identify it as a white-tip, I call it a Galápagos shark. It may not be the scientific method, but it usually works.

Hammerhead Sharks — They have a very distinctive appearance, with their eyes and nostrils located at the ends of the lateral hammer-like projection. Aside from any improvements to their field of vision, the enlarged snout amplifies the already astounding electro-sensitivity of the animal. Capable of sensing one-millionth of a volt, sharks can detect an animal's natural electrical output from a long distance.

White-tipped Sharks — Called *tintorera* in Spanish, they prefer shallow water and can be seen in several of the sheltered lagoons fringed with mangrove trees, such as Black Turtle Cove (Caleta Tortuga Negra). Their white tip is easily recognizable, and a good photographic subject (see Photo #17).

CRUSTACEANS

These are the arthropods (jointed-limbed creatures) having a segmented body surrounded by a tough "crusty" shell. Commonly-seen crustaceans include the following (lobsters and shrimps will not be discussed):

Barnacles — These sedentary crustaceans are often seen at the tide line adhering to the base of mangrove trees, where they filter-feed on suspended particles in the seawater.

Ghost Crabs — You will see their burrows and trails on sandy beaches much more frequently then you'll see the "ghosts." This elusive nature, in addition to their speed and nocturnal activity, is the source of their name. If you're fast and resourceful, however, the "ghost" can be captured on film. I have seen photographs of one in its burrow with only the large eyes visible, protruding vertically as antennae.

Hermit Crabs — Lacking the hard, external skeleton typically associated with crustaceans, these "hermits" live in discarded houses — the empty shells of snails and slugs. These beggars are choosy, and will select a shell of just the right size — not too small as to be uncomfortable and not too large as to restrict mobility. They change shells continuously as they grow.

Sally Lightfoot Crabs — These beautifully-colored crabs are everywhere to be seen on the black lava rocks, a scene offering striking contrast and great photographic opportunities (see Photo #47). They are named for their nimble, "light-footed" scurrying motion, sometimes up & down or upside-down, across the rocks and over the water.

ECHINODERMS

Echinoderms (spiny-skinned creatures) are typically built with five-sided or radial bodies. As adults, they live on the seabed. Commonly seen echinoderms include the following (sea cucumbers will not be discussed):

Green Sea Urchins — Endemic to the Galápagos, their round, sculptured skeletons (often seen on beaches — see Photo #48) are composed of a series of interlocking crystals. Sea urchins are nocturnal herbivores, slowly grazing on algae scraped from the ocean floor by a complex feeding/locomoting network of "tube-feet," which are extended from the mouth.

Pencil Sea Urchins — Seen on the ocean bottom, they are not to be stepped on, as the sharp spines are poisonous. Their skeletons are often spotted washed up on beaches (see Photo #49). The spines are supposedly "pencil shaped," while some say the name is derived from the ability to use a spine as a writing instrument on rocks. Don't try it; remember it's illegal to pick up or touch the wildlife!

Starfish — Often seen while snorkeling, star fish are most colorful, usually a deep purple. This beauty does not extend to eating habits, which consists of extruding the stomach, wrapping it around and externally digesting the food.

PLANT LIFE

It comes as little surprise that there are only about 600 indigenous plant species in the Galápagos (compared to upwards of 20,000 on mainland Ecuador). The archipelago has a relatively small land area to begin with, about 3,000 square miles. Also, it is still in its early stages of formation, especially the western islands, where the flora are actually in the "primordial stage," of pioneering plants. These "pioneers" seem to grow out of the lava itself, while providing the humus for future generations of more advanced plant life. Helping keep the number of plant species down is the lack of pollinating insects (consisting of basically the carpenter bee and a few butterfly species). For this reason, then, large colorful flowers are less likely to survive, and therefore occur less frequently than non-pollinators. In general, we have a pretty harsh environment without a lot of very rich soil; for the most part, the Galápagos is not exactly your typical orchid jungle.

As you've gathered from our look at the animals of the Galápagos, the life forms are fairly basic. So it is with the plants, but for somewhat different reasons. With the animals it was related to arrival and survival factors. While any exotic plant seed could have arrived, perhaps stuck on the wings or feet of a bird, surviving once there was another matter. And once the formula for survival was achieved, it had to be modified from island to island. Thus, the process of adaptive radiation is as much a factor in the evolution of the prickly pear cactus and scalesia as it is the giant tortoises, mockingbirds, and Darwin's finches.

The result of adaptive radiation is endemism — new, unique species. Thus, the evolutionary process has resulted in one-third of the Galápagos plants being endemic to the islands. This is the same pattern we saw with the animals — species-poor and endemic-rich. I would suspect that this high rate of endemism will decrease in the future, as the islands are studied more thoroughly and new species discovered, especially in the relatively humid and soil-rich highland areas.

With this orientation, we will take a look at the different growing environments (typically referred to as Vegetation Zones) and get a feel for the plant communities in these areas.

Note: Once again, this section is intended to be an overview, an introduction to the plant life of the Galápagos. For a comprehensive treatment of this subject, you are referred to **FLORA OF THE GALAPAGOS** by Wiggins and Porter; for a compact field guide, there is Eileen Schofield's **PLANTS OF THE GALAPAGOS ISLANDS** (see the Literature section).

COASTAL AREA PLANTS

The coastal plant community grows in what is frequently referred to in the texts as the Littoral (Latin for "shore") Zone. These plants can be described as having, of necessity, a high salt tolerance and form two distinct groups.

MANGROVES

These are the evergreen trees you will see along the shore throughout the islands, forming groves in and around sheltered lagoons. There are several species, including the black, button, red, and white mangrove, each readily identifiable by leaf structure. The red is the most common and arrived in the Galápagos on its own; the pod-shaped seedlings, typically dispersed by sea, were able to float across the ocean, root in the mud, take hold, and grow.

The black mangrove has the highest salt tolerance, as its leaves are equipped with special salt-excreting glands. Actually, several of the varieties have root systems that filter out salt, allowing the leaves to receive fresh water.

Depending on the location, these same roots will anchor the tree to the rocks, gather material all around to help stabilize the beach or lagoon shore, and/or project into the air for breathing purposes.

SAND DUNES

The Galápagos beaches are kept intact by and are a home for several salt-tolerant herbs, shrubs, and vines found on these shores.

Beach Morning Glory — Sometimes called *Ipomoea*, this is a creeping vine that helps stabilize beaches. It is recognized by the purple, funnel-shaped, daylight-opening flower (characteristic of morning glories).

Salt Bush — A most prominent beach plant, the salt bush has heart-shaped, puckered leaves; they even look (and supposedly) taste salty. Some of the Guides will call it *Cryptocarpus*, part of its Latin name.

Sesuvium — During the dry season, this herb turns red and is among the most colorful plants in the Galápagos, forming extensive mats (see Photo #8). The small, star-shaped flowers are quite distinctive. It is seen near the shore of several islands, most notably on South Plaza.

DRY AREA PLANTS

Arid conditions prevail throughout most of the Galápagos. Thus, it is no surprise that drought-resistant, dry area flora dominates much of the harsh landscape. On many islands, this is the only Vegetation Zone. There are several broad groupings in this category.

CACTI

Cacti are succulents, a classification of plants having thick, fleshy leaves or stems for the purpose of storing and conserving moisture. In the case of the cactus Family, it is the leaf-like stems (called pads) that achieve this function. Aside from serving as water-storage vessels, the pads also replace leaves as the photosynthetic organs. Spines have also evolved as a means of protection.

Candelabra Cactus — Named for its characteristic shape and endemic to the Galápagos, the candelabra cactus can also be readily distinguished by its tube-like pad segments. It is readily observed (from your boat) on the cliffs at Academy Bay, outside the town of Puerto Ayora, Santa Cruz Island.

Lava Cactus — On islands that are still dominated by lava formations, such as Bartolomé and Sombrero Chino (and especially the younger western islands), the endemic lava cactus is one of the few visible plants; it is considered a "pioneer" or colonizing plant. With bright yellow-tipped coloring and micro-phone shapes, the clumped formations are visually appealing and dramatically stand out from the barren fields of lava (see Photo #52).

Prickly Pear Cactus — Also called by its Spanish name, *opuntia*, the prickly pear is an outstanding example of adaptive radiation. In all, fourteen species of

#19

The word Galápagos is the Spanish name for the giant tortoise. With the facial features that were actually used to create the visage of E.T. (#19), these gentle giants are generally thought to live upwards of 125 years. While there is no precise method of determining the age of older tortoises, there are growth rings on the shells of younger animals, as seen in a 2 year old (#20) and 8 year old (#21).

#21

#20

#22

You'll be able to observe the aggressive male "posturing" behavior, 2-3 tortoises stretching their necks skyward and at each other (#22), seeing who will back down or get a bloody nose (#23) and who will reign supreme and eat a victory dinner of straw pasta al dente (#24).

#23

#24

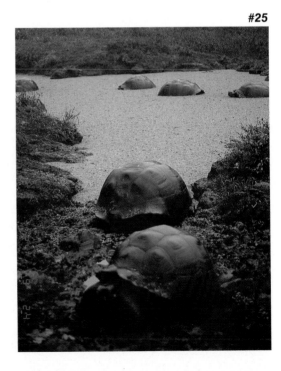

With a visit to the lush Highlands of Santa Cruz Island, you may get the opportunity of photographing several tortoises in a colorful duckweed-covered pond (#25).

#26

#27

The red-billed tropicbird is the most beautiful and graceful bird in the Galápagos. Hearing their piercing cries as they fly back and forth near the steep cliffs, either solo (#26) or in squadrons (#27), your eyes are drawn upwards, riveted by the long, streaming tails. Occasionally, one can get a surreal in-motion shot as the tropicbird fights the off-shore wind to land safely in its cliffside nest (#28).

#28

#29

#31

Your tour of the islands will include views of the sometimes dried-and-cracked lagoon bottom on Floreana Island (#29) and Bartolomé Island (#30)—including Pinnacle Rock (#31).

#30

#32

#33

#34

#35

Whether singly (#32) or in groups (#33), close-ups (#34) or wide-angle shots (#35), the marine iguanas will provide you with endless colorful photo opportunities of Beauty on the Beast. While fewer and harder to find, the land iguana will show you its colors as well (#36).

#36

#37

#38

Frigatebirds are the pirate ships of the air, a name earned by reputation and habit. They are built for and look the part (#37). It takes the juveniles (#38) over a year to learn the flying skills required for survival. The bright red, inflated, balloon-like sac of the male is used for display purposes during courtship (#39).

#39

shrubs and trees have evolved. Some of the trees are impressively tall (see Photo #53), a survival necessity from the days that tortoises roamed the islands in great numbers, seeking food and water from the fleshy stems. The trunks are now well-protected with spines and a heavy bark. The flat pads of the *opuntia* shrubs are also covered with clusters of spines; this armor notwithstanding, the prickly pear pads are a major food and water source of land iguanas as well as tortoises. While the land iguanas are known to roll the pads on the ground to break the sharp spines, they frequently are seen eating the pad as is, spines and all!

CUTLEAF DAISY

There's no mistaking that this beautiful plant is a daisy. Endemic and only seen by visitors at Punta Cormorán on Floreana Island, the cutleaf daisy is sometimes called *Leocarpus*, its partial Latin name, by the Guides.

LANTANA

This endemic shrub has beautiful little white flowers (usually five-lobed) with a yellow center and is readily observed on Tower (Genovesa) Island. The indigenous species was once prolific on Punta Cormorán, Floreana, but is now in some danger; an introduced lantana species is winning the competition for the available water and taking over. Brought to the islands in 1938 as an ornamental for a family garden, the introduced lantana is readily dispersed by the native birds and roots easily. It has spread to over 5000 acres, where the dense thickets have inhibited the access of the endangered dark-rumped petrel to its nesting area.

LEATHER LEAF

Leather leaf grows in the Galápagos as either a large shrub or small tree; it is easily recognized by the vertical orientation of the flat, yellow-green leaves. The net effect here is energy conservation, minimizing the leaf surface area exposed to the heat of the sun, also reducing water loss. Your Guide may refer to this plant by its partial Latin name, *Maytenus* (pronounced, "my tennis").

MANZANILLO

This large fruit tree is the only indigenous toxic plant in the Galápagos, and is also called the "poison apple" tree. Touching the sap causes dermatitis, and eating the fruit can be lethal to humans (although it is a favored food of the tortoises, doing no harm to their primeval digestive systems). A *manzanillo* (Spanish for "little apple") tree, complete with warning label, adorns the grounds of the Hotel Galápagos, next to the Darwin Station in Puerto Ayora, Santa Cruz Island.

MOLLUGO

This endemic herb looks more like a weed and is the most widely-distributed pioneering plant (or "colonizer") in the islands; it is seen growing on many of the lava fields.

MUYUYO

Easy to recognize by its large, brilliant yellow flowers, the large shrub is common throughout the dry regions of the Galápagos. The muyuyo is often referred to by its Latin name, *Cordia lutea*.

PALO VERDE

These trees are characterized by long, green, leafless stalks, giving rise to its name which is Spanish for "green stick." The Guide may also refer to it by its partial Latin name, *Parkinsonia*. The arched branches have several extremely sharp spines, which have impaled many a juvenile blue-footed booby during an attempted flight. Palo verde trees are seen near the blue-footed booby colony on Seymour Island and along the lagoon on Punta Cormorán, Floreana Island.

TIQUILIA

This endemic woody herb is recognized by the dull grey coloring, and mat-like growth, usually standing out against the sandy areas that it pioneers. It is pronounced "ta-keel-ee-yah" and is not related to the stuff that margaritas are made from!

TRANSITION AREA PLANTS

The Dry Zone gradually gives way, and the cacti-dominated landscape changes to a still somewhat arid, usually leafless forest of palo santo trees.

PALO SANTO

In an effort to conserve moisture, these trees are leafless for much of the year. They have a lichen-covered bark which is silvery-grey in appearance and grow in forests which dot the rolling hills on several islands (see Photo #51). The view has a mystical quality to it, and the feeling is not lessened by the name *palo santo*, which is Spanish for "holy stick." This name actually has a couple of other derivations. First, the tree takes leaf and blooms around Christmas, which happens to correspond with the beginning of the rainy season. Second, the palo santo is related to frankincense, and the sap contains an aromatic resin. The branches are shipped to the mainland where they are burned as incense in churches. Supposedly the branches are also burned locally to repel insects. The Guide may also refer to the tree by its partial Latin name, *Bursera*.

HUMID AREA PLANTS

Some of the islands have highlands, typically starting at about 900 ft, that receive an almost constant misty precipitation (called a *garúa*) for a good portion of the year (see the section on Climates in Chapter II). This lush, humid area is typically classified into several regions — the Scalesia, Miconia, and Fern-Sedge Zones. If you visit the Highlands of Santa Cruz Island, you will ascend into and through many of the Vegetation Zones; the differences in the plant communities will be most obvious and quite fascinating to behold.

BRACKEN FERNS

There are about 100 fern species in the Galápagos. Many of those seen near the road in the moist Highlands of Santa Cruz Island are bracken ferns, characterized by their large curving fronds.

MICONIA

Endemic to the Galápagos, the tall miconia shrub is one of the only plants in the islands with red flowers.

SCALESIA

Having evolved into twenty species ranging from shrubs to 45 ft trees, scalesia is an excellent example of adaptive radiation. Related to daisies, several species have beautiful yellow flowers, characteristic of the sunflower family to which they belong.

Note: When the topic of "conservation of the Galápagos wildlife" is raised, many of us think of endangered tortoises and land iguanas. This is certainly what I was thinking of when Dr. Daniel Evans, former Director of the *Charles Darwin Research Station*, (in an answer to my question concerning the progress made by the conservation programs), stated, "We're winning the battles and losing the war." I was very surprised when Dr. Evans went on to explain that the "war" referred to plants — introduced plants. Since 1985, over 100 new plants have been introduced by man on Santa Cruz Island alone. Not only do these introduced plants take over an area and threaten several species of indigenous (and sometimes endemic) plants, they also drastically upset the entire biological community by altering habitats and breaking several food chains. To date, there is no ready fix for this problem, although plans for quarantine and education/awareness programs are underway.

CHAPTER IV

CHOOSING A TOUR

It is the fate of most voyagers, no sooner to discover what is most interesting in any locality, than they are hurried from it....
                                                        Charles Darwin, 1845

There are many ways to tour the Galápagos and have an exciting 1-2 week experience. Depending on your interest, comfort level, pocketbook, and resourcefulness, you can cruise the islands at a cost ranging from $75-$400/day per person. In each case, all meals are included and the boat is fully-crewed, complete with a Guide trained at the *Charles Darwin Research Station* in the Galápagos. The cost depends on a number of factors that we will discuss and will require you to make a number of decisions. The first of your decisions, however, concerns the duration of your visit to the Galápagos.

DURATION OF YOUR TOUR

The great majority of Galápagos Island tours are 8 days, 7 nights. Actually, only 7 full days are spent touring the islands, because the first and last days are partials, with an early afternoon arrival and departure. Throughout this book, these are referred to as 1 week tours. The itineraries are, for the most part, well-planned, and a diversity of wildlife can be observed. I would classify this as the **minimum** recommended tour duration (to come away with a good feeling and a good feel for the Galápagos). While there are 3-4 day tours, you will spend so much of your time getting there, getting unpacked, repacked, and ready to leave that the irritations of travel, especially South American travel, will probably outweigh the brief experience itself.

A 2 week tour of the Galápagos Islands is recommended for maximum observation, photographic opportunities, and just plain enjoyment. Each island is different, with its own unique ecosystem and wildlife distribution. Not only are many species endemic to the Galápagos Islands, they are often endemic to a specific island. In other words, each island has plants and animals that you're not going to see on any other island. So, the more islands you visit, the more unique wildlife you're going to see. If you want to see the red-footed booby, you have to go to either Tower (Genovesa) Island or Punta Pitt on San Cristóbal Island. If you want to see the flightless cormorant, you have to go to Hood (Española) Island. And the list goes on.

There are official touring areas, called Visitor Sites (established by the *Galápagos National Park Service*) on ten (out of thirteen) major islands as well as on several of the islets (including Rábida, Seymour, and Sombrero Chino). In many cases, there are two or more Visitor Sites per island, with a total of over forty Visitor Sites in the Galápagos. While several of the central islands can be viewed on a two-a-day basis, there are an equal number that will require a single day unto themselves. In addition, tours of the outer islands (such as Española, Tower, and Isabela) require significant inter-island travel time. A tour of Isabela itself can be a 3-5 day process to adequately see the resident wildlife, especially if a hike up the Alcedo Volcano is included.

When I recommend a 2 week tour as being ideal, I am referring to 14 days actually spent in the islands. Many of the 1 week trips are advertised as 10-14 day tours, whereas 2-6 of those days are spent in mainland Ecuador. On a typical "12 day tour," Day 1 is "in-flight" to Ecuador (usually Quito), Day 2 is usually spent touring Quito, and it's not until Day 3 that you actually travel to the Galápagos. Your 1 week Galápagos Island tour ends on Day 10 when you fly back to Quito; you then spend Day 11 touring Quito and depart for home on Day 12. I would do everything you could to swing an 18 day vacation. This allows for 2 days of travel to and from mainland Ecuador, 2 shopping/touring days in Quito and a 14 day Galápagos Island cruise. If you have a total of 2 weeks of vacation time, the best you can do is a 10 day Galápagos tour, of which there are only a few to choose from.

Many tours have optional "trip extensions" in the mountains and jungles of Ecuador as well as Peru. My feeling is that if you want to visit the Andes, the Amazon, the Inca ruins at Machu Picchu, etc., do it on another trip. It simply isn't feasible to take a comprehensive tour of the Galápagos and have time left over unless you have several weeks to spend. On this subject, there's some interesting feedback from the Tour Operators. Many of them say that the 1 week Galápagos tours with "trip extensions" are easier to sell (and generate more profit). They go on to say, however, that a lot of customers who bought these packages expressed regret for not spending more time in the Galápagos.

SELECTION OF A TOUR

Once you've selected the duration of your tour, you are faced with the decisions of what type of tour and boat you want to go on. Let's start by looking at what determines the cost of a Galápagos Island vacation.

As pointed out above, tour prices can vary significantly. Some of the price differences are directly related to very tangible factors. A tour on a converted fishing vessel with bunk beds, shared toilet facilities, and a common shower (located on-deck) is going to cost less than one on a modern yacht that has features such as cabins with double beds and private bathrooms. If the Tour

Operator provides an expert-class Tour Leader (often a biologist), you would expect to pay a bit extra for this service. Also, some Tour Operators provide specialty tours, such as dive packages and photographic workshops; professional guidance and instruction are provided, and a premium price is justified.

But sometimes the cost differential is little more than a series of markups (through the tour network distribution system) of prices originally set by an Ecuadorian-based Tour or Boat Operator. There may or may not be sufficient value added (such as airport transfers, lodging, food, local tours of Quito, etc.) to justify the higher price. So it is possible to save a reasonable amount of money by booking what I will refer to throughout this book as a "Base Rate" tour. Here you are only paying for the cost of the Galápagos tour itself; hotels, meals, local tours in mainland Ecuador, and local transportation are purchased separately. There are several Tour Operators offering Base Rate tours of the Galápagos Islands; they are listed later on in this chapter. You can also deal directly with the Ecuadorian Tour and Boat Operators via FAX; for your convenience, some of the larger Ecuadorian Operators have a U.S. representative with a TOLL FREE number.

You can possibly save even more by going to mainland Ecuador and arranging your tour once you arrive. A Boat Operator may have a couple spaces available on a yacht ready to leave the next day and might be willing to settle at a very reasonable price to fill the boat. On the other side of the coin, part of the price you pay for the possibility of saving money is time, as it may take up to a week to arrange a suitable tour. And at that, you may not save much (if at all). There is also a chance you may not get an English-speaking Guide. Is it worth it? That depends on the situation, which we will now try to define. Let's take it one step at a time.

CRUISE SHIPS VS. PRIVATE YACHTS

First off, would you prefer to tour the Galápagos Islands on a 90 passenger cruise ship or an 8-20 passenger yacht? The larger ships may appeal to you for reasons of comfort, convenience, security, social activities, etc. It will be the least difficult transition to make for those who do not enjoy the feeling of ocean travel. If you're thinking this would be the best choice for you, turn to the section on Cruise Ships in this chapter. You could be swayed over to this category by the newest member of the Galápagos Cruise Ship fleet, the ISABELA II; she's a beautiful ship and holds but 38 passengers, so you get the comfort of a large vessel and some of the privacy of a small yacht. If you're not sure what type vessel is best for you, read the section on Life At Sea in Chapter IX, which discusses a typical day in the Galápagos on both yachts and Cruise Ships.

The smaller yachts do provide for a more personal, relaxed, and thorough tour of the Galápagos Islands. Your island tour-walks will be in groups of about 10 people. Cruise Ships bring their passengers ashore in groups of 20, the maximum allowed by the National Park. With the larger groups, it's a little harder to take pictures, there's less of an opportunity to ask questions, and there's more time spent waiting—either for your opportunity to go ashore or for the last groups to return to the ship.

Another difference between a yacht and ship tour is that the Cruise Ships are only allowed access to certain islands, presumably the larger, safer anchorages. In addition, there are presently no Cruise Ships with itineraries longer than 1 week. If your choice is to see as much of the Galápagos wildlife (and thus as many of the islands) as possible, a tour on a small yacht is the way to go. It is my personal preference and recommendation as well.

GENERAL TOURS VS. SPECIALTY TOURS

If you have decided that touring the islands on a 8-20 passenger yacht is for you, look at the tour categories listed below and see where you fit.

Birding Tours — You're a serious birder and want to identify and observe the maximum number of Galápagos avifauna. Birding Tours are accompanied by an experienced leader in addition to the required Galápagos Guide.

Diving Tours — You're interested in exploring the underwater world of the Galápagos. Dive trips are available, but you must be a Certified Diver.

General Tours — You want to see and photograph the unique wildlife of the Galápagos archipelago. I put myself in this category.

Photography Tours — You want to concentrate on (forgive the pun) developing your photographic skills in this visual paradise. Tours are typically led by noted wildlife photographers, several with extensive Galápagos shooting experience. There are evening workshops, etc.

TOUR LEADER VS. NO TOUR LEADER

If you have opted for a General Tour, you now have to decide whether or not you want to select a tour that offers a Tour Leader (TL). Think of a TL as a natural history expert. This is much the same concept as a Specialty Tour emphasizing birding or photography and offering an expert leader.

The expertise of a Tour Leader will heighten your understanding of the many natural forces at work in the Galápagos. Several TLs have graduate degrees in the biological sciences; some are PhDs. Many have conducted research, written scientific papers, and authored books on the Galápagos Islands. I take several groups to the Galápagos each year and am impressed with the Tour Leaders I meet; they tend to be excellent teachers and raise the level of the tour experience quite a few notches.

The Licensed Guide Program — The Tour Leader is there in addition to the Licensed Guide, who will conduct your tour-walks and point out the wildlife along the way. While the Guides are all trained at the Darwin Station, some are more knowledgeable than others. Several Tour Operators will refer to "our Naturalist Guide." There are two misnomers here. First, the Guide is not "theirs," but rather a crew member required and trained by the *Galápagos National Park Service*. The Guide is also a representative of the Park Service and is requested to explain and enforce the National Park Regulations. The Park rules state that one Guide per 16 passengers be on-board each touring vessel.

The second misnomer is the term "Naturalist Guide." Not all Licensed Guides are Naturalist Guides, a title reserved for bilingual college graduates in the biological sciences who have successfully completed an extensive Guide course at the *Charles Darwin Research Station.* Most Guides hold an Auxiliary license; the required background is a high school education, some bilingual ability, and the successful completion of a more limited course at the Darwin Station. In general, their knowledge of the wildlife and English-speaking ability are also more limited.

The result is that if you happen to get a true Naturalist Guide or one of the top Auxiliary Guides who speaks fluent English, the Guide and the Tour Leader will probably work as a team. This is an ideal situation; you'll have two sources of information and more of an opportunity for private discussions. If you happen to get an Auxiliary Guide whose background is weak and/or whose English is not that great, the TL will make all the difference.

In addition to providing the services of an expert naturalist to you and your shipmates, the Tour Leader typically meets you at the airport, confirms your reservations, checks you in at the hotel, conducts excursions in and around Quito, and often accompanies you on your flights to and from the Galápagos. You're very well taken care of. By now you may be asking, "Why shouldn't I select a tour that has a Tour Leader?" It's a good question. To provide an answer, let's look at the alternatives.

1. A General Tour without a Tour Leader at "tour-led" premium prices (about $2000/week per person, excluding airfare). The U.S.-based Tour Operator will usually have an Ecuadorian affiliate meet you at the airport, provide transportation to the hotel, and take care of your flight arrangements. The price will usually include airport transfers, hotels, most meals in Quito or Guayaquil, and some local sightseeing. Your tour of the Galápagos, however, will be led only by the Licensed Guide. There is no on-board Tour Leader; even though their brochure states "On Tuesday we do this," they really mean, "you do this" because "they" aren't there. Quite often, you're not getting the same value for your money (as with a tour providing a TL). The tours in this category will be referred to as Premium Tours throughout this book.

2. A General Tour without a Tour Leader for about half to two-thirds the price. You can get a 1 week "Base Rate" tour for about $1100-$1800. It's a significant difference in cost and definitely worth considering, but remember that this price is for the boat cruise only; all expenses in mainland Ecuador (including hotels, all meals, local tours, etc.) are extra. If you like to study up on where you're going, enjoy getting around on your own, or prefer to experience nature for yourself, you may not need or want a Tour Leader, If you're a photographer, you may find that, on tour, you're more interested in taking full advantage of every photo opportunity than in listening to what the Guide or Tour Leader has to say. The books in the Literature section (the Jackson **GUIDE** in particular), will greatly supplement the information presented by the Guide on your tour; the combination (including this book) will give you a comprehensive orientation to the Galápagos wildlife.

3. A General Tour without a Tour Leader for as little as one-third the price. Sounds great, doesn't it? It can be done, but it's by no means a sure thing. It's also going to cost you some time, perhaps a lot of time. It will depend on a lot of factors, including the Tour Operator, the time of the year, the amount of the discount, your personality, and luck! It involves flying to Ecuador without a prearranged tour. Then, once in Quito or Guayaquil you will make the rounds of

Tour Operators and negotiate the best deal you can. If you're the resourceful type, **and** if you have some time on your hands, this is a definite opportunity for you. This book will provide you with the necessary details (airline information, the Tour Operators, pricing structures, etc.), but ultimately it will be up to you to put things together and make it happen.

FAMILIES

Before we get into the Galápagos Tour Operations, let's discuss the subject of bringing the kids along. As wonderful and exciting as the Galápagos is, it is not the place for most children. There are several factors to consider:

Safety — There are slippery rocks and cliff edges to deal with on the island tours. While kids are more agile than many of us adults, they also tend to be less careful. Which makes falling overboard another point of concern.

Lack of Medical Facilities — If by chance an accident should occur that requires medical attention, you will have to interrupt your vacation and get the child to the mainland. There are emergency facilities in the Galápagos, but in general they are not recommended for anything more than immediate first aid. The Cruise Ships have either a doctor or nurse on-board, but the rule of getting to the mainland for medical attention still applies.

The Restrictive Environment — On the island tours, kids can not even wander 1-2 ft off the trail and must be quiet while the Guide is lecturing. Compared to most places, including your house, the yachts have cramped quarters. Everyone's "space" has to be respected, which is sometimes difficult enough for adults to achieve. If you have a problem with a child on-board the boat, everyone shares that problem with you. Also, there are no bathrooms on most islands, and it is illegal to "go behind a bush," because of the danger of introducing organisms to the island. Even most yachts have marine toilets with pump handle flushing mechanisms; all the boats require that toilet paper be disposed of in a separate receptacle and not flushed.

With the above in mind, many of the yachts and Cruise Ships do not allow children on-board under the age of 7; I would tend to raise that to 10-12. Even then, I would not take children to the Galápagos unless they were extremely well-behaved, tended to not be "accident-prone," and had a demonstrated interest in natural history and wildlife.

For those who have decided to make the Galápagos a family adventure, there are several options:

Cruise Ships — They have less confined quarters, ample deck space, lounging areas, and onboard medical facilities.

Chartering a Small Yacht — There are a few 4-8 passenger yachts that would give a family (or perhaps a couple of families) the opportunity to be by themselves.

Day Trip Programs — Once you're on a week-long cruise, there's no turning back, with the exception of an emergency. So if you have a problem, you can't just get off. With a series of Day Trips, you always return to port in the evening. One or more members of the family can decide to skip a day or two, staying at the hotel and perhaps touring the surrounding area.

Special "Family Trips" — I suspect there will be more of these offered in the future. At this time the following U.S. Tour Operators offer Family Trips to the Galápagos:

ADVENTURE EXPRESS, 650 Fifth St., #505, San Francisco, CA 94107. PHONE: (415) 442-0799; TOLL FREE: (800) 442-0799, FAX: 415-442-0289. Ask for information about their "Rascals in Paradise" Program.

OVERSEAS ADVENTURE TRAVEL, 349 Broadway, Cambridge, MA 02139. PHONE: (617) 876-0533, TOLL FREE: (800) 221-0841, FAX: 617-876-0455.

WILDERNESS TRAVEL, 801 Allston Way, Berkeley, CA 94710. PHONE: (510) 548-0420, TOLL FREE: (800) 247-6700, FAX: 510-548-0347.

WILDLAND ADVENTURES, 3516 N.E. 155th, Seattle, WA 95155. PHONE: (206) 365-0686, TOLL FREE: (800) 345-4453, FAX: 206-363-6615.

GALAPAGOS TOUR OPERATIONS

During the last few years, there have been some major changes in the dynamics of Galápagos tour operations — some for better and some for worse. On the "better" side, we have more boats to choose from. A lot of money has recently been invested in a number of very attractive yachts. The listing below is significantly different than in the first edition of this book. You will notice that many of these boats have only been in service since 1992-93. Also, the vessels are now generally a lot safer than they were just a few years back. The BARTOLOME disaster in 1990, where 5 passengers died in a fire that quickly sank the yacht, resulted in several safety measures; there are now strict regulations regarding equipment in addition to annual inspections and rescue courses for crew members. While there are still incidents (mostly on the lesser Economy Class and Day Trip Yachts), the safety situation has improved tremendously.

Now for the negative side. With all the investment in newer yachts, the "marketing plan" of the investors was evidently to promote the boats through the U.S. Travel Agent Network, more or less in the same way that the Galápagos Cruise Ships are sold. These newer boats have even gone so far as to mimic the 3-4 night itineraries of the Cruise Ships. This "fake full week" concept is discussed more fully in the Boat Operators in Ecuador section at the end of this chapter.

Unfortunately at this time, there's not a chance that (with very few exceptions) travel agents can help you, even if they wanted to, with your plans to visit the Galápagos — and most of them don't want to. Unless it's on their computer screen, they don't want to know about weirdo nature tours. Thus, they will sell only the Cruise Ships and the newer yachts with the "3 and 4 night programs." And up to now, most travel agents can't even decipher that there are 2 airports in Galápagos, not to mention which boats operate out of which airport harbor. Some day this will probably change, which is great. But it hasn't changed as of this writing, and for those still trying to work through travel agents to pick a Galápagos tour, it ain't so great.

The problems aren't limited to travel agents. At least they have an excuse — the lack of information. There are those that know better — alumni tours, museum groups, zoological associations, etc., that offer short trips on Cruise Ships — simply because they need that many passengers to amortize the national marketing and advertising costs. And the worst of all is offered by those who should know best of all — organizations such as the *National Audubon Society* who offer Galápagos cruises that basically pass through the islands without much of a stop. These cruises are on ships that are not even formally registered as Galápagos touring vessels. No doubt, these organizations (and there are a growing number of them) have letters of permission from someone in the Ecuadorian government (above the level of the conservation-oriented *Galápagos National Park Service* and the *Charles Darwin Research Station*) basically approving all this.

These letters of permission to pass through the Galápagos are also being given to a few "around the world" cruise ships — each carrying several hundred passengers (many of them probably wearing an "I'm an Ecotourist" button). These ships are given permission to anchor in the harbor of one of the large towns (Puerto Ayora or Puerto Baquerizo Moreno) and let the passengers go ashore. The store owners love it — lots of T-shirts get sold. The ship owners and operators love it too; they can show a photo of a blue-footed booby and a giant tortoise on the cover of their brochure.

Which brings us face to face with the symbol of change in Galápagos tourism — the slick brochure. Not that fancy brochures necessarily reflect an undesirable tour of the Galápagos. It just means you have to concentrate harder to find out what you're really getting. And that's what the rest of this chapter is going to help you do.

BOATS OF THE GALAPAGOS

This section will list most of the boats that sail the Galápagos archipelago. The yacht listings are to be used in conjunction with the Tour Operator sections later on in this chapter. The section on Cruise Ships is more of a complete guide and contains pricing information as well as the primary sources to book your tour with.

First, a word on yacht classification. During the first printing of this book, I used the categories "Tourist Class Yachts" and "Luxury Class Yachts." In retrospect, the terms are somewhat inappropriate. Basically, I used the term "Luxury Class" to denote yachts that had air-conditioned cabins and hot water showers. In reality, the air conditioning is not reliable on many of these yachts, nor is it necessary for a good part of the year. Further, some of the "Tourist Class" Yachts are more spacious and offer a higher degree of overall service (including the food) than some of the "Luxury Class" boats. So it comes down to evaluating each yacht on its own merits and overall reputation.

Another sort of misunderstanding involves the yacht designation "motor-sailer." Everyone loves a sailboat, or nearly everyone, but the "motor-sailers" in the Galápagos are almost "all motor" and "no sail." By necessity, the motors (diesel inboards) need to be running to get the vessel from island to island each night. You want to be at the next island by sunrise, wind or no wind. It's generally too much trouble for the crew to hoist the sails at 2:00 a.m. — the passengers aren't awake to appreciate it, so why bother. And during daylight hours, travel is at a minimum, typically from one side of the island to the other (usually less than an hour). So the sails are hoisted during the first day of the cruise (leaving the harbor), the last day (returning to the same harbor), and maybe a couple other times. And that's about it for most motor-sailers.

Now for the real bad news. By necessity, sailing vessels need to be sleek in design. That results in better performance under sail. It also results in a very crowded interior, with small cabins, and a minimum of deck space (with lots of cleats to trip on as well). The common area is often reduced to a multi-purpose dining room/lounge. My idea of a 1-2 week cruise is to have as much privacy as possible for those times you don't want to be with the other passengers. And that's just what you don't get with many of the motor-sailers in the Galápagos.

While there are notable exceptions to this negative-sounding description, it's true enough to encourage you to think twice after seeing the pretty photos of the motor-sailers in the brochure — these yachts are pretty (if and when the sails are up), but do look at the available space with regard to the number of passengers before you make a decision.

NOTE: Some yachts do advertise their "superior service," but it must be understood that a tour of the Galápagos Islands is more of an adventure than a luxury cruise. The islands are isolated and depend on air cargo service to bring in a lot of the food consumed on-board the boats. The fancier the menus, the greater the chance that a key ingredient will be missing. So if you can't do without your favorite mustard or brand of coffee, the Galápagos may not be the best destination for you. If you're on a particular diet, this should be discussed with the Tour Operator as early as possible.

Finally, as Galápagos tourism expands, yachts are constantly being upgraded and new yachts are added. Occasionally, and for various reasons, boats are also withdrawn from service on either a temporary or permanent basis.

Here then are the registered Galápagos yachts:

AHMARA (Motor Sailer) — A sister ship of the ESCAPADA (see below) having identical specifications, with the exception that all 5 double cabins on the AHMARA have double beds. The yacht is owned and operated by NIXE CRUISES and began its Galápagos Island service in 1993.

ALBATROS — The ALBATROS, an 80 ft steel-hulled, air-conditioned yacht, was built in Ecuador specifically for Galápagos service, which began in 1992. The air-conditioned, spacious yacht carries 12 passengers and a crew of 8, including a university-level Naturalist Guide. There are 6 double cabins, each with 2 lower beds and private bathroom with hot shower and electric toilet. The yacht is equipped with a water maker, ice machine, VCR, satellite navigation controls, and an electric diving compressor. The ALBATROS is operated by GALAMAZONAS in Ecuador and represented by TEMPTRESS CRUISES in the U.S.

AMIGO I — The 62 ft AMIGO I carries 14 passengers with a crew of 7. The yacht has 6 double and 2 single cabins, each with a ventilating fan and 110 VAC outlet. There are 5 bathrooms, each with a shower. The singles on the upper decks have commanding views. There is a VCR and a full bar on-board. A large lounging area is located on the upper deck. The AMIGO I is an older boat; it has a friendly feel to it, but it is a bit cramped. The yacht is represented by GALAPAGOS HOSTAL C.A. in Ecuador.

ANDANDO (Motor Sailer) — Completely refurbished in 1988 and in great demand, the 90 ft yacht is most spacious both topside and below. She is a charming blend of a square-rigged brigantine fitted with modern conveniences (including air conditioning) and navigation equipment. The 22 ft beam allowed the vessel to be fitted with 6 comfortably-sized double cabins, each having an upper single & a double lower berth and a private bathroom with hot shower. This yacht carries 12 passengers with a crew of 6, including a university-level Naturalist Guide. An ice maker and a large supply of fresh water are carried on-board. Beverages are complimentary. The ANDANDO is owned and operated by Captain Fiddi Angermeyer and Jane Davies. Fiddi was born and raised in the islands and carries on the tradition of the well-known Angermeyer family of expert navigators who have sailed the waters of the Galápagos archipelago. Charters are handled through ANDANDO TOURS.

ANGELIQUE (Motor Sailer) — The spacious 97 ft double-masted brigantine began its Galápagos cruising operations in March, 1990. She carries 12 passengers and a crew of 6; there are 6 double cabins, each with an upper double & single lower berth, private bathroom, and shower. The yacht, equipped for diving, has an ice machine and satellite navigation instrumentation. There always seems to be festivities on-board, which can often be heard by adjacent vessels at anchor. The ANGELIQUE is owned and operated by Captain Franklin Angermeyer, a long-time Galápagos resident. The yacht is represented by ETNOTUR.

ANGELITO I — Built in 1992, this 70 ft yacht carries 12 passengers and a crew of 7. There are 6 double cabins (U/L berths), each with a private bathroom and shower. The ANGELITO I is represented by ANGERMEYER'S ENCHANTED EXCURSIONS.

BEAGLE III — Formerly the research vessel used by the *Charles Darwin Research Station* and converted for passenger cruising in 1978, the BEAGLE III is 66 ft long and carries 10 passengers with a crew of 5, including a university-level Naturalist Guide. There are 5 double cabins on-board, with 2 large bathrooms and 1 hot shower. The BEAGLE III is owned and operated by Captain Agosto Cruz, a Galápagos native, and his wife Georgina; the yacht is marketed by METROPOLITAN TOURING and can be booked through their U.S. representative, ADVENTURE ASSOCIATES.

CACHALOTE (Motor Sailer) — This popular 70 ft vessel carries 10 passengers and a crew of 5. The CACHALOTE (Spanish for sperm whale) was built in 1971, reconditioned in 1988, and is equipped for diving. The stable Motor Sailer has 5 double cabins and 3 bathrooms, each provided with a hot shower. The owner/operator, Martin Schreyer, is frequently the captain; he is a long-time resident and knows the islands extremely well. A university-level naturalist guide is also aboard. The yacht is represented by ANGERMEYER'S ENCHANTED EXCURSIONS.

CORAL — This classic 110 ft steel-hulled vessel was totally refitted & reconditioned, and began its Galápagos service in 1991. She carries 20 passengers and a crew of 10, including 2 university-level Naturalist Guides. The CORAL has 10 exterior cabins located on 3 decks, including 6 doubles (each with a twin bed), 2 doubles with U/L berths, and 2 double suites; each cabin has a polished wood interior, a private bathroom, and hot shower. This very spacious air-conditioned yacht is equipped with 2 water makers, an ice machine, VCR, satellite navigation, and 2 compressors for diving. There is a formal dining room, outside terrace dining, and a large lounge & bar area (2 complimentary cocktails per passenger offered daily). The CORAL is operated by KLEINTOURS.

CRUZ DEL SUR — This 75 ft yacht was built in 1989 and began its Galápagos touring operations in December of that year. The CRUZ DEL SUR is a sister ship of the ESTRELLA DEL MAR and DORADO (see below) and has identical specifications. The yachts is operated by GALASAM CIA LTDA.

DARWIN EXPLORER — Formerly the ISABELA I, this 108 ft yacht was totally refitted and modernized, returning to Galápagos service as the DARWIN EXPLORER in 1992. She carries 12 passengers and a crew of 8, including a university-level Naturalist Guide. There are 4 double cabins (3 with U/L berths and 1 suite), a triple, and a single cabin on board, each with a private bathroom and hot shower. The yacht is equipped with satellite navigation and is extremely spacious both inside and out, including lots of outdoor lounging area. The DARWIN EXPLORER is operated by TURGAL TURISMO.

DIAMANTE (Motor Sailer) — The 97 ft fiberglass brigantine schooner is a modern scaled-down version of the classic naval training ships. Built in 1987, completely refit in 1991, she began her Galápagos service in 1993. The yacht accomodates 8 passengers in 4 large air-conditioned cabins, each with a double bed (1 with a king-size bed), bathroom, and shower. She carries a crew of 6, including a university-level Naturalist Guide. The beamed main salon is tastefully decorated with beautiful mahogany and teak; extras include VCR, a water maker, and satellite navigation. The DIAMANTE is operated by ECOCRUCEROS S.A.

DORADO — This 75 ft yacht was built in 1988, carries 16 passengers with a crew of 8, including a university-level Naturalist Guide, and is owned and operated by GALASAM CIA LTDA. The air-conditioned DORADO is very spacious throughout, and the interior is very nicely laid out and furnished. It is a very reasonably-priced yacht for the features and high class of service offered.

There are 8 cabins (all have a lower twin and upper single berth), each with a private bathroom and hot shower; 2 of the cabins are on the upper deck and are considered suites. The dining room and lounge area are very large and comfortable; the full-service bar is beautifully designed.

ENCANTADA (Motor Sailer) — This 70 ft staysail schooner has a red hull and is one of the most photogenic boats in the islands. It carries 10 passengers with a crew of 6, including a university-level Naturalist Guide. Fully renovated in 1992, the ENCANTADA is fitted with 5 double cabins (1 of which has a double bed), 3 bathrooms (with shower and electric toilets), 1 hot shower, a full bar, an ice maker, and is equipped for diving. The power supply is 24 VDC. The yacht is operated by METROPOLITAN TOURING and their U.S. representative, ADVENTURE ASSOCIATES.

ERIC — Inaugurated in January, 1991, this beautiful 83 ft yacht carries 20 passengers and a crew of 10, including 2 university-level Naturalist Guides. She has 10 double cabins located on 3 decks; each cabin has lower twin beds (some have a larger double bed), a private bathroom, and hot shower. The ERIC is very spacious throughout and has a beautiful polished wood interior; its large windows provide dramatic panoramic views. The air-conditioned yacht is equipped with a VCR and satellite navigation instrumentation. The ERIC and her 2 sister ships, FLAMINGO and LETTY, are operated by SITUR and their U.S. representative, GALAPAGOS NETWORK.

ESCAPADA (Motor Sailer) — This 45 ft catamaran was built in 1989 by Philippe Jeantot (3-time around-the-world sailing champion) and began its Galápagos service in February, 1990. She carries 12 passengers and a crew of 5, including a university-level Naturalist Guide. The yacht is fitted with 5 double cabins (4 with U/L berths and 1 with a double bed), each with private bathroom and hot shower. Other features include a large dining room, fully-equipped bar, water maker, ice machine, gas stove, microwave oven, VCR, and video library. A gourmet-style menu is offered for each meal, with which complimentary beer and wine are served. The yacht is equipped with an electric compressor for diving; windsurfing is also available on request. ESCAPADA is owned and operated by NIXE CRUISES.

ESTRELLA DEL MAR — This 75 ft yacht joined the fleet of yachts owned and operated by GALASAM CIA LTDA in 1990. The ESTRELLA DEL MAR is a sister ship of the CRUZ DEL SUR and DORADO (see above) and has identical specifications.

FLAMINGO — This beautiful 83 ft yacht began her Galápagos service in November, 1991. She has identical specifications as her 2 sister ships, ERIC and LETTY (see the description of ERIC above); the 3 sisters are operated by SITUR and their U.S. representative, GALAPAGOS NETWORK.

GABY — Built in the Galápagos and completed in 1989, the GABY is 71 ft long and carries 12 passengers with a crew of 6, including a university- level Naturalist Guide. There are 6 large double cabins, each with a lower twin &

upper single bed, private bathroom, and shower. The yacht has ample deck space, including lounge chairs in both sun and shade locations. There is a full bar and spacious dining area on-board. GABY is equipped for diving and is available through most major Tour Operators in Ecuador.

GALAPAGOS ADVENTURE — Built in Ecuador specifically for Galápagos service, the 90 ft yacht was launched in 1991. She carries 20 passengers in 10 double cabins (3 with double beds and 7 with 2 lower beds), each with its own bathroom and hot water shower. There are 8 crew members on-board, including a university-level Naturalist Guide. The GALAPAGOS ADVENTURE is very modern & spacious, and is equipped with VCR (although BETA) and satellite navigation; it is represented by NUEVO MUNDO EXPEDITIONS.

GALAPAGOS AGGRESSOR — see PODEROSO II below.

ISLAS PLAZAS — This 66 ft yacht was built in Ecuador and began its Galápagos service in 1992. The ISLAS PLAZAS carries 12 passengers and a crew of 8, including a university-level Naturalist Guide. There are 6 double cabins, each with 2 lower beds, private bathroom, and hot shower. There are 4 downstairs cabins; each has electric flush toilets. There are also 2 upper cabins featuring panoramic windows and a lower double bed (along with an upper single). The air-conditioned yacht is quite modern in appearance and has a very comfortable outside lounge on the upper deck. The ISLAS PLAZAS is operated by GALASAM CIA LTDA.

LAMMAR LAW (Motor Sailer) — Designated one of the largest trimarans in the world, the 93 ft LAMMAR LAW was designed by the well-known team of Duncan and Annie Muirhead; it joined the fleet of yachts operated by QUASAR NAUTICA, S.A. in 1990. Equipped for diving, the LAMMAR LAW is very spacious throughout and carries 18 passengers with a crew of 6, including a university-level Naturalist Guide. There are 9 double cabins, each with a private bathroom and hot shower. Many of the beds are queen-sized doubles that convert to twins. The amount of deck space is vast as is the lounging room down below, fitted with soft comfortable chairs and sofas. There is a large capacity water maker, ice machine, and VCR on-board. The yacht is fitted with the latest instrumentation, including satellite navigation. The LAMMAR LAW is represented in the U.S. by TUMBACO, INC.

LETTY — This beautiful 83 ft yacht began her Galápagos service in 1993. She has identical specifications as her 2 sister ships, ERIC and FLAMINGO (see the description of ERIC above); the 3 sisters are operated by SITUR and their U.S. representative, GALAPAGOS NETWORK.

LOBO DE MAR — The 73 ft yacht carries 12 passengers and a crew of 7. There are 6 double cabins (L/L), each with a private bathroom and shower. The LOBO DE MAR is represented in Ecuador by NUEVO MUNDO EXPEDITIONS.

MARIGOLD — The 55 ft fiberglass-hulled yacht carries 8 passengers with a crew of 4. It is fitted with 2 double cabins and 1 quad cabin, each with U/L berths, private bathroom, and shower. There is a water maker and VCR (BETA format) on-board. The air-conditioned MARIGOLD, equipped for diving, is owned and operated by Jorge and Patricia Valdivieso; reservations can be made through most Ecuadorian Tour Operators.

MISTRAL II — The 66 ft MISTRAL II carries 12 passengers and has a crew of 6, including a university-level Naturalist Guide. There are 6 double cabins — 3 with a lower twin and an upper single, 1 with U/L berths, and an adjoining 2-cabin suite; there are 5 bathrooms with hot showers. Equipped for diving, the very attractive air-conditioned yacht is fitted with a VCR, ice machine, 2 water makers, and satellite navigation equipment. The MISTRAL II is owned and operated by QUASAR NAUTICA, S.A. and represented in the U.S by TUMBACO, INC.

NORTADA — Built in France in 1986, the 66 ft NORTADA carries 10 passengers with a crew of 5, including a university-level Naturalist Guide. The sleek, very attractive, air-conditioned yacht has 5 double cabins (U/L berths) and 3 bathrooms with hot showers. Owned and operated by QUASAR NAUTICA, S.A., she is equipped for diving, and fitted with a VCR, 2 water makers and satellite navigation instrumentation. The U.S. representative for QUASAR is TUMBACO, INC.

ORCA — The 54 ft ORCA carries 8 passengers with a crew of 4 and is represented by ETNOTUR. The yacht is fitted with 4 double cabins, each with a private bathroom and shower. This is an extremely stable vessel, providing a very smooth ride.

PANCHITA (aka SEA CLOUD) — Constructed in 1984 as the SEA CLOUD (one of the well-known Cloud Series, of which approximately 10 were built), the 85 ft fiberglass-hulled ketch began her Galápagos service in 1992. Carrying a crew of 5, including a university-level Naturalist Guide, she accommodates 8-10 passengers in 4 cabins, each with a double and single berth (U/L), private bathroom, and hot shower. This attractive air-conditioned yacht, equipped for diving, has rich teak paneling throughout; facilities include VCR, a water maker, and satellite navigation instrumentation. The PANCHITA is operated by SITUR and their U.S. representative, GALAPAGOS NETWORK.

PODEROSO II (aka GALAPAGOS AGGRESSOR and JESUS DEL GRAN PODER) — This is an excellent dive boat, although the name and ancestry are a bit confusing. The original PODEROSO (aka JESUS DEL GRAN PODER) was an Economy Class Yacht. The new PODEROSO II, an 80 ft steel-hulled yacht, was built in Ecuador specifically for Galápagos service, which began in 1992. The air-conditioned, spacious yacht carries 12 passengers and a crew of 9, including a university-level Naturalist Guide and a certified Dive Master. There are 6 double cabins, each with 2 lower beds and private bathroom with hot shower and electric toilet. The yacht is equipped with a water maker, VCR, satellite navigation controls, and an electric diving compressor. The PODEROSO II is operated by GALAMAZONAS in Ecuador and represented by GALASAM CIA LTDA. and marketed through the prestigious AGGRESSOR FLEET (of excellent live-aboard dive boats) in the U.S.

PULSAR — This 50 ft fiberglass catamaran was constructed in 1981 and reconditioned for Galápagos service, which began in 1992. She has a capacity of 10 passengers in 4 double cabins and 2 singles; all cabins have a private bathroom (5 of the 6 have wash basins), and there are 2 hot water showers on-board. The PULSAR carries a crew of 4 and is owned & operated by GALAPAGOS CRUISES 2000 S.A.

RACHEL III (Motor Sailer) — The 85 ft Formosa vessel was built in 1990 and began her Galápagos service in 1993. The yacht accomodates 8 passengers in 4 large air-conditioned cabins, each with a double bed, bathroom, and shower. Fitted with a beautiful teak interior, she carries a crew of 6, including a university-level Naturalist Guide. Additional equipment includes a VCR, water maker, and satellite navigation. The RACHEL III is operated by ECOCRUCEROS S.A.

REINA SILVIA — Named after the Queen of Sweden, the REINA SILVIA began its Galápagos Island service in December of 1989. This 90 ft vessel sails with 16 passengers and a crew of 7, including a university-level Naturalist Guide. The yacht is extremely spacious and impressively equipped. There are 6 double cabins (each with upper and lower full-size beds), 2 single cabins, and 1 luxury suite (called the "owner's cabin") with king-size bed and complete sound system. All cabins have a private bathroom with hot shower as well as a piped-in music system (on/off switch). The galley is restaurant-scale and includes a commercial-size freezer, ice machine, and water maker. The rates include pre-dinner cocktails from the fully-equipped bar. Other features include a washer/dryer, video system, swimming platform, extended bow-bridge for dolphin watching, and the latest in safety equipment. The REINA SILVIA is equipped for diving, including a large capacity electric compressor. It has a large power plant, enabling a 1 week itinerary that includes the outer islands of Tower, Española, Fernandina, and Isabela (Tagus Cove only). The REINA SILVIA is operated by PLACES SPACE CONTROL AB in Sweden.

RESTING CLOUD (Motor Sailer) — Built in 1985, carrying 10 passengers with a crew of 5 (including a university-level Naturalist Guide), this 84 ft air-conditioned ketch joined the fleet of yachts operated by QUASAR NAUTICA, S.A. in December, 1989. There are 5 staterooms, each with reading lamps, 110VAC outlets, a lower twin and an upper single berth, as well as a private bathroom with hot shower. There is a large capacity water maker and ice machine on-board. The fiberglass-hulled RESTING CLOUD is equipped for diving and is fitted with a VCR and satellite navigation instrumentation. The galley is quite large and in addition to the gas stove and oven is equipped with 3 refrigerators, a freezer, and a microwave oven. The U.S. representative for QUASAR NAUTICA is TUMBACO, INC.

SAMBA (Motor Sailer) — This classic 78 ft steel-hulled trawler was built in 1966 and totally refitted in 1993 for Galápagos service. She carries 10 passengers and a crew of 5, including a university-level Naturalist Guide. The yacht is equipped with 5 air-conditioned double cabins, each with private bathroom and hot shower; there is a water maker and VCR on-board. The SAMBA is owned and operated by Captain Fiddi Angermeyer and Jane Davies, who did an excellent job of reconditioning the ANDANDO (see above), making it one of the most popular boats in the islands. They are working towards a similar success with the SAMBA, which can be chartered through ANDANDO TOURS.

SAMOA I — Built in 1986 and refitted in 1989, this 72 ft yacht carries 16 passengers with a crew of 8, including a university-level Naturalist Guide. There are 2 single cabins and 7 air-conditioned double cabins, each with a private bathroom and shower. A complimentary evening cocktail is served from the fully-equipped bar; there is also a water maker and ice machine on-board. The SAMOA I has a natural history library, is equipped for diving, and is owned and operated by SAMOA TURISMO, S.A.

SANDPIPER (Motor Sailer) — This 56 ft air-conditioned ketch began her Galápagos service in 1993. She carries 6 passengers and a crew of 5, including a university-level Naturalist Guide. There are 3 double cabins, each with a lower twin berth and single upper, bathroom, and hot shower. The yacht, finished with rich teak throughout the interior, is equipped with a water maker, ice machine, VCR, and satellite navigation instumentation. An ideal yacht for a family or a group of friends, the SANDPIPER is marketed by QUASAR NAUTI-CA S.A., and their U.S. representative, TUMBACO, INC.

SAN JACINTO — The 80 ft. SAN JACINTO was built in in 1989 and began its Galápagos cruising operations in 1990. She carries 12 passengers and a crew of 9, including a university-level Naturalist Guide. The vessel has 8 double outside cabins, each with 2 lower berths (the beds in the 4 aft cabins slide together), private bathroom (with electric flush toilets), and shower. The yacht is very spacious throughout; there are 3 decks, including a sundeck with lounge chairs. The interior has attractive wood paneling, with a large lounge area, most suitable for evening Workshop discussions. The dining room is also quite spacious, as is the well-stocked bar area. The SAN JACINTO is represented by GALAPA-GOS TRAVEL in the U.S.

SEA CLOUD — See PANCHITA above.

SULIDAE (Motor Sailer) — The 60 ft ketch is a classic; built in 1907, it is kept in beautiful appearance and condition. She carries 8 passengers and a crew of 5 (including a university-level Naturalist Guide) and is fitted with 4 double cabins (U/L berths), 3 bathrooms (2 with showers), and a deck shower; there is also an ice maker on-board. The SULIDAE (named for the family of boobies and gannets) is very popular, owing in part to the expertise of captain Pepe Salcedo, an internationally-licensed Dive Master who owns and operates the yacht. The SULIDAE, equipped for diving, is operated by (and can be booked directly through) SULIDAE CHARTERS. The charter price includes all beverages, including sodas, beer, and wine.

SYMBOL (Motor Sailer) — This 37 ft ketch carries 4 passengers with a crew of 3. It has an outside shower, connecting (semi-private) cabins and 1 bathroom.

Equipped for diving, the SYMBOL is ideal for a small family or a group of 3-4; the yacht is operated by ROLF WITTMER/TURISMO GALAPAGOS CIA. LTD.

TIP TOP II — A very popular boat, the steel-hulled TIP TOP II was built in 1983, is 70 ft long, and holds 12 passengers with a crew of 6, including a university-level Naturalist Guide. Accommodations are 6 double cabins (U/L berths), each with a private bathroom and shower. Captain Rolf Wittmer is the first natural resident of Floreana Island, born in 1933; he knows the islands extremely well, and the crew is spoken of with respect by a number of Tour Operators. Passengers are treated to a special experience — a family-style dinner at the Wittmer Pension on Floreana Island. The TIP TOP II, fitted with satellite navigation instrumentation and equipped for diving, is operated by ROLF WITTMER/TURISMO GALAPAGOS CIA. LTD.

YOLITA — Completely refurbished in 1985, the YOLITA is 53 ft long, carries 12 passengers with a crew of 5, and is operated by GALASAM CIA LTDA. The yacht has 6 cabins (which are rather small and have no reading lights), 4 with private bathrooms; there is 1 shower on-board. The YOLITA is a bit cramped for 12 passengers.

ECONOMY CLASS YACHTS

The boats in this classification have both private (double) and shared (quad) cabins with bunks, as well as shared bathroom and shower facilities. Occasionally the cold water showers are located on-deck (enclosed). While these vessels are typically recommended for budget travelers, I would have to disagree. As a classification, the Economy Class Yachts have a poor track record with regard to customer satisfaction. I have heard numerous complaints regarding overcrowding, not fulfilling full week tour obligations, the Guides, and just general hassles. For a few hundred dollars more per week, you can book a yacht on which the comfort and service levels are up at least a notch; more important, you're less likely to have unpleasant surprises. In all fairness, you'll probably do just fine with an Economy Class Yacht; I just can't recommend taking a reasonable chance on spoiling a once-in a-lifetime adventure while saving a small percentage of the total cost of the vacation.

   NOTE: Your chance of getting an Auxiliary Guide with non-fluent English ability is higher in this category than the others. If it is important for you to have a university-level, licensed Naturalist Guide, communicate this to the Tour Operator and have it included in the contract. You may be told that a more expensive yacht will be required. Shop around!

   Designated Economy Class Yachts include the AIDA MARIA, ANGELITO (reputedly the best of the lot), ANTARTIDA, CORMORANT, DAPHNE, DARWIN, ELIZABETH, ESPANOLA, FENIX, FLAMINGO, GOLONDRINA, ISLAS GALAPAGOS II, KICKER ROCK, MOBY DICK, POSEIDON, SAN JUAN, VALIANT, and XAVIER.

DAY TRIP YACHTS

By definition, these boats cruise by day, and you sleep ashore (at one of several hotels). As a classification, it's really a mixed bag ranging from overcrowded, poorly conducted budget operations that are giving a black eye to Galápagos tourism to organized programs offering a series of 1 day mini-adventures.

We'll start from the bottom and work our way up, although there's not a single option I can recommend. Somehow, a lot of people show up in the Galápagos each year without a prearranged tour. Many of them fit the "backpacking through South America" category. There are a number of Boat Operators that cater to these budget travelers. While some of them do a reasonable job, others have blatantly violated the laws of the National Park. This includes overloading the boats, which is unsafe as well as illegal. Some have an insufficient number of Licensed Guides on-board (sometimes none). Another regulation that is sometimes violated is the one that calls for the captain to report the ship's itinerary to the Port Captain and receive clearance to sail to the requested island(s). This law is meant to reduce the impact of tourism by controlling the number of visitors per day to each island.

The end result is not good. The tourists are not controlled and are free to wander off the trails, thus damaging the fragile terrain and in many ways upsetting the ecology of the islands. The effects are amplified by the number and frequency of these tours, as well as by the fact that many of the trips visit the same close-by islands, such as South Plaza and North Seymour. These islands are said to have already been impacted, as evidenced by a reduction in the numbers of animals seen as well as trail erosion. The information received from the Guides on these tours is often quite minimal.

Many well-intentioned travelers think that you can get a standard tour of the islands cheaper once you arrive there. At first glance, this isn't an unreasonable concept, especially considering the lack of objective information written about Galápagos touring. However, it turns out that almost all the Tour Operators have their reservation and office operations in mainland Ecuador. The better Tour Operators do keep an operations office in the Galápagos, mainly to handle day-to-day logistics such as maintenance and supplies. The bottom line is that you can't expect to show up in the Galápagos and put together a cruise on any of the better boats; this includes the vessels listed in this book, and the ones of like quality that I may have missed for one reason or another.

These visitors are then "stuck" on the islands without a tour, typically in the town of Puerto Ayora on Santa Cruz Island. They usually wind up staying in one of the hotels and taking a series of Day Trips to the islands close by. These boats, which are advertised on signs throughout town, provide a reasonable service and, by and large, conform to the National Park regulations. But they do add to the overload on the close-by islands. In addition, the experience is not one of the best. Often, you have to board a bus at 5:30 a.m. which bounces across Santa Cruz island to the channel near Baltra Island, where the boat is anchored. This process is reversed in the evening, and you often arrive back at the hotel after dark. Then there's the 2-3 hour boat ride each way as well as the island tour itself, often conducted by a non-English-speaking Guide. It isn't very informative, and it isn't very relaxed or pleasant. And it also isn't necessary. You can avoid this type of experience by not going to the Galápagos until you have arranged a tour. If you want to put together your own tour on a direct basis and possibly save some money, do it in mainland Ecuador (see the section, Galápagos Tour Operations in Ecuador, towards the end of this chapter).

Finally, there are many people who simply do not enjoy the experience of sleeping on a boat, regardless of the comfort level. There are also families that don't find the arrangements to be practical or convenient. Still there's too much back-and-forth time, and the near-by islands are the ones most frequently visited.

The most organized program of the bunch is run by METROPOLITAN TOURING; their high speed yacht, the 36 passenger DELFIN II, is capable of single day round-trips to some of the central islands. Nights (including dinner and breakfast) are spent at the Hotel Delfin, one of the few First Class hotels in the Galápagos. The yacht anchors in Academy Bay, Puerto Ayora with transfers to/from the hotel via quick dinghy (*panga*) rides. Two university-level Naturalist Guides are on-board and also provide evening lectures and briefings at the hotel. The problem is the itinerary. They have a 4 day program (which visits 3 nearby islands) and a 5 day program (which does about the same, with the addition of a day in the highlands of Santa Cruz Island); there is also a combined 1 week program (which misses more than it sees).

While there are several other the Hotel/Day Trip Programs, I do not feel it appropriate to present this option (Day Trips) as a viable alternative to touring the Galápagos Islands.

GALAPAGOS CRUISE SHIPS

There are presently five Cruise Ships which tour the Galápagos Islands — the AMBASADOR I, CORINTHIAN, GALAPAGOS EXPLORER, ISABELA II, and SANTA CRUZ. The AMBASADOR I carries 86 passengers, THE CORINTHIAN carries 48, the GALAPAGOS EXPLORER carries 100, the SANTA CRUZ carries 90, and the ISABELA II carries 38. To conform with National Park regulations, each ship carries 1 Guide per 16 passengers. Each passenger is thus assigned to a group (based primarily on language) of up to 16 people. Due to the relatively large numbers, the land tours tend to be more regimented.

Breakfast and lunch are typically served buffet style, while dinners are seated. These ships require a formal attire (no shorts) for the evening meal, which is a marked difference from the casual atmosphere of the smaller yachts. After dinner, the Guides conduct briefings on the islands to be toured the following day; in addition, there are Galápagos videos that are shown a few times per week. At some point in the evening, things get decidedly less formal, the music begins, and people stroll out to the center of the lecture room (which is now a disco) to do their best blue-footed booby imitations. Welcome and farewell cocktails are served.

The air-conditioned cabins are very spacious and comfortable, with ample storage space, private bathrooms with hot showers and flush toilets, as well as piped-in music (via on/off switch). There is a P.A. system that lets you know about upcoming activities well in advance. Snorkel equipment is available on a rental basis; snorkeling activities are more restricted (in the time allotted and where they let you go) than on the smaller yacht tours.

Here then are the Galápagos Cruise Ships:

AMBASADOR I — Built in 1958 and totally refurbished in 1993, the 298 ft AMBASADOR I began its Galápagos service in September, 1993. She has 4 decks and carries 86 passengers & a crew of 66, including 4-6 university-level Naturalist Guides. Ship features include a swimming pool, solarium, boutique, beauty salon, library, and grand lounge with nighly entertainment/dancing. Electricity is 220 VAC (110 VAC adaptors on request). Satellite telecommunication is also available. Children under 7 not permitted.

COMMENTS: The AMBASADOR I operates out of Baltra Island. As the second edition of this book was going to press, the ship was just beginning its Galápagos service and experiencing some problem in booking passengers.

CRUISES:

> Itinerary "A" — Sunday to Wednesday (3 nights)
>
> Itinerary "B" — Wednesday to Sunday (4 nights)
>
> Combined Itinerary "A" / "B"

CABINS: There are 62 cabins (43 outside and 19 inside), including singles (inside and outside), doubles (L/L & U/L), triples, quads, and Deluxe Suites.

RATES: Priced by cabin type and cruise selection.

> Double cabins are about $200-$275/night (per person, double occupancy). Deluxe doubles are higher. Single cabins are about $325-$350/night. Triple cabins are about $125-$175/night (per person, triple/quad occupancy).

RESERVATIONS: The AMBASADOR I is owned and operated by **ISLAS GALA-PAGOS TURISMO Y VAPORES C.A.,** Av. República del Salvador 935, (P.O. Box 135-A), Quito. PHONE: 011-593-2-446-883 or 011-593-2-240-247, FAX: 011-593-2-446-882. Reservations can also be made through their U.S. representative, **GALAPAGOS ADVENTURES, INC.,** 1790 Broadway, New York, NY 10019. PHONE: (212) 581-0100, FAX: 212-265-6214.

CORINTIAN — A former research vessel operating in Alaska, the 195 ft CORINTHIAN was renovated in 1993 and is scheduled to begin service in the Galápagos in 1994. She will carry 48 passengers and a crew of 30, including 2-3 university-level Naturalist Guides. The spacious dining room (1500 sq ft) has large picture windows. Other features include an observation lounge, solarium, jacuzzi, boutique, and library. There is a full time doctor on-board.

COMMENTS: The CORINTHIAN will operate out of San Cristóbal Island. While she will be just beginning her Galápagos service, the Boat Operators and their U.S. Representative have a lot of positive experience in the islands. There is an ownership affiliation with SAETA and SAN Airlines, and convenient, attractively-priced package plans are sometimes offered. The ship's clock is set on mainland Ecuador time (rather than on Galápagos time) which is convenient for quick in-and-out trips but a bit confusing at first for those that have spent some time in the islands prior to the voyage and have gotten used to local time.

CRUISES:

> Itinerary "A" — Thursday to Sunday (3 nights)
>
> Itinerary "B" — Sunday to Thursday (4 nights)
>
> Combined Itinerary "A" / "B"

CABINS: There are 25 double cabins located on 2 decks. The upper deck cabins have large windows. All cabins have twin lower beds.

RATES: Priced by cabin type and cruise selection.

Double cabins are about $150-$175/night (per person, double occupancy). Single occupancy is about $200-$225/night.

RESERVATIONS: The CORINTHIAN is owned and operated by **SITUR,** Av. C.J. Arosomena — Km 2, Guayaquil. PHONE: 011-593-4-201-516, FAX: 011-593-4-201-153. Reservations can be made directly with SITUR, although it may be more convenient for you (or your travel agent) to work through their U.S. representative, **GALAPAGOS NETWORK,** 7200 Corporate Center Dr., Ste. 204, Miami, FL 33126. PHONE: (305) 592-2294. TOLL FREE: (800) 633-7972, FAX: 305-592-6394.

GALAPAGOS EXPLORER — The largest (314 ft, 4 decks) and fastest ship operating in the islands, the GALAPAGOS EXPLORER was built in 1962 and completely refurbished in 1985. She carries 100 passengers and a crew of 75, including 5-6 university-level Naturalist Guides. Amenities include a large swimming pool, solarium, 2 bar areas, boutique, library, and live evening entertainment in the disco. Electricity is 220 VAC (110 VAC transformers provided on request). Bar and boutique (gift shop) bills are settled on the last day via cash (U.S. dollars or sucres), traveler's checks, or major credit card. There is a medical facility and a doctor on-board the GALAPAGOS EXPLORER. No children are allowed under the age of 7.

COMMENTS: The GALAPAGOS EXPLORER operates out of San Cristóbal Island. There is an ownership affiliation with SAETA and SAN Airlines, and convenient, attractively-priced package plans are sometimes offered. The ship's clock is set on mainland Ecuador time (rather than on Galápagos time) which is convenient for quick in-and-out trips and a bit confusing at first for those that have spent some time in the islands prior to the voyage and have gotten used to local time.

CRUISES:

Itinerary "A" — Wednesday to Saturday (3 nights)

Itinerary "B" — Saturday to Wednesday (4 nights)

Combined Itinerary "A" / "B"

CABINS: There are 53 cabins, including singles, doubles (L/L & U/L), triples (2L/1U), quads, and Deluxe Suites.

Top (León Dormido) Deck — 1-2 occupants

Second (Albatross) Deck — 2 occupants

Main (Marchena) Deck) — 1-4 occupants

Lower (San Cristóbal) Deck — 1-3 occupants

RATES: Priced by cabin type and cruise selection.

Upper and boat decks are about $250-$300/night (per person, double occupancy) and about $300-$325/night for single occupancy.

Main and lower decks are about $200-$275/night (per person, double occupancy), about $175/night (per person, triple/quad occupancy), and about $275/night for single occupancy.

RESERVATIONS: The GALAPAGOS EXPLORER is owned and operated by **CAN-ODROS S.A.**, Urdenata 1418 and Av. del Ejèrcito (P.O. Box 8442), Guayaquil. PHONE: 011-593-4-285-711, FAX: 011-593-4-287-651. Reservations can be made directly with CANODROS, although it may be more convenient for you (or your travel agent) to work through their U.S. representative, **GALAPAGOS, INC.**, 7800 Red Road, Suite 112, South Miami, FL 33143. PHONE: (305) 665-0841, TOLL FREE: (800) 327-9854, FAX: 305-661-1457.

ISABELA II — The 166 ft Cruise Ship made its first Galápagos Island voyage in December, 1988. It is fully-carpeted, has 3 decks, a large salon and bar, as well as a spacious dining area. For relaxation, there is a covered sun deck with comfortable lounge chairs, a jacuzzi, sauna & exercise room, and a library/reading room. The dining and reading rooms are entirely non-smoking areas. The ISABELA II has a modern water purification system on-board. In addition to the main engines, there is a bow-thruster which adds to the maneuverability of the vessel, an item of importance when negotiating the tricky anchorages of the archipelago.

COMMENTS: Carrying 38 passengers with a crew of 24 (including 3 university-level Naturalist Guides) and a doctor, the ISABELA II is literally in a class of its own. It has the comfort of a Cruise Ship with almost the same degree of privacy as the larger Luxury Class Yachts. The ISABELA II is in great demand and is booked solidly by the Tour Operators.

CRUISES: All tours are on an 8 day/7 night (Tuesday-Tuesday) itinerary and visit many of the major islands of the Galápagos. Due to its high speed capability, the ISABELA II is one of the few boats that allows the outer islands of Tower (Genovesa), Fernandina, and Isabela (Tagus Cove only) to be visited on a 1 week tour.

CABINS: There are 19 spacious, exterior twin cabins (14' X 9' 4" — lots of storage room) with 2 lower berths; these cabins open onto a promenade.

RATES: Prices are about $2000 per person (double occupancy) and $2400 for single occupancy.

RESERVATIONS: All tours on the ISABELA II are booked through **METROPOLITAN TOURING**, Av. Republica de El Salvador 970 (P.O. Box 17-12-0310), Quito. Phone: 011-593-2-464-780, FAX: 011-593-2-564-702. Reservations can be made directly with METROPOLITAN, although it may be more convenient for you (or your travel agent) to work through their U.S. representative, **ADVENTURE ASSOCIATES**, 13150 Coit Rd., Suite 110, Dallas, TX 75240. Phone: (214) 907-0414, TOLL FREE: (800) 527-2500, FAX: 214-783-1286.

SANTA CRUZ — Built in 1980, the 3-decked SANTA CRUZ sails with 90 passengers and a crew of 50, including 6 university-level Naturalist Guides. Almost all of the 45 cabins are exterior, although there are some inside triples and singles on the upper and main decks. The SANTA CRUZ is fully-carpeted, with a spacious dining room and cocktail lounge. Bar bills are settled on the last day via cash or traveler's checks — no charge cards. There is a full-time doctor on-board.

CRUISES:

Itinerary "A" — Monday to Thursday (3 nights)

Itinerary "B" — Thursday to Monday (4 nights)

Combined Itinerary "A" / "B"

CABINS:

Twin (L/L) — Main Deck/Boat Deck/Upper Deck

Triple (2L/1U) — Main Deck/Boat Deck

Quad — Main Deck

Inside Triple (2L/1U)

Inside Single

RATES: Priced by cabin type and cruise selection.

Twin cabins are about $225-$275/night (per person, double occupancy).

Triple cabins are about $200-$225/night (per person, triple occupancy).

Quad cabins are about $175/night (per person, with 4 occupants).

Inside triple cabins are about $200/night (per person, triple occupancy).

Single cabins are about $300/night.

RESERVATIONS: All tours on the SANTA CRUZ are booked through **METRO-POLITAN TOURING** who are represented in the U.S. by **ADVENTURE ASSO-CIATES**. For details, refer to the section above on the "ISABELA II."

GENERAL TOURS WITH TOUR LEADERS

The value of a Tour Leader has been discussed in detail earlier in this chapter (see the section "Tour Leader vs. No Tour Leader").

TOUR OPERATORS PROVIDING GENERAL TOURS WITH TOUR LEADERS

NOTE: Prices do not include airfare, Galápagos National Park entrance fee, Ecuador departure taxes, or gratuities unless noted.

AMERICAN MUSEUM OF NATURAL HISTORY/DISCOVERY CRUISES, Central Park West at 79th St., New York, NY 10024-5192.

PHONE: (212) 769-5700   **FAX:** 212-769-5755

TOLL FREE: (800) 462-8687

BOATS: ISABELA II (Cruise Ship).

TOUR LEADER: 2 museum lecturers accompany the trip (see Comments).

PRICE RANGE: 1 week tour (+ 6 nights in Quito and tours of the surrounding area, incl. museums) for $5000.

COMMENTS: Two AMERICAN MUSEUM lecturers accompany each trip (1-2 Galápagos trips per year); each is truly an expert. Dr. Charles Cole, Curator, *Department of Herpetology and Ichthyology,* is a specialist in amphibian & reptile evolution and genetics; Dr. Cole has accompanied several AMERICAN

MUSEUM trips. Carol Townsend is an Associate in the same department and has also lectured on several AMERICAN MUSEUM voyages to the Galápagos.

BIOLOGICAL JOURNEYS, 1696 Ocean Drive, McKinleyville, CA 95521.
PHONE: (707) 839-0178 or (510) 527-9622   **FAX:** 707-839-4656
TOLL FREE: (800) 548-7555
BOATS: ANDANDO, CACHALOTE.
TOUR LEADER: Ron LeValley or Ronn Storro-Patterson (see Comments).
PRICE RANGE: 2 week tour (+4 days in Quito) for $4200-$4600 incl. Quito-Galápagos round-trip airfare, National Park entrance fee, and all beverages on-board the yacht.
COMMENTS: Ron LeValley has been actively teaching bird-watching classes for 15 years. He has a long involvement with the *Point Reyes Bird Observatory* and spent 2 years as a biologist at the *Farallon Islands Research Station*. Ron is a former Northern California Regional Editor for **AMERICAN BIRDS**. Ronn Storro-Patterson is one of the leading authorities on whales and has been a member of the Scientific Committee of the *International Whaling Commission*. He founded and directed the *University of California* Extension Programs on Natural Environmental Studies and Photography.

CHEESEMAN'S ECOLOGY SAFARIS, INC., 20800 Kittredge Road, Saratoga, CA, 95070.
PHONE: (408) 867-1371 or (408) 741-5330   **FAX:** 408-741-0358
TOLL FREE: (800) 527-5330
BOATS: ANDANDO
TOUR LEADER: Various and have included Luis Tam.
PRICE RANGE: 1 week tour (+10 days in the Amazon Basin and the Andes) for $3100 incl. some meals in Quito.
COMMENTS: The Cheesemans are very highly regarded, as is Tour Leader Luis Tam. Doug Cheeseman is a Professor of Zoology; his wife Gail is a birder. Their trips are birding-oriented and are described as being ". . . for people who enjoy being in the field all day and are non-smokers."

GALAPAGOS TRAVEL, P.O. Box 1220, San Juan Bautista, CA 95045.
PHONE: (408) 623-2920   **FAX:** 408-623-2923
TOLL FREE: (800) 969-9014
BOATS: SAN JACINTO
TOUR LEADER: Various, including Barry Boyce, the author of this book.
PRICE RANGE: 11 day tour (+3 nights in Quito) for $2550 incl. most meals in Quito and all non-alcoholic beverages on the cruise; 2 week tour (+3 nights in Quito) for $3150 incl. most meals in Quito and all non-alcoholic beverages on the cruise. This tour emphasizes the western islands of Isabela and Fernandina and includes a hike/horseback ride to and around the rim of the Sierra Negra Volcano (or, on some itineraries, a 3 day hike/camp-out along the rim of the Alcedo Volcano).
COMMENTS: GALAPAGOS TRAVEL offers a series of workshop-oriented tours of the Galápagos. The 11 day format allows sufficient time to visit the outer islands and to see a significant representation of the plant and animal species; the 2 week trips present a rare opportunity to explore the western islands of Fernandina and Isabela in depth. In addition to the daily guided island visits,

evening workshop sessions focus on topics such as island formation and history, wildlife distribution, evolution, and conservation. An emphasis is placed on providing optimum photographic opportunities and guidance to each passenger.

NATURAL HABITAT WILDLIFE ADVENTURES, One Sussex Station, Sussex, NJ 07461.
PHONE: (201) 702-1525   **FAX:** 201-702-1335
TOLL FREE: (800) 543-8917
BOATS: GALAPAGOS ADVENTURE
TOUR LEADER: Various, including Gary Miller (see Comments).
PRICE RANGE: 1 week tour (+2 nights in Quito) for $3100 incl. round-trip airfare from Miami, National Park entrance fee, and all meals in Quito.
COMMENTS: Gary Miller has a PhD in Ecology and is an assistant professor at the *University of New Mexico.*

NATURE EXPEDITIONS INTERNATIONAL, P.O. Box 11496, Eugene, OR 97440.
PHONE: (503) 484-6529   **FAX:** 503-484-6531
TOLL FREE: (800) 869-0639
TOUR LEADER: Various scientists and teachers (see Comments).
BOATS: AMIGO I, BEAGLE III, SULIDAE, TIP TOP II.
PRICE RANGE: 1 week tour (+1 week touring mainland Ecuador) for $2900 incl. National Park entrance fee and most meals in mainland Ecuador (except in Quito); 2 week tour (+3 nights in Quito) for $3300 incl. National Park entrance fee. Meals in Quito not included.
COMMENTS: NEI has offered wildlife and natural history expeditions since 1974. Company President David Roderick states, "We especially take pride in our Trip Leaders, who are specialists in anthropology, natural history, or biology. In addition to broad field experience in the host country, every NEI leader is required to have an M.A., Ph.D., or equivalent professional training, and teaching experience on the college level."

NEW YORK BOTANICAL GARDEN, ATTN: Carol Gracie, Bronx, NY 10458-5126.
PHONE: (718) 220-8647   **FAX:** 718-562-6780
TOUR LEADER: Carol Gracie, former Travel Program Coordinator for the New York Botanical Garden.
BOATS: REINA SILVIA
PRICE RANGE: 1 week (+1 week in Quito and tours of the surrounding area) for $3800 incl. all meals in Quito and round-trip airfare from Miami.
COMMENTS: This is one of the few tours that emphasize the plants of the Galápagos Islands. Extensive educational material is provided to each participant.

OCEANIC SOCIETY EXPEDITIONS, Fort Mason Center, Building E, San Francisco, CA 94123.
PHONE: (415) 441-1106   **FAX:** 415-474-3395
TOLL FREE: (800) 326-7491
BOATS: TIP TOP II.
TOUR LEADER: Various experts, including Al Molina and Craig Strang (see Comments).

PRICE RANGE: 1 week tour (+ 2 nights in Quito/1 night in Guayaquil) for $3300 incl. round-trip airfare from Miami; 12 day tour (+ 2 nights in Quito/1 night in Guayaquil) for $4000 incl. round-trip airfare from Miami.

COMMENTS: Tour Leader Al Molina (M.A., Botany) is Director of the Bolinas Marine Lab, a college biology instructor, and has been leading trips for over 20 years. Craig Strang is the Director of Marine Activities Resources & Education (MARE) at the Science Museum/Education Center of the *University of California, Berkeley.*

SIERRA CLUB, 730 Polk St., San Francisco, CA 94109.
PHONE: (415) 923-5630
BOATS: Economy Class Yachts
TOUR LEADER: See Comments.
PRICE RANGE: 5 day tour (+9 nights in mainland Ecuador) for $3600-$4000 incl. several local tours (and some meals) in mainland Ecuador.
COMMENTS: The *Sierra Club* is a conservation-oriented organization. As stated in their **OUTINGS** brochure, "Unlike ordinary tour agencies, the Sierra Club seeks to promote an understanding of environmental issues on all its outings. . . . Trips are led by experienced and competent leaders. . . ." The style of travel is not First Class, but it is most informative. Participants must be members of the *Sierra Club.*

VOYAGERS INTERNATIONAL, P.O. Box 915, Ithaca, NY 14851.
PHONE: (607) 257-3091   **FAX:** 607-257-3699
TOLL FREE: (800) 633-0299
BOATS: CRUZ DEL SUR, DORADO, ESTRELLA DEL MAR.
TOUR LEADER: See Comments.
PRICE RANGE: 1 week tour (+2 nights in Quito) for $2500 — $3000 incl. round-trip airfare from Miami.
COMMENTS: VOYAGERS, INTL. markets tours with various nature organizations, such as the *California Center for Wildlife*, the *Center for Environmental Study, Brukner Nature Center*, and the *National Association of Biology Teachers* (NABT). These organizations provide a Tour Leader which have included Dr. Kay Dodge, Director of the *Center for Environmental Study*, and Dr. Alton Biggs, President of NABT. These trips are open to the general public.

WILDERNESS TRAVEL, 801 Allston Way, Berkeley, CA 94710.
PHONE: (510) 548-0420   **FAX:** 510-578-0347
TOLL FREE: (800) 368-2794
BOATS: ANDANDO, CACHALOTE, ENCANTADA, SULIDAE.
TOUR LEADER: Various (see Comments).
PRICE RANGE: 1 week tour (+7-10 days in either the Andes/Amazon or Peru) for $3100-$3400; 2 week tour (+3 nights and most meals in Quito) for $3200-$3800 incl. a 3 day hike to the Alcedo Volcano.
COMMENTS: WILDERNESS TRAVEL has over the years recruited excellent Tour Leaders including several authors and scientists who have done academic research in the islands.

WILDLAND ADVENTURES, 3516 NE 155th St., Seattle, WA 98155.
PHONE: (206) 365-0686   **FAX:** 206-363-6615
TOLL FREE: (800) 345-4453
BOATS: ANDANDO, CACHALOTE, RESTING CLOUD.
TOUR LEADER: See Comments.
PRICE RANGE: 2 week tour (+3 nights in Quito) incl. a 3 day hike to the Alcedo
   Volcano for $3200 (CACHALOTE)/$3800 (ANDANDO).
COMMENTS: Formerly called JOURNEYS, the company has been in operation
   since 1978 and has led tours to the Galápagos since 1980. They have talent-
   ed Tour Leaders, including scientists who have done academic research in
   the islands. Part of the proceeds go to the *Earth Preservation Fund,* a non-profit organization founded in conjunction with WILDLAND ADVENTURES, supporting conservation projects and community development in host countries.

ZEGRAHM EXPEDITIONS, 1414 Dexter Ave. N., Ste. 327, Seattle, WA 98109.
PHONE: (206) 285-4000   **FAX:** 206-285-5037
TOLL FREE: (800) 628-8747
BOATS: FLAMINGO.
TOUR LEADER: Jack Grove, Peter Harrison.
PRICE RANGE: 1 week tour (+2 nights in Quito) for $3000 incl. most meals in
   Quito and all non-alcoholic beverages on the cruise.
COMMENTS: Tour Leader Jack Grove is the author of **GALAPAGOS FISHES: A
   COMPREHENSIVE GUIDE TO THEIR IDENTIFICATION** (see the Literature
   section). Jack also worked as a Licensed Galápagos Guide for 7 years. Other
   credentials include being recognized as Underwater Photographer of the
   Year by the BBC. In his "spare time," he also serves as a Research Associate
   at *Hubbs-Sea World Research Institute* in San Diego. Tour Leader Peter
   Harrison is one of the world's leading authorities on sea birds. His **SEABIRDS:
   AN IDENTIFICATION GUIDE** is the definitive book on the identification of
   sea birds. Jack and Peter co-founded ZEGRAHM EXPEDITIONS in 1990. The
   other co-founders are equally impressive — and they each lead their own
   trips. By the way, their company name, "ZEGRAHM," is some sort of conflu-
   ence of their names put together, and there's about 6 of them!

CANADIAN TOUR OPERATORS PROVIDING
GENERAL TOURS WITH TOUR LEADERS

QUEST NATURE TOURS, c/o WORLDWIDE ADVENTURES, 36 Finch Avenue,
   West, North York, Ontario, M2N 2G9.
PHONE: (416) 221-3000   **FAX:** 416-221-5730
TOLL FREE: (800) 387-1483 U.S. & CANADA
TOUR LEADER: Biologists and graduate-level professionals (see Comments).
PRICE RANGE: 1 week tour (+2 nights in Quito) for U.S.$1750.
COMMENTS: Barry Griffiths, President of QUEST, states, "Quest's well-
   researched programs offer our participants a rare insight into wildlife, cul-
   tures, and peoples, enabling them to acquire a stimulating and in-depth
   perspective of the regions in which they are travelling. The strong educational focus adds a very personal touch and distinctive dimension to our interna-

tional nature tour program. Whether you are a birder, a botanist, or a lover of all nature, you will find our expertly-led tours provide you with a memorable and worry-free vacation; no special knowledge required!"

Several of QUEST's Tour Leaders are residents of the countries visited. Barry Griffiths also leads many of the nature tours. He is an educator, an author, and a widely-published wildlife photographer. Barry is a former President of the *Federation of Ontario Naturalists* and *Director of the Canadian Nature Federation.*

GENERAL TOURS WITHOUT TOUR LEADERS

Many Galápagos Island General Tours without Tour Leaders are offered at Premium or value-added ("Package") prices. Basically, you're paying a higher price than the retail cost of a weekly tour on a particular boat. We'll take a look at some of the extras that **might** be provided:

Airfare — Round-trip to Ecuador and/or between Ecuador and the Galápagos.

Hotels — This can include one or more nights in mainland Ecuador, typically in a First Class Hotel.

Meals — This can include 1-3 meals per day in mainland Ecuador.

Day Tours — Escorted trips in and around Quito.

Airport Transfers — Rides to and from the airport in mainland Ecuador, including check-ins and baggage assistance.

Pre-Trip Briefing Material — literature, etc.

As stated above, some or all of the above services may or may not be provided by a particular Tour Operator. While this book endeavors to list as many of these value-added extras as possible, it is up to you to verify which ones are included in the tour price. Operators who provide Premium ("Package") Tours should prove to you that they are providing tangible premium services.

TOUR OPERATORS PROVIDING
GENERAL TOURS WITHOUT TOUR LEADERS

NOTE: Prices do not include airfare, Galápagos National Park entrance fee, Ecuador departure taxes, or gratuities unless noted.

ELDERHOSTEL, 75 Federal Street, Boston, MA 02110-1941.
PHONE: (617) 426-7788   **FAX:** 617-426-8351
BOATS: CRUZ DEL SUR, DORADO, ESTRELLA DEL MAR.
PRICE RANGE: 1 week tour (+ 3 nights in Quito, most meals and some local touring) for $2500 incl. round-trip airfare from Miami.
COMMENTS: ELDERHOSTEL is a non-profit, educational organization that serves older adults. Every year, thousands of people age 60 and older (spouses may be under 60) participate in programs at educational and cultural institutions (including national parks) in the U.S., Canada, and in 43 countries

overseas. Although their Galápagos itinerary requires that "Elderhostelers be physically fit and vigorous, as it is a strenuous program," the groups tend to be mixed in physical ability; possibly for this reason, it has been observed that their walks are somewhat limited on certain islands.

GEO EXPEDITIONS, P.O. Box 3656, Sonora, CA 95370.
PHONE: (209) 532-0152   **FAX:** 209-532-1979
TOLL FREE: (800) 351-5041
BOATS: CORAL, ISABELA II, MISTRAL II, NORTADA, REINA SILVIA, RESTING CLOUD, SANDPIPER.
PRICE RANGE: 1 week tour (+ 3 nights in Quito) incl. most meals in mainland Ecuador for $2400-$2600 ($3100 for the ISABELA II).
COMMENTS: GEO has been offering tours to the Galápagos since 1982 and has a most knowledgeable staff.

HIMALAYAN TRAVEL, 112 Prospect St., Stamford, CT 06901.
PHONE: (203) 359-3711   **FAX:** 203-359-3669
TOLL FREE: (800) 225-2380
BOATS: Several, including Economy Class Yachts as well as modern, air-conditioned boats.
PRICE RANGE: 1 week tour (+2 nights in Quito) for $1100-$1700.
COMMENTS: HIMALAYAN TRAVEL was founded in 1977 and offers a wide range of adventure travel trips throughout the world. They have operated in South America since 1980 and added the Galápagos in 1987.

HOLBROOK TRAVEL, INC., 3540 NW 13th St., Gainesville, FL 32609.
PHONE: (904) 377-7111   **FAX:** 904-371-3710
TOLL FREE: (800) 451-7111
BOATS: CRUZ DEL SUR, ESTRELLA DEL MAR.
PRICE RANGE: 1 week tour (+2 nights in Quito) for $2200 incl. round-trip airfare from Miami.
COMMENTS: HOLBROOK TRAVEL has over 20 years of experience in the Galápagos and know the travel logistics in this part of the world very well.

INCA FLOATS, 1311 63rd St., Emeryville, CA 94608.
PHONE: (510) 420-1550   **FAX:** 510-420-0947
BOATS: ANDANDO, BEAGLE III, CORAL, ENCANTADA, GALAPAGOS ADVENTURE, LAMMAR LAW, MARIGOLD, MISTRAL II, NORTADA, REINA SILVIA, RESTING CLOUD, SANDPIPER.
PRICE RANGE: 1 week tour (+2 nights in Quito) for $2200-$2800 incl. most meals in Quito; 1 week tour (+2 nights in Quito and 1 night at the HOTEL GALAPAGOS) for $2100-$2700 incl. most meals in Quito; 1 week tour (+ 3 nights in Quito and 3 nights at the HOTEL GALAPAGOS w/day treks on Santa Cruz Island) for $2800-$3000 incl. most meals in Quito; 1 week tour (+ 9 days in Peru W/Machu Picchu, 3 nights in Quito and 1 night at the HOTEL GALAPAGOS) for $3700-$4300 incl. some meals in Peru and Quito; 2 week tour (+2 nights in Quito and 1 night at the HOTEL GALAPAGOS) for $5200 incl. most meals in Quito — for optional 4 day Alcedo Volcano hike/camp-out, add $500.

COMMENTS: INCA FLOATS (started in 1976) specializes in the Galápagos and offers over 60 tours a year to the islands. Owner Bill Roberson was a Licensed Galápagos Guide, and his knowledge of the islands is extensive. They are one of the few U.S. Tour Operators that have a resident manager in the Galápagos to look after their passengers (before and after the boat tours).

INTERNATIONAL EXPEDITIONS, INC., One Environs Park, Helena, AL 35080.
PHONE: (205) 428-1700   **FAX:** 205-428-1714
TOLL FREE: (800) 633-4734
BOATS: GALAPAGOS ADVENTURE, LOBO DE MAR.
PRICE RANGE: 1 week tour (+3 nights in Quito) for $3000 incl. all meals in Quito, round-trip airfare from Miami, and National Park entrance fee; 11 day tour (+4 nights in Quito) for $4000 incl. all meals in Quito, round-trip airfare from Miami, and National Park entrance fee.

MOUNTAIN TRAVEL.SOBEK, 6420 Fairmount Ave., El Cerrito, CA 94530.
PHONE: (510) 527-8100   **FAX:** 510-525-7710
TOLL FREE: (800) 227-2384
BOATS: AHMARA, BEAGLE III, ENCANTADA, MISTRAL II, RESTING CLOUD, SULIDAE.
PRICE RANGE: 1 week tour (+2 nights in Quito) for $1900-$2400 incl. most meals in Quito.
COMMENTS: MOUNTAIN TRAVEL has been in the adventure travel business since 1968 and acquired SOBEK EXPEDITIONS in 1990. They have handled Galápagos excursions since 1971 and currently offer about 12 trips per year.

OCEAN VOYAGES, INC., 1709 Bridgeway, Sausalito, CA 94965.
PHONE: (415) 332-4681   **FAX:** 415-332-7460
BOATS: Several.
PRICE RANGE: 1 week tour for $950; 2 week tour for $1700; 3 week tour which includes a hike up to the Alcedo Volcano for $2600.
COMMENTS: Director Mary Crowley has made over 10 trips to the islands; through these visits, she has been able to establish and maintain good working relationships with some of the independent Boat Operators. Mary is a professional sailor, ocean researcher, and has published articles on the Galápagos. She and I strongly agree on one important point; a 2 week tour is necessary to fully experience and appreciate the unique beauty of the Galápagos. She makes this possibility affordable and stresses it to her customers, and I am stressing it to you.

OVERSEAS ADVENTURE TRAVEL, 349 Broadway, Cambridge, MA 02139.
PHONE: (617) 876-0533   **FAX:** 617-876-0455
TOLL FREE: (800) 221-0814
BOATS: ESTRELLA DEL MAR, ISLAS PLAZAS, SAN JACINTO, TIP TOP II.
PRICE RANGE: 1 week tour (+ 2 weeks in the Andes/Amazon) for $3500; 1 week tour (+ 4 nights in Quito) for $2200-$2400 incl. sightseeing day trips in the mainland.
COMMENTS: OVERSEAS ADVENTURE TRAVEL, in business since 1979, has a very impressive, professional operation with a most knowledgeable staff. Special "Family Trips" are offered 1-2 times per year.

VOYAGERS INTERNATIONAL, P.O. Box 915, Ithaca, NY 14851.
PHONE: (607) 257-3091   **FAX:** 607-257-3699
TOLL FREE: (800) 633-0299
BOATS: CRUZ DEL SUR, DORADO, ESTRELLA DEL MAR.
PRICE RANGE: 1 week tour (+2 nights in Quito) for $2500 incl. round-trip air-fare from Miami.
COMMENTS: VOYAGERS does an excellent job of providing pre-trip briefing information.

WILDERNESS TRAVEL, 801 Allston Way, Berkeley, CA 94710.
PHONE: (510) 548-0420   **FAX:** 510-578-0347
TOLL FREE: (800) 368-2794
BOATS: ANDANDO, CACHALOTE, ENCANTADA, SULIDAE.
PRICE RANGE: 1 week tour (+3 nights in Quito) for $2000-$2300 incl. most meals in Quito.
COMMENTS: WILDERNESS TRAVEL has, over the years, put together excellent Galápagos packages.

WILDLAND ADVENTURES, 3516 NE 155th St., Seattle, WA 98155.
PHONE: (206) 365-0686   **FAX:** 206-363-6615
TOLL FREE: (800) 345-4453
BOATS: GALAPAGOS ADVENTURE, LOBO DE MAR, MISTRAL II, NORTADA, RESTING CLOUD.
PRICE RANGE: 1 week tour (+3 nights in Quito) for $2200.
COMMENTS: Formerly called JOURNEYS, the company has been in operation since 1978 and has led tours to the Galápagos since 1980. Part of the pro-ceeds go to the *Earth Preservation Fund*, a non-profit organization founded in conjunction with WILDLAND ADVENTURES, supporting conservation pro-jects and community development in host countries.

CANADIAN TOUR OPERATORS PROVIDING GENERAL TOURS WITHOUT TOUR LEADERS

GALAPAGOS HOLIDAYS, 745 Gerrard Street East, Toronto, Ontario M4M 1Y5.
PHONE: (416) 469-8211   **FAX:** 416-463-5131
TOLL FREE: (800) 661-2512 U.S. & CANADA
BOATS: Several, including Economy Class Yachts as well as modern, air-condi-tioned boats.
PRICE RANGE: 1 week tour (+6 nights in Quito and tours of the surrounding area) for U.S.$2600 incl. round-trip airfare from Miami. 2 week tour with an overnight trek to the Alcedo Volcano (+2 nights in Guayaquil) for U.S.$2800 incl. round-trip airfare from Miami. Meals in Guayaquil not included.
COMMENTS: GALAPAGOS HOLIDAYS works exclusively on Galápagos Island tours, and also offers several selections of "on-your-own" packages and specialty tours (diving, etc.). The owner, Ingrid Versteeg, lived in Ecuador and owned a travel agency in Quito from 1969 to 1982. Their prices are very rea-sonable, considering that airfare and hotel rooms are included.

GALAPAGOS SPECIALTY TOURS

NOTE: Prices do not include airfare, Galápagos National Park entrance fee, Ecuador departure taxes, or gratuities unless noted.

BIRDING SPECIALTY TOURS

Of land-birds, I obtained twenty-six kinds, all peculiar to the group and found nowhere else, with the exception of one lark-like finch from North America.

Charles Darwin, 1845

Since the historic visit by that well-known Galápagos birder, the number of indigenous species of land birds has reached twenty-nine, twenty-two of which are endemic to the islands. While the resident land birds are quite approachable and their locations more or less predictable (based on zonal vegetation), it will take an experienced eye to identify the majority of the Darwin's finches. This is part of the reason that you may want to choose a specialized Birding Tour, with an expert-class Tour Leader.

Birding Tours make even more sense when the sea birds and coastal species are considered. With the vast ocean everywhere around, the Galápagos have no sparsity of sea birds, with totals estimated at well over one and a half million. There are nineteen resident species of pelagic avifauna, as they are called, five of which are endemic to the islands. To see them all requires some planning and often a special orientation; for example, the endemic waved albatross is typically absent from January-March. In addition, the availability of food in a given year may alter the distribution of a particular species from island to island. Finally, there are many migrants amongst the species found along the more than 800 miles of Galápagos coastline and tidal lagoons; this would require a trip during the northern winter. The Birding Tour Operators will be more apt to know these variables in advance and compensate for them in the selected itinerary. Birding itineraries allow for a continuous, yet comfortable pace of bird watching, providing each member with clear views of as many species as possible. Small groups, therefore, are often the rule. The days are apt to begin a bit earlier on these tours, to match pace with the activity cycles of the birds.

TOUR OPERATORS OFFERING BIRDING TRIPS

BIOLOGICAL JOURNEYS, 1696 Ocean Drive, McKinleyville, CA 95521.
PHONE: (707) 839-0178 or (510) 527-9622   **FAX:** 707-839-4656
TOLL FREE: (800) 548-7555
BOATS: ANDANDO, CACHALOTE.
TOUR LEADER: Ron LeValley (see Comments).
PRICE RANGE: 2 week tour (+4 days in Quito) for $4200-$4600 incl. Quito-Galápagos round-trip airfare, National Park entrance fee, and all beverages on-board the yacht.

COMMENTS: Ron LeValley has been actively teaching bird-watching classes for 15 years. He has a long involvement with the *Point Reyes Bird Observatory* and spent 2 years as a biologist at the *Farallon Islands Research Station*. Ron is a former Northern California Regional Editor for **AMERICAN BIRDS**.

CHEESEMAN'S ECOLOGY SAFARIS, INC., 20800 Kittredge Road, Saratoga, CA, 95070.
PHONE: (408) 867-1371 or (408) 741-5330   **FAX:** 408-741-0358
TOLL FREE: (800) 527-5330
BOATS: ANDANDO
TOUR LEADER: Various and have included Luis Tam.
PRICE RANGE: 1 week tour (+10 days in the Amazon Basin and the Andes) for $3100 incl. some meals in Quito.
COMMENTS: The Cheesemans are very highly regarded, as is Tour Leader Luis Tam. Doug Cheeseman is a Professor of Zoology; his wife Gail is a birder. Their trips are birding-oriented and are described as being ". . . for people who enjoy being in the field all day and are non- smokers."

FIELD GUIDES, INC., P.O. Box 160723, Austin, TX 78716-0723.
PHONE: (512) 327-4953   **FAX:** 512-327-9231
TOUR LEADER: Various professional birders, including Chris Benesh.
PRICE RANGE: 12 day tour (+2 nights in Guayaquil) for $3300, incl. National Park entrance fee and round-trip airfare from Guayaquil.
COMMENTS: FIELD GUIDES is one of the leading birding Tour Operators. Director Allan Griffith states, "All of our tours are birding tours. At FIELD GUIDES INCORPORATED we believe that experienced and personable leadership is the most important feature of a tour. Our guides know their areas thoroughly and make every effort to provide each participant memorable views of as many species as possible. Emphasis is placed on area specialties, rarities, and behaviorally interesting birds. We spend most of every nontravel day in the field, often departing before dawn to reach birding areas for the height of activity and song."

GALAPAGOS TRAVEL, P.O. Box 1220, San Juan Bautista, CA 95045.
PHONE: (408) 623-2920   **FAX:** 408-623-2923
TOLL FREE: (800) 969-9014
BOATS: SAN JACINTO
TOUR LEADER: Various, including Barry Boyce, the author of this book.
PRICE RANGE: 11 day tour (+3 nights in Quito) for $2550 incl. most meals in Quito and all non-alcoholic beverages on the cruise; 2 week tour (+3 nights in Quito) for $3150 incl. most meals in Quito and all non-alcoholic beverages on the cruise. This tour emphasizes the western islands of Isabela and Fernandina and includes a hike/horseback ride to and around the rim of the Sierra Negra Volcano (or, on some itineraries, a 3 day hike/camp-out along the rim of the Alcedo Volcano).
COMMENTS: GALAPAGOS TRAVEL offers a series of workshop-oriented tours of the Galápagos. The 11 day format allows sufficient time to visit the outer islands and to see a significant representation of the plant and animal species;

the 2 week trips present a rare opportunity to explore the western islands of Fernandina and Isabela in depth. In addition to the daily guided island visits, evening workshop sessions focus on topics such as island formation and history, sea birds (2 sessions), land birds, shore birds, wildlife distribution, evolution, and conservation. An emphasis is placed on providing optimum observational and photographic opportunities to each passenger.

MASSACHUSETTS AUDUBON SOCIETY, South Great Road, Lincoln, MA 01773.
PHONE: (617) 259-9500   **FAX:** 617-259-8899
TOLL FREE: (800) 289-9504
BOATS: CRUZ DEL SUR, DORADO
TOUR LEADER: See Comments.
PRICE RANGE: 1 week birding tour (+2 nights in Quito) for $3000, incl. round-trip airfare from Miami, National Park entrance fee, and all meals in Quito.
COMMENTS: The Natural History Travel program is part of the *Massachusetts Audubon Society's* Conservation Department; a diverse array of conservation-oriented travel is offered across the country and throughout the world. Tour Leaders have included Dr. Gerard Bertrand, president of *Massachusetts Audubon*, and field ornithologist Wayne Petersen, one of the country's best-known birders.

VOYAGERS INTERNATIONAL, P.O. Box 915, Ithaca, NY 14851.
PHONE: (607) 257-3091   **FAX:** 607-257-3699
TOLL FREE: (800) 633-0299
BOATS: CRUZ DEL SUR, DORADO, ESTRELLA DEL MAR.
TOUR LEADER: Various ornithologists throughout the year.
PRICE RANGE: 1 week tour (+3 nights in Quito) for $3000 incl. round- trip airfare from Miami.
COMMENTS: There are occasional visits with Paul Greenfield, one of Ecuador's best birders. VOYAGERS INTL. markets tours with many leading birding groups and organizations, including the *American Birding Association, Connecticut Audubon Society, Cornell Laboratory of Ornithology*, and the *Detroit Audubon Society*. Individuals as well as groups are invited to call or write for information. VOYAGERS does an excellent job of providing pre-trip briefing information.

DIVING SPECIALTY TOURS

In 1986, with the creation of the *Galápagos Marine Resources Reserve*, the Galápagos National Park was extended to the waters surrounding the islands (a 15 nautical mile boundary zone was established). This event received extensive media coverage, and the wonders of this underwater world came to the attention of many divers.

The waters of the Galápagos are nutrient-rich (a result of strong upwelling activity), attracting a multitude of unique wildlife. About 10 percent of the 400 or so Galápagos fish species are endemic to the islands; the figure would be around 20 percent if the pelagic species were excluded. As you explore and perhaps photograph the unique subtidal life, sea lions will be your constant dive companions, swimming alongside you and seemingly sharing your curiosity (see Photo #15). Other occasional native swimmers and divers include penguins, marine turtles, flightless cormorants, and marine iguanas. Several species of rays are commonly seen, as well as white-tipped and hammerhead sharks. Then there's the yellow-tailed surgeonfish, parrotfish, pufferfish, creolefish, grouper, and king angelfish, not to mention the yellow-bellied triggerfish, moorish idol, and hieroglyphic hawkfish.

Caution: While an exciting experience, diving in the Galápagos is not easy and is definitely not recommended for the inexperienced. The seasonal upwelling activity (especially in the waters off the western and northern islands) that has resulted in the diversity and abundance of marine wildlife, is itself a result of mixing of strong ocean currents (up to 2-4 knots) that the diver must contend with. The upwelling also causes prolific plankton growth, and the waters tend to be murky for the first 40-50 feet; it is thus relatively easy to lose your points of reference. In addition, the waters are often cold (60-65 Deg. F) and quarter-inch wet suits must be worn. Finally, there is virtually no emergency medical help available in the islands. The closest operational decompression chamber is found at Howard Air Force Base in Panama, which is an expensive 1000 mile journey at best (there is the possibility of a new facility opening in Guayaquil).

Added to the above cautions, it is my recommendation that you do not dive the Galápagos until your second trip there. Much of the fascination and beauty of Galápagos is on land, and mixing a land-dive tour simply doesn't work. It's like ordering "steak and lobster;" you get the worst of both. The majority of the great dive sites (e.g., Darwin & Wolf Islands, Roca Redonda) are not anywhere near a land Visitor Site. Even if you're a diver, I recommend that your first trip to the Galápagos be on a non-dive tour, but one that visits as many of the islands as possible (a 10 day or 2 week tour) and allows you to do quite a bit of snorkeling (free-diving there is most rewarding). Then, if you can, go back to the islands on a dive trip that emphasizes the best dive sites.

To dive the Galápagos, you must be a Certified Diver; beginning or Certification Courses are not offered. Bring full scuba diving gear, including full wet suit (1/4"), gloves, hood, boots, fins, mask, snorkel, weight belts (weights are provided), regulator, gauges, and fish slates. Several yachts are equipped for diving (see the section in this Chapter on Boats of the Galápagos). A compressor is on-board these boats, and tanks are provided. For a discussion of photographic equipment, see the Underwater Photography section in Chapter VII.

To formally book your dive trip, many of the Tour Operators will want a copy of your current Dive Card and a letter from your physician stating that you are in good health for diving.

For more comprehensive information about the underwater world of the Galápagos, there are some excellent books on the subject, including **SUBTIDAL GALAPAGOS** by James Cribb, **GALAPAGOS: A MARINE AND TERRESTRIAL PHENOMENON** by Paul Humann, **MARINE LIFE OF THE GALAPAGOS** by Pierre Constant, and an issue of **OCEANUS** entitled **THE GALAPAGOS MARINE RESOURCES RESERVE**; see the Literature section at the end of this book.

Finally, while the Dive Master will be sure to caution you, remember the rule about waiting at least 24 hours after your last dive before getting on the airplane for the flight back to Ecuador.

TOUR OPERATORS OFFERING DIVE TRIPS

NOTE: Prices do not include airfare, Galápagos National Park entrance fee, Ecuador departure taxes, or gratuities unless noted.

AQUATIC ENCOUNTERS, INC., 1966 Hardscrabble Place, Boulder, CO 80303.
PHONE: (303) 494-8384   **FAX:** 303-494-1202
BOATS: REINA SILVIA.
DIVE GUIDE: Marc Bernardi, the owner of AQUATIC ENCOUNTERS.
PRICE RANGE: 1 week diving tour (2-3 dives per day) + 4 nights (and some meals) in Quito for $2700.
COMMENTS: AQUATIC ENCOUNTERS offers several Galápagos diving trips each year. Every trip is led by owner Marc Bernardi. Marc, who has a lot of diving experience in the Galápagos, states that each trip "always includes the high voltage diving at the northern islands of Darwin and Wolf."

LANDFALL PRODUCTIONS, 39189 Cedar Blvd., Newark, CA 94560.
PHONE: (510) 794-1599   **FAX:** 510-794-1617
TOLL FREE: (800) 525-3833
BOATS: LAMMAR LAW
DIVE GUIDE: Locally provided.
PRICE RANGE: 1 week diving tour (2-3 dives per day) for $2100 (hotel, meals, and transfers in Quito not included.
COMMENTS: LANDFALL PRODUCTIONS, a dive tour operator, is the "stateside booking office" for the owners of the LAMMAR LAW, the largest trimaran in the world.

SEE & SEA, 50 Francisco St., Suite 205, San Francisco, CA 94133.
PHONE: (415) 434-3400   **FAX:** 415-434-3409
TOLL FREE: (800) 348-9778
BOATS: ENCANTADA, LAMMAR LAW, MISTRAL II.
DIVE GUIDE: Ned De Loach and Paul Humann, noted underwater photographer and author of an excellent book, **GALAPAGOS: A TERRESTRIAL AND MARINE PHENOMENON** (see the Literature section).
PRICE RANGE: 10 day diving tour (2-3 dives per day) for $2800 (hotel, meals, and transfers in Quito not included); 2 week diving tour (2-3 dives per day) for $3900 (hotel, meals, and transfers in Quito not included).
COMMENTS: SEE & SEA is generally well-known and one of the leading companies in the dive travel industry; they have led Galápagos dive trips since 1972. Carl Roessler, the owner of SEE & SEA, is an internationally-acclaimed author and underwater photographer with several beautifully-illustrated books to his credit (**DIVER'S GUIDE TO THE CAYMAN ISLANDS, THE CORAL KINGDOMS**, and **THE UNDERSEA PREDATORS**). About 6 trips per year are offered.

WILDERNESS TRAVEL, 801 Allston Way, Berkeley, CA 94710.   Called
PHONE: (510) 548-0420   **FAX:** 510-578-0347   12\ 19
TOLL FREE: (800) 368-2794

BOATS: SULIDAE.
DIVE GUIDE: Jonathan Green (see Comments).
PRICE RANGE: 1 week dive tour (+3 nights in Quito) for $2500 incl. most meals in Quito.
COMMENTS: These trips will combine diving and land experiences on most days. Jonathan Green is a certified Dive Master and is currently completing a book on the Galápagos. He is also a Licensed Galápagos Naturalist Guide and knows the waters here extremely well. In addition, Captain Pepe Salcedo of the SULIDAE is one of the most respected Dive Masters in the islands.

CANADIAN TOUR OPERATORS PROVIDING DIVE TRIPS

GALAPAGOS HOLIDAYS, 745 Gerrard Street East, Toronto, Ontario M4M 1Y5.
PHONE: (416) 469-8211   **FAX:** 416-463-5131
TOLL FREE: (800) 661-2512 U.S. & CANADA
BOATS: MARIGOLD.
DIVE GUIDE: Locally provided.
PRICE RANGE: 1 week dive tour (+2 nights in Guayaquil) for U.S.$2600 incl. round-trip airfare from Miami.
COMMENTS: GALAPAGOS HOLIDAYS works exclusively on Galápagos Island tours, and also offers several selections of "on-your-own" packages and specialty tours (diving, etc.). The owner, Ingrid Versteeg, lived in Ecuador and owned a travel agency in Quito from 1969 to 1982. Their prices are very reasonable, considering that airfare and hotel rooms are included.

PHOTOGRAPHY SPECIALTY TOURS

These trips are accompanied by a professional photographer in addition to the Licensed Guide. During the daily tours, photographic opportunities will be suggested, and guidance will be offered as requested. Evening workshop sessions will be held, and a variety of topics will be discussed, based on the interest of the group and the Tour Leader. The photography experience level of the tour members will vary quite a bit, from beginner to professional, and is generally not a factor; the common denominator is that everyone enjoys photography and wants to learn more. Photographic information will typically be supplied with the pre-departure briefing packet.

These trips offer a real opportunity to improve your photographic technique and to develop your "eye." As a photographer, I have never failed to learn a great deal from the instructor and the fellow members of a photographic field trip. Also, on a trip that is oriented towards photography, you are in a better position to take advantage of lighting conditions. The equatorial sun produces harsh shadows and bleaches out a lot of the rich natural color; some of the best shooting times occur on overcast days and during twilight (which is extremely brief on the equator). A photography group will be more apt to get up extra early in order to get on the first Visitor Site right at dawn and take advantage of the morning twilight. In the evening, the members will usually prefer to stay on the island a bit later for some twilight shots rather than go swimming or back to the boat for a "cold one."

Another advantage to a Galápagos photography tour is that if you're doing something wrong, there's a high probability that someone will notice and point it out; better to find out on the second day of your tour that your polarizer or sun shade wasn't on than after you get home and start looking at the results of the 35 rolls of film you shot.

The only real negative (did I say that?) to a photographic safari of the Galápagos Islands is that it might be an overload situation. The main emphasis in the Galápagos is the wildlife. Many visitors, myself included, spend the evenings and early morning hours reading up on (and discussing) the flora and fauna to be observed on the next couple of islands to be visited. If there's going to be an evening photography discussion, I would want it to be relevant to what we're going to be seeing tomorrow, as opposed to a discussion of advanced photofinishing techniques. While on tour, you are dividing precious time (you're only on an island for 1-3 hours and have to keep moving) between listening to the Guide/Tour Leader, being awed by what you're seeing, and trying to take pictures. There's not a lot of extra time for discussion.

Before deciding on whether to take a photographic specialty tour of the Galápagos, you might think about taking a photography field trip at home. In any case I recommend that, whenever possible, you speak directly with the Photo Tour Leader (Tour Operators often provide their phone numbers), and get a feel for the orientation of the trip that they're coordinating. In addition, you might ask if they've been to the Galápagos Islands before. One thing to watch out for is a "big name" photography Tour Leader who doesn't understand that a Tour Leader's prime responsibility concerns logistical details - and lots of them. Also, you don't want a laid-back, "do your own thing because all pictures are wonderful" type of instructor on your once-in-a-lifetime trip to the Galápagos Islands. What you do want is a photographer who will provide you with and alert you to the unique photographic opportunities on each island and how best to take advantage of them.

TOUR OPERATORS OFFERING PHOTOGRAPHY TRIPS

NOTE: Prices do not include airfare and yachts are Tourist Class unless otherwise noted.

GALAPAGOS TRAVEL, P.O. Box 1220, San Juan Bautista, CA 95045.
PHONE: (408) 623-2920   **FAX:** 408-623-2923
TOLL FREE: (800) 969-9014
BOATS: SAN JACINTO
TOUR LEADER: Various, including Barry Boyce, the author of this book.
PRICE RANGE: 11 day tour (+3 nights in Quito) for $2550 incl. most meals in Quito and all non-alcoholic beverages on the cruise; 2 week tour (+3 nights in Quito) for $3150 incl. most meals in Quito and all non-alcoholic beverages on the cruise. This tour emphasizes the western islands of Isabela and Fernandina and includes a hike/ horseback ride to and around the rim of the Sierra Negra Volcano (or, on some itineraries, a 3 day hike/ camp-out along the rim of the Alcedo Volcano).

COMMENTS: GALAPAGOS TRAVEL offers a series of workshop-oriented tours of the Galápagos. The 11 day format allows sufficient time to visit the outer islands and to see a significant representation of the plant and animal species; the 2 week trips present a rare opportunity to explore the western islands of Fernandina and Isabela in depth. In addition to the daily guided island visits, evening workshop sessions focus on topics such as island formation and history, wildlife distribution, evolution, and conservation. These sessions always include a photography briefing for the following day. An emphasis is placed on providing optimum photographic opportunities and guidance to each passenger.

JOSEPH VAN OS PHOTO SAFARIS, P.O. Box 655, Vashon Island, WA 98070.
PHONE: (206) 463-5383   **FAX:** 206-463-5484
BOATS: MISTRAL II, NORTADA.
TOUR LEADER: Various photographers, including Wayne Lynch and David Middleton (see Comments).
PRICE RANGE: 1 week photo tour (+2 nights in Quito) for $3400 incl. round-trip airfare from Miami and all meals in Quito.
COMMENTS: JOSEPH VAN OS PHOTO SAFARIS has been offering quality photo tours and workshops since 1980. Occasional Group Leader David Middleton is a photographer, naturalist, and writer; a recent publication is **ANCIENT FORESTS: A CELEBRATION OF NORTH AMERICA'S OLD GROWTH WILDERNESS**. Wayne Lynch has travelled to over 40 countries, and his photographs have been published extensively around the world; he has recently written **THE BEARS OF THE NORTHERN WORLD**.

VOYAGERS INTERNATIONAL, P.O. Box 915, Ithaca, NY 14851.
PHONE: (607) 257-3091   **FAX:** 607-257-3699
TOLL FREE: (800) 633-0299
BOATS: CRUZ DEL SUR, DORADO, ESTRELLA DEL MAR.
TOUR LEADER: Several photographers throughout the year including John Gerlach, Ron Rosenstock, Leonard Lee Rue, John Shaw, and Bill Thomas.
PRICE RANGE: 1 week photo tour (+2 nights in Quito) for $2700 - $3000 incl. round-trip airfare from Miami and some meals in Quito.
COMMENTS: Owner David Blanton has worked as a professional photographer for several years and has authored a book on nature photography. VOYAGERS conducts a unique series of photographic workshops led by prominent nature and travel photographers throughout the year; brochures are offered describing the background and orientation of each of the photographic instructors. VOYAGERS does an excellent job of providing pre-trip briefing information.

CANADIAN TOUR OPERATORS PROVIDING PHOTOGRAPHIC TRIPS

QUEST NATURE TOURS, c/o WORLDWIDE ADVENTURES, 36 Finch Avenue, West, North York, Ontario, M2N 2G9.
PHONE: (416) 221-3000   **FAX:** 416-221-5730

TOLL FREE: (800) 387-1483 U.S. & CANADA
TOUR LEADER: (see Comments).
PRICE RANGE: 1 week tour (+2 nights in Quito) for U.S.$1750.
COMMENTS: QUEST organizes several photographic tours a year to the Galápagos and other international destinations. These tours are always led, in addition to local Naturalist Guides, by an expert wildlife photographer. Barry Griffiths, President of QUEST, is a popular nature and photo tour leader who has led tours around the world for the past 25 years. He is an educator, an author, and a widely-published wildlife photographer. Barry is a former President of the *Federation of Ontario Naturalists* and the Director of the *Canadian Nature Federation.*

GALAPAGOS TOUR OPERATIONS IN ECUADOR

The prices you will be quoted by the Ecuadorian Operators will be about the same as you have received from their U.S. representatives and Tour Operators. These are reputable Ecuadorian Tour and Boat Operators, not discount houses! You may have some bargaining power, however, if you travel to Ecuador and personally visit their offices. Occasionally there are a few vacancies on a boat scheduled to sail in the next couple of days, and the Operator may decide to offer you a discounted price to fill the empty slot(s). I do want to make it clear that there's no telling how often, when, or even if this opportunity will present itself.

The amount of any discount is totally open to negotiation; depending on you and the situation, a $1000 1 week cruise could wind up costing anywhere from $600-$1000 and anywhere from 5 minutes to a week or more of your time. This kind of activity can only occur in Ecuador with the Boat Operator and only during the week before the boat is scheduled to sail. There will be those companies, however, that will not want, or need, to offer a discount for whatever reason. The Cruise Ship Operators, for example, are used to sailing with vacancies and rarely discount.

Before you visit a particular Ecuadorian Tour Operator, look at their listing in this Chapter (see the section below) and make a note as to which boats they operate and/or directly represent. The point here is that while they will act as an indirect representative for just about anyone's boat, they are only in a position to lower the price to fill a vacancy, as they deem necessary, on the boats they are directly involved with. To determine which boats you're potentially interested in, turn to the section, Boats of the Galápagos, earlier in the chapter and note who the Boat Operator and/or direct representative is.

As you make the rounds of the Tour Operators in Quito and/or Guayaquil, ask the following series of questions:

1. "Do you have any available space on 1-2 week Galápagos tours in the next week or so"? If there isn't anything available, thank them for their time, and ask if they know of another company that has something available.

2. "What boats are they on?" (Refer to the listing as discussed above.) Let them know which airline (SAN or TAME) you have reservations on. As discussed in Chapter V (FLIGHT PLANS), SAN only flies to the island of San Cristóbal and TAME only to Baltra. A particular boat will be leaving from one or the other

island, and this must be clearly understood. The section below on Ecuadorian Tour Operators states the island the boat typically sails from, but this is subject to change. This detail must be worked out with the Tour Operator.

3. "Does the Guide speak English"? After they say, "Yes," you can ask the follow-up question, "Does the Guide have a Naturalist or Auxiliary license?" (See the Tour Leader vs. No Tour Leader section at the beginning of this chapter.) At this point, they will begin to think you're smarter than you look.

4. "What is the price of the tour"? After this question is answered, you can decide if the tour sounds good and the price is acceptable. If you want a better price, proceed to the following questions.

5. "When is this tour scheduled to leave"?

6. "How many vacancies are there"? Go on to say that you would like to be on the tour, but you're looking for something less expensive. At this point, the Tour Operator will get the idea of what you're up to and either they'll want to play or they won't. If they do, the rest is up to you; this is where your negotiating skills go to work.

If you don't come to an agreement, let the Tour Operator know which hotel you're staying at (just in case the situation changes). If you do agree to terms, you will be required to pay in advance for your tour. Once you agree on a tour, the Operator will also help you confirm your flight arrangements to the Galápagos. This is an important detail as the TAME flights to Baltra, in particular, are often overbooked; those passengers that have a firm tour are given priority consideration. Also, the Tour Operator may be escorting some of their other passengers to the airport, in which case they can arrange for you to join them (usually for an "airport transfer" charge). Again, this is not a minor detail as you may need some "inside help" at the airport (read Chapter V for a blow-by-blow description). In addition, they will be happy to assist you with local tours and excursions to the surrounding areas before or after your Galápagos cruise.

If you're not immediately successful in putting together an acceptable tour, you're going to have to make some contingency plans. You can stay in Quito and/or Guayaquil for a few days and wait to be contacted by one of the Tour Operators you visited. While you're waiting, you can do some shopping (which you would have done at the end of your vacation), tour Quito, and/or take Day Trips to the outlying areas. The amount of time you spend in the mainland depends on how tight your schedule is; the more time you appear to have, the better your negotiating position. Also, most cruises are 1 week in duration, and a particular boat may be sold out this week and have several vacancies the next.

Caution: At some point you'll decide on a particular tour and you'll be off to the islands. Do not, however, under any circumstances, go to the Galápagos without having purchased a tour. People do this, thinking they can get a cheaper or better tour directly from a local agency, the boat owner, or captain. This situation is a disaster - for you and the Galápagos. As pointed out earlier in this chapter (in the section on Day Trip Yachts, which is worth rereading at this time), virtually all the Tour Operators have their reservation and office operations in mainland Ecuador, so you can't just show up in the Galápagos and put together a cruise on any of the better boats. You then get stuck with the Day Trip companies which, once again, won't do you or the islands much good. **Please heed this warning!**

BOAT OPERATORS IN ECUADOR

Note: All phone numbers are local. When calling from the U.S., you must first dial the international access code "011" followed by the country code for Ecuador "593" followed by the city code for Quito "2" or Guayaquil "4" and then the local number. When calling Guayaquil from Quito, dial "04" followed by the local number; when calling Quito from Guayaquil, dial "02" followed by the local number. If you place an international call, remember that mainland Ecuador is on Eastern Standard Time throughout the year.

The FAX numbers listed below include the international, country, and city codes. For some reason, it is a lot easier for Ecuador to receive than to send a FAX communication; don't be surprised if it takes several attempts to get a message to you.

Caution: Unfortunately, in the name of "progress," many of the newer yachts (and there are many of them) are imitating the itineraries of the Cruise Ships by offering 3 and 4 night (4 and 5 day) programs. This means that, if you've purchased a full week cruise, you might really be getting 2 partial weeks put together. Thus, you're making an extra stop at an airport and losing some fellow passengers while picking up others. In my opinion, aside from losing time, it takes away from the overall feeling of the trip. The problem is that the Tour Operator probably won't tell you that your 1 week cruise is really Cruise A + Cruise B. Be careful in your selection! See the Comments sections below to get an idea which of the yachts may follow this practice. But you still need to be cautious; other boats may change their operations at any time. By the way, this type of situation is avoided by booking through a U.S. Tour Operator who has chartered the yacht for the entire length of the Cruise.

BOAT OPERATORS IN QUITO

ANDANDO TOURS, P.O. Box 17-21-0088
LOCAL PHONE: 241-813   **FAX:** 011-593-2-443-188
CONTACT: Charo Beate
BOATS: ANDANDO and SAMBA which operate out of Baltra Island on Wednesdays.
PRICE RANGE: Available typically only on a charter basis. Approximate charter prices are: ANDANDO = $18,000/ week; SAMBA = $14,000/ week.
COMMENTS: The ANDANDO is a very popular boat, and is booked solid by U.S. Tour Operators. The same degree of popularity is forecast for the SAMBA. Reservations should be made well in advance.

ANGERMEYER'S ENCHANTED EXCURSIONS, Foch 769 (off Av. Amazonas).
LOCAL PHONE: 569-960 or 231-713   **FAX:** 011-593-2-569-956
CONTACT: Judy Carvalhal (General Manager), Consuelo (Sales Representative), Sergio Bernardi (Operations Manager).
BOATS: ANGELITO I and CACHALOTE. ANGELITO I typically sails from Baltra on Sundays; the CACHALOTE typically sails from Baltra on Wednesdays.
PRICE RANGE: Available both on a charter and per-passenger basis.

Approximate charter prices are: ANGELITO I = $15,000/ week; CACHALOTE = $11,000/ week. Approximate per-passenger prices are: ANGELITO I = $1300/ week; CACHALOTE = $1200/ week.

COMMENTS: Owner and General Manager Judy Carvalhal lived in the Galápagos for several years and knows the islands very well.

ECOCRUCEROS S.A., Av. Colon 1480, Pa. Co. Building, 7th Floor.
LOCAL PHONE: 509-881 or 509-882
CONTACT: Eliana Rhor
BOATS: DIAMANTE and RACHEL III, which operate from San Cristóbal on Thursdays.
PRICE RANGE: Available only on a charter basis for approximately $16,500 - $17,500/ week.
COMMENTS: This new operation seems to have a keen sense of the right type and size boats that are appropriate for and needed in the Galápagos.

ETNOTUR, Luis Cordero 1313 and Juan León Mera (P.O. Box 4770).
LOCAL PHONE: 230-552 or 564-565   **FAX:** 011-593-2-502-682
CONTACT: Patricia de Arteaga (General Manager), Nelson de la Torre.
BOATS: ANGELIQUE and ORCA. ANGELIQUE sails from Baltra Island on Wednesdays or Saturdays; The ORCA operates from San Cristóbal on Tuesdays or Fridays.
PRICE RANGE: Available both on a charter and per-passenger basis. Approximate charter prices are: ANGELIQUE = $14,000/ week; ORCA = $7500/ week. Approximate per-passenger prices are: ANGELIQUE = $1300/ week; ORCA = $1000/ week.
COMMENTS: The ORCA is a very comfortably-riding boat, and the ANGELIQUE is a classic brigantine motor sailer.
U.S. REPRESENTATIVE: FORUM TRAVEL INTERNATIONAL, INC., 91 Gregory Lane, #21, Pleasant Hill, CA 94523. Phone: (510) 671-2900, FAX: 510-946-1500.

GALAPAGOS CRUISES 2000 S.A., Reina Victoria 447 and Roca, Ste. 4C.
LOCAL PHONE: 528-303 or 569-120   **FAX:** 011-593-2-569-121
BOATS: PULSAR, which operates from Baltra Island.
CONTACT: Patricio Teyssedre, President.
PRICE RANGE: Available both on a charter and per-passenger basis. Charter price is about $10,500/ week. Approximate per-passenger price is $900/ week.
COMMENTS: This is a new venture, and, as of 1993, still trying to get organized. The boat is a nice-looking catamaran, well-suited for diving cruises. This is, however, one of the boats offering full week and "fake full week" (3 + 4 night) programs; insist on a full week — see the Caution above.

ISLAS GALAPAGOS TURISMO Y VAPORES C.A., Av. República del Salvador 935, (P.O. Box 135-A).
LOCAL PHONE: 446-883 or 240-247   **FAX:** 011-593-2-446-882
BOATS: Cruise Ship AMBASADOR I which operates out of Baltra.
PRICE RANGE: See the section on Cruise Ships for pricing information.

COMMENTS: As the second edition of this book was going to press, the ship was just beginning its Galápagos service and experiencing some problems in booking passengers.
U.S. REPRESENTATIVE: GALAPAGOS ADVENTURES, INC., 1790 Broadway, New York, NY 10019. PHONE: (212) 581-0100, FAX: 212-265-6214.

KLEINTOURS, Av. Shyris 1000.
LOCAL PHONE: 430-345   **FAX:** 011-593-2-442-389
BOATS: CORAL, which operates from Baltra Island on Wednesdays and Sundays.
CONTACT: Francisco Jarrin
PRICE RANGE: Available both on a charter and per-passenger basis. Charter price is about $28,000/ week. Approximate per-passenger price is $1650-$1900/ week (double occupancy and based on cabin type).
COMMENTS: This is a classic yacht and should do very well. Once again, this is a boat offering full week and "fake full week" (3 + 4 night) programs; insist on a full week - see the Caution above.

METROPOLITAN TOURING, Av. Republica de El Salvador 970 (P.O. Box 17-12- 0310).
LOCAL PHONE: 464-780   **FAX:** 011-593-2-464-702
CONTACT: Monica Cordova, Director of Tourism.
BOATS: Yachts BEAGLE III and ENCANTADA; Cruise Ships ISABELA II and SANTA CRUZ. Most of these boats sail from Baltra Island on Tuesdays; the Cruise Ship SANTA CRUZ sails from Baltra on Mondays and Thursdays. A combination hotel/ Day Cruise program is offered in affiliation with the Hotel Delfin (yacht DELFIN II) on Santa Cruz Island.
PRICE RANGE: (yachts available on a charter basis only): BEAGLE III = $11,000/ week; ENCANTADA = $13,000/ week. Hotel Delfin/ Day Cruise 1 week program (Wednesday/ Wednesday or Sunday/ Sunday) for about $1300/person. For pricing information on the ISABELA II and SANTA CRUZ, see the Section on Cruise Ships.
COMMENTS: METROPOLITAN TOURING is the Ecuadorian company that carefully and professionally introduced tourism to the Galápagos Islands. METROPOLITAN is very highly respected in the industry and is the largest Boat and Tour Operator in the islands, offering a variety of yachts, Cruise Ships, and tour programs. All their Guides are university-level Naturalists and go through a special training program in addition to the formal course prepared and administered by the Darwin Research Station and the National Park.
U.S. REPRESENTATIVE: ADVENTURE ASSOCIATES, 13150 Coit Rd., Suite 110, Dallas, TX 75240. PHONE: (214) 907-0414, TOLL FREE: (800) 527-2500, FAX: 214-783-1286.

NIXE CRUISES, S.A., El Comercio 125 Y Shyris (P.O. Box 6646, CCI).
LOCAL PHONE: 467-980 or 468-507   **FAX:** 011-593-2-437-645
CONTACT: Martha García (Sales Manager), Federico Dreyer (General Manager).
BOATS: AHMARA and ESCAPADA, which typically sail from Baltra on Saturdays.

PRICE RANGE: Available on a charter basis only for about $15,000/ week.
COMMENTS: NIXE CRUISES operates a pair of beautiful catamarans, very well suited for dive trips. The operations manager in the Galápagos (and part owner), Polo Navarro, is extremely knowledgeable and helpful in all logistical details. These boats, however, offer full week and "fake full week" (3 + 4 night) programs; insist on a full week — see the Caution above.

NUEVO MUNDO EXPEDITIONS, Av. Amazonas 2468 (P.O. Box 402A).
LOCAL PHONE: 552-617 or 552-816 or 552-839 FAX: 011-593-2-565-261
CONTACT: Oswaldo Muñoz (President), Maria Rueda.
BOATS: GALAPAGOS ADVENTURE and LOBO DE MAR, which sail from Baltra Island on Fridays.
PRICE RANGE: Available both on a charter and per-passenger basis. Approximate charter prices are: GALAPAGOS ADVENTURE = $29,000/ week; LOBO DE MAR = $17,000/ week. Per passenger price is about $1400-$1600/ week.
COMMENTS: NUEVO MUNDO is a very professional, well respected Tour Operator; they are very active in many conservation programs.

QUASAR NAUTICA, S.A., Gaspar de Villaroel and Av. Sheiris.
LOCAL PHONE: 459-162   **FAX:** 011-593-2-436-625
CONTACT: Dolores Diez, Operations Manager.
BOATS: LAMMAR LAW, MISTRAL II, NORTADA, RESTING CLOUD, and SANDPIPER; these boats generally operate out of San Cristóbal Island.
PRICE RANGE: Available both on a charter and per-passenger basis. Approximate charter prices are: SANDPIPER = $10,000/ week; MISTRAL II, NORTADA, and RESTING CLOUD = $17,000-$19,000/ week; LAMMAR LAW = $31,000/ week. Per-passenger price for all yachts is about $1900-$2000/ week.
COMMENTS: QUASAR NAUTICA is a very established company. Their boats are all attractive, modern, and very popular with many of the U.S. Tour Operators. The yachts are all well-equipped for diving.
U.S. REPRESENTATIVE: TUMBACO, INC., 7855 NW 12th St., Suite 115, Miami, FL 33126. PHONE: (305) 599-9008, TOLL FREE: (800) 247-2925, FAX: 305- 592-7060.

SAMOA TURISMO, S.A., Ramirez Dávalos 151 & Amazonas (P.O. Box 9107, Suc. 7).
LOCAL PHONE: 239-892 or 524-135   **FAX:** 011-593-2-500-944
CONTACT: Mariana Almeida (General Manager), Consuelo Gavela (Tour Operations Manager).
BOATS: SAMOA I, which typically sails from Baltra on Thursdays.
PRICE RANGE: Available both on a charter and per-passenger basis. The approximate charter price is about $17,000/ week; per-passenger price is about $1200/ week.
COMMENTS: The SAMOA is another of the yachts that offer full week and "fake full week" (3 + 4 night) programs; insist on a full week — see the Caution above.

TURGAL TURISMO GALAPAGOS CIA. LTDA., Robies 653 (off Av. Amazonas), Proinco Bldg., #1110, (P.O. Box 17-03-739).
LOCAL PHONE: 549-733 or 524-878   **FAX:** 011-593-2-503-740
BOATS: DARWIN EXPLORER, which operates out of San Cristóbal Island on Mondays.
CONTACT: Carlos Pacheco, General Manager.
PRICE RANGE: Available both on a charter and per-passenger basis. Approximate charter prices are: $15,000/ week; per-passenger price is about $1300/ week.
COMMENTS: The DARWIN EXPLORER is another of the yachts that offer full week and "fake full week" (3 + 4 night) programs; insist on a full week - see the Caution above.

ROLF WITTMER/ TURISMO GALAPAGOS CIA. LTDA., Valderrama Accesso 57 and Mariana de Jesus, Department 11 (P.O. Box 17-07-8989).
LOCAL PHONE: 449-337   **FAX:** 011-593-2-448-173
BOATS: SYMBOL, TIP TOP II; these yachts operate out of Baltra Island on Fridays.
CONTACT: Enrique and Elizabeth Wittmer, General Managers.
PRICE RANGE: TIP TOP II is available both on a charter ($15,000/ week) and per-passenger ($1400/ week) basis. The SYMBOL is only available on a charter basis ($4500/week).
COMMENTS: TURISMO GALAPAGOS is owned by Captain Rolf Wittmer (the first natural resident of Floreana Island) who knows the islands extremely well. The SYMBOL is ideal for a small family wanting their own private charter. Diving programs are offered on both yachts.

BOAT OPERATORS IN GUAYAQUIL

NOTE: Any branch offices in Quito are also listed.

CANODROS, S.A., Urdenata 1418 and Av. del Ejèrcito (P.O. Box 8442).
LOCAL PHONE: 285-711 or 280-143   **FAX:** 011-593-4-287-651
CONTACT: Luis Hidalgo
BOATS: Cruise Ship GALAPAGOS EXPLORER which operates out of San Cristóbal on Wednesdays and Saturdays.
PRICE RANGE: See the Section on Cruise Ships for pricing information.
COMMENTS: The GALAPAGOS EXPLORER has an ownership affiliation with SAETA and SAN Airlines, and convenient, attractively-priced package plans are sometimes offered.
U.S. REPRESENTATIVE: GALAPAGOS, INC., 7800 Red Road, Suite 112, South Miami, FL 33143. PHONE: (305) 665-0841, TOLL FREE: (800) 327-9854, FAX: 305-661-1457.

GALAMAZONAS, T. Martinez 102.
LOCAL PHONE: 563-333   **FAX:** 011-593-4-563-771
CONTACT: Peter Witmer

BOATS: ALBATROS and PODEROSO II (aka GALAPAGOS AGGRESSOR). Both yachts sail from San Cristóbal Island on Thursdays.

PRICE RANGE: Available both on a charter and per-passenger basis. Approximate charter prices for both yachts are $21,000/ week. Approximate per-passenger prices for both yachts are $1900/ week.

COMMENTS: These are both excellent dive boats with high profile U.S. marketing offices.

U.S. REPRESENTATIVES: The PODEROSO II (aka GALAPAGOS AGGRESSOR) is represented by **AGGRESSOR FLEET LIMITED,** P.O. Drawer K, Morgan City, LA 70381. PHONE: (504) 385-2628, TOLL FREE: (800) 348-2628, FAX 504-384- 0817.

The ALBATROS is represented by **TEMPTRESS CRUISES**, 1600 N.W. LeJeune Rd., Suite #301, Miami, FL 33126. PHONE: (305) 871-2663, TOLL FREE: (800) 336-8423, FAX: 305-871-2657.

GALAPAGOS HOSTAL C.A., Luis Urdaneta #313 and Escobedo (P.O. Box 6941).

LOCAL PHONE: 562-028 or 563-571   **FAX:** 011-593-4-563-251

CONTACT: Eric Galvez, Sales Manager

BOATS: AMIGO I, which sails from San Cristóbal Island on Mondays.

PRICE RANGE: Available primarily on a charter basis for about $15,000/ week.

COMMENTS: The AMIGO I also offers full week and "fake full week" (3 + 4 night) programs; insist on a full week — see the Caution above.

GALASAM CIA. LTDA., Av. 9 de Octubre 424, Gran Pasaje Bldg., #1106.

LOCAL PHONE: 306-093 or 306-289 or 313-724   **FAX:** 011-593-4-313-351

CONTACT: Antonio Samán (General Manager), Gianna (Reservations).

BOATS: CRUZ DEL SUR, DORADO, and ESTRELLA DEL MAR, which operate out of San Cristóbal Island on Mondays; ISLAS PLAZAS and YOLITA, which sail from San Cristóbal on Saturdays and from Baltra on Wednesdays.

PRICE RANGE: Available both on a charter and per-passenger basis. Approximate charter prices are: CRUZ DEL SUR, DORADO, and ESTRELLA DEL MAR = $21,000/ week; ISLAS PLAZAS = $15,000/ week; YOLITA = $11,000/ week. Approximate per-passenger prices are: CRUZ DEL SUR, DORADO, ESTRELLA DEL MAR and ISLAS PLAZAS = $1200/ week; YOLITA = $850/ week.

COMMENTS: GALASAM is well-known to budget travelers, especially those from Europe. They operate several Economy Class Yachts on a budget basis which results in several problems and inconveniences for the average tourist. The YOLITA is a step up, but not a big step. The other yachts listed here, on the other hand, are excellent throughout, a good value, and highly recommended. You should be aware, however, that the ISLAS PLAZAS and the YOLITA have full week and "fake full week" (3 + 4 night) programs; insist on a full week - see the Caution above.

QUITO OFFICE: Pinto 523 and Av. Amazonas. **LOCAL PHONE:** 550-094 or 551-233.

U.S. REPRESENTATIVES:

FORUM TRAVEL INTERNATIONAL, INC., 91 Gregory Lane, #21, Pleasant Hill, CA 94523. Phone: (510) 671-2900, FAX: 510-946-1500.

KLEINTOURS, Tungurahua 502A and Av. 9 de Octubre.
LOCAL PHONE: 361-855   **FAX:** 011-593-4-361-855
BOATS: CORAL
PRICE RANGE: See section above,"Tour Operators in Quito."
QUITO OFFICE: Their Main Office is in Quito; see above.
COMMENTS: The CORAL also offers full week and "fake full week" (3 + 4 night) programs; insist on a full week — see the Caution above.

SITUR, Av. C.J. Arosomena - Km 2.
LOCAL PHONE: 201-516   **FAX:** 011-593-4-201-153
CONTACT: Ilse Tugenhadt
BOATS: ERIC, FLAMINGO, and LETTY (which operate out of San Cristóbal Island on Tuesdays and Fridays), as well as the PANCHITA (aka SEA CLOUD) which sails from San Cristóbal on Mondays; the Cruise Ship CORINTHIAN which sails out of San Cristóbal on Thursdays and Sundays.
PRICE RANGE: PANCHITA is available on a charter basis for approximately $14,000/ week. ERIC, FLAMINGO, and LETTY are available both on a charter (about $30,000/ week) and per-passenger basis (about $1500-$1800/ week, based on deck level/ cabin size).
COMMENTS: SITUR has an ownership affiliation with SAETA and SAN Airlines, and convenient, attractively-priced package plans are sometimes offered. It also means that these yachts are in the travel agent computer systems and can be readily booked by them. You should be aware, however, that the ERIC, FLAMINGO, and LETTY offer full week and "fake full week" (3 + 4 night) programs; insist on a full week - see the Caution above.
QUITO OFFICE: A. Amazonas and Santa Maria 510. **LOCAL PHONE:** 564-969.
U.S. REPRESENTATIVE: GALAPAGOS NETWORK, 7200 Corporate Center Dr., Ste. 204, Miami, FL 33126. PHONE: (305) 592-2294, TOLL FREE: (800) 633-7972, FAX: 305-592-6394.

SULIDAE CHARTERS, P.O. Box 09-01-0260
LOCAL PHONE: 201-376   **FAX:** 011-593-4-323-478
BOATS: SULIDAE, which typically sails from Baltra Island on Tuesdays.
CONTACT: Cecilia Salcedo, Reservations.
PRICE RANGE: By charter only for about $9500/week.
COMMENTS: The SULIDAE is a popular, professionally-maintained boat, owing in part to well-known Captain Pepe Salcedo, an internationally-licensed Dive Master who owns and operates the yacht.

REPRESENTATIVES OF ECUADORIAN BOAT OWNERS/OPERATORS

The companies in this list are direct U.S. (or worldwide) representatives for the leading Tour and Boat Operators in Ecuador; these reps work with U.S. Tour Operators, Travel Agents, and the general public. The reps typically will quote the same retail list prices for a Galápagos Tour as their affiliated Ecuadorian Tour/Boat Operator. This arrangement makes it very convenient to book a

Galápagos Tour in the U.S. at Base Rate prices. By the way, Base Rate means just that; it is the retail or base price of a Galápagos tour as established by the Boat Operator in Ecuador. Base Rate also means no "welcome" and "farewell" dinners in Quito. Airport transfers, hotels, local tours, and meals in mainland Ecuador are on your own, although the Tour Operators listed below will help you with all the necessary reservations.

The companies listed below will give you a wide variety of tour boats to choose from - Cruise Ships to all the yacht classifications. Let them handle your flight reservations as well.

NOTE: The following companies are not necessarily exclusive representatives of the Boat Owner/Operator.

ADVENTURE ASSOCIATES, 13150 Coit Rd., Suite 110, Dallas, TX 75240.
PHONE: (214) 907-0414   **FAX:** 214-783-1286
TOLL FREE: (800) 527-2500
BOATS: Yachts BEAGLE III and ENCANTADA; Cruise Ships ISABELA II and SANTA CRUZ; a combination hotel/Day Cruise program is offered in affiliation with the Hotel Delfin (yacht DELFIN II) on Santa Cruz Island.
PRICE RANGE: For the yachts and the DELFIN II program, see the METROPOLITAN TOURING listing in the Section on Boat Operators In Ecuador. For the ISABELA II and SANTA CRUZ, see the Section on Cruise Ships.
COMMENTS: ADVENTURE ASSOCIATES is the U.S. representative for METROPOLITAN TOURING, the Ecuadorian company that carefully and professionally introduced tourism to the Galápagos Islands. METROPOLITAN is very highly respected; they are the largest Boat and Tour Operator in the islands, offering a variety of yachts, Cruise Ships and tour programs.

AGGRESSOR FLEET LIMITED, P.O. Drawer K, Morgan City, LA 70381.
PHONE: (504) 385-2628   **FAX:** 504-384-0817
TOLL FREE: (800) 348-2628
BOATS: PODEROSO II (aka GALAPAGOS AGGRESSOR).
PRICE RANGE: See the GALAMAZONAS listing in the Section on Boat Operators In Ecuador.
COMMENTS: AGGRESSOR FLEET LIMITED operates and represents high-quality live-aboard dive boats throughout the world; they are very well known in the diving community. As they will probably learn (they just began their Galápagos operations in 1993), these islands are more than a series of Dive Sites.

FORUM TRAVEL INTERNATIONAL, 91 Gregory Lane, #21, Pleasant Hill, CA 94523.
PHONE: (510) 671-2900   **FAX:** 510-946-1500
BOATS: ANGELIQUE, CRUZ DEL SUR, ESTRELLA DEL MAR, ISLAS PLAZAS, ORCA, and YOLITA.
PRICE RANGE: See the ETNOTUR and GALASAM CIA. LTDA. listings in the Section on Boat Operators In Ecuador.
COMMENTS: FORUM has been putting together Galápagos trips since 1965, and according to Director, Dr. Nicolas Hetzer, they were the first North American company to offer tours to the islands.

GALAPAGOS ADVENTURES, INC., 1790 Broadway, New York, NY 10019.
PHONE: (212) 581-0100 **FAX:** 212-265-6214
BOATS: Cruise ship AMBASADOR I.
PRICE RANGE: See the Section on Cruise Ships for pricing information.

GALAPAGOS, INC., 7800 Red Road, Suite 112, South Miami, FL 33143.
PHONE: (305) 665-0841 **FAX:** 305-661-1457
TOLL FREE: (800) 327-9854
BOATS: Yachts CRUZ DEL SUR, DORADO, ESTRELLA DEL MAR, ISLAS
PLAZAS and YOLITA; Cruise Ship GALAPAGOS EXPLORER.
PRICE RANGE: For the yachts, see the GALASAM listing in the Section on Boat
Operators In Ecuador. For the GALAPAGOS EXPLORER, see the Section on
Cruise Ships.

GALAPAGOS NETWORK, 7200 Corporate Center Dr., Ste. 204, Miami, FL
33126.
PHONE: (305) 592-2294 **FAX:** 305-592-6394
TOLL FREE: (800) 633-7972
BOATS: Yachts, ERIC, FLAMINGO, LETTY, and PANCHITA (aka SEA CLOUD);
Cruise Ship CORINTHIAN.
PRICE RANGE: See the SITUR listing in the Section on Boat Operators In
Ecuador; for the CORINTHIAN, see the Section on Cruise Ships.
COMMENTS: The operator of these yachts, SITUR, has an ownership affiliation
with SAETA and SAN Airlines, and convenient, attractively- priced package
plans are sometimes offered. It also means that these yachts are in the travel
agent computer systems and can be readily booked by them. Finally, the staff
at GALAPAGOS NETWORK are most knowledgeable about Galápagos operations — especially their manager, Doris Welsh.

GALAPAGOS TRAVEL, P.O. Box 1220, San Juan Bautista, CA 95045.
PHONE: (408) 623-2920 **FAX:** 408-623-2923
TOLL FREE: (800) 969-9014
BOATS: SAN JACINTO
PRICE RANGE: The SAN JACINTO is available only on a charter basis for about
$16,500/ week.
COMMENTS: GALAPAGOS TRAVEL, the publisher of this book, maintains an
office in Quito. In addition to its Galápagos operations, a number of extension
trips are offered in mainland Ecuador.

PLACES SPACE CONTROL AB, S-104 40 (P.O. Box 14235), Stockholm,
Sweden
PHONE: 011-46-8-301-645 **FAX:** 011-46-8-301-135
BOATS: REINA SILVIA, which sails from Baltra Island on Wednesdays.
PRICE RANGE: Available mostly on a charter and occasionally on a per-pas-
senger basis. Approximate charter price is $18,000-$24,000/week.
Approximate per-passenger price is $1300-$2500/week. The per-passenger
price variation is based on cabin selection, with the top of the line being the
luxury suite they refer to as the "owner's cabin." The charter price variation is

based on the number of passengers and whether the "owner's cabin" will be occupied.

COMMENTS: The REINA SILVIA is an excellent, well-managed yacht. PLACES TRAVEL, although in Sweden, seems on top of most logistical details and very well organized.

TEMPTRESS CRUISES, 1600 N.W. LeJeune Rd., Suite #301, Miami, FL 33126.
PHONE: (305) 871-2663   **FAX:** 305-871-2657
TOLL FREE: (800) 336-8423
BOATS: ALBATROS.
PRICE RANGE: See the GALAMAZONAS listing in the Section on Boat Operators In Ecuador.
COMMENTS: The ALBATROS is an excellent boat for natural history and dive tours of the Galápagos. TEMPTRESS CRUISES is well established in Costa Rica and began their Galápagos operations in 1993. Evidently, they are trying to operate their Galápagos program the same way as in Costa Rica, asking passengers if they want "a soft tour or hard-core natural history." If you book a tour through them, tell them you want the real stuff.

TUMBACO, INC., 7855 NW 12th St., Suite 115, Miami, FL 33126.
PHONE: (305) 599-9008   **FAX:** 305-592-7060
TOLL FREE: (800) 247-2925
BOATS: LAMMAR LAW, MISTRAL II, NORTADA, RESTING CLOUD, and SANDPIPER.
PRICE RANGE: See the QUASAR NAUTICA listing in the Section on Boat Operators In Ecuador.

CHAPTER V

FLIGHT PLANS

The only flights to the Galápagos Islands are from mainland Ecuador. You have a choice of flying to either Quito or Guayaquil, with little difference in cost. If you're part of a tour group, the decision of whether to fly to Quito or Guayaquil will be made for you. More than likely you will fly to Quito with your group or meet your group in Quito.

If you're going over without having booked a Galápagos tour in advance, I would recommend getting round-trip air tickets to Quito; there are many more Ecuadorian-based tour operators in Quito than in Guayaquil (see Chapter IV, CHOOSING A TOUR).

Most Tour Operators function as travel agencies and will offer to make flight arrangements for you. Take them up on it; they will usually get you at least as good a fare as you can get on your own. Besides, it'll save you the time and effort which you can use to read up on the Galápagos. If you are waiting to book your Galápagos tour in Ecuador, read the following flight information and make your airline reservations directly with the airline or through your travel agent. If you opt for the latter, tell the agent the flights you want as well as the quoted fares. If you do it this way, there will be no price difference between what the airline and the travel agency quotes you. I don't mean to imply that travel agents mark-up the prices; the agencies make their money in the form of a discount off the list price. It's just that there are not many travel agencies that are familiar with flights and airfares to Ecuador, not to mention the Galápagos Islands. There are several nuances and special "tied-fares" that are not in the travel agent's computer. Let's discuss them.

GETTING TO ECUADOR

There are currently four main air routes from the U.S. to Ecuador — direct flights from Miami (via AMERICAN, ECUATORIANA, and SAETA AIRLINES), flights from New York City (SAETA direct and ECUATORIANA through Miami), flights from Los Angeles (SAETA direct and ECUATORIANA through Mexico

City), and flights from Houston (CONTINENTAL AIRLINES through Panama City). The direct travel time is approximately 4 hours from Miami, 6 hours from New York City, and 11 hours from Los Angeles. There are also several connecting flights to these international gateways, often with discounted through-fares.

FLIGHT SCHEDULES TO ECUADOR

As with prices, the following schedules are subject to change; verify the current schedule before making your reservations. Remember that mainland Ecuador remains on Eastern Standard Time throughout the year.

To/From Miami:

AMERICAN AIRLINES — AMERICAN has daily direct late afternoon and evening flights to Quito. There are also daily direct flights from Quito to Miami with morning departures.

AMERICAN has a daily direct evening flight to Guayaquil. There is also a daily direct flight from Guayaquil to Miami with a morning departure.

Comments: The AMERICAN flights to Ecuador are quite convenient as they provide same-day connecting flights and through-fares from most U.S. cities; this service is especially attractive to those beginning their journey from the West Coast (where overnighting in Miami is currently required to make the international connections on some of the other carriers). AMERICAN also provides separate daily flights to both Quito and Guayaquil, which knocks about an hour off the arrival time to the second city on a combined Quito/Guayaquil or Quito/Guayaquil flight. Finally, there's the frequent flyer miles you can earn (as well as using frequent flyer awards to fly to Ecuador). On the negative side, AMERICAN cannot ticket you to the Galápagos, making it both more difficult and expensive for you to fly to the islands (see the section below, From Ecuador to the Galápagos).

ECUATORIANA AIRLINES — ECUATORIANA has direct red-eye flights to Quito 2 nights/week and indirect red-eye fights 2 nights/week (stopping in Panama City and/or Guayaquil). There are indirect morning flights from Quito to Miami 4 days/week (stopping in Guayaquil and/or Panama City).

ECUATORIANA has indirect red-eye flights to Guayaquil 4 nights/week (stopping in Panama City and/or Quito). There are indirect morning flights from Guayaquil to Miami 4 days/week (stopping in Quito and/or Panama City).

Comments: ECUATORIANA (Spanish for Ecuadorian) is in fact an Ecuadorian government-owned airline. They have an affiliation with TAME, another government airline (operated by the military) that runs flights within Ecuador and from the mainland to the Galápagos. There is a special "tied-fare" between the two (see the section below, From Ecuador to the Galápagos).

ECUATORIANA is known to not operate on a very consistent or timely schedule for whatever reason. The TAME flights to the Galápagos have a tendency of being seriously overbooked, causing all kinds of confusion. Also, ECUATORIANA is currently in serious financial difficulties, and their future (at least in the way that they are now structured) is somewhat uncertain.

SAETA AIRLINES — SAETA has daily direct afternoon flights to Guayaquil (with continuing service to Quito). There are also daily direct morning flights from Guayaquil to Miami; these flights originate in Quito.

    Comments: SAETA (*Sociedad Ecuatoriana de Transportes Aeros*) is a privately owned Ecuadorian airline. They are affiliated with SAN, an Ecuadorian airline that operates flights within Ecuador and from the mainland to the Galápagos. There is a ''tied-fare'' between the two (see the section below, From Ecuador to the Galápagos).

    SAETA operates on a very business-like schedule and has very competitive prices. Their service is excellent; the times I've flown with them to Ecuador, every seat on the plane was treated as First Class, with complimentary champagne prior to takeoff, complimentary cocktails during the flight, tasty appetizers (including Ecuadorian specialties) and your choice of 3 entrees served with very fine wines. Finally, SAETA will soon have affiliations with U.S. carriers for through-fares from most major cities as well as earning frequent flyer miles on SAETA flights.

To/From Los Angeles:

ECUATORIANA AIRLINES — ECUATORIANA has indirect red-eye flights 2 nights/week to Quito (stopping in Mexico City). One of these flights stops in Quito first, offering continuing service to Guayaquil; the other flight stops in Guayaquil first, with continuing service to Quito.

    ECUATORIANA offers 2 indirect morning flights/week from Guayaquil to Los Angeles (stopping in Mexico City); these flights originate in Quito.

    Comments: See above.

SAETA AIRLINES — As of this writing, SAETA will soon be offering direct red-eye flights 2 nights/week from Los Angeles to Guayaquil, with continuing service to Quito. They will also offer direct morning flights 2 days/week from Guayaquil to Los Angeles; these flights will originate in Quito.

    Comments: See above.

To/From New York:

ECUATORIANA AIRLINES — ECUATORIANA has indirect red-eye flights to Quito/Guayaquil (or Guayaquil/Quito) 4 nights/week (with a stop in Miami or stops in Miami/Panama City).

    ECUATORIANA has indirect morning flights from Quito/Guayaquil (or Guayaquil/Quito, to New York City 4 days/week (with a stop in Miami or stops in Miami/Panama City).

    Comments: See above.

SAETA AIRLINES — SAETA has direct red-eye flights to Guayaquil 4 nights/week (with continuing service to Quito). There are also direct late morning flights from Guayaquil to Miami 4 days/week; these flights originate in Quito.

To/From Houston:
CONTINENTAL AIRLINES — CONTINENTAL has an early afternoon departure to Quito 4 days/week (with a stop in Panama City). There are 4 flights/week from Quito to Houston with morning departures, also stopping in Panama City.

CONTINENTAL has an early afternoon departure to Guayaquil 3 days/week (with a stop in Panama City). There are 3 flights/week from Guayaquil to Houston with morning departures, also stopping in Panama City.

Comments: CONTINENTAL is the newest player in the "fly to Ecuador" game. No doubt, they do offer Texans convenient flights to Ecuador as well as through-fares from the cities that CONTINENTAL serves. Then there's the frequent flyer miles you can earn and the prospect of flying to Ecuador on frequent flyer awards. It would appear, though, that their customer base is limited; the disadvantages (limited schedule, indirect flights, and financial uncertainty) seem to outweigh the advantages in most cases. Also, CONTINENTAL cannot ticket you to the Galápagos, making it both more difficult and expensive for you to fly to the islands (see the section below, From Ecuador to the Galápagos.

AIRFARE TO ECUADOR

Fares to Ecuador are quite reasonable, although, as with the rest of the airline pricing schedules, they are constantly being adjusted and should be verified before purchasing a ticket. At the time of this writing, you can buy a 30 day maximum Excursion Fare round trip Miami/Quito ticket for about $425. These tickets are in coach class and must generally be purchased at least 2 weeks in advance. Some carriers vary the price based on high/low seasons. The fares from New York are about $550-$600, $750-$850 from Los Angeles, and $700-$900 from Houston.

Warning: Quite often (usually as soon as people decide that they're going to the Galápagos) they rush out and buy a round trip ticket to Ecuador. The fact is they didn't know they would have to pay $375 more to get to the Galápagos. They also didn't know that there were special "tied-fares" to the Galápagos. Neither did the airline or travel agent who sold them the tickets. Nor do their computers show that there are 2 airports in the Galápagos. Carefully read the section, From Ecuador to the Galápagos.

DEPARTURE TAX

In addition the the above airfares, each person must pay a $25 departure tax, payable in U.S. dollars or sucres, at the airport in Ecuador on the day of international departure (for the flight back to the U.S.).

DISCOUNT TICKET HOUSES

There are airfare discount houses (known in the trade as "bucket shops"). You see their ads in the travel section of the Sunday newspaper, offering "the lowest prices to anywhere." If you were going to London or flying from New York to Los Angeles, they could probably save you some money. These are common routes, and they have legitimate access to a certain amount of heavily-discounted tickets. However, they're not going to beat the Excursion Fares to an out-of-the-way destination such as Ecuador, and there's no way that they're going to have "tied-fare" tickets to the Galápagos Islands.

SEAT SELECTION

Flights to and from Quito pass over the Andes, and the views are spectacular. Window seats are recommended if you will be flying during daylight hours. See the section below, Airplane III, South American Rules.

FROM ECUADOR TO THE GALAPAGOS

The cost of most flights within Ecuador is about U.S.$50; the round-trip airfare from Quito to the Galápagos is about U.S.$375 (about U.S.$325 from Guayaquil), which is extremely high. Things actually reached the absurd level in December, 1989 when the Ecuadorian government increased the fare by 30 percent (to about U.S.$480); this impulsive fare hike came under a lot of pressure and was rescinded only a month later. Even the present $325-$375 round-trip fare is very "unfair" when you consider that it's for foreigners (*extranjeros*) only; Ecuadorians pay only about U.S.$150 for the same flight, and Galápagos residents pay even less.

Part of the problem is that Ecuador is a poor country; the rest of the problem is poor policy. Even though Ecuadorians require domestic air service for business purposes, they cannot afford to pay very much for the airfare. So the government sets a very low fare on these flights, which therefore operate at a loss. In turn, the government figures it can balance the books on the deep pockets of the *gringo* taking the flight to the Galápagos.

TIED-FARES TO THE GALAPAGOS

While there are no discounted fares from Ecuador to the Galápagos, the "tied-fare" options mentioned above are as follows:

AMERICAN AIRLINES and **CONTINENTAL AIRLINES** — If you fly AMERICAN or CONTINENTAL to Ecuador, you must pay full price for your Ecuador/ Galápagos tickets (on either TAME or SAN airlines).

ECUATORIANA AIRLINES — If you fly ECUATORIANA AIRLINES from the U.S. to Ecuador, there is currently a "tied-fare" for the Ecuador-Galápagos flights. As stated above, ECUATORIANA is affiliated with another Ecuadorian government-owned airline called TAME (pronounced "tami"). TAME (*Transportes Aereos Militares Ecuatorianos*), is operated by the military and has a daily morning flight from Quito (stopping in Guayaquil) to the Galápagos (Baltra Island Airport). At Baltra, you will either meet your boat or take local transportation to the town of Puerto Ayora on Santa Cruz Island. Return flights to mainland Ecuador are also daily, leaving Baltra early in the afternoon and flying to Guayaquil and then on to Quito. Some return flights are direct to Quito.

The round-trip "tied-fare" from Miami to Baltra Island in the Galápagos is currently $730 (or $1000-$1150 from Los Angeles) for stays (in the Ecuadorian mainland and/or the Galápagos) of at least 7 days with excursion fare penalties and restrictions. For minimum 21 day stays, the "tied-fare" from Miami drops to $659. You can save $25-$50 more by flying to Guayaquil instead of Quito.

SAETA AIRLINES — If you fly SAETA AIRLINES from the U.S. to Ecuador, there is also currently a "tied-fare" for the Ecuador-Galápagos flights. As described above, SAETA is affiliated with another Ecuadorian airline, SAN (*Servicios Aereos Nacionales*). SAN has a daily late morning flight from Quito (stopping in Guayaquil) to the Galápagos (San Cristóbal Island Airport). At San Cristóbal, you will either meet your boat or take local transportation to the town of Puerto Baquerizo Moreno. Return flights to mainland Ecuador are also daily, with an early afternoon flight to Guayaquil and then on to Quito.

While the town of Puerto Ayora on Santa Cruz Island is the hub of social and commercial activity, Puerto Baquerizo Moreno is the political capital of the Galápagos. Recently, efforts have been made to develop Puerto Baquerizo Moreno from the fishing and farming community that it was to a second tourist center, rivaling Puerto Ayora. In this regard, the San Cristóbal Island Airport was completed in 1986, and several boat tours now leave from the harbor at Puerto Baquerizo Moreno. While the tourist-oriented facilities are still basic compared to Puerto Ayora, the development push of this area is under way.

As part of the effort to promote tourism in (and their flights to) San Cristóbal, SAETA AIRLINES (in conjunction with SAN) is currently offering a special "tied fare" price of about $700 round trip from Miami to San Cristóbal Island in the Galápagos (for stays of up to 30 days). Considering the price as well as the excellent international service of SAETA, you may well want to consider this attractive option.

Warning: As stated above, buying a Galápagos ticket from a travel agent can be a bit risky. The airline computers only show 1 airport in the Galápagos (the one in Baltra); at present, the airport in San Cristóbal does not come up on the computer when you "enter" Galápagos (code "GPS"). The 2 airports are on separate islands, and there is no dependable inter-island ferry service. Basically, you have a problem on your hands. This problem gets worse when you find out that the Galápagos ticket can not be exchanged (for tickets to the "correct" island).

It would be convenient for all the tour operations if SAN and TAME would accept each others tickets, but they are fiercely competitive. Since TAME and the Baltra Airport are operated by the military, they are not going to make life easy for SAN. At the same time, SAN and SAETA are winning over customers (many of them Tour Operators), from ECUATORIANA and TAME. As more Tour Operators change their base of operations from Puerto Ayora to Puerto Baquerizo Moreno, there will be more pressure put on TAME to accept SAN tickets and/or open up Baltra to SAN. For now, however, it's the tourist that once again pays the price, which in this case is inconvenience.

FLIGHT RESERVATIONS

If you're part of a group tour, the flight reservations will be taken care of for you. It is somewhat surprising to note, however, that several of the Tour Operators that have been booking Galápagos trips for many years do not know about some of the "tied-fare" options. By all means, let them handle your flight reservations, but do get them to quote you airfares before you agree to a ticket purchase. Compare the prices with those listed above, and if there's a significant difference, ask why. There very well could be a valid reason for the difference, such as a recent price hike, peak season rates, or the leg from Des Moines to Miami could be as costly as from Miami to Quito.

If you're not part of a group tour, you may wish to book your own flight reservations; the Toll Free numbers for the airlines with service to Ecuador are as follows:

AMERICAN AIRLINES
  (International Reservations):   (800) 634-6262
CONTINENTAL AIRLINES
  (International Reservations):   (800) 231-0856
ECUATORIANA AIRLINES: (800) 328-2367
SAETA AIRLINES: (800) 338-3975

You may also choose to have your travel agent make your flight reservations for you. If you opt to do this, inform them of the "tied fare" situation, and once again compare the prices they quote you to those listed above. Remember, they probably have booked very few flights to the Galápagos, if any, and you want to double-check all the details.

Note: Mainland Ecuador is on Eastern Standard Time while the Galápagos Islands are on Central Standard Time (with a 1 hour time difference between the two locations) throughout the year.

CONFIRMING YOUR FLIGHTS

Once you arrive in Ecuador, it is extremely important for you to confirm your flights to and from the Galápagos with TAME or SAN (24-48 hours in advance). The TAME flights are typically overbooked, and priority is given to those with firm tour reservations. If you have booked a tour with a U.S. Tour Operator, their Ecuadorian affiliate company will take care of this detail for you. If you book your tour in Ecuador, the Tour Operator there will be sure to help you; the last thing they want is for you to miss their boat! Always ask for your Record Locator Number, which is your computer reservation number, thus "confirming your confirmation."

Flight confirmation is not a detail to be passive about, as is evidenced by the following quote from a U.S. Tour Operator who has been offering trips to the Galápagos Islands since 1969:

> "It's essential to have an operating office in Quito. We send someone to the airport 3 times to personally check the manifest. They go 30 days before the flight; this is the first day that the airline [TAME or SAN] will print out the manifest for a particular flight. If someone's not on the manifest, they [our affiliate] show them the international coupon that says 'Galápagos.' Well, the week before the flight we do it again, to catch the people that were dropped off the original manifest so that someone's brother could get on the flight. The third time is the day before the flight. There's actually a fourth time, because the people from the local office actually accompany the people to the airport."

While in the Galápagos, visit the TAME or SAN office while you are in Puerto Ayora on Santa Cruz Island (all tours go there) and reconfirm your flight back to Ecuador. In most cases your Guide or Tour Leader will take care of this for you. Finally, once you get back to Ecuador, confirm your flight home with the international carrier. Once again, the Tour Operator will typically handle this detail, but it's up to you to verify the situation; ask for the Record Locator Number.

BAGGAGE REGULATIONS

On the international flights to and from mainland Ecuador, each person is allowed 2-3 pieces of checked baggage. The actual number of checked bags and the allowed weight varies by airline; the best is to ask the carrier, your Tour Operator, or travel agent. Two carryons are also allowed. The flights to and from the Galápagos, however, limit you to one checked bag and 2 carryons.

Note: When you travel as a group, all your checked bags may go on as "Group Luggage," which provides more margin for "overages" in the number of bags and for a particular bag that may be over the weight limit.

A suggestion for you to consider is to take 3 bags to Ecuador — 1 checked piece and 2 carryons. While in Quito or on a vist to one of the markets, you can purchase a leather travel bag and use it to store the sourvenirs, gifts, and other items you purchase. This leather bag will then be the second piece of checked luggage on your flight home. For a complete discussion of this subject, see the section on Luggage in Chapter VI. Also, see the section on Film in Chapter VII for a discussion on getting your photographic equipment and film through airport x-ray security machines.

Warning: If you are changing airline carriers between your domestic and international flights (in Miami, New York, Los Angeles, or Houston), pick up your luggage at the baggage claim area and take it to the international ticket counter. Do not depend on the domestic carrier to make the transfer. If your bags don't make it to Ecuador with you, you probably won't get them in time for your flight to the Galápagos, and there's not an efficient way for the bags to catch up to you; remember, you're going to be on a boat, cruising from island to island. Don't get yourself in this situation!

Also, do not pack your film or alcoholic beverages in your checked luggage. Quality film is not an item you can easily replace, and glass bottles will break!

AIRPLANE III — SOUTH AMERICAN RULES

Airport conduct is somewhat less defined in South America than it is in the U.S. I'm not referring to flight safety or security, but rather some basic situations, such as standing in line. Let me cite a few examples.

1. Many of the flights to and from the Galápagos are on an open-seating basis. The rule is — don't linger; get on the boarding line as soon as it "forms" (if that is the correct verb to describe the activity). Now mind you, my airport behavior back home is very low-key; I try to be patient and avoid the rush of humanity. In South America, however, the airport situation is less structured, and one has to be a bit more aggressive.

For the best views of the Andes (at least on the days when the clouds decide to part), sit on the left side of the aircraft when flying from Quito and on the right side when flying to Quito. It is hoped that not everyone on-board the plane has read this section and that there will be sufficient passengers seated on both sides to maintain a balanced aircraft.

2. If you're not part of a group tour and are waiting in line at the Quito airport for your Galápagos flight, you may find the check-in procedure to be interesting. You may be third or fourth in line, and after a wait of a half hour or so, you may still be third or fourth in line. What's happening is that the Tour Leaders for the various groups are checking-in all the passengers (while the passengers themselves are comfortably seated in the terminal). As you will find, each group can take quite a while.

That's the way it's done, and it's another advantage of signing up for a tour that has a Tour Leader. This is also part of an optional service (called an "airport transfer") provided by the Ecuadorian affiliate of U.S. Tour Operators. If you booked your tour in Ecuador, discuss this option with the local company (see the section on Tour Operations in Ecuador in Chapter IV).

On the return flight from the Galápagos, things will be much easier, because your Guide and/or Tour Leader will assist you with this procedure. While you're at the airport waiting for your return flight from the Galápagos to mainland Ecuador, make sure you have your Guide or Tour Leader take your passport to the National Park official, who will stamp it with the official *Parque Nacional Galápagos* seal (actually it's a tortoise). Really, it's a nice souvenir to have, and the officials won't do it unless asked.

Warning: With all the potential sources of confusion in the airports, combined with a tight schedule, you may be wandering back and forth from your place in line to clarify and/or expedite the situation for you and your group. During these times especially, keep track of your camera bags; they have a way of disappearing. Which brings us to the following topic.

TRAVEL PROTECTION INSURANCE

A variety of comprehensive travel insurance packages are available through the Tour Operators, travel agencies, and the insurance carriers themselves. The Tour Operators all recommend these packages. They do so for several reasons:

1. Without knowing the habits, history, and travel experience profile of every customer, from their point of view it's good advice. They have certain up-front costs (such as chartering or reserving space on a yacht) which is justification for the non-refundable deposit they ask for. Thus, they tell the customer, "To protect yourself, we recommend Trip Cancellation Insurance."

2. They earn a commission from the insurance carriers.

3. It is in the best interest of the Tour Operator for you to be covered. If a situation does occur that possibly requires your being compensated, it's taken care of by the insurance company. No matter what waiver forms you sign, given certain bad situations, you can find an aggressive attorney who will suggest that you can and should go after the Tour Operator. With Travel Protection Insur-

ance, you are less likely to need or seek legal aid (also typically an expensive ordeal in its own right).

THE COST

A standard Travel Protection Insurance package will cost about $75-$150 per person for a 1-3 week vacation; family rates for a 1-3 week vacation are $150-$250. Many Tour Operators carry Group Policies, and as a courtesy, will pass the Group Rate on to you. There may be an additional cost for certain types of medical evacuation coverage.

Let's look at the various kinds of situations and coverages in a standard Travel Protection Insurance package.

TRIP CANCELLATION/INTERRUPTION INSURANCE

Standard Trip Cancellation Insurance is a one-time-only policy that reimburses you for non-refundable air and land costs (including all deposits) should you have to cancel the trip (or part thereof) due to personal or family illness and/or accident.

The Coverage — Usually the full amount you prepaid.

What it Usually Covers — These policies typically cover cancellations (on your part) due to sickness, injury, or death of/to you, a traveling companion, or member of your immediate family.

What it May Cover — Some policies cover cancellations/interruptions due to jury duty, financial default of an airline, Tour or Boat Operator, terrorist incidents, and traffic accidents en route to a scheduled departure. There may be a separate section of the policy that covers certain costs related to Trip Delays (including hotel rooms, rebooking flights, meals, etc.) incurred for reasons beyond your control; such reasons include bad weather, carrier or Operator delays, and lost or stolen passports or money.

What it Usually Doesn't Cover — Not covered are cancellations due to a change in your plans, business obligations, financial circumstances, inability to obtain required travel documents, or a pre-existing sickness or injury (unless this condition is controlled by prescription medication). There are also the usual exclusions, such as self-inflicted harm, etc.

Analysis — The insurance companies have covered the odds on their side of the table; it's up to you to do the same on your side. Look at what's covered and not covered.

It is very important to note that the Galápagos Islands have very basic medical facilities, equivalent to a first aid station; at that, it is not recommended. Some of the Cruise Ships have an onboard physician or nurse. Even so, just about any serious illness or injury requiring medical treatment will most probably result in the patient being flown to at least mainland Ecuador. From the standpoint of a medical situation interrupting your trip, Trip Cancellation/Interruption Insurance begins to make sense, especially for families.

BAGGAGE PROTECTION INSURANCE

This one-time-only policy covers, to a limit, the loss of or damage to your baggage.

The Coverage — Actual cash value at the time of loss (replacement cost less depreciation as defined by the insurance carrier) up to a limit, which is usually less than $1000 per traveler.

What it Usually Doesn't Cover — Not covered items include breakage to cameras or other "fragile" items such as musical instruments and electronics, any loss or damage to eyeglasses, contact lenses, false teeth, animals, automobiles, boats, motorcycles, etc. The loss of money, securities, or documents is typically not covered.

Analysis — There is a section of your airline ticket called, NOTICE OF BAGGAGE LIABILITY LIMITATIONS. It reads as follows:

> *For most international travel (including domestic portions of international journeys) the liability limit is approximately $9.07 per pound for checked baggage and $400 per passenger for unchecked baggage. For travel wholly between U.S. points federal rules require any limit on airline's baggage liability to be at least $1250 per passenger. Excess valuation may be declared on certain types of articles. Some carriers assume no liability for fragile, valuable or perishable articles. Further information may be obtained from the carrier.*

From the above, you've already got Baggage Protection Insurance each time your bags are checked in at an airport; in fact, some policies specifically state that their coverage is "secondary to any coverage provided by a common carrier." However, Baggage Protection is part of most Travel Insurance packages, and it doesn't pay to exclude it. At the same time, if you're not buying a Travel Insurance Package, it may not make sense getting Baggage Protection by itself. Ecuador is a very safe country; the Galápagos Islands are even more safe. The most common loss is a camera bag theft at the airport.

EMERGENCY EVACUATION INSURANCE

The Coverage — This policy covers expenses (up to a maximum) incurred if an injury or sickness commencing during the course of the scheduled trip results in a necessary emergency evacuation.

What it Usually Covers — Covered expenses include transportation costs as well as medical services and supplies.

What it May Cover — This is important. Some policies exclude the cost of medical evacuations resulting from injuries and medical emergencies related to certain activities, such as scuba diving or mountain climbing. Also, some policies require that the emergency evacuation must be ordered by a legally licensed physician, typically not available in the Galápagos in an emergency situation.

What it Usually Doesn't Cover — The cost of medical evacuations resulting from pre-existing illnesses or conditions are typically not covered.

Analysis — As discussed above, the Galápagos have very basic medical facilities, and a serious injury or illness will most probably result in the patient being flown to at least mainland Ecuador. Whether a commercial flight will suffice depends on the extent of the illness or injury.

If you are on a diving trip to the Galápagos, the nearest decompression chamber is in Panama, a thousand miles and several thousand dollars away. Your diving trip Tour Operator will probably require you to have an emergency evacuation policy; the one that they provide or recommend will no doubt cover scuba diving.

TRAVEL ACCIDENT INSURANCE

The Coverage — This is generally a blanket policy covering the loss of life or limb and the cost of local medical treatment as a result of a travel accident.

What it Usually Doesn't Cover — Pre-existing medical conditions and injuries are typically not covered.

Analysis — Between your personal life insurance, major medical coverage, and the liability of the airlines and boat owners, this could be largely redundant coverage. On the other hand, if you're going to buy any part of the package, it's nice to have this as secondary protection.

Note: If you presently carry medical insurance, it would be a good idea to contact the carrier and verify the extent, if any, of your international coverage. While speaking with them, inquire as to the proper reporting procedure in the event that medical attention is necessary. Let them know that you will be in Ecuador. If you opt to get Travel Protection Insurance, make sure you understand the reporting procedures before you depart.

CHAPTER VI

PREPARE FOR DEPARTURE

The Galápagos Islands are a natural paradise and are anything but developed. From a social point of view, the bad news for some is that there are very few night clubs and discos; the real good news for most of us is that the dress code is very casual. Unless you plan to tour the islands on a 90 passenger Cruise Ship, there is no need to wear anything more formal than short pants and sleeves once you leave the Ecuadorian mainland.

The orientation of this book is to encourage you to visit the Galápagos Islands, to assist you in planning your trip, and to guide you in preparing for your tour. An important part of this orientation is to strongly suggest and recommend that, for the full appreciation of the islands and the diversity of wildlife that awaits you, this trip be an exclusive Galápagos odyssey (with the addition of a few days on the Ecuadorian mainland prior to and after your tour). Save the other "nearby" travel spots (the ones that the Tour Operators are pushing) for another trip. You'll silently thank me after your Galápagos tour is complete for harping on this subject every chapter.

While a relatively small blessing, the packing job for a Galápagos-only trip is a lot easier than for a whirlwind tour of South America. The game plan is simple — travel light and travel smart. We'll go through the items by category. A check list is provided at the end of this chapter; combine this list with the one found at the end of Chapter VII, PHOTOGRAPHING THE GALAPAGOS ISLANDS.

HOTEL RESERVATIONS

This is a category you don't have to think about if you are part of a group or package tour. If you have selected a Base Rate tour, the Tour Operator will usually offer to help you with these reservations. My advice is to take them up on the offer, assuming they quote you about the same room rates as you can get on your own (a list of the top hotels in Quito and Guayaquil appears in the

Hotels sections of Chapter VIII, WELCOME TO ECUADOR). If you've decided to make your own hotel reservations, you can FAX or phone in your reservation. For most hotels, there's a more convenient alternative known as Overseas Reservation Services. These are authorized U.S. agents of selected hotels that take care of the reservation details for you. There is no extra charge for this service, and you do not have to pay in advance (as required with most Tour Operators); you settle your room bill on check-out. The Hotel section in Chapter VIII includes the phone and FAX numbers of any Overseas Reservation Service(s) for each hotel.

TRAVEL DOCUMENTATION

A valid passport is required for travel to mainland Ecuador and the Galápagos Islands. Tourists are allowed a stay of up to 90 days; visas are not necessary for U.S. or Canadian citizens travelling to Ecuador on a tourist basis. Locate your passport a month or so before your departure, and verify that it is current and will remain current throughout your trip (check the expiration date). This will give you sufficient time to not only find out where your passport really is, but to get it renewed or replaced if necessary. When you find or get your passport, take two photocopies of the identification page along with any travel/tour vouchers, the I.D. numbers of your traveler's checks, an inventory of expensive personal items (including Model/Serial Numbers, when appropriate), and your airline itinerary. Keep one copy at home and take one with you. The purpose here is in case of loss or theft (see the section on Safety and Security in Chapter VIII).

Carry your passport with you in Quito and Guayaquil. Actually. it's a legal requirement, and theoretically you could be asked for it by an official at any time. Besides, you will need it when exchanging money, buying airline tickets, paying with traveler's checks, and other situations requiring identification. On-board your boat in the Galápagos, you will have to surrender your passport to the captain who is required to properly register and be accountable for all tourists on the vessel. This is part of the visitor control program of the *Galápagos National Park*. Your passport will be returned upon completion of the tour.

On your flight to Ecuador, you will be asked to fill out a T3 Tourist Information Card. On arrival, you will hand this card to the Immigration Officer. Part of it will be stapled to your passport and returned to you. Do not tear it out and throw it away; it will be requested by the Passport Control Officer when you leave the country.

CUSTOMS REGULATIONS IN ECUADOR

Each person is allowed to bring one bottle of liquor and 300 cigarettes into Ecuador duty-free as well as a "reasonable" quantity of perfume, gifts, and personal effects. There are the usual forbidden items — narcotics, firearms, and ammunition. In addition, fresh and dry meat as well as all plants and vegetables are illegal to bring into Ecuador.

MONEY

How much money should you bring? Well, you have already paid for the airfare. If you have selected a general or specialty tour, the cost of the hotel rooms and usually at least half of the meals in mainland Ecuador are included. If you have selected a Base Rate tour or are going to book your tour in Ecuador, you can put the hotel bill (at the better hotels) on a credit card. The same is true for meals at the finer restaurants in Quito and Guayaquil as well as local tours. Many Galápagos Packages include day and overnight tours of Quito and the surrounding area.

With this in mind, allowing $50-$100 per day per person in mainland Ecuador for cash expenses is more than enough; cash here refers to currency and traveler's checks. Remember you're in a country where the dollar is very strong and goes a long way; a typical taxi fare is about 25 cents. The per diem covers 1-2 meals on your own, perhaps a bottle of wine for the room, incidental purchases, cocktails in the evening, and gambling in the hotel casino.

While you're on tour in the Galápagos, allow about $150 per person total cash expenses. This covers the National Park Entrance Fee ($80 per person, payable in U.S. dollars or sucres), tipping the Guides and crew ($50-$75 per passenger per week — U.S. dollars always appreciated), your beverage tab on the boat (settled in currency or traveler's checks on the last day of the cruise), buying a couple of bottles to bring on-board, and incidental purchases in Puerto Ayora or Puerto Baquerizo Moreno (the two principal towns in the islands).

After your tour, it's shopping time in Quito. Allow $200 per person, figuring that the real expensive items can be put on a a credit card.

If you add everything up, taking into account your personal tendencies and the number of days you are going to be on the Ecuadorian mainland, the total varies between $500-$1000 per person. Of this, I would bring at least $200 in currency per person (mostly in U.S. dollars and about $50 in sucres) and the balance in traveler's checks.

TRAVELER'S CHECKS

You should be able to get travelers' checks without having to pay a service charge at the bank where you do the bulk of your checking. I say **should** because banks do vary in "service." Even with no service charge, the banks are still using your money interest-free. Yes, and they encourage you to get your traveler's checks early. Sure they do, so they can use your money longer. They also know that you'll probably hold on to the unused checks for a month or so after you return. Play it smart and get your traveler's checks as late as possible and exchange the unused ones as soon as you return.

AMERICAN EXPRESS has a very organized service network and a complete set of traveler services in addition to traveler's checks. If you are going to use their traveler's checks, make sure you pick up a copy of their booklet of travel tips; it's called the **AMERICAN EXPRESS TRAVELER'S COMPANION**. AMERICAN EXPRESS has a 1 percent service charge if you buy traveler's checks directly from them (unless you hold one of their PLATINUM CARDS).

The BANK OF AMERICA has extensive operations in South America, including Ecuador. If you have a B of A GOLD CARD, they waive the service charge when you buy their traveler's checks. Should you be challenged on this, have the teller call the B of A traveler's check service number at (800) 227-3460.

CREDIT CARDS

As stated above, major credit cards (including MASTER CARD, VISA, and AMERICAN EXPRESS) are accepted at all major hotels in Quito and Guayaquil. The same is true of most of the finer restaurants and gift shops. Having this option means that you can carry less cash and traveler's checks.

Take your Telephone CALLING (Credit) CARD with you. While there is virtually no phone service in the Galápagos, you may need or want to call the U.S. from mainland Ecuador. Using your CALLING CARD will be less expensive than charging the call to your hotel room. If you're not calling from the hotel, it will save you the bother of paying for the call (with your somewhat limited supply of cash) at that time.

MONEY POUCH

While Ecuador is a relatively safe country, you may feel more secure with a money pouch, worn on the body (see the section on Safety and Security in CHAPTER VIII).

LUGGAGE

On the international flights between the U.S. and Ecuador, you're allowed two pieces of checked luggage per person weighing up to a total of 140 pounds; two carryons are also permitted. For flights between Ecuador and the Galápagos, however, you're limited to one checked bag weighing up to 40 pounds and two small carryons.

My suggestion for the international flight to Ecuador is to take three bags — one checked piece and two carryons. For the check-on, I recommend a backpack with internal frame (see the section below). For the carryons, I suggest a multi-purpose tote and a camera bag.

After your tour of the Galápagos, you'll probably want to do a little sightseeing and shopping in Quito. Since one of the best items to buy are leather goods, get yourself a leather travel bag. They have several styles that fold and zip-up into a small, convenient carrying bag; when unzipped, it becomes a full size piece of luggage. Use it to store all your gifts and bulky wool sweaters (another item in the "best buy" category). The bag will then be a second piece of checked luggage on your return flight from Ecuador.

BACKPACK

Instead of a suitcase, I recommend a backpack that has an internal frame; the frame is inside the lining and cannot be seen. There are many advantages:

1. It's very efficient and comfortable. Put the pack on your shoulders, and adjust the straps so that the weight is on your hips. If you haven't worn one of these before, it will pleasantly surprise you. If the straps are adjusted right, you will hardly feel any weight or discomfort on your shoulders, even after an extended period of time. Believe me, your hips are very strong and can easily

and comfortably handle the load. Next chance you get, go into a mountaineering or camping store, and try one of these packs on. Have one of the clerks show you how to adjust the straps for comfortable weight distribution.

2. You don't have to carry it. In an airport situation, having your hands free is a major advantage.

3. It has a professional appearance; it doesn't look like you're hitchhiking on the Interstate when you wear one of these packs. I've used them for years while traveling on business.

4. There are several compartments, so you can segment your stuff. This makes it real handy to find most anything you need "on the fly." The large compartment can hold a pair of snorkel fins, and there are two vertical side compartments just right for stowing a water bottle and flashlight.

5. You can zip-up the cover flap over the shoulder straps while standing in line at the airport ticket counter. This will keep the straps from being eaten by the baggage conveying equipment.

6. On-board the boat, it's pliable and stores easily in the often somewhat-tight storage facilities in your cabin.

CLOTHING

As discussed at the beginning of this chapter, while on tour you'll be wearing either shorts or a bathing suit. Bring a couple or three pairs of each. Pack your favorite bed clothes, and bring about 1 week's worth of T-shirts, socks and underwear. All boats have a clothesline of some sort, so you can wear these items twice during the cruise portion of your trip. Also, you'll probably supplement the supply by purchasing a few Galápagos T-shirts in the islands.

Pack a sweat shirt, jacket, or sweater for the evening. I don't recommend that you bring more than one sweater, because you will probably buy several beautiful wool sweaters in Quito. One pair of pants and 2-3 shirts (or a skirt and 2-3 blouses) will suffice for the few days you'll spend in Quito and the plane rides. If you plan on staying in mainland Ecuador for a longer period of time and/or will be touring the islands on-board a Cruise Ship (which has a somewhat more formal evening meal and social scene than the smaller yachts), you may need to add to this list, but not by much. I can't think of any reason to bring a suit, sport jacket, tie, or dress.

FOOTWEAR

The hiking isn't all that formidable, unless your tour includes a trek up the Alcedo Volcano on Isabela Island. For the general Galápagos itinerary, athletic shoes (sneakers) seems to be the best all-around answer. You'll be doing a lot of up and down hiking over smooth lava rock, so you want a pair that will give you excellent traction. For maximum ankle support, wear high-tops. These tennis shoes are going to get wet, salty, sandy, and scuffed up. Rather than buying a new pair and getting them old quickly, this may be a great farewell performance for an older, comfortable pair with some decent traction; put the white polish to them, and they'll look just as good as a new pair.

An alternative to athletic shoes is a light pair of hiking boots. You will get more traction and support; remember, you're also going to get them soaked with salt water and filled with sand. And from a cosmetic standpoint, you may not look that great in a bathing suit and hiking shoes.

Thongs are not recommended; your feet will turn into broiled lobster claws. The last thing you want is to be hobbled by sunburned feet (see the section on Suntan Lotion). If you're feet are well-tanned, you may want to consider wearing a pair of Tevas®, best described as ATV sandals — heavy tread, built rugged, and strong support. The advantage here is that you can wear them ashore during wet landings and keep them on as you traverse over rocky, lava terrain.

Note: To keep the boats from getting full of sand and grit, most of the yachts do not allow you to wear shoes on-board (see the section, Life at Sea in Chapter IX).Thongs are okay as long as you don't wear them on-deck (because of the sunburn problem referred to above); socks and sandals would be a good choice. I usually remain barefooted while down below and wear socks on deck.

Whatever your footwear, bring along an extra pair of laces.

HEAD WEAR

It is recommended that you wear a hat while you're on tour. You're going to be in and directly under the equatorial sun. Pack a couple of your favorites or buy a straw hat in Quito. You do want something that fits rather snug so it doesn't blow off while you're sailing the blue waters. You could also lose a hat to the wind on some of the islands; on South Plaza, for example, you'll be walking on trails near rocky cliffs where the gusts are fairly strong.

For those who tend to perspire quite a bit, I suggest you pack a sweatband. It's no fun getting perspiration in your eyes (or on your camera lens as you're trying to take a picture).

TOILETRIES

Bring along a supply of your favorite brands, because you may not be able to find exactly what you're looking for once you arrive in Ecuador, and most probably not in the Galápagos. If you stay over in Miami prior to your international departure, take stock and make sure you didn't forget anything; if you did, there are excellent drugstores located in the Miami Airport.

You want as many of the toiletries as possible to be packaged in small plastic bottles and containers. You may not have a private bathroom on-board the boat. Private or not, chances are the facilities will be a bit more compact than what you're used to. You will no doubt be packing and unpacking your toiletry kit and trying to balance all those neat little bottles on a small, narrow ledge while the boat is chopping through the waves. If you've got the picture, you can see that you don't want to bring glass jars with you. It's also better to bring three small containers of shampoo with you rather than a single large one. If your favorite brand only comes in large sizes or in glass containers, you can buy small plastic transfer bottles with flip-up spouts.

A check list of toiletries is found at the end of this chapter.

RECOMMENDED UTILITY ITEMS

Binoculars — This is an essential item. You want a small, rubber or plastic-coated pair that you can wear around your neck along with a camera. On your daily island tours, you will be transported ashore in the dinghy (*panga*). As you ride along the rocky shores, you will have unique glimpses of several animals you may not see very often during your visit — the Galápagos penguin being a good example. You'll be scanning with the binoculars and then possibly wanting to take a couple of quick photos. Thus, you want both the binoculars and the camera handy. You can't dig into your pack very easily in the crowded little *panga*. Also, if your camera and binoculars were not secured around your neck, you could lose your grip and drop one of them if you get jostled about by a wave or another person.

For those of you who wear eyeglasses, as I do, it is very inconvenient (once the animal is spotted with the eye) to take off your glasses, raise, aim, and look through the binoculars. Often, the animal has moved, or you've looked in the "wrong tree;" you've then got to repeat the process, sometimes more than once. To even attempt this, you have to either be wearing Croakies® (see below) or to raise the glasses to a precarious position on your forehead. The answer to this problem is actually quite simple, assuming your binoculars have little suction cups at each eyepiece. Just bend the little rubber cups back, and you now see through the binoculars with your eyeglasses on. I can't believe all the years I didn't know you could do that!

Here's another little hint about the wonders of the binocular device. If you look through the "wrong end" of the binoculars and focus on an object held just a few inches away, your binoculars become a magnifying glass. This works great for the little stuff you see while tide-pooling.

Regarding specifications for binoculars, a 7 × 25 pair, for example, has a magnification power of 7 and a 25mm objective lens (the one furthest from your eye) diameter. If you divide the lens diameter by the magnification, you get the brightness factor, which in this case is 3.57. The higher the brightness factor, the more light will hit your eyes, making it "easier" and more comfortable for you to see the subject. This is especially true when viewing in a low-light situation (such as trying to see a penguin against dark, shadowy rocks). Thus, if I had a choice between a 7 × 25 and a 8 × 22 pair of binoculars, I would opt for the 7 × 25.

Another specification number is the field of view. Thus, a particular model may have a "376 ft field at 1000 yds," meaning that at 1000 yards the field of view is 376 feet wide. All things being equal or near-equal (including price), I would select the pair with the widest field of view. Try them out in the store before purchasing, using fixed boundaries to determine the "effective" field of view; also, look into a corner that isn't well lit.

Business Cards — You will meet a lot of interesting people and want to stay in touch with them. Instead of scribbling your name on a corner of a well-worn hotel brochure, hand them one of your cards. To save time, put your home address and phone on the blank side of a number of cards before you leave.

Croakies® — This is a little band that either clips on or slips over your eyeglasses and keeps them from falling off. These prove very useful in all outdoor and water-related activities. For those near-sighted individuals, this allows you to take off your glasses while reading (supported, they rest on your chest), without having to set them down (and possibly break or lose them).

Daypack — You'll use a daypack on your daily tours to the islands; commonly-stowed items will include a water bottle, bandages, first aid cream, guide book, film, and camera equipment. You'll have to decide whether you want to carry the photographic accessories in your camera bag or daypack; you don't want the burden of carrying both. If there are two of you, a good compromise would be for one to carry the pack and the other the camera bag.

Another option, one that I use, is a fanny pack. The advantage here is that it puts the weight where you can best support it (on your hips) and still leaves your hands free. You can even wear these things sideways, so you can get at your field guide or suntan lotion without having to take the pack off. Fanny packs are available in many sizes; I strongly recommend one large enough to hold all the items you would normally carry with you in a day pack. The model I have can even hold my camera and extra lenses. The better ones (available through mountaineering stores and their mail order catalogs) have adjustment/support straps to insure a snug, comfortable fit.

Whatever type of pack you opt for, I recommend treating it with two coats of a water-repellent spray (such as ScotchGard® about a week or so before you leave. The same holds true for your camera bag.

Earplugs — The cabin on board your boat is a lot smaller than your bedroom. Some of us have a tendency to snore, and a pair of earplugs will go far in insuring a good night's sleep.

Extra Pair of Eyeglasses (or Contact Lenses) — You don't want to be in a situation where you break or lose your glasses and can't see what you came all this way to look at. An old pair will do just fine as a backup; now's the time to start looking for them. Also, ask your eye doctor to write out and give you your correction lens prescription. This is a handy piece of paper to carry with you. While there's not too many eye doctors in the Galápagos, you could get a pair made in Ecuador if necessary, depending on the timing and the circumstances.

First Aid Kit — This is yet another reminder that you will be isolated once you reach the Galápagos, and someone in your group will probably have occasion to use most of the following recommended items to pack in your first aid kit: aspirin, bandages, first aid cream, foot powder, insect repellant, IMODIUM®, skin cream, topical anaesthetic skin spray (for sunburn, insect bites, cuts, and scratches), and throat lozenges.

Flashlight/Book Light — You'll find these to be a couple of useful items to have along. The flashlight is especially important; a small plastic one will do just fine. You're likely to spend at least one night in Puerto Ayora on Santa Cruz Island, where the town's electricity is turned off at midnight; carry your flashlight if you're out and about. Your flashlight will also come in handy on-board the boat for finding your way after hours. Bring extra batteries.

If you like to read in bed, your cabin may not be equipped with a reading lamp (or the generator could be off). You might want to consider packing one of those handy little book lights and a supply of batteries. You can also use it as a flashlight. It's an important item for me.

Plastic Bags — Oh so many uses! So many, in fact, that this item appears in two check lists (this chapter and the one on photography). The various applications include stowing dirty clothes, wet bathing suits (on your flight back to mainland Ecuador after swimming that morning), shaving cream, shampoo, tooth brushes, snacks, disposables, etc. Don't forget the twist ties.

Rain Gear/Pancho — Actually a windbreaker will do just fine. Something light weight that doesn't take up much room and easily stuffs into your day pack. During the first half of the year, there can be an hour or so of rain per day. The second half of the year brings a mist (called a *garúa* — see the section on Climate in Chapter II) to the higher-altitude islands. Many tours take a trip to the highlands of Santa Cruz Island, where it is often quite misty. You may also need the rain gear in Quito, which can get some rain (usually afternoons and/or evenings) from October to May.

Sunglasses — What's a vacation without sunglasses? You might want to consider prescription sunglasses. I wear "photo grey" glasses, the ones that are photosensitive and darken in the sunlight. I never enjoyed the continual changing of glasses as I went from indoors out into the sunlight and then back again. I was always forgetting to take a pair from home or leaving my sunglasses in some dimly-lit restaurant!

Suntan Lotion — An absolutely essential item. Bring lots; the selection is very limited in the Galápagos, and the heaviest screen value available is a 4. Start off with a full screen block and gradually (after a few days, depending on your complexion) lighten up. Keep the suntan lotion on-deck in your snorkel bag (see the Snorkeling Equipment section below). When the Guide announces that it's time to get ready for the next island tour, start applying the lotion. Don't forget the feet! There will be times when, after snorkeling, you'll be sitting on the beach with bare feet for an hour or so; that's when you get zapped. After lunch, when you're taking a *siesta* on-deck, wear your socks (as stated in the Footwear section, you're not allowed to wear shoes on-board many of the yachts because they don't want sand all over the place). You're also advised to wear a hat.

Swiss Army Knife — Always handy, this multi-purpose tool is especially useful in an isolated environment such as the Galápagos. You will no doubt have several interesting applications. If you are going to purchase one of these little gems, you probably already know that there are a million-and-one options, with some of the cases being as wide as they are long. Aside from the knife portion, the options that seem to get frequent use are the cork screw, screw drivers, and scissors. Remember that a knife is considered to be a weapon, and you are not allowed to have it in your possession on-board an aircraft; pack it with your check-on luggage.

Tape Player — There are many occasions where the sound of your favorite music forms a perfect background for the activities going on around you. I can think of several such times for me — lying on-deck after lunch while sailing towards the next island, "escaping" from the noisy kids across the aisle on the airplane, and beating the boredom of the 4 hour bus and ferry excursion from Baltra Airport to the town of Puerto Ayora on Santa Cruz Island. Many of the yachts have cassette players, so you can entertain your shipmates and the crew during meals and the evening "bull" sessions. Be sure to bring spare batteries.

Vitamins — Don't forget them! International travel has a way of fatiguing and stressing the body. You are also in contact with people carrying and spreading all sorts of little germs. Taking your vitamins could make the difference and keep you healthy.

Watch, Water-Resistant — Be the last one on your block to get one of these inexpensive wonders. You never have to think about where you left it because you're always wearing it, even while snorkeling and in the shower. Almost all of them have built-in alarm clocks, so you don't have to figure out how to arrange a wake-up call.

Water Bottle, Plastic — It can get fairly hot in the Galápagos, and some island tours (Bartolomé and Santa Fe are good examples) require a bit of an uphill trek, so you could get thirsty. There is bottled water on-board the boat to fill your container with. Make sure the bottle you choose will fit into one of the side pouches on your backpack.

SNORKELING EQUIPMENT

You will have the opportunity to snorkel almost every day, and it's an experience that you want to take maximum advantage of. While the cool Humboldt Current keeps the island waters at temperatures below that at which a fully-developed coral reef system can form, the surface water is not that bad (except off the western and northern islands, where the upwelling is extensive). In fact, there are a few coral reefs in the Galápagos, around which you will see beautiful parrotfish, yellow-tailed surgeonfish, angelfish, moorish idols, and several other lovelies. The real treat is the sea lions, which will swim up to, with, and around you. The first time this happens, your composure will probably go south. For some reason, we tend to have a negative mindset regarding large, sleek, finned creatures brushing past us in the water. It takes a while to get used to it, but when you do, you'll treasure the experience and will welcome your further "encounters," which will be numerous.

Mask & Tube — You don't want to be without snorkel equipment. Forget what the Tour Operator's brochure says or what they told you on the phone about the equipment being provided; bring your snorkel gear with you! The boats may or may not carry snorkel equipment, and if they do, it will have to be shared. And when it's your turn, you may find out that the mask leaks! The same is true of the large selection of masks available (for rent) on the Cruise Ships; I've seen Cruise Ship passengers basically waste an entire snorkeling session fooling with a mask that leaked. Maximize your opportunity of viewing the 400 or so species of fish that swim the waters of the Galápagos (over 10 percent of which are endemic to the islands). Bring at least a mask and snorkel tube (along with a spare tube strap that attaches the tube to your mask).

Incidentally, if you wear glasses or contacts and are nearsighted, most major brands of face masks offer lens inserts to match your correction. While these lens inserts are not precise corrections (being available in increments of 0.5 diopters), they are more than good enough for the intended purpose and will truly increase your appreciation of the underwater world. These lenses do take into account the natural correction that the water provides, which is about -1.3 diopters. The dive shop where you buy the mask will install the lenses for you, which will cost about $75 for the pair. Call your eye doctor and have the office send you the correction prescription for each eye; they will not read you the prescription over the phone. It will take the dive shop 2-3 weeks to receive and install your lens inserts.

If you already have a mask, go to the shop where you bought it or a local dive shop and see if custom lens inserts are offered for that particular mask. If not, you might decide it's time for a new mask, or you could take your old mask to the eye doctor who will have totally custom lenses ground (to match your prescription) and inserted into the mask. If you have some unique visual anomalies (such as astigmatism), you may wish for the eye doctor to do this for you anyway. Going this route will take a bit longer (allow 4-6 weeks) and will cost a lot more (my guess is about $150).

Fins — I recommend that you bring fins as well. It may be quite a distance from the place where you enter the water to where the majority of the fish are (over by the rocks — it's not deep, just far). Without fins, unless you're a good swimmer, you'll probably give up trying to reach the area where the other snorkelers are, being content to stay in one general location, and hoping that ''a bunch of fish will decide to come by.'' So, without fins you'll most likely miss out on seeing the best fish, but I won't press the point. Packing space is at a premium, and fins are bulky; so are all those clothes that I'm trying to convince you not to take! As discussed earlier, the fins will fit in the large compartment of an internal frame backpack.

There is a chance that there will be a pair of fins on-board the boat, but only a small chance. Most of the Cruise Ships do have an adequate selection that they rent out. By the way, if you're borrowing the fins from a friend, make sure they fit!

Booties — If I've convinced you to bring your fins, then you'll also want to get a pair of slip-on diving booties. First, if you're a tenderfoot like I am, with booties on you'll be able to comfortably walk from the place you took off your shoes to the water. Often, this hike is not insignificant, being over lava rocks and other little nasties that like to hurt your feet. Second, the booties allow you to easily get your fins on and off. They also keep the fins from riding on the back part of your heel and wearing off the skin. Finally, on a few of the islands, there's a tour followed by a swim on Beach #1 which is in turn followed by a swim on Beach #2. After all this, you return to Beach #1 where the *panga* is waiting. The booties save you the time and trouble of repeatedly getting into and out of your shoes, especially with wet, sandy feet.

Gear Bag — While you're at the dive shop, buy a mesh diving gear bag. They cost about $10-$20 depending on the size and whether the bag has handles or a drawstring. These gear bags will easily hold 3-4 sets of masks and fins as well as any underwater camera equipment you may have. Once you get to the islands, you can put all your snorkel stuff inside the bag and keep it there. On the boat, leave the gear bag on the aft deck. They usually have a few plastic equipment containers back by the *panga*, and you can store the bag in there. When you take a shower, bring the gear bag in with you and give the snorkel and underwater camera gear an instant fresh water rinse job. Always load the gear bag into the *panga* before going ashore unless the Guide convinces you that there will absolutely be no snorkeling opportunities. Sometimes they're not sure if there will be enough time for swimming, and to save the time of rounding all the stuff up, they may tell people not to carry their masks and fins. With a gear bag being so convenient to load into the *panga* and leave onshore (without a sea lion being able to cart it off to play with), they'll say, "Sure, take it; we may have time."

Buoyancy Vest — Speaking to those who do not feel comfortable snorkeling in the ocean, there's no reason for you to miss out on all the fun and fascination. Get a buoyancy vest at the dive shop, and you'll be right in there with the others. You manually inflate them just a little bit, and wear it as a vest. You'll feel like you can't sink, because you can't!

Wet Suit — Finally, if you're one who can't deal with water that is colder than 78 Deg F, bring a wet suit. I personally don't feel it's necessary for snorkeling in the Galápagos, but I've seen several people not snorkel because they were convinced the water was too cold.

MEDICAL CONSIDERATIONS

A vacation in the Galápagos Islands can be put into the classification of adventure travel. While you will not be partaking in activity as strenuous as mountain climbing, there will be a reasonable amount of daily physical activity. This includes hiking (sometimes up steep hills and over rocky terrain), swimming, and snorkeling. The conditions will often be full sun/ tropical heat. You will most likely experience the high altitude (9300 ft) of Quito where you may be under some pressure to get a lot of shopping (and therefore walking) done during a brief stay.

Needless to say, it is preferable that you be in reasonable physical condition. For the elderly and those with heart conditions or high blood pressure are advised to check with their physicians considering the advisability of the trip. Remember there are virtually no medical facilities in the Galápagos. Perhaps one of the larger Cruise Ships that carry a doctor or nurse on-board may be somewhat more practical for some travelers.

If you're not accustomed to working out on a regular basis, but in otherwise good health, you might want to consider starting on an exercise program a couple of months prior to your departure. As always, consult your physician whenever appropriate.

Altitude Sickness — A more serious version of the symptoms described in the section below on Motion Sickness occurs on the last day of the tour when you spend the morning on the boat (cruising to the airport), the afternoon on the airplane, and the evening in Quito (at 9300 ft). Some people just feel the shortness of breath and the fatigue associated with a sudden change to a high altitude. Other people get fairly sick, and are out of commission for a day or so.

Alcohol seems to be a predisposing factor relative to altitude sickness (as does smoking and eating heavily). If you're flying from the States directly to Quito, bear this in mind on your flight over. Also, you might want to take it easy the last night on-board your boat; have your "farewell party" the night before last. If you're taking any medication, including preventatives for motion sickness and/or altitude sickness, the use of alcohol is typically contraindicated; be very cautious.

There is a preventative medication for altitude sickness; it is an acetazoleamide diuretic marketed under the brand DIAMOX®. This drug is used, among other things, to treat glaucoma, as it relieves sinus and cranial pressure; thus, it can prevent some of the symptoms, including headaches, associated with altitude sickness. There are some side effects, and it seems to me that the high altitude dries you out enough as it is. Consult your physician regarding this medication. Good old aspirin does quite a bit of good for me, relieving the headache and malaise associated with the first day of life at 9300 ft. I still feel a decided loss of energy, which fades after 24-36 hours.

The air **is** drier at high altitudes, which, for one, causes the skin to crack. This is where the skin cream and lip balm come in very handy. The dry air also causes the eyes to be irritable; those that wear contacts might consider leaving their lenses out whenever possible in Quito.

Dental — If you have any nagging dental problems or concerns, get them taken care of before you leave. You don't want to be thinking about a dentist while you're anchored off Española Island.

Don't forget to pack your dental floss. You'll probably find some unique uses for it. I've seen some people use floss instead of Croakies® to tie between the ear holders of their glasses. Also, if you have any caps on your teeth, take some POLI-GRIP® along in case one comes loose.

Food — In Quito and Guayaquil, the rule is don't eat uncooked food, including peeled fruits and vegetables (due to the water used in washing them). Salads seem to be one of the main culprits. In the better restaurants (including the major hotels), you probably won't have any problems; use your judgment. In other establishments, it's best to be careful.

Speaking of being careful, I am extra-cautious during my stay in Quito (or Guayaquil) before the Galápagos, not wanting to risk an intestinal problem prior to the cruise; I'm slightly bolder after Galápagos, with the thought that I'll soon be home. I refrain from any fruit or even fruit juice for breakfast at the fancy hotel coffee shops (in my paranoid state, I picture Julio adding water to the juice at 4:00 a.m., and other such images). Getting back to basics, one of the first phrases to learn in Spanish is "*sin hielo*" (without ice), a must expression in bars and restaurants as well as on the flights to and from the Galápagos.

On your boat, there shouldn't be any problem. The cooks do a good job, and the food is well prepared. Still, if you have a sensitive tummy, it's best not to take any chances and minimize the possibility of discomfort. You're not going to starve in any case, and the daily experience of sitting around the dining room of the boat and being served good food while watching the Galápagos show going on around you generally raises the meal rating from "very good" to "memorable feast."

As a precaution, it is highly recommended that you take along some IMODIUM®, an excellent over-the-counter medication that will usually plug you up pretty quick.

Medication — If applicable, make sure you have an ample supply, and have your written prescription(s) with you. There are several pharmacies in Quito and Guayaquil (there's even a couple in the Galápagos), that dispense most major medications; please do note that the dosages are a lot stronger, so be aware of any potential side effects. Also, consult your physician regarding any potential side effects relative to high altitude, heat, and being at sea for an extended period of time. Make note of your blood type, as well as any allergies and allergic reactions you may have.

Caution: It is vitally important for those of you with an extreme allergy response (possibly leading to anaphylactic shock) to identify this condition in advance to the Tour Operator, Tour Leader, and Guide. Let them know specifically what you are allergic to. In particular, there are a growing number of introduced wasps on Floreana Island; these wasps are being carried (mostly by the tour boats) to several other islands. Typical allergy medication (including BENADRYL® is not strong enough for an anaphylactic reaction. Bring 1-2 norepinephrine jabber sticks with you (it's like a needle but simpler to use — consult your physician), and make sure you have them with you at all times; also instruct the Tour Leader and Guide as to the location of this medication.

Motion (Sea) Sickness — While the seas are generally calm in the Galápagos, it can get a bit rough if you travel to the western, northern, or southern islands (depending on the currents). Generally, if you don't take anything for motion sickness, there's no reason to in the Galápagos. If you're accustomed to taking something, pack whatever brand or type works best for you. If nothing else, you'll feel more secure having the stuff with you.

Many of the pills are antihistamines and have undesirable side effects, such as drowsiness and disorientation. There are now alternate forms of motion sickness medication. A popular preventative is TRANSDERM SCOPE®, a skin patch worn behind the ear that slowly releases its scopolamine (a nervous system depressant) medication through the skin. Each patch is effective for about 3 days. Another new approach is SEA BANDS®, worn on both wrists. There is no medication involved; they are said to operate by the exertion of pressure (by a button embedded in the band) on the acupressure point on the wrist, the spot that (according to Chinese medicine) controls nausea. The product is manufactured in England and imported by SOUWEST BAND CORP., West Palm Beach, FL.

Bear in mind that all the various forms of medication are preventative in nature. It will do you no good to start taking them once the effects of motion sickness have begun. Follow the instructions; they typically recommend that you begin using the product several hours prior to boarding. Since SEA

BANDS® contain no medication, you can begin wearing the device after the onset of the symptoms, according to the manufacturer.

Note: After touring the Galápagos by boat for several days, you may have a tough time getting your "land legs" back. This will be noticeable if you stop at Santa Cruz Island after a few days at sea. What seems to be happening is that the equilibrium center of the inner ear is still rocking back and forth while the rest of you is staying in one place. The brain doesn't particularly care for contradictory signals, and the result is a feeling of dizziness. The effect is intensified inside a building (due to the fixed rectangular visual cues); going outside will make you feel better. The symptoms typically go away after a few hours.

Vaccinations — No inoculations are required in mainland Ecuador or the Galápagos Islands. However, if you plan to visit the Amazon region of Ecuador, a yellow fever shot (good for 10 years) and malaria tablets are typically recommended. You are urged to consult with your physician on this matter.

Water — As the saying goes, don't drink the water (unless it's bottled — GüTIG® is the local brand). You wil typically find 2-3 bottles in your hotel room; use this water for drinking as well as for brushing your teeth. There is always bottled water on-board the boat as well as bottled soft drinks and beer (cerveza).

PACKING CHECK LIST

Use this list in conjunction with the Photography Check List at the end of Chapter VII, PHOTOGRAPHING THE GALAPAGOS ISLANDS.

CLOTHING

☐ Bathing Suits   ☐ Pajamas, etc.   ☐ Blouses
☐ Dress Shirts   ☐ Hats   ☐ Jacket
☐ Pants   ☐ Shoelaces (spare)   ☐ Shoes
☐ Shorts   ☐ Skirts   ☐ Socks
☐ Sweatband   ☐ Sweat Shirt   ☐ T-shirts
☐ Underwear   ☐ Rain Gear/Pancho

Notes _____

_____

FIRST AID KIT

☐ Aspirin   ☐ Bandages   ☐ First Aid Cream
☐ Foot Powder   ☐ Insect Repellant   ☐ IMODIUM®
☐ POLI-GRIP®   ☐ Throat Lozenges   ☐ Sunburn Treatment
☐ Cortisone Skin Cream (Heat Rash)

Notes _____

_____

SNORKELING EQUIPMENT

☐ Booties   ☐ Buoyancy Vest   ☐ Fins
☐ Gear Bag, Mesh   ☐ Mask   ☐ Tube
☐ Wet Suit

Notes _____

_____

TOILETRIES

☐ Contact Lens Solutions   ☐ Contraceptive Materials
☐ Combs & Brushes   ☐ Cosmetics   ☐ Dental Floss
☐ Deodorant   ☐ Hair Spray   ☐ Lip Balm
☐ Nail Clipper   ☐ Plastic Bottles   ☐ Razors
☐ Shampoos   ☐ Shave Cream   ☐ Skin Cream
☐ Soap   ☐ Tampons   ☐ Toothbrush/Paste

Notes _____

_____

ITEM	NOTES
☐ Backpack, Internal Frame	_____
☐ Binoculars	_____
☐ Book Light/Batteries	_____
☐ Books	_____
	_____
☐ Business Cards	_____
☐ Contact Lenses (extra pair)	_____
☐ Credit Cards (MC, VISA, AM EXPRESS)	_____
☐ Croakies®	_____
☐ Daypack	_____
☐ Earplugs	_____
☐ Eyeglasses (extra pair)	_____
☐ Flashlight/Batteries	_____
☐ Hotel Reservations	_____
	_____
☐ Medication	_____
☐ Money/Traveler's Checks	_____
☐ Money Pouch	_____
☐ Motion Sickness Treatment	_____
☐ Passport	_____
☐ Photocopies of all Documentation/Tickets	_____
☐ Plastic Bags/Twist Ties	_____
☐ Sunglasses	_____
☐ Suntan Lotion	_____
☐ Swiss Army Knife	_____
☐ Tape Player/ Cassettes/Batteries	_____
☐ Telephone Credit (Calling) Card	_____
☐ Vitamins	_____
☐ Watch, Water-resistant	_____
☐ Water Bottle	_____
☐ Misc. Items	_____

CHAPTER VII

PHOTOGRAPHING THE GALÁPAGOS ISLANDS

As a general rule don't take anything from the islands that belongs there. Take only photographs, and leave only your footprints.
General Rule, from the LIST OF RULES,
Galápagos National Park, Ecuador

The subject of preparing for your trip to the Galápagos Islands is incomplete without a discussion of photography and the photographic equipment that you take along. The advice that will be offered in this chapter can be briefly summarized (in the same fashion as the General Rule stated above) — bring lots of film and extra batteries, get a zoom lens, consider buying an underwater camera, test all your equipment before you leave, always be ready, and leave your tripod home.

FILM

You cannot bring too much film to the Galápagos Islands! There are so many opportunities for spectacular shots that the rolls will appear to sprout wings, flying out of your bag and into the camera, soon followed by a fast return flight. Shooting three or four rolls per day is not unusual. If you run out of film while touring the islands on a yacht, you are also out of luck. Some of the Cruise Ships may have a limited supply of film for sale, but I would consider this option below the level of a fallback. Just the thought of running low on film is enough to drive me to distraction. In Puerto Ayora (the largest town in the Galápagos), or even in mainland Ecuador, such film as is available may be close to or past the expiration date, and the cost is extremely high (double or triple the U.S. price). So please, bring lots of film. Even if you have several rolls left over, you will absolutely have no problem selling them at cost to a very grateful tourist who didn't get this friendly advice.

Film selection is always a personal choice. I like to keep photo albums at home to document my trips, so I generally shoot prints. Many of the people I know prefer transparencies because it keeps the processing cost down. They also enjoy sharing their vacation adventures with friends in the form of a slide show after the dinner dishes have been cleared away. With today's processing technology, (including laser-scanned internegatives and the Cibachrome® process, where the internegative phase is bypassed altogether), you can get professional quality prints made from your best slides. It's your choice, but do bring an assortment of film speeds. I find that a mixture of 25% ASA (ISO) 64-200 and 75% ASA 400 is reasonable. You'll be doing a lot of medium-to-long telephoto work and will want to be able to "close down" as much as possible (to get the sharpest picture quality) and at the same time be able to shoot at 1/125th to 1/250th of a second to avoid blurring the action. More on this later.

Note: Regarding the different systems used to rate film speed, ASA (*American Standards Association*) and ISO (*International Standards Organization*) numbers are the same. Thus, ASA 400 is equal to ISO 400. There is a numerical difference, however, when ISO or ASA sensitivity values are compared to European system DIN (*Deutsche Industrie Norm*) values.

Plan on using 1-2 rolls per day of 400 ASA film. If you intend to do any underwater photography, increase the allowance by half a roll per day. Since I use mostly ASA 400, I buy rolls of 36 exposures, and am interrupted by having to reload film one-third less often; for 72 shots, that's one reload instead of two. In the Galápagos there are times when that's important as well as convenient, especially when it lets you continue shooting a key sequence. For the slower films, which I use less often, I buy rolls of 24 exposures; this makes a necessary change to ASA 400 that much easier.

Remember to change the ASA dial on your camera when you change film speeds! If you're partially into a roll and decide to change film speeds, there is a way to deal with this situation and not waste film. Note the exposure you're on, and write it in your notebook (also write it on the film leader after rewinding). Rewind the roll, taking care not to rewind the film leader into the film canister. If you goof, there's always the film extractor (see the section on Accessories to Consider). When you want to use this roll again, make sure the lens cap is securely on before loading. Then, in a fairly dark location, advance the film to about two shots past the number you left off at (for a margin of safety).

Speaking of changing film, when you finish a roll, **do** wind the film leader into the canister. This will avoid that sinking, confused thought, "Is this a new roll of film, or did I already shoot it today?"

FILM PROCESSING

Don't have your film developed in Ecuador; the word is that the processing is not the best. On the other hand, it is not recommended that you keep undeveloped film for an extended period of time, especially in a warm climate. If you're planning a trip of longer than 2 months, try to bribe a departing friend into having your film processed and then keeping the prints or slides for you. This will give you both a good reason to get together after your return. To facilitate the accounting process, you could buy pre-paid processing film packs, and then your friend simply has to put them in the mail. While we're on the subject, don't post any photographic material from Ecuador; you're taking too much of a chance, and you'll always be wondering if the package arrived home safely, or if at all.

FILM STORAGE

Film emulsion chemistry is fairly sophisticated, designed to remain stable for a long time. But not forever! Check the expiration date before purchasing or packing film for your trip. Film chemistry is also affected by heat. Thus, you want to store unused film in a cool location, such as a refrigerator, taking care to pack the film in a plastic bag or moisture-proof container. Please note, however, that if the film is suddenly transferred from cold storage to a warm environment and then opened, moisture may condense on it. Let the film warm gradually before opening the container and loading the film.

THE CAMERA

As discussed throughout this book, taking pictures in the Galápagos is a continual sequence of opportunities, ones that lend themselves very nicely, and in many cases uniquely, to a hand-held 35mm camera. Many of these situations happen quickly and change from minute to minute as you're splashing through the waves in a dinghy shoulder-to-shoulder with eight other passengers. There's no time or room (or even a foundation) for a tripod set-up.

If you read this chapter and still have the motivation to drag a 4×5 view camera out to the Galápagos — go for it! Your patience will be well-rewarded with the quality, detail, and extreme resolution of your final product. Remember, though, you're going to have to take your equipment ashore in the dinghy (*panga*), you can't walk off the trails to get a better angle, and you must stay with the Guide (and therefore with the rest of the group). The same flexibility limitations are true (although to a lessor degree) for those who use medium format cameras. To all of you that are dedicated to the "bigger piece of film," I can only say, "Bring a 35mm camera in addition to your larger format camera so you won't miss out on a lot of 'right now' opportunities."

Now I turn to all of you that haven't used and/or are afraid to use a 35mm camera. There are several 35mm automatic cameras on the market today that are perfectly acceptable and will allow you to take great shots of the Galápagos wildlife. These cameras are self-loading, they recognize and adapt to what film you're using, will automatically rewind and advance the film to the next shot, have built-in flash, and set the exposure to get consistently good results. And they're reasonably priced — starting at about $100. You do have to spend about $250 to get two of the best features — autofocus and dual-lenses. With the second feature, you can change from a wide-angle to a telephoto lens with the push of a button. If you're going to buy one of these for the trip, here's an idea. For about the same price, you can get a sports version of a 35mm automatic camera that does all the above and you can take it snorkeling with you. If you're interested, see the section on Underwater Photography.

LENS SELECTION

Choosing the right lens for the situation is another highly personal decision, being a function of what you're trying to accomplish. There are times when just about any wide-angle, telephoto, or standard lens would be ideally suited (based on the given situation). The everyday reality of Galápagos Island touring does strongly indicate, however, the extreme suitability of a 70-210mm zoom lens (for a 35mm SLR camera). Here's why:

1. Opportunities occur suddenly and often unpredictably. You're panning the sky trying to get the perfect spread-wing hawk shot when your

companion tells you to look down; much to your surprise a land iguana, has stopped in his tracks, his lunch of "cactus leaf salad" in mouth, about 5 ft from you. The telephoto is too much lens, and if you tried to move back or change lenses, the little creature would probably scurry off. With the zoom, you can go from 210mm, where you have been scanning the skies, to 70 mm or whatever it takes to perfectly frame the iguana.

2. The scene described above is very common. So is the reverse situation. You're honed in on two blue-footed boobies waiting for their "dance" to begin when, suddenly, you hear the war cry of the photographer, "Wow, look at that!" You spin around and your companions' heads are all tilted skyward. There, lazily circling above you, is a male frigatebird, perfectly posed (see Photo #37). There's no time to change lenses, but you don't have to; just zoom in!

3. Similar situations occur on the daily *panga* rides. You may not realize it at first, but these little boats present you with many unique photo opportunities, so once you get seated have your camera out, ready, and protected (see the section on A Day at Sea in Chapter IX). This is the closest you're going to get (on the water) to the rocky cliffs, which serve as home for many Galápagos sea birds and shore birds. The *panga* ride may also provide the best (sometimes the only) chances of observing and photographing penguins, white-tipped sharks, and possibly "pairs" of three mating sea turtles (see Chapter III).

Opportune situations are not without their challenges. Aside from the varying distances of the subjects, your little *panga* is bouncing up and down, you're occasionally getting splashed, and the quarters are very tight. The end result is that you don't have the time or the opportunity to change lenses, which is exactly what you need to do. Unless you have a zoom lens.

4. Once ashore and touring a Visitor Site, you must stay on the narrow trail, due to the fragile environment. Thus, if the picture composition isn't right, you don't usually have the luxury of backing up or moving forward. This problem can be solved by letting the zoom lens do the moving for you. The alternative is to change lenses and hope that you're exactly the right distance away to get the composition you want.

5. Speaking of composition (an art for some and an acquired skill for the rest of us), the zoom lens is an excellent instructional tool. As you zoom in, aside from getting a close up view of the subject, the background changes dramatically, sometimes for better or worse. When time allows, it's fascinating to slowly zoom in and out, observing the continual change in composition. At some point, you stop and say, "Perfect, that's it!" Most of us can recognize excellent composition better than we can achieve it, and what the zoom lens is actually doing is showing us hundreds of shots, allowing us to pick the one with the best composition. As we analyze it further, we can see that the composition was right because the amount of sky was reduced or a certain rock was added to the foreground, etc.

The use of composing the shot "on-the-fly" is somewhat more important when shooting slide film, because you don't have the option of cropping as you do with prints.

6. The zoom lens is more than the compromise that it used to be. With today's lens-making technology, end-product results from a zoom lens are, for most purposes, of the same quality level as those from a fixed focal length lens.

A 70-210mm zoom allows you to focus to about 5 ft (depending on the lens), and even closer with macro zoom lenses. Read the following section,

Exposure, for a discussion of correct aperture and shutter-speed determination with a telephoto (zoom) lens.

EXPOSURE

While I'm somewhat of a purist about preferring to set my own shutter speeds and apertures (as opposed to letting the camera make the decisions for me), in the Galápagos I usually leave the camera on Automatic. As described several times in this chapter, the photo situations in the islands are fast-paced, with both the subject matter and the lighting quickly changing on a shot-to-shot basis. Even within a single shot, there can be sudden and drastic changes to the amount of light entering the camera. A good example occurs as you pan the camera, following the flight of the tropicbird, waiting for the perfect composition; you alternate from bright sunlight to full shade several times. Keeping my camera in Automatic saved many such situations in addition to all the times I would have forgotten to take light meter readings and set new exposure values between shots (of different scenes, often from the same spot).

You can still override (offset) the Automatic with the Exposure Compensation Dial (using + 1, + 2 to increase the exposure or add light and using − 1, − 2 to decrease the exposure). In the bright equatorial sun of the Galápagos, you may have to increase the exposure, thereby compensating for the somewhat dominating effect of the overall ambient light on your camera's light meter. On the other hand, underexposing color film by a half to a full stop actually puts more pop into the color. So you have a trade-off situation. This is where a spot meter comes in handy (see the section, Accessories to Consider). The ASA Film Speed Dial can be used in the same manner. For example, if you want to underexpose the effect of the automatic setting, and you're shooting ASA 400 film, you can set the ASA Film Speed Dial to 800, thereby decreasing the exposure by one stop. Exposure compensation is especially important when shooting slide film, because the film in the camera becomes the end-product. With prints, you do have the option of exposure (and color) correction during the printing process.

Some of today's cameras are equipped with onboard microprocessors and their associated memory functions. Basically you can take a close-up light reading (with the camera's built-in meter) of the subject and lock in that reading. Thus, when you step back (on foot or with the zoom lens) to take the shot, the camera is basing the exposure value of the scene on the locked-in light reading.

TELEPHOTO (ZOOM) LENS EXPOSURES

When using a telephoto or a telephoto zoom lens, special consideration must be given to the exposure values. Your first concern is shutter speed. To avoid motion blur, you want a shutter speed with about the same numerical value as the focal length of the lens. Thus, with a 250mm lens, the shutter speed should be at least 1/250th of a second. With a 70-210mm zoom lens, the shutter speed should be set to at least 1/125th to 1/250th of a second, depending on the amount you're zooming.

If you're shooting from an airplane (and the peaks of the Andes above the clouds **are** beautiful), use shutter speeds of 1/500th to 1/1000th of a second and keep the focus set at infinity. Also, in aerial photography make sure you have the skylight filter on the lens. A polarizing filter, on the other hand, may produce unwanted rainbows, as you're shooting through a plastic window.

Picture sharpness is affected by the depth of field, which increases as the lens aperture decreases (*i.e.*, as you close the lens). Since telephoto lenses have less depth of field than lenses of shorter focal lengths (for a given f/stop setting), you want to close the lens down as much as possible, even if underexposing slightly. If you are using an automatic camera with shutter-priority, choose the slowest acceptable exposure time; at that, you may want to compensate (override) the aperture setting that the camera has selected to achieve sharper detail. If you are using an automatic camera with aperture-priority, look through the view finder and close down the aperture reading as much as possible until the camera has selected an acceptable shutter speed. Once again, you may need to override the Automatic.

If your camera lets you choose between aperture and shutter-priority, select shutter-priority because you know the required minimum shutter speed. Since you want to shoot as fast as possible **and** to close the lens as much as possible, it is an advantage to be shooting fast film, and ASA 400 is recommended (see the section on Film).

LIGHTING

As stated in other sections, the equatorial sun of the Galápagos tends to be harsh, often washing out the beautiful colors. Overcast days will produce more dramatic photographs (the lighting is softer and more diffuse) and should be taken advantage of. You can warm up the bleached midday colors by photographing subjects that are in the shade or by using a polarizing filter (see the section, Recommended Accessories).

Twilight also produces very warm colors. Unfortunately, with the Galápagos being on the equator, "twilight time" is very short; it gets light fast, and it gets dark fast! Still, your best lighting on most days will be early morning and late afternoon, and this is the time when you want to be "on the trail." The problem is that most of your other shipmates may want to be having a second cup of coffee or getting back to the boat for "a cold one." Unless you and your photography-oriented group are chartering the entire boat, your options are limited in this regard. You can select a Photography Tour (see the section on Specialty Tours in CHAPTER IV). If you're on a General Tour, while the captain and Guide do have a daily schedule to adhere to, there is a degree of flexibility based on the makeup and wants of the passengers. Thus, you can use your negotiating and teaching skills to advantage by suggesting to the other passengers that they can get better pictures by starting out earlier, taking a longer *siesta* in the afternoon, and staying on the island later, towards the evening.

Sunset light is often shifted to the orange-red part of the spectrum, often producing dramatic results. Aside from the "obligatory" sunset shots, it's a good time to take some pictures of your fellow passengers, as the coloring adds a warm, flattering glow to skin tones.

TRIPODS

The tripod is a wonderful piece of equipment that I recommend for most situations due to the excellent stability it provides. Even at shutter speeds as fast as 1/1000th of a second, highly magnified prints of shots taken with and without a tripod show a significantly sharper image when a tripod was used. Another good feature of the tripod is that it helps your eye relax and take in the total composition, thus facilitating the necessary adjustments. With hand-held shots, we often tend to see what's in our mind rather than what's in the view finder. The tripod also allows us the time to take detailed light readings and analyze them, enabling us to get the perfect exposure for the situation.

As useful a tool as it is, the tripod is usually (and unfortunately) large, heavy, awkward, and time-consuming to set up. It is my opinion, therefore, that in most cases the tripod is not suitable for use on the Galápagos Islands. Mind you, I said, "in most cases." I can think of beautiful shots of lava texture, the spatter cones on Bartolomé, the geological formations on Sombrero Chino Island that would be greatly enhanced by the use of a tripod. There are even some animal shots (the marine iguana warming up on his favorite rock or a blue-footed booby with a recently-hatched chick) where the tripod would be most beneficial. The problems, as documented earlier, are those of logistics and practicality. It's difficult getting the tripod on-shore, you must set up on the trail, and stay with the Guide.

There are small tripods on the market that would be more practical as far as transportation goes. There are other accessories available such as "chest-pods" and "bean bag" camera supports. But, in general, with these devices you're giving up the most important reason for having a tripod — stability. While not an easy decision, and a question that I've given a lot of thought to, my conclusion is to leave the tripod home. Again, this is a personal decision. There are those who thought I was somewhat impractical for toting a pair of swim fins half way out to nowhere. I decided I needed them, and I brought them.

RECOMMENDED ACCESSORIES

Batteries, Spare — Bring spare batteries for your camera(s). Make sure you get the right type, quantity, and voltage. Several models will take either two 1.55V silver-oxide batteries or a single 3V lithium battery. Consult your camera instruction manual.

Don't forget the spare batteries for your other photographic equipment, such as a spot meter or data back.

Instruction Manual(s) — There's a story about Albert Einstein at a party, where he is found looking over an instruction manual for a piece of equipment. Asked what he was doing, Albert merely replied, "You know how it is; you forget the stuff!" You do, and stuff happens too! So if you do or when it does, you'll need the instruction manual to figure it out. It might be a relatively simple "how-to" situation, such as using the self-timer, or making multiple exposures. A good idea is to make a photocopy of the Manual to take with you, keeping the original safe at home.

Lead Foil Film Bags — If you don't already use them, I recommend that you get a couple of lead foil film bags to protect your film from airport X-ray systems. These film shields typically have a layer of lead foil laminated (or sandwiched) between an outside layer of strong, puncture-resistant polyester and a black, barium-impregnated interior layer. Lead foil bags cost about $20 and are sold at most camera and travel stores.

Even with this level of protection, there is a disclaimer printed on the bag stating that it can keep only so much of the radiation out. Some airports are known to use "super-zapper" equipment, and there's no sure film protection available. The problem is intensified if you are shooting sensitive high-speed film (over ASA 400) and also by (repeated) multiple doses. The best way to deal with this situation is to hand the film (in the lead foil bag) to the Security Inspector as you walk through. Hand the Inspector the camera also, if it is loaded. Within the U.S., the FAA mandates that passengers have the right to hand their film to the Security Inspectors; on the other hand, most of the known "super-zappers" are outside the U.S. Aside from being a minor inconvenience, the procedure works quite well. There are times, though, when I've forgotten to do this (or quite frankly, have been too lazy), and that's when I'm glad that I had the lead foil bags.

Lens Tissues, Cleaner, & Dust Brush — Camera care is a very important detail, very often neglected. It's a matter of consistency and discipline. Your camera is a precision piece of mechanical equipment and a carefully engineered optical system. You will visit a beach every day, and an accumulation of sand will stall that precise machine. Your daily supply of fingerprints on the lens will produce smeared photos despite your superior optics. The first step is to bring lots of lens cleaning tissue, a dust brush, and a plastic bottle of lens cleaning solution.

I usually choose the morning, when I feel fresh, to methodically clean the lenses. I also use this time to pack away the film shot the previous day as well as to sort through the remaining film, transferring a sufficient supply into my camera bag for the day's shooting.

Lens Hood — Lens hoods, as they are called, are perhaps better described as lens shades, as these round extensions (made of metal, plastic, or rubber) shade the lens from stray light, thus helping to prevent lens flare. Without a lens hood attached, the stray light can easily hit the front glass surface, bounce around inside the lens and then strike the film, showing up as a flare.

Each lens should have its own hood, based on the characteristics of the lens (primarily the focal length). If you try putting a long telephoto lens hood over a wide-angle lens, you may cut off the corners in the final product, giving a spyglass effect called vignetting.

Even with the lens hood in place, you still have to guard against lens flare. If your eye can see it, your lens can. Occasionally, you can use your hand to shade the sun from the lens.

Neck Strap — You'll be in a lot of precarious, unstable situations where people are apt to bump into you or a sudden wave could cause you to lose your balance. The last thing in the world you want to do is drop your camera or get it wet. If you don't already have one, you are strongly advised to buy a neck strap and get in the habit of wearing it.

Note Pad — Keep a little note pad and pencil in your camera bag. You think you can remember that the "X" on the film cartridge means to push the development one stop, but you may inadvertently make a similar mark on another cartridge with a completely different meaning. Write it down!

Taking another example, you may decide to experiment with different exposure settings and bracket a series of shots. While it's fresh in your mind, take the time to write down what you're doing. You'll learn from the situation and will be able to make better exposure decisions. Then, when you try to figure out how you got that great shot, you just might be able to. And that, my friends, is a real practical way to acquire a skill.

Plastic Bags — I've advised you to wear the camera around your neck and have it ready to fire when you're riding in the *panga*. But do take every precaution to keep the camera dry. Keep it covered as best you can in a plastic bag. Do this also when you're on-deck. Take a supply of plastic bags with you. They can be used to store film and will come in handy for general purpose use as well (see Chapter VI). In addition, I recommend treating your camera bag with two coats of a water-repellent spray (such as Scotch-gard®) about a week or so before you leave. The same holds true for your daypack.

Polarizing Filter(s) — A polarizing filter is used to selectively reduce or eliminate reflected (polarized) light, often from glass or water, thus allowing one to photograph what is inside a window or under the water (instead of photographing a reflection). In the Galápagos, you will want to use a polarizer when photographing dolphins, marine turtles, white-tipped sharks, rays, and other underwater subjects.

Also, the lighting is often harsh in the islands. Since the light reflected off the subject is less saturated, the use of a polarizer will result in richer, more intense colors. A polarizing filter will also deepen a blue sky (by decreasing the reflections from very small particles in the atmosphere). This also adds contrast between clouds and sky, thus "bringing out" the clouds. You are cautioned, however, about using a polarizer when photographing from an airplane; you may get an unwanted rainbow effect as you shoot through the plastic window.

Polarized light, which causes reflections and glare, vibrates in only one plane (unlike ordinary light waves). A polarizer is a two-piece filter, each with a grid of fine lines, and the external filter can be manually rotated. When both filters have their grids aligned, the polarized light passes through. Then, as the external filter is rotated, the polarized light is increasingly blocked. The maximum blockage occurs when the grids are at right angles to each other. Functionally, with an SLR camera, you don't look at the front of the camera and rotate the external filter 90°; instead, you study the subject through the view finder and rotate the filter until the right amount of glare is removed, the animal can be seen underwater, the color of the sky is darkened, or the color tone of the subject is sufficiently enriched.

When the two filter pieces are aligned, no light is absorbed. Thus, you can use the polarizer as a lens protector, instead of a skylight filter. When the external element is rotated, polarized light is absorbed, thus decreasing the total light that hits the film. You effectively lose about 1-2 f/stops (i.e., the filter factor is 1-2), and with a telephoto lens, you will probably need 400 ASA film (to allow you to shoot at 1/125th to 1/250th of a second and be closed down for sharpness).

You will need a polarizer for each lens diameter. If your lenses are of the same diameter, you may choose to interchange the polarizing filter between lenses.

Scissors — Occasionally a roll of film doesn't have a straight edge (on the leader) and may be thus troublesome to load. A pair of scissors, kept at the ready in the camera bag, will quickly solve this problem. You will surely find some other applications for this useful tool.

Skylight Filter(s) — A skylight filter is primarily used as a lens protector and is typically left on the lens at all times. Thus, you should have one for each lens. A skylight filter also cuts out haze (to reveal more detail) and removes the bluish cast of color shots taken at a great distance (from an airplane, for example).

Unlike most filters, a skylight filter does not reduce the amount of light entering the camera; it therefore does not affect the exposure value.

ACCESSORIES TO CONSIDER

Data Back — An accessory that I have found very functional is the data back, an add-on piece of equipment available for several quality cameras. Basically, a data back replaces the standard "back" of the camera and imprints user-selectable data onto the film, on any and every shot that you choose, for the purpose of keeping lasting records. The data can be the date, time of day, shot number, etc. The NIKON® model that I use displays the user's choice of either Year/Month/Day, Day/Hour/Minute, or Frame Number. This information can be imprinted on the film as described above. The Frame Number can actually be any numbering system you have in mind; it will automatically sequence the number (each time the shutter is released) from -2 up to 2000. The unit that I have also has an alarm clock function. I've never used this feature, but I suppose you could set it to remind yourself that at 10:30 a.m., it's time to put the polarizer on, etc.

The imprinting is done by a six-digit LED (see Photo #31), the intensity of which is automatically adjusted (based on the film speed, which you manually enter). Once again, what the data back does is to give you a permanent record of each roll of film, allowing you to figure out months or years later which roll is which. Here's how I use it:

At the beginning of each roll, before I release the shutter 2-3 times (to advance the film to the zero point), I turn the print button to the "ON" position, allowing the data to appear on the film. I make sure that the lens cap is securely on before pressing the shutter. The result is a black background with the data neatly imprinted in the lower right hand corner. The data that I typically choose to imprint in the Galápagos, where I'm shooting several rolls per day, is Year/Month/Day on the first shot followed by Day/Hour/Minute on the second shot. I then turn the print button to the "OFF" position, so that the data doesn't appear on the "real shots."

Bring along spare batteries for the data back.

Film Extractor — This inexpensive gadget that looks like a pair of tweezers will reclaim a roll of film (by extracting the film leader) that has accidentally been rewound back into the cartridge.

Masking Tape — I find masking tape useful to label film canisters, plastic bags, and camera equipment. It's very easy to write on and can be easily removed if necessary (unless it has seen a lot of sunlight).

Neutral Density Filter(s) — There may be times when you actually have too much light coming into the camera. This may happen on Bartolomé Island; after your climb to the top, you may want to put a wide-angle lens on the camera to get a great panoramic view of the islands (see Photo #30). The problem is that you're still shooting ASA 400 film, and even with the wide-angle lens closed down and set at maximum speed, the light meter reads "overexposed." A neutral density filter, which basically cuts down the amount of light entering the camera, can solve this problem. These filters are not color-selective and can be used in series to achieve the results.

Spot Meter — The camera's built-in light meter works on a weighted average system. It takes an overall reading of the ambient light, and it also takes a reading of the central zone (usually a circled area located at the center of the view finder). It then calculates the exposure, giving importance (or weight) to the central area. This helps to somewhat negate the bright background when you're trying to get detailed definition in your subject. To cite an example, a center-weighted system, when used properly, will let the sky "go white" and fill in facial detail in the subject (rather than getting a blue sky at the expense of an underexposed face).

The center-weighted system can only do so much, however. Your subject may not be in the center of the picture, or the contrast may be so great that the weighted-average is still not correct in terms of the detail you want. This is where a spot meter can help.

A spot meter is just that; it's a hand-held light meter that selectively meters a very small angle of view (or spot). In the PENTAX® model that I use, the angle of view is 1° (with a total view angle of 26°) which provides accuracy even from a distance. If you want facial detail, you aim the little spot meter (about the size of a water pistol) at the subject's face. The reading you get will orient (or center) the exposure around the facial features. You can then take a couple of other spot readings (of other areas of the picture) to determine how much variation there is. You then weigh these numbers and make a decision regarding the exposure value. If the overall contrast is too high, you either don't take the shot, fill with flash, or decide where to give up the detail.

Typically, the alternative to a spot meter is to walk up to the subject, aim the camera at the face, and take a reading. Based on this reading, you manually adjust the exposure or, if available, use the camera's memory exposure system to enter the reading. You then go back to the original location and take the shot. Again, the potential problem here is that you're not allowed off the trail; you could use a zoom lens to do the "walking," however, zooming in and then back.

Reinforcing some of my earlier statements, you don't have time to be taking detailed readings and calculating average exposures on every shot. You do have a couple of minutes on each island to get an overall feel for the situation. What I usually try to do is compare the spot meter reading with that of the camera. If I think that there's a bias in the camera's reading, I'll change the exposure settings if I'm in Manual, or adjust the Exposure Compensation Dial if I'm in Automatic.

As usual, bring spare batteries.

UNDERWATER PHOTOGRAPHY

You will get many underwater photo opportunities in the Galápagos, and the investment in an underwater camera is highly recommended. Believe me, the first time you spot a sea lion through your snorkel mask about 3 ft in front of you, you will appreciate the true value of that little yellow camera. Regarding the selection of an underwater camera, I have mixed feelings (as described in the following section).

LITTLE YELLOW CAMERAS

There are several brands of underwater automatic cameras in the $200-$300 range that are good pieces of equipment. They are sealed against sand and dust so you can use them on the beach. You can also take them skiing, down the rapids, and into the pool. Typically, they can be used down to a depth of 15 ft, which is about all you need for snorkeling. They generally have all the automatic camera features, including autofocus, motor-driven film advance, autorewind, automatic exposure, built-in flash, etc.

You can use these cameras on land as well as in and under the water. In fact, the autofocus feature typically only works above water; underwater, they are fixed focus cameras. The MINOLTA® model that I use has an underwater focus range of 4-12 ft, with a close-up button that sets the focus from 1.4-4.3 ft. My camera is also a dual-lens type; pressing a button will switch between a standard underwater (35mm) and mild telephoto (50mm) lens. As you can tell by these numbers, underwater optics are different.

The problem with these cameras, at least underwater, is that you don't have the same control over the light, and therefore the quality of the end product, as you do on land with a full-function 35mm SLR. Thus, what you wind up with are underwater snapshots. It is definitely much better than not having an underwater camera at all, just to be able to document a sea lion coming straight at you! But many of us are used to a certain level of accomplishment with the camera, and I've not been able to get that kind of quality with the automatic underwater cameras. Put it this way, none of the underwater shots that I've taken are hanging on my walls.

PROFESSIONAL UNDERWATER CAMERAS

For top quality underwater shots, we are left with the option of going all the way with a complete underwater photographic system, starting with a NIKONOS V® camera. It has through-the-lens metering capability with aperture-priority Automatic and Manual operation, interchangeable lenses, full focusing control, and is rated to a depth of 160 ft. The NIKONOS V® does have its limitations in that it is a bit inconvenient to use. The viewfinder does not see through the camera's lens, and a potential parallax problem is created; you have no way of "seeing" if you're in focus. There is a focus range indicator on the front of the lens along with the f/stop indicator (not exactly a convenient location). The biggest limitation, though, is that it has a NIKON® price — about $500 with the standard 35mm lens. And that's just the beginning! If you want to get into wide-angle underwater photography, good quality 24mm and 15mm lenses can cost around $1000 each.

Then there's the cost of the strobe system. The Galápagos waters are, for the most part, murky (due to the upwelling activity and the resulting plankton formation). A strobe light (a fancy word for a remote flash unit) is required for professional quality shots. Cameras with built-in flash tend to light up suspended particles in the water, creating back-scatter, which a strobe unit mounted (or held) away from the camera helps eliminate. A good strobe (such as the IKILITE® units) provide 500 flashes with relatively fast 5 second recycle times.

There are various size underwater strobes available, varying in both power and angle of coverage (narrow to wide-angle) depending on the kind of shooting you will be doing. A standard strobe unit with through-the-lens metering circuitry (synchronized with the camera) is about $400 including bracket and flash bar. Another cost adder is a strobe unit with a built-in aiming light. What happens is that when you aim the strobe unit at the subject, you're aiming at where you see the subject, not where it really is (due to the angle of refraction). The better aiming lights are built-in to the strobe unit; this assures that the strobe will fire where you want it to. Some of the lesser quality aiming lights are located under the strobe unit, and you wind up having to make adjustments — which is what you're trying to avoid by using an aiming light. At any rate, the strobes with the built-in aiming lights can cost around $800.

The bottom line is expensive; it can cost $1000-$1500 to get started with a reasonable quality underwater camera to get the same kind of results beneath the surface as you do topside. If you're not ready to shell out that kind of money, the little yellow cameras will certainly document your subtidal encounters. You will have to be patient and take your shots only in very clear, sunlit waters, which tend to occur in small isolated pockets. It's not at all like shooting in the Florida Keys or the Grand Cayman Islands where the visibility is crystal clear.

If neither of the above alternatives to underwater photography appeals to you, there is another option. KODAK® has a disposable underwater camera on the market called the WEEKEND 35®. This camera, which sells for about $15, is preloaded with a 24 exposure roll of ASA 400 print film, has a plastic housing and is rated for underwater use to a depth of 12 ft.

PHOTOGRAPHY CHECK LIST

Use this list in conjunction with the Packing Check List at the end of Chapter VI, PREPARE FOR DEPARTURE.

ITEM	NOTES
☐ Camera Batteries, spare	
☐ Film	
☐ Film Extractor	
☐ Instruction Manual(s)	
☐ Lead Foil Film Bag(s)	
☐ Lens Cleaner/Tissue/ Dust Brush	
☐ Lenses/Caps/Hoods	
☐ Light Meter/Spot Meter/ Batteries	
☐ Masking Tape	
☐ Neck Strap	
☐ Neutral Density Filter(s)	
☐ Note Pad	
☐ Plastic Bags	
☐ Polarizing Filter(s)	
☐ Scissors	
☐ Skylight Filter(s)	
☐ Underwater Camera/ Equipment	

CHAPTER VIII

WELCOME TO ECUADOR

From the standpoint of this book, mainland Ecuador is a base camp, a point of departure to (and return from) the Galápagos Islands. In addition, some of you will use the stay in Quito or Guayaquil to put together your tour of the islands. On the return trip, Quito becomes a city of shopping opportunity, a source of gifts for your friends and family as well as for yourself. While this may sound a bit cold and calculated, it's meant to be. The purposes of this book are to get you to go to the Galápagos Islands, to make you aware of all the touring possibilities, to get you there in an efficient manner, and to keep you there for as long as your vacation time allows. Being a travel guide to Ecuador is not one of these purposes. There are other books that do an excellent job of this (see the Literature section).

As the saying goes, something's got to give. And what's giving, if you accept the guidance offered here, is an extensive tour of Ecuador. For now anyway. If you like, consider this brief encounter to be a scouting mission for your next visit to Ecuador. I suspect that once you see the snow-capped peaks of the Andes and the beautiful city of Quito, you may well want to return for an extensive stay. At that time you can tour the Amazon jungles and visit the Andean highlands, travelling the length of the "Valley of the Volcanoes." But for now you're passing through. Maybe with enough time to catch a peak or two (as the saying sort of goes), especially in and around the Quito area. Many of you on a Galápagos group tour may be provided with the opportunity of several Day Trips. With this orientation, then, let's take a brief look at Ecuador.

ABOUT ECUADOR

Ecuador is located on the west coast of South America and, as its name suggests, on the equator. Its neighbors are Columbia to the north and Peru to the east & south. The country has a population of about 10 million people and is a constitutional republic with an elected president and a House of Representatives. Ecuador consists of 21 provinces, including the Galápagos Islands, and is the second smallest Latin American country in South America (Uruguay is the smallest); the Guianas (Guyana, Suriname, and French Guyana), while smaller, are not considered to be part of Latin America.

Ecuador is divided into three geographic regions, more like three different worlds. First there is *La Sierra*, framed by the majestic Andes, with volcanic peaks as high as 20,000 ft. Running the length of Ecuador from Columbia to Peru, two Andean ranges are separated by the 25-40 mile wide Central Valley (termed the "Avenue of the Volcanoes") in which Quito is situated. To the west of the Andes is *La Costa* or coastal region, where Guayaquil is located; this is mostly lowland and Ecuador's main agricultural export area. To the east is *El Oriente*, the upper Amazon region with its tropical rain forests.

Until substantial oil discoveries were made in the 1970s (in the northern *Oriente* region, close to the Columbian border), Ecuador was a typical "banana republic." In fact, Ecuador is still the world's largest exporter of bananas. Coffee, though low yielding, is the most extensive of Ecuador's cash crops, accounting for about 20 percent of the total agricultural land. Other agricultural exports include sugar, cocoa, rice, cattle, and (yes) shrimp farming. Ecuador is also the world's leading producer of balsa wood. While employing about a third of the labor force, agriculture foreign exchange earnings fell to about 15 percent of Ecuador's total as petroleum exports rose to first place. By the 1980s, oil accounted for about half of the country's export earnings. Fishing and tourism are also growing industries.

With all that, Ecuador remains a Third World country with serious economic problems. With the big drop in oil prices in the mid-1980s, Ecuador's national income was greatly reduced (by about 50 percent). To make matters worse, in 1983 an extreme *El Niño* (a weather phenomenon associated with warming of the normally cool ocean waters) caused severe flooding of agricultural lands and completely disrupted the fishing industry. And then in 1987 a major earthquake hit Ecuador, causing great damage and loss of life. Over 30 miles of the nation's Trans-Andean oil pipeline were destroyed, and oil exports came to a standstill for almost 6 months. As a result, the economy is in a weakened condition, with considerable debt and a currency that has seen significant devaluation.

In terms of politics, Ecuador is relatively stable despite occasional shows of force by the opposing conservative and liberal factions as well as by the military. The tranquil setting seems to dominate the spirit of the people and in turn has kept Ecuador from the turmoil of other South American countries.

It wasn't always that way. As part of the Inca empire, Ecuador was not spared by the Spanish conquistadors, and fell in 1535 to the armored, cannon-firing forces of Francisco Pizarro. Ecuador then became a Spanish colony, and remained so until 1820 when the great liberator, Simón Bolívar, led the successful battle for independence which was fully achieved in 1830. Ecuador went to war with Peru in 1941, the result of which was a new border line between the neighboring countries, a boundary still in dispute as this book is being written.

Through it all, an air of dignity has prevailed, a characteristic that best describes the Ecuadorians themselves, proud descendants of Indian and Spanish cultures. About 40 percent of the population are native Indians, progeny of the Inca empire, living mostly in the highlands of the *Sierra*. An equal number are *mestizo* (mixed Indian and Spanish); about 10 percent are European with the balance of the population made up of Africans and Asians. The *Sierra* and *Costa* regions each have about half of Ecuador's total population, with the sparse remainder (less than 500,000) living in the rain forests of *El Oriente*, where development is slowly beginning.

The blend of Indian and Spanish cultures is also evident in the tradition of artistic achievement and expert craftsmanship. Made with skills handed down from Inca forefathers, today's Indian art ranges from intricately-woven tapestries, leatherwork, and hat-making to handsome wood carvings, ceramics, and finely-detailed jewelry. The dress of the Indians is an art form in itself, with the women wearing beautifully embroidered blouses and ornately-colored head cloths.

When the Spaniards departed, they left behind a vast collection of colonial art (mostly sculptures and paintings) and a legacy of religious architecture — superb churches and cathedrals with their golden altars, colored columns, gilded balconies, and richly sculptured facades.

And that is a very brief look at Ecuador. Fasten your seat belts and get ready for a real look, with your own eyes.

ARRIVAL IN ECUADOR

Whether you arrive in Quito or Guayaquil, your first goal is to get out of the airport, into a taxi or tour van, and be on the way towards your hotel. First however you will have to go through the Passport Control area, where, in addition to your passport, you must present the T3 Tourist Information Card that you filled out on the airplane. You may also be asked for your return airline ticket. If asked your purpose for being in Ecuador, respond that you are on vacation, and that you will be visiting the Galápagos Islands. You will also be asked how long you intend to stay in Ecuador. Respond with the actual length of your stay. U.S. and Canadian citizens touring Ecuador are allowed a visit for up to 90 days without a visa. A part of the T3 card will be returned to you, stapled to your passport. Do not throw this portion of the card away; it states the legal duration of your visit (they usually write in 30 days), and will be required by any Ecuadorian official checking your passport as well as by the Passport Control Officer when you leave the country.

Note: If it turns out that you will be spending more time in Ecuador than allotted by the Immigration Officer, you will have to visit the Immigration Department in either Quito or Guayaquil and get an extension stamped on your passport and T3 card. The process is easy, but the wait is not very pleasant. You are advised to let the Tour Operator you are working with or your Tour Leader take care of this detail on your behalf. They do this kind of thing all the time and know their way around Immigrations pretty well.

During your visit, when asked where you are from, always respond, "The United States," or "The U.S." It's better than saying you're from "America" because South Americans are "Americans" too!

By the way, don't try to impress the Immigration Officer by saying that you're there on business; you may be detained, because businessmen require a business visa. While we're on the subject of being detained, it just about goes without saying that you don't want to bring anything illegal into Ecuador. We all know about the reputation of South American prisons. End of subject.

After Passport Control, you'll go to the Baggage Claim area to gather up your checked baggage and then proceed to Customs. Remember, each person is allowed to bring in, duty-free, one bottle of liquor, 300 cigarettes as well as a "reasonable" quantity of perfume and gifts. All of your bags will usually be inspected, quickly, neatly and thoroughly! Waiting in line, you will see some of the largest suitcases ever made.

As you leave the Customs area, you will sometimes be met by a virtual wave of humanity — a greeting committee waiting for their friends, family, and loved ones to exit the hallowed gates of Customs. They all look happy, very excited, with lots of waving and yelling. The first time I went through this, I didn't exactly know what was going on. Images came to mind of visiting team outfielders staring up at the bleachers of Fenway Park or Wrigley Field.

At the fringes of this congregation you will find a currency exchange window called a *cambio* (see the section below on Currency) where you should exchange up to U.S.$100 so you can leave tips, pay for a taxi to the hotel, and mostly to have some pocket money. After the currency is exchanged, give the person behind the counter a 5000 sucre bill and request, "small bills, please" (*billetes pequenos, por favor*). If you're part of a group tour, a van will take you to the hotel, and you can exchange money a bit later if you like.

TAXIS

Next come the porters and taxis, both official and unofficial. The official porters wear uniforms; the unofficial ones are mostly kids. It doesn't really matter; they'll all do a good job carrying your bags to a taxi. The job is worth about 1000 sucres per full-size bag. If you haven't changed money, you can leave 50 cents per bag. U.S. currency is always welcome and actually preferred in Ecuador where the sucre is constantly being devalued.

Make sure you get a yellow taxi. They are official; the black ones are not. A cab ride from the Quito airport to your downtown hotel will cost no more than 5000 sucres with the meter off (about U.S. $3.00, depending on the exchange rate), and a bit less with the meter on. From Guayaquil, the unmetered fare is about 7000 sucres (about U.S $4.00). No tips. The unofficial cabs can cost twice as much.

Agree on the fare in advance. If you're not up to trying this in Spanish, just say, "Hotel Colón (or the name of your hotel), *por favor* (please)." Keep a firm grip on your bags, because the driver will begin to put them into the taxi. Before the bags go in, agree on the price. Ask him how much, "*¿quantos?*" Chances are he will answer in English, and the price will be within the above-specified limits. He may point to the meter in which case everything is fine. If the driver answers in Spanish and you're not sure what he said, hand him a pen and piece of paper and once again say, "*por favor.*" He'll understand. If the amount he writes is too much, write the amount you want to pay. You shouldn't have any problem.

You will find taxis to be a convenient, inexpensive way to travel in Quito and Guayaquil. Many of the hotels have a list of estimated fares to various locations. Negotiate the fare in advance if you don't see a meter with the fare numbers lit up.

CAR RENTALS

Renting a car in Ecuador is generally not necessary, nor is it recommended. The condition of many of the cars is suspect, and traffic can be congested in the business districts. Outside the cities, the roads are often unpaved, there is a lack of road signs, and trucks and buses are wild and loose. There are several reports of blown tires in remote locations, not a very comforting thought. Besides, taxis are cheap enough, and there are many organized tours of Quito and Guayaquil as well as excursions to the outlying areas.

If you insist on renting a car, do so at the airport where HERTZ®, INTER-NATIONAL®, AVIS®, BUDGET® and others have cars for about U.S. $50 (including mandatory insurance and tax) per day with unlimited mileage. The steering wheel is on the left (just like home).

CURRENCY

The monetary unit of Ecuador is the sucre. While money may be sweet, that's not the origin of the sucre. During the battle for Ecuadorian independence from Spain, it was General Antonio José de Sucre, who defeated the Spanish at the decisive Battle of Pichincha (the mountain that dominates the view from Quito) and became a national hero.

The sucre (often written as S/) has undergone a severe devaluation in recent years, due to the downturn in Ecuador's economy (primarily related to the drop in oil prices). For you, that's good news, in that your dollars are strong — very strong in fact. This will be evident to you in restaurants, hotels, clothing stores, and gift shops. The exchange rate in 1993 was about 1800 sucres per dollar (compared to about 650 sucres early in 1990), with a 10 sucre daily variation. There are bills of 10,000, 5000, 1000, 500, 50, 20, 10, and 5 sucres. There are also 50 and 20 sucre coins. When you consider that a sucre is currently worth a fraction of a penny, and that the sucre itself, until just recently, was divided into 100 centavos (with 50, 20, 10 and 5 centavo coins), you have an insight into the extent of the Ecuadorian currency devaluation.

There are several money exchange houses (*casas de cambio*) in Quito and Guayaquil. You will find them more accessible and convenient to use than banks in that there is rarely a line. The banks, on the other hand, are usually crowded, and they are not really set up for this function. *Cambios* and banks are open 9:00 a.m. to 1:30 p.m., Monday through Friday. Your passport will be required as proof of identification if exchanging traveler's checks.

Most banks and *cambios* will offer about the same exchange rates. So will the *cambio* in your hotel. A difference of 5 sucres in the exchange rate is a difference of only about a penny; on an exchange transaction of $500, this adds up to about $5.00. While we all want the best exchange rate, I don't recommend giving up valuable vacation time to get a little better exchange rate, especially if your time in mainland Ecuador is short, and there's shopping to be done and sights to be seen. Also, you'll get about the same exchange rate for cash dollars and traveler's checks.

The exchange rates in mainland Ecuador are much better than you will get at the U.S. departure airport, where you still may want to exchange about U.S.$50 for instant pocket money.

You will get a better exchange rate in Quito and Guayaquil than in the Galápagos. There are no official *cambios* in the islands, although a number of shops have *cambio* signs in their window and the current exchange rate that they offer. They are providing this service to earn a little extra money. Very few will exchange traveler's checks, the Bodega Blanca (located next to the Hotel Galápagos) being the most notable.

Try to estimate out-of-pocket expenses on the last couple of days in Ecuador so you can use up most of your sucres and won't have to exchange them back to U.S. dollars.

LOCAL TIME

Mainland Ecuador is on Eastern Standard Time. The flight from Miami is almost due south. Since Ecuador is, logically enough, on the equator, there is an equal amount of night and day throughout the year. There is no need for, and therefore, no Daylight Saving Time. The Galápagos Islands, 600 miles west of the Ecuadorian mainland, are on Central (Chicago) Standard Time, year-round.

BUSINESS HOURS

Stores are generally open Monday through Saturday from 9:00 a.m. to 1:00 p.m. and from 3:00 p.m. to 7:00 p.m., with a mid-day *siesta* in between. Some of the tourist-oriented gift shops do not close for *siesta*. This is also true of the growing number of shopping centers. Some stores may only be open Monday through Friday, and others remain open for half a day on Saturday. If you find a shop that you like and plan on going back to buy more items or to "finalize" an expensive purchase, verify their business hours.

LANGUAGE

One way or another, you'll have to come to terms with Spanish. To be honest, in the tourist-oriented circle in which you will travel, you can get by completely without a single word of Spanish. It would be somewhat rude, though, not to make an attempt to learn at least the basic greetings. Besides, it's fun and part of the total travel experience. It can also be very practical! Being able to read a menu, even with a dictionary at the table, certainly has its advantages. So does asking the maid for an extra pillow (without having to phone the main desk) and finding out if a store has a larger sweater of the same color, etc. It's also nice to be able to ask directions (and find out how to get to the store in the first place).

Take a phrase book and dictionary with you; I recommend Barron's **SPANISH AT A GLANCE: PHRASE BOOK & DICTIONARY FOR TRAVELERS** (see the Literature section). There are enough word similarities between English and Spanish that you'll soon be putting sentences together. Do the best you can; the Ecuadorians will know you're trying and appreciate the effort.

In the Galápagos, many of you will find that learning the names of the animals in Spanish to be as interesting as learning about the animals themselves. Some of my favorites are sea lions (*lobos marinos*, or sea wolves), the dove (*paloma*), heron (*garza*), turtle (*tortuga*), penguin (*pingüino*), and blue-footed booby (*piquero patas azules*). The word *Galápagos* itself is the Spanish name for the giant tortoise.

Incidentally, Ecuador has two official languages — Spanish and Quechua (spoken by the majority of the native Indians). Several other indigenous languages are also spoken, although not to a great extent.

TIPPING

A 20 percent surcharge is added to your hotel bill to cover tax (10 percent) and gratuities (10 percent). This includes meals at the hotel restaurant. Restaurants outside the hotel add a 10 percent service charge. Thus, leaving an additional 5 percent tip at a restaurant is customary. For a porter at the airport, a 1000 sucre tip per full-size piece of luggage is adequate. While you're not required to tip the porters at the hotel, you'll probably feel better by handing the porter about 1000 sucres; remember, this is just over 50 cents!

ELECTRICITY

The electric power in mainland Ecuador and the Galápagos Islands is 110 VAC, 60 cycles (the same as in the U.S. and Canada).

TELEPHONE

Ecuador has upgraded its local and international telephone service over the last few years. Calling and sending a FAX to and from Ecuador is a lot smoother than it was 3 years ago. Keep in mind though that it does cost about 4 times more to place a call or send a FAX from Ecuador to the U.S. than it does for us to call or FAX Ecuador from the U.S.; the differential is even more, of course, if your call or FAX is charged to your hotel room.

When calling or sending a FAX to Ecuador from the U.S., you must first dial the international access code "011" followed by the country code for Ecuador ("593"), the city code for Quito ("2") or Guayaquil ("4"), and then the local number. To place a call or send a FAX from Ecuador to the U.S., dial the international access code to the U.S. ("001") followed by the area code and local number. If you want to charge the call to your telephone "calling card," or place a collect call, you can quickly access a U.S. operator by dialing "119." This last system has been recently introduced and seems to work very well.

If you place an international call, remember that mainland Ecuador is on Eastern Standard time throughout the year.

When calling Guayaquil from Quito, dial "04" followed by the local number. When calling Quito from Guayaquil, dial "02" followed by the local number.

TOURIST INFORMATION

Once you arrive in Ecuador, there is an excellent guidebook available called **THIS IS ECUADOR**. This booklet is published monthly and is available at all the major hotels and travel agencies. It contains handy maps, a calendar of events, useful sightseeing information, and advertisements of interest for restaurants, gift shops, Tour Operators, etc. There is also a listing of many useful phone numbers that is more current than those found in the telephone directories.

The Ecuadorian government operates a National Tourist Board called *CETUR (Corporación Ecuatoriana de Turismo)*. There is at least one *CETUR* office in all the major cities and towns (including one in Puerto Ayora on Santa Cruz Island in the Galápagos). They have several brochures and maps, and can help you find a specific location, store, etc. *CETUR* (formerly *DITURIS*) will also tell you where the important museums and key points of interest are located. They generally have an English-speaking person working at each office.

While *CETUR* is a good source of general information, don't depend on them to help you put together a tour of the Galápagos. That is not their function. The best they can do is tell you where the Tour Operators are located. If you run into a problem regarding a price negotiation, the quality of a product or service, or a refund not received, it would be worth going there in a peaceful attempt to settle the matter. I've heard that *CETUR* will occasionally intervene in this type of situation. Also, if they receive a number of complaints about a particular company or organization, they may take action.

Also, the Department of Ecuador Tourism has a U.S. office, and you may want to send away for some literature. Their address is P.O. Box 526532, Miami, FL 33152-6532. TOLL FREE: (800) 553-6673; FAX: 305-577-0531.

QUITO

Quito, the capital of Ecuador is a quiet, beautiful city (see Photo #1). Flanked by the tall, snow-capped peaks of the Andes, Quito itself is at 9300 ft, yet located almost directly on the equator. On a clear day, as they say, you can see the snow cones of the volcanic peaks, giving the city an air of a mountain retreat. Based on your expectations of a bustling South American city, the serenity and the dramatic setting takes you by pleasant surprise. While the population of Quito is over a million people, making it the second largest city in Ecuador (Guayaquil is the largest), it has a tranquil small town feel to it (the rush hour and center-city traffic notwithstanding). The people, the city, and the setting seem to blend together, all part of the rich artistic and cultural heritage.

Here at the foot of 15,700 Mt. Pichincha, an active volcano, you are in the Andean highlands in what was once an Inca city. When the approaching conquistadors finally fought their way here in 1534, they found Quito in ruins. The Incas chose to destroy their city rather than surrender it. So the city was rebuilt in the grand colonial style architecture described at the beginning of this chapter. This legacy was formally recognized by *UNESCO* in 1978, proclaiming Quito a "Cultural Patrimony of Mankind," and sanctions were passed to preserve the character and architectural integrity of what is called Old Town.

Old Town is located in the central section of Quito, called *el centro* (I told you Spanish was easy). The modern business and main shopping district is in the north. This is also where the finer hotels are located.

THE AIRPORT

Mariscal Sucre International Airport is located on Av. de la Prensa, 6 miles north of the business, shopping, and major hotel district. This is an older airport (compared to the modern facility in Guayaquil) that tends to be somewhat crowded, especially the section for domestic flights; the international terminal is relatively tranquil.

Note: There is a $25 Departure Tax on international flights, payable in sucres or U.S. dollars.

TOURIST INFORMATION

There are three *CETUR* offices in Quito at the following locations:

Main Office: Reina Victoria 514 and Roca. **Local Phone:** 527-002 or 522-387 or 527-074

Municipal Palace (*Palacio Municipal*) Office: In the Old Town district, located in the Municipal Palace (City Hall) on the southeast side of Plaza Independencia. **Local Phone:** 514-004

Airport Office: Mariscal Sucre Airport, in the arrival hall of the international terminal. They don't seem to be open all that often. **Local Phone:** 246-232

CLIMATE

The combination of the equatorial and mountain setting give Quito an ideal climate of pleasant, warm days (in the 70s Deg F) and brisk, cool evenings, with temperatures in the 50s Deg F. The rainy season is from October to May, with frequent afternoon and/or evening showers. The heaviest rainfall is typically in April.

HOTELS

There are several First Class hotels in Quito at extremely reasonable rates. While Quito does have a complete selection of accommodations, including $2 hostels and pensions as well as $10-$15 clean, budget-style hotels, my recommendation is to stay with the best. And why not? For about $85, you can have a spacious, elegantly-furnished double room at most of the finer hotels in Quito. Generally, they have excellent restaurants serving international cuisine as well as Ecuadorian specialties. There are also shopping arcades, lounges, and meeting rooms; some have casinos. These hotels are all centrally located, close to the finer gift shops, restaurants, *cambios*, and museums. From a security standpoint, they are your best choices. Finally, the staff speaks excellent English and will be able to help you with directions, confirming flights, etc.

By the way, the casinos are an experience. The slot machines take 25 sucre tokens (about 5 cents) and they seem to be programmed to pay off more often than the ones in the U.S. You don't really win much, but you don't seem to lose money either. You just keep playing . . . and playing. Finally, you're at the point where you want to lose, so you can go upstairs and get some sleep! There's also blackjack, *chemin de fer*, and roulette for the serious gambling types. I would suspect that playing these games of chance, you can get to go upstairs a lot faster.

Now, some special advice for those who are arriving in Quito without having booked a tour to the Galápagos. Make reservations at one of the finer hotels for 2 nights. By the second day, you'll have a good idea on the progress you're making with the Ecuadorian Tour Operators. If you think that you'll be staying on in Quito for a few days more, you may choose to switch to a lower price hotel. The following list contains some of the best hotels in the Tourist Class category. They all have clean, well-furnished rooms with a private bath, and they're in the same modern section of town as the premium hotels. Laundry service is provided, and the rooms have a telephone, refrigerator, and color TV with cable broadcasts from the U.S. These Tourist Class choices are also for those on a budget and for the traveler that doesn't especially care for fancy hotels with casinos and all the other glitz.

Note: The sink and shower faucets at some of the hotels are marked differently than you're used to, which could be cause for confusion as well as a potential problem. The left (hot) faucet is marked "C" for *Caliente*; the right (cold) faucet is marked "F" for *Frío*.

Many of the hotels provide bottles of mineral water in each room for drinking and rinsing when brushing your teeth.

All phone numbers are local. The FAX numbers listed below include the international, country, and city codes.

Here then are the recommended hotels of Quito and their affiliated U.S. Reservation Service(s). Add 20% to all prices for tax and service.

First Class Hotels:

HOTEL ALAMEDA REAL — Roca 653 and Av. Amazonas (P.O. Box 358-A).
Local Phone: 554-100 or 562-345   **FAX:** 011-593-2-565-759
Rooms: Rooms are very nicely furnished; all have refrigerators. For $5-$15 extra, you can get suites with living rooms, kitchenettes, etc. Room service is available 24 hours a day.
Price Range: Single — U.S.$70;   Double — U.S.$80;   Triple — U.S.$90.
Comments: I recommend the Alameda Real very highly. It is said that, of the finer hotels, they have the most personal service. The comments I hear time and again are, "I have stayed at all of the best hotels in Quito, and the staff at the Alameda Real get to know you real fast. You're treated more as an individual rather than as a number." My experiences strongly support this impression.
U.S. Reservation Services: Latin American Reservation Center (LARC), TOLL FREE: (800) 327-3573 Nationwide; FAX: 813-439-2118; **Steigenberger Reservation Service** (SRS), TOLL FREE (800) 223-5652 U.S. & Canada; FAX: 407-679-3361.

HOTEL COLON INTERNACIONAL — Av. Amazonas and Patria.
Local Phone: 560-666 or 561-333 or 562-888   **FAX:** 011-593-2-563-903
Rooms: All rooms are finely furnished; the higher-priced suites are exceptional.
Price Range: Single — U.S.$105; Double — U.S.$120; Triple — U.S.$135.
Comments: You would have to describe the Hotel Colón as the best hotel in town. It has very good restaurants, a nice disco, an excellent mall consisting of several very fine stores, fourteen convention and meeting rooms, an exercise facility with sauna and jacuzzi, and a large casino.
U.S. Reservation Services: Utell International (UI), TOLL FREE: (800) 223-9868, Nationwide.

HOTEL QUITO — González Suárez 2500 at Av. 12 de Octubre (P.O. Box 2201).
Local Phone: Switchboard, 230-300 or 544-60O; Reservations, 543-631   **FAX:** 011-593-2-567-284
Rooms: Refurbished — great views.
Price Range: Single — U.S.$80;   Double — U.S.$90;   Triple — U.S.$100.

Comments: If you want a room with a view, this is the place. The Hotel Quito is located on a hilltop just a few blocks from the central business and shopping district. The top floor restaurant and lounge, El Techo del Mundo (Roof of the World), provides a truly special panoramic vista of the city and surrounding peaks in addition to good food at a reasonable price. Being a bit removed from the heart of the city, there are no street sounds. With the beautiful gardens, it is a very peaceful location. Other features include a full-size outdoor pool, tennis courts, casino, and night club.

U.S. Reservation Services: Best Western Hotels (BW), TOLL FREE: (800) 222-2378 Nationwide, ask for the international desk, **Utell International** (UI), TOLL FREE: (800) 223-9868, Nationwide.

HOTEL ORO VERDE QUITO — Av. 12 de Octubre 1820 and Cordero
Local Phone: 566-497 or 568-128   **FAX:** 011-593-2-569-189 or 569-106
Rooms: All rooms in the 14 story complex have a safe deposit box, mini-bar, and are provided with 24 hour room service. Suites have a separate reception area and valet service.
Price Range: Single — U.S.$140;   Double — U.S.$170;   Suites — U.S.$200-$300.
Comments: Opened in Quito during the summer of 1990, the Oro Verde follows in the tradition of First Class hotel service it has established during many years of operation in Guayaquil. Amenities include a shopping mall, baby-sitting services, a heated swimming pool, fitness center including racquetball, and a full casino.
U.S. Reservation Services: The Leading Hotels of the World (LHW). TOLL FREE: (800) 223-6800 U.S. & Canada.

Tourist Class Hotels:

HOSTAL LOS ALPES — Tamayo 233 and Jorge Washington.
Local Phone: 561-110 or 561-128   **FAX:** N/A
Price Range: Single — U.S.$32; Double — U.S.$42.
Comments: Charming throughout and nicely decorated. The best of the Tourist Class hotels that I have visited. The name is appropriate because it does have a rustic Swiss Inn feel to it. The warm personality of the general manager, Claudio Facchinei, adds to the special flavor.

HOTEL AMARANTA INTERNACIONAL — Leonidas Plaza 194 and Jorge Washington (P.O. Box 4967).
Local Phone: 560-585 or 543-619   **FAX:** 011-593-2-560-586
Price Range: Single — U.S.$28; Double — U.S.$43;
    Apartments (for up to 8) — U.S.$115
Comments: All rooms are suites with kitchenettes.

HOTEL CHALET SUISSE — Reina Victoria and Calama (P.O. Box 17-07-8703).
Local Phone: 562-700   **FAX:** 011-593-2-563-966
Price Range: Single — U.S.$50;   Double — U.S.$60.
Comments: Spoken of very highly by several guests; they have a fine international restaurant and a casino. Amenities include a gym, jacuzzi, and steam room.

HOTEL EMBASSY — Av. Presidente Wilson 441 and 6 Deciembre (P.O. Box 17-01-1314).
Local Phone: 561-990 or 563-179   **FAX:** 011-593-2-563-192
Price Range: Single — U.S.$20;   Double — U.S.$25;   Triple — U.S.$30.

HOTEL SEBASTIAN — Almagro and Cordero (P.O. Box 17-07-9377).
Local Phone: 527-577 or 233-461 or 566-322   **FAX:** 011-593-2-565-261
Price Range: Single — U.S.$52; Double — U.S.$62.
Comments: Opened in 1993, the Sebastian is owned and operated by one of the major Ecuadorian Tour Operators, NUEVO MUNDO EXPEDITIONS (see Chapter IV, CHOOSING A TOUR). I would expect to see some package programs in the coming years.

HOTEL TAMBO REAL — Av. 12 de Octubre and Patria (P.O. Box 2143).
Local Phone: 563-822 or 563-823 or 563-824   **FAX:** 011-593-2-554-964
Price Range: Standard (kitchenettes available at no extra charge), Single — U.S.$45;   Double — U.S.$55; Suites (with living room and kitchenette), Single — U.S.$55;   Double — U.S.$65;   Triple — U.S.$80.
U.S. Reservation Services: Utell International (UI), TOLL FREE: (800) 223-9868, Nationwide.

MEDICAL

Quito is at an altitude of 9300 ft. Be sensitive to the symptoms of altitude sickness (see the section, Medical Considerations, in Chapter VI). If medical attention is required, the First Class Hotels typically have a house doctor on call. For medical emergencies, contact Hospital Metropolitano (Av. Mariana de Jesus). **Local Phone:** 431-520 or 431-457 or 439-336 (Emergency — 450-287). Another recommendation is the Hospital VozAndes (Vilalengua 267 and 10 de Agosto, next to VozAndes, the "Voice of the Andes" radio station). **Local Phone:** 449-374.

If your medical insurance has international coverage or you have Travel Protection Insurance, you may have to report the situation to the attention of the carrier ASAP (see the Travel Protection Insurance section of Chapter V).

RESTAURANTS

The eating schedule is a bit different in South America. If you enter a restaurant at 6:00-7:00 p.m., it will probably be almost empty. You may think that you've chosen the wrong place to eat. Along about 8:00, people will begin to arrive, and at 9:00 the place will be full. This is related to the 2 hour afternoon *siesta* and the subsequent work schedule, often til 7:00 p.m.

The list that follows is a brief one and does not include the hotel restaurants, which are of a much higher class of food and overall quality than American hotel restaurants. By the way, the *ceviches* (marinated seafood served with popcorn and toasted corn on the side) are wonderful appetizers everywhere in Ecuador.

ARLEQUIN — (Av. Orellana 155 and 12 de Octubre). The gentle, live guitar in the background and the beautiful art on the walls complement the international cuisine — all have local flavor.

BENTLEYS — (Juan León Mera 404 and Robles) Americanized throughout; highly recommended (closed Saturday and Sunday).

LA CHOZA — (Av. 12 de Octubre and Cordero) Excellent local atmosphere. A spacious, open setting; the 2-story white walls are tastefully decorated with Andean *artesanías*. Even the chandeliers are beautifully crafted out of gourds. I recommend the *locro de queso* (a potato and cheese soup served with avocados) and the *llapingachos mondados* (mashed potato pancakes filled with cheese and served with peanut sauce on the side). A good lunch stop after shopping at the famous FOLKLORE gift store owned by designer Olga Fisch, just a couple of blocks away. No alcoholic beverages are served.

DELMONICOS — (Mariano Aguilera 331 and La Pradera) An excellent restaurant. The *orgia de mariscos* is delicious and just what it sounds like — an orgy of shellfish.

EXCALIBUR — (Calama 380 and Juan León Mera) Cozy, romantic atmosphere with a good selection of recorded music; a nice quiet spot to enjoy a well-prepared lunch. The mushroom or cheese *tortillas* are not what we're used to; they're actually very delicious omelettes, a meal in itself for under $2.

PIMS — (Calama 413 and Juan León Mera; they have grown and recently opened at a second location — Mariano Aguilera St.) A lively, cheerful eating and drinking spot for the young Ecuadorian working set, many of whom appear to have a college background. Open from 4:00 — 11:00 p.m., Pims is a great place to go with friends and share the day's adventures while Piaf-genre music plays in the background. I recommend the sea bass with mushrooms (*corvina con champignones*).

LA QUERENCIA — (Eloy Alfaro 2530 and Catalina de Aldaz) Frequented by many tour groups and featuring typical Ecuadorian cuisine.

LAS REDES — (Av. Amazonas 845) A highly-recommended seafood lunch spot; excellent ceviche and shrimp dishes to choose from.

LA REINA VICTORIA — (Reina Victoria 530 and Roca) Their business card states that they are "a cross between an English Pub and American Bar;" the description is apt. La Reina Victoria is the only establishment in town (including the hotels) with enhanced Cable TV, pulling in the major U.S. networks (ABC, CBS, and NBC). I watched the World Series from there. While you're viewing the game, you can feast on very appropriate sports food, including pizza, tacos, subs, Reuben sandwiches, and whatever else owner Dorothy Albright feels like cooking. Dorothy, who's from Chicago, is thus far resisting customer pressure for her to work on weekends, and the place is closed on Saturday and Sunday.

RINCON DE FRANCIA — (Roca 779 and 9 de Octubre) Ecuadorian and French selections. A favorite spot for entertaining; very elegant.

RINCON LA RONDA — (Bello Horizonte 400 and Almagro) Elegant dining complete with strolling musicians.

LA TERRAZA DEL TARTARO — (Av. Amazonas and Veintimilla) Take the rear elevator to the top floor of the Amazonas Building (*Edificio Amazonas*). Excellent food (my favorites are the filet mignon and the langostinos) with a great panoramic view of the city and surrounding mountains.

SHOPPING

At the focus of the modern business and shopping district is the main thoroughfare, Avenida Río Amazonas (Amazon River Avenue). Amazonas, as it is called, starts at the Hotel Colón at Parque El Ejido, the largest park in Quito, and heads north all the way to Plaza Olmedo by the airport. For the best shopping, stay between Av. Amazonas and Juan León Mera (which is to the east of, and parallel to, Amazonas — to your right as you're walking away from the Hotel Colón). Between these two avenues, and on the side streets between them, you will find many excellent shops selling arts & crafts, jewelry, books, clothes and leather goods. If you get hungry, you will probably take more than a passing look at some of the best restaurants in Quito, sidewalk cafes, and pastry shops. And for taking care of business, this is where you will find the airline ticket offices, Tour Operators, and *cambios* — exchange houses, remember?

If you have a limited time in Quito, you will want to set aside at least one afternoon for shopping. You'll have several categories of souvenir and gift items to choose from, including clothing and jewelry. Some of the better and well-known stores are listed below, but you'll no doubt find several others to your personal liking as well. There is very little bargaining, unless you're buying from one of the outdoor stalls or actually travel to one of the Indian markets (see the section on Touring below).

Indian handicrafts (*artesanías*) will stare at you from many of the shop windows. You'll see a lot of wood carvings; some you'll like, and some you won't. Included in this category are figures made of balsa wood, carved in the Amazon rain forests of *El Oriente*. Ecuador is famous for its leatherwork, and the prices are quite reasonable. You will walk past a lot of shop windows displaying several styles of good looking wallets, handbags, jackets, and luggage. Also high on the shopping list are the rugged, coarse-woven wool sweaters and vests. Many beautiful colors and attractive patterns are available for about U.S.$20-$30. The sweaters made of alpaca wool are very high quality, extremely fine to the touch (the fibers only 25 microns thick), and naturally command a higher price, often a lot higher. The alpaca, by the way, is related to the llama, and both are raised, as they have been for centuries, by native Indians in the Andean highlands.

The jewelry is of very high quality. Also relatively expensive. The precious stones are more reasonable, but not cheap. Oh well, you can always buy a Panama hat, for sale everywhere! It'll make a good sun shade for the Galápagos too, if it doesn't blow off.

Note: Keep the receipts from your purchases so that, if necessary, you can convince U.S. Customs Officials that you really bought all that stuff so cheap! Each person (children included) is allowed to bring back U.S.$400 worth of merchandise.

Be aware that black coral is an endangered species. You will see stores with signs advertising that they sell gift items made of black coral. Often the products are quite beautiful and usually quite expensive as well. Less often, but frequently the items are fake. While at present there are no laws prohibiting these stores from selling goods made of black coral, from the standpoint of conservation, it is strongly suggested that you refrain from purchasing such items. At the same time, the store owners are often not to be blamed, as they themselves may not understand the significance of the issue. Thus, it is not suggested that you refrain from shopping at their stores; just don't purchase their black coral products.

A small selection of some of the better known gift shops in Quito include:

ARTE FOLKLORE DALMAU — (Bello Horizante 123 and Manuel Iturrey) Exclusive handicraft and jewelry designs.

ARTICULOS DE CUERO — (In the arcade mall of the Hotel Colón, the airport, and several other business district locations). Leather goods.

LA BODEGA — (Juan León Mera 614) Opposite the Libri Mundi bookstore.

FOLKLORE OLGA FISCH — (Av. Colón 260) Probably the best known gift store in Quito, owned and operated by the family of the late Olga Fisch, internationally-acclaimed designer. There are also branches in the Hotel Colón and Hotel Oro Verde, Quito.

GALERIA LATINA — (Juan León Mera 823) Next to Libri Mundi. For my taste, the best overall selection of quality products that I have found.

LA GUARAGUA — (Jorge Washington 614) Good selection of *artesanías* and antiques.

HAMILTON — (Av. Amazonas 171) Ecuadorian gold and silver handicraft. In front of the Hotel Colón.

LIBRI MUNDI — (Juan León Mera 851) Without a doubt the best bookstore in Ecuador. They have a comprehensive selection of Galápagos literature. The one stop to definitely make before you leave for the islands. While there is a smaller branch in the arcade mall of the Hotel Colón, the main store is just a few blocks away.

LA LLAMA — (Av. Amazonas 149) Ecuadorian handicrafts available for export.

PETER MUSSFELDT — (Juan León Mera 838) The main factory outlet for designer Peter Mussfeldt's colorful motifs — bags, clothes, tapestries. Across from the Libri Mundi bookstore.

OCEPA — (Calle Carrion 1236 and Versalles) Government *artesanía* store; also located near the Hotel Colón at Jorge Washington 252 and Av. Amazonas.

PRODUCTOS ANDINOS — (Urbina 111 and Cordero) An artesian co-operative with reasonably priced goods.

H. STERN JEWELERS — In the arcade mall of the Hotel Colón.

TOURING

On your return from the Galápagos, you may have some time for sightseeing in and around Quito. If you're on a group tour, the arrangements have most likely already been made. If you're on your own, there are several options; in each case the Tour Operator you worked with on your Galápagos excursion can handle all the arrangements for you. In fact, the following list is but a small representation of the vast number of half-day and full-day mainland tours that are standardly offered. The more time you have, the greater the number of possibilities. I won't elaborate, because as you well know by now, the orientation of this book is to get you to spend the maximum amount of time in the Galápagos.

THE AMAZON — Located in the eastern portion of Ecuador (or *El Oriente*, as the area is called), is the rich neotropical rain forest of the upper Amazon region. The area is also rich in other natural resources, namely oil, which is now Ecuador's leading source of export revenue.

While the Ecuadorian Amazon would be a great natural history destination all by itself (in much the same way that Costa Rica is), it is with mixed feelings that I recommend this area for an extension trip before or after the Galápagos Islands. Actually, except for hardcore naturalists (especially birders), I strongly recommend it as a pre-extension only — that is, to visit the Ecuadorian Amazon before the Galápagos. What happens is that, simply put, the Galápagos spoils you. You get used to seeing and photographing the animals within 4-6 ft; these animals have few natural predators and have not learned fear. This is not the case in the Amazon, where the animals need (and expertly use) the jungle as camouflage. The result is that "you can hear them, and you can see one way up there (between the fourth and fifth branches of the third tree to the right of that patch of red soil) but you don't usually get a close look." At least not for any length of time. Which reduces photography to the lush scenery. And since you can't observe the animals as closely as in Galápagos, you have to bring more knowledge with you. This need is amplified because, while the Guides here are good and very knowledgeable, they are not trained to interpret nature as thoroughly as they are in Galápagos. However, the Ecuadorian Amazon *will* get you warmed up and ready for the Galápagos.

The other problems with the Amazon are logistical. It takes a minimum of 5 days to get any feel for this special place; the Amazon is the largest neotropical rain forest in the world. Of the 5 days, 2 of them will be spent getting in and out. Since the 1987 earthquake, the road system (such as it was) was reduced to the level of "undependable." Most Ecuadorian Amazon programs now include a flight from Quito to the town of Coca, located on the Napo River (a major tributary of the Amazon River). Even so, transportation each way will take up the greater portion of a day.

There are many Amazon tours to consider, including several newer lodges that have yet to distinguish themselves. Logistics and comprehensive interpretive programs are essentials; don't sign up unless you're convinced! The largest Tour Operator in Ecuador, Metropolitan Touring, runs a popular floating hotel in the Amazon, called, oddly enough, the Flotel Orellana. This tripledecker sleeps 40 passengers and has 4 & 5 day programs. It's not my idea of adventure travel but neither is touring the Galápagos on a Cruise Ship.

La Selva Lodge — In 1992, La Selva Lodge in the Ecuadorian Amazon was named and awarded the "Best Ecotourism Destination" by the World Congress on Tourism and the Environment. La Selva ("the jungle" in Spanish) overlooks a beautiful lake, consists of 16 double cabins and features an exceptional restaurant. More important, they have excellent itineraries that blend guided dugout canoe rides and trail walks. If you're a birder, they have specialized programs (a full week is recommended) and excellent birding Guides; bring your tape recorders and a copy of **BIRDS OF COLOMBIA** — both are essential.

Their general programs are not as individualized as the brochures indicate ("tailor-make your own jungle adventure"). In fact, their brochures and advertising do much to hurt their programs, in my opinion, by calling attention to "our exotic, gourmet cuisine." What happens is that they get some "Cruise Ship" passengers (sorry for the generalization, but it's mostly deserved) who aren't much interested in an educationally-oriented program. The problem is that these passengers can be put in the same group as some serious natural history types, and the Guides take the easy way out — "here's the stuff the natives dye their faces with, folks." If you have your own group, this problem is avoided.

There are 4-day programs for $585 and 5-day programs for $685.

Note: Full rain gear is essential for touring the Amazon. In addition, yellow fever shots and malaria pills are recommended for this area in some of the literature; consult your physician.

COTOPAXI NATIONAL PARK — Cotopaxi, at 19,700 ft, is the world's highest active volcano. If you have the time, it's definitely worth a look. There are organized full-day tours. The driver will take the Pan American Highway south for about 35 miles along the Central Valley, flanked by two parallel ranges of high mountain volcanoes (most are still active). This is the famous "Avenue of the Volcanoes," aptly named by the German explorer, Alexander von Humboldt.

Cotopaxi National Park, established in 1975, offers spectacular views of lava fields, colorful highland flora, llamas, deer, wild horses, and mountain birds, including an occasional glimpse of an Andean condor. When the clouds decide to part, you will be treated to a beautiful sight — the higher slopes of glaciatic blue ice and the snow-covered peak, a perfect cone if ever there was one.

Lunch is included on the full-day tour. Many trips take lunch at Hacienda La Cienega, a beautiful 300 year old estate now functioning as a country inn. If you have the time, you can overnight (advanced reservations required) at this romantic hacienda (many of the rooms have 20 ft ceilings) and make this a 2-day tour, taking in a traditional market on the return to Quito (the Saturday Zumbuhau Market and Quilotoa Crater Lake are highly recommended).

The price of a full-day tour of *Cotopaxi National Park,* including lunch, ranges from $50/person for a group of ten to $85/person for a group of two. The 2-day program (including an overnight at La Cienega) ranges from $145/person for a group of ten to $250/person for a group of two.

CUENCA — Cuenca is considered by many to be the most beautiful city in Ecuador. Not as crowded as Quito, without the extensive high-rise business district, Cuenca offers the rich flavor of colonial history and traditional architecture. In all, Cuenca is a recommended visiting area for those that have 3-4 days to spend and have a cultural orientation — especially those who were interested in seeing Machu Picchu in Peru. Outside of Cuenca (2 hours north), one can visit the most significant Inca ruins in Ecuador — the Ingapirca Fortress. No, it's not Machu Picchu, but it's safer than Peru, more logistically feasible (for starters, you don't have to overnight in Lima), and a lot less expensive. A 3-day visit would start with a morning flight from Quito and include a half-day City Tour of Cuenca. In addition to viewing cathedrals, museums, and pre-Columbian ruins, you will have the opportunity to visit one or more of the factories where "Panama" hats are made. On the second day, you will tour the scenic Gualaceo Valley. In addition to the beautiful landscapes, you will visit several markets, with an emphasis on ceramics, jewelry, and hand-woven tapestries and sweaters. After visiting the Ingapirca ruins on the third day, you fly back to Quito.

The price of a 3-day tour of Cuenca ranges from $240/person for a group of ten to $350/person for a group of two (flights, hotels, and most meals included).

EQUATORIAL MONUMENT — If you always wanted to be right on the equator, here's your chance. There are tours to *La Mitad del Mundo* (Center of the World) located 15 miles north of Quito at latitude 0°00'00''. In addition to the monument, there is a museum describing the 18th century expedition that established the exact location of the equator; there is also an interesting display of local Indian cultures. It's customary to have your picture taken straddling the northern and southern hemispheres; with the drifting clouds and the beautiful mountain scenery, some of the shots can be quite dramatic (see Photo #2).

The price of a half-day tour to the Equatorial Monument ranges from $15/person for a group of ten to $25/person for a group of two. Prices do not include lunch.

OLD TOWN — In 1978, *UNESCO* declared Quito as one of the world's cultural heritage sites, and the Old Town section is now controlled so far as development is concerned. Thus, entering Old Town and walking down the narrow, winding cobblestone streets, one is immediately immersed in 16th century colonial architecture, by whitewashed walls, red-tiled roofs, heavy wooden doors, and fountained courtyards.

Starting at the *Plaza de Independencia*, your tour of Old Town takes in the *Palacio Municipal* (City Hall), *Palacio de Gobierno* (the Presidential offices), *La Catedral* (the site of the first church in Quito), and *Palacio Arzobispal* (the Archbishop's Palace), now a series of shops. Nearby is the most impressive architectural treasure Quito has to offer, *La Compañia* Church, whose interior is a virtual blaze of gold. It is decorated in renaissance style, and almost entirely in gold leaf; I've never seen anything quite like it.

Other attractions include the Church of *San Francisco* (the largest of Quito's 86 churches) and *La Merced*, housing Quito's oldest clock. As you wander through Old Town, you will notice scaffolding almost everywhere; in 1987, a severe earthquake damaged several of these structures, which were subsequently closed. Repair work is proceeding slowly, paced by available funds and the required expertise.

While you could visit Old Town on your own, it is highly recommended that you take one of the City Tours offered by virtually all the Tour Operators. The Guides are well-versed in the architectural and general history of Quito. Almost as important as the Guides' knowledge of the subject matter is their familiarity with the "unusual" visiting hours of the various churches and museums, which is sometimes only a couple of hours at a time. They will also take you up to Panecillo Hill for a fine panoramic view of the city (see Photo #1). Optionally you can also tour some of the fine museums, including the Archaeological Museum of the Central Bank; here you will find the most complete collection of pieces from Ecuadorian prehistory, dating back to 10,000 B.C.

The price of a half-day Colonial Quito City Tour (including the Archaeological Museum) ranges from $20/person for a group of ten to $30/person for a group of two. Prices do not include lunch.

OTAVALO MARKET — Ecuador is noted for its native markets, a tradition that predates even the Incas, to a time when agricultural products were first carried down from the Andean highlands (on the backs of llamas) and traded for goods from the Amazon region, which were also transported to the "marketplace." Of these markets, none is more famous than the one at Otavalo, a few hours drive to the north of Quito, where one can experience the sights and sounds of the Saturday Market (if you have a free Saturday, that is).

Today's market is now more oriented to selling handicrafts to the tourist audience than it is to "local" trading. The market opens early every Saturday, the outdoor stalls displaying the most popular items — ponchos, blankets, scarves, sweaters, belts, tapestries, and rugs. The Otavalo region is known for their skilled weavers, but there may be as many (or more) mass-produced, synthetic items as hand-woven woolen products. Bargaining is the rule, and transactions are in sucres.

Even if you're not interested in this type of shopping, the photo opportunities may be worth the trip. The traditional dress is very striking and most colorful. This is a very crowded area, though, so don't set your camera bag down, and be wary of pickpockets.

The price of a full-day tour to the Otavalo Market, including lunch, ranges from $45/person for a group of ten to $85/person for a group of two.

Note: While the "traditional" Otavalo Market is on Saturday, there is an "open" market at Otavalo several days a week. In fact, tours to the Otavalo area (the Imbabura Province) are offered daily. For the same price as the Otavalo Market trip, you can visit several towns (including Otavalo) and quietly shop for quality handmade products, leather goods, wooden crafts, sweaters, tapestries, and bread dough figurines. For you non-shoppers, the Imbabura Province trip also offers excellent views of the Andes.

GUAYAQUIL

With a population approaching 2 million people, Guayaquil (pronounced gwah-yah-keel) is the largest city in Ecuador as well as the economic and industrial center of the country. Guayaquil has a coastal location on an unusually long 30 mile inward reach of the Gulf of Guayaquil, and is the major port (called *Puerto Nuevo* or New Port) of Ecuador. The city also has inland water access, being situated on the Guayas River, which winds down from the north. Almost all of Ecuador's imports (and about half of its exports) are handled here. Guayaquil is also surrounded by the major export farming areas of Ecuador and is the agricultural center of the country.

The potential economic importance of Guayaquil as a major trading center was recognized by the Spanish conquistadors, who founded the city in 1537 and developed it to its present status as an international port. Due to its business orientation, Guayaquil politics tend to favor government nonintervention with free trade. It is therefore labeled as "conservative," in contrast to the more "liberal" Quito, where, due to a greater incidence of poverty, government-sponsored social programs are favored.

While recognized as the business center of Ecuador, Guayaquil does not rank very high as a tourist attraction. It doesn't really try to be. There is a serious work orientation, and aside from the hotels and some Tour Operators, the tourist is not really catered to, almost ignored. I like Guayaquil. In many ways it reminds me of New York City; it has its own special personality which you can decide to become part of. Unfortunately, I feel that most tourists would decide not to become part of Guayaquil. There is simply too much street noise and congestion. It is not until one spends some time there that this perception begins to change. Considering the short 1 night pre-Galápagos stay here (at the most), there will be no attempt to introduce the reader to the restaurants, shops, and touring possibilities of Guayaquil.

THE AIRPORT

The Simón Bolívar Airport is very modern, located 3 miles north of the business district, shopping sector, and major hotels.

Note: There is a $25 Departure Tax on international flights, payable in sucres or U.S. dollars.

TOURIST INFORMATION

There are two *CETUR* offices in Guayaquil at the following locations:

Business District Office: Aguirre 104 and the Malecón
Local Phone: 328-312 or 325-607   **FAX:** 011-593-4-329-377
Airport Office: Símon Bólivar Airport

CLIMATE

During the warm rainy season from December-May, the average temperature is 80-85 Deg F. The heat and humidity tend to be on the uncomfortable side from January through April. Guayaquil is dry during the rest of the year, although the skies are frequently overcast and the evenings cool. The driest months are July-October when temperatures reach the 70s (Deg F) during the day and drop to the 50s (Deg F) at night.

HOTELS

As in Quito, there are many First Class hotels in Guayaquil. The prices are still reasonable but tend to be somewhat higher (than those in Quito).

Note: The sink and shower faucets at some of the hotels are marked differently than you're used to, which could be cause for confusion as well as a potential problem. The left (hot) faucet is marked "C" for *Caliente*; the right (cold) faucet is marked "F" for *Frío*.

Many of the hotels provide bottles of mineral water in each room for drinking and rinsing when brushing your teeth.

All phone numbers are local. The FAX numbers listed below include the international, country, and city codes.

Here then are the recommended hotels of Guayaquil and their affiliated U.S. Reservation Service(s). Add 20% to all prices for tax and service.

First Class Hotels:

HOTEL CONTINENTAL — Chile and 10 de Agosto
Local Phone: 329-270   **FAX:** 011-593-4-325-454
Rooms: All rooms have an AM/FM/tape player in addition to color TV. Room service is available from 5:00 a.m. til midnight.
Price Range: Single — U.S.$135; Double — U.S.$140; Jr. Suite — U.S.$170.
Comments: The El Fortin restaurant is highly-rated. There is also a music hall with nightly entertainment.
U.S. Reservation Services: Golden Tulip Hotels International (GT), TOLL FREE: (800) 344-1212 Nationwide; **Loews Reservations International** (LRI), TOLL FREE: (800) 223-0888 Nationwide; **Utell International** (UI), TOLL FREE: (800) 223-9868 Nationwide.

GRAND HOTEL GUAYAQUIL — Boyacá 1600 (between Clemente Ballén and 10 de Agosto — P.O. Box 9282).
Local Phone: 329-690   **FAX:** 011-593-4-327-251
Rooms: Courtesy in-room coffee heaters and 24 hour room service.
Price Range: Single — U.S.$85; Double — U.S.$115; Triple — U.S.$130.

Comments: Their brochure describes the Grand Hotel as "the only hotel in the world to share a whole city block with a cathedral." I certainly have never seen another hotel with that particular characteristic! The features include a swimming pool area with tropical waterfall and barbecue. There is also a mini-shopping mall and gymnasium with two squash courts, sauna, steam bath, and massage room.

U.S. Reservation Services: Selective Hotel Reservations (SHR), TOLL FREE: (800) 223-6764 U.S. & Canada; **Utell International** (UI), TOLL FREE: (800) 223-9868 Nationwide.

HOTEL ORO VERDE — Av. 9 de Octubre and Garcia Moreno (P.O. BOX 9636).
Local Phone: 327-999   **FAX:** 011-593-4-329-350
Rooms: Finely-appointed rooms with mini-bars and video rentals.
Price Range: Single — U.S.$140; Double — U.S.$.$170; Suites — U.S.$210-$290.
Comments: Generally rated as the finest hotel in Guayaquil, the Oro Verde has four restaurants, including Le Gourmet, offering award-winning French cuisine. There is also a restaurant by the pool. Other amenities include the casino, sauna, and gymnasium.
U.S. Reservation Services: The Leading Hotels of the World (LHW), TOLL FREE: (800) 223-6800 U.S. & Canada.

HOTEL RAMADA — Malecón and Orellana (P.O. Box 10964).
Local Phone: 565-794 or 562-475 or 566-798   **FAX:** 011-593-4-563-036
Price Range: Single — U.S.$70;   Double — U.S.$80;   Triple — U.S.$90.
Comments: The Ramada is located on the waterfront with a view of the Guayas River, but it is somewhat out of the way and approaching an area a bit unsafe to walk after dark. There is a casino at the Ramada.

UNIHOTEL — Clemente Ballén 406 (P.O. Box 563).
Local Phone: 327-100   **FAX:** 011-593-4-328-352
Rooms: Very comfortable and 24 hour room service.
Price Range: Single — U.S.$90;   Double — U.S.$110;   Triple — U.S.$125.
Comments: I would rate the Unihotel as the best First Class hotel for your money in Guayaquil. Features include a sauna, whirlpool, gymnasium, and casino. The hotel complex contains an eighty store shopping mall.
U.S. Reservation Services: Steigenberger Reservation Service (SRS), TOLL FREE: (800) 223-5652 U.S. & Canada; FAX: 407-679-3361; **Utell International** (UI), TOLL FREE: (800) 223-9868 Nationwide.

Tourist Class Hotels:
HOTEL CASINO BOULEVARD — Av. 9 de Octubre 432 (P.O. Box 7524).
Local Phone: 562-888 or 566-700   **FAX:** 011-593-4-560-076
Rooms: This used to be an apartment building, so each room is actually a suite with kitchenette and mini-bar.
Price Range: Single — U.S.$47;   Double — U.S.$67; Suites — U.S.$77.
Comments: As the name indicates, they have a casino.

HOTEL SOL DE ORIENTE — Aguirre 603 and Escobedo (P.O. Box 5875).
Local Phone: 325-500 or 325-702   **FAX:** 011-593-4-329-352
Price Range: Single — U.S.$45;   Double — U.S.$55;   Triple — U.S.$65.
Comments: The Sol De Oriente is quite reasonably priced, and they have a
   good Chinese restaurant.

MEDICAL

If medical attention is required, the First Class Hotels typically have a house
doctor on call. For medical emergencies, contact the Clínica Guayaquil (P.
Aguirre and General Córdova). **Local Phone:** 563-555. Another recommendation is the Clínica Kennedy (Av. San Jorge and Kennedy). **Local
Phone:** 286-963.

   If your medical insurance has international coverage or you have Travel
Protection Insurance, you may have to report the situation to the attention of the
carrier ASAP (see the Travel Protection Insurance section of Chapter V).

SAFETY & SECURITY

South America does not have the best reputation as far as theft is concerned.
Some of the countries, notably Peru and Columbia, have unfortunately earned
this reputation. Not so with Ecuador. I would say that Quito is safer than most
U.S. cities, especially in the downtown hotel and business district. The
Galápagos is extremely safe in this regard. With the modern day atmosphere of
Guayaquil, however, comes some of the less desirable aspects of contemporary
life, including a higher rate of theft, pickpocketing, etc.

   No matter how safe Ecuador may be, never forget that you easily stand out
as a "rich *gringo* tourist." Thus, you want to take reasonable precautions:

   1. Crowded airports are a prime location for rip-offs, and camera bags
are the number one casualty. I've even seen people "lose" their cameras at
Baltra Island Airport in the Galápagos. Keep track of your carryon bags at all
times.

   2. The major portion of your money should be in traveler's checks.

   3. Don't leave valuables in your hotel room any more than absolutely
necessary. The major hotels have security boxes (*cajas de seguridad*) for money
and jewelry. There are also safe storage areas for larger items. You are advised
to take advantage of this service. In recent years, there have been occasional
rashes of break-ins by professionals said to be from Peru or Columbia.

   4. If you're going shopping, take your camera with you. It's a good way
to keep track of it, and the inner compartments of the camera bag make
convenient, practical locations to store your money.

   5. Do the bulk of your shopping on your return trip from the Galápagos.
You'll have fewer valuables to keep track of and worry about. Besides, it's not
real practical to be carting a lot of stuff out to the islands. There are also airline
baggage and shipboard space limits to contend with. If you do purchase some
items prior to your tour, you can store them at most of the major hotels.

6. Men shouldn't carry a wallet in their hip pocket. While in a city, keep your money in an inner compartment of your tote or camera bag. You may also choose to wear a money pouch.

7. In general, it's not real smart to walk the streets by yourself late at night. This is less of a risk in the central hotel and business district of Quito.

8. Always carry your passport and T3 Tourist Information Card with you. Aside from the value of these documents as identification when you want to cash a traveler's check, it is a legal requirement that you have them in your possession. While an unlikely scenario, if you fail to present a passport when requested to do so by an official, you could be detained. And you don't want to be detained, so carry your passport!

9. Report a theft to the police ASAP. If items are missing from your hotel room, notify the management immediately and before contacting the police.

10. If you are on a group tour, report any loss or theft to your Tour Leader immediately. Part of their job is to provide assistance in this type of a situation. They will advise you on contacting the police.

11. Report a loss or theft of traveler's checks ASAP as follows:

AMERICAN EXPRESS has a number that you can call collect 24 hours a day, (801) 964-6665, to report lost or stolen AMERICAN EXPRESS traveler's checks. For lost or stolen AMERICAN EXPRESS CARDS, call collect (919) 333-3211.

The BANK OF AMERICA has a number that you can call collect 24 hours a day, (415) 574-7111 to report lost or stolen B OF A traveler's checks and B OF A credit cards. Refunds of lost or stolen B OF A traveler's Checks are coordinated with the BANK OF AMERICA offices in Quito and Guayaquil.

12. Report a loss or theft of your airline ticket(s) to the airline ticket or branch office ASAP. The way it usually works is that you purchase a replacement ticket and then fill out a lost ticket application form. You will get a refund from the carrier after 120 days if the original ticket was not used, thus making it urgent that you make this report as soon as possible.

13. Report a loss or theft of your passport to the U.S. consulate at the U.S. Embassy in Quito or Guayaquil. Have your passport number handy when you contact them (see Item 15 below). If you haven't made a copy of your passport identification page, your hotel has your passport number on the registration sheet that you filled out.

The U.S. EMBASSY locations are as follows:

Quito — Av. Patria 120.
  Local Phone: 562-890
Guayaquil — Av. 9 de Octubre and García Moreno.
  Local Phone: 323-570

The U.S. Consulate will usually issue a new passport within 24 hours.

14. If you have Travel Protection Insurance, report a loss or theft of any personal items to the carrier (see the Travel Protection Insurance section of Chapter V).

15. For purposes of reporting lost or stolen items, it will be helpful to have some backup documentation. Remember, before you leave home, take two

photocopies of the identification page of your passport, any Travel Vouchers, the I.D. numbers of your traveler's checks, an inventory of expensive personal items (including Model/Serial Numbers, when appropriate), and your airline itinerary. Leave a copy at home and take the second copy with you, keeping it in a secure location (such as the hotel security box).

CHAPTER IX

TOURING
THE GALAPAGOS ISLANDS

This chapter will serve as an orientation to the Galápagos Islands, to most of the Visitor Sites, as well as the on-board and daily activities that will make up your exciting adventure.

WELCOME TO THE ENCHANTED ISLES

The entrance point to the Galápagos is the airport at either Baltra or San Cristóbal Island. As you step down off the airplane and look around, perhaps trying to catch sight of a giant tortoise, you will most likely be underwhelmed; the view will be noticeably disappointing. Baltra, in particular, is pretty desolate, and you'll be looking at dry area vegetation. You will have to wait until you get on-board your yacht and are under way to the first Visitor Site (in about an hour or two) before you can begin to see and enjoy the Galápagos wildlife. For now, proceed to the terminal and prepare to line up one more time.

ENTRANCE FEE

While the line you wait on is "immigration-oriented" (you are entering a regulated National Park), and your passport will be examined, the main purpose here is to collect your $80 *Galápagos National Park* entrance fee. This fee is payable in U.S. dollars or sucres and is rarely included in the tour price. In return for your $80, you will receive an official entrance permit which you should keep with your passport. Once on-board, your Guide will ask for these documents; in turn, they will be handed over to the captain, who is required to keep them for the duration of the trip and to report your passport and entrance permit numbers to the Galápagos port officials. This is all part of the tourism control system of the *Galápagos National Park Service*.

NATIONAL PARK REGULATIONS

The Entrance Officer will also give you a list of *Galápagos National Park* Rules, which ask you not to disturb or remove anything (not even a rock or shell), not to touch or feed the animals, and to stay on the marked trails. With an increasing number of tourists visiting the Galápagos Islands each year, it becomes a matter of extreme importance that you not only follow these rules, but that you set an example for others, showing that tourists can be conservation-minded. There are those that look at the expansion of tourism as a double-edged sword, feeling that the delicate natural order of the archipelago will be adversely affected by the very visitors who want to experience this special place on earth. Man does not have a very good track record in the Galápagos; it won't take much in the way of insensitive behavior on the part of a few to result in the outraged cries of "enough."

My views on this subject are quite specific and have been stated in the section on Growth, Tourism, and Conservation in Chapter III. Once again, I am a strong believer in responsible and controlled tourism, with an emphasis on the need for tighter (translate that as "enforced") controls. With the revenue that Galápagos tourism is generating, the enforcement responsibility is Ecuador's.

GETTING TO YOUR BOAT

For most of you, the majority of the work is over, and your Galápagos vacation has really begun. Your Guide (perhaps the captain as well) will be waiting for you just past the "immigration" line. On passenger pick-up day, the crew all wear cute little white or tan shorts and matching shirts (typically bearing the name of the boat). A few of them also hold up signs announcing the boat. Some of you will be wearing a sign as well, a tag put on by the Tour Operator in the mainland. Once you and your Guide find each other, you will be warmly greeted and assisted in the collection of your check-on baggage, which will be stowed on the bus that takes you on a short journey to the harbor and, at long last, your boat. Skip to the section, "Life at Sea."

Alas, some of you will have to wait a bit more for the fun to begin. For those that have flown TAME to Baltra and have to meet their boat in Academy Bay on Santa Cruz Island, read the section below, Getting to Puerto Ayora. For those that have flown SAN to San Cristóbal and have to spend the night before boarding the boat, read the section below, "Getting to Puerto Baquerizo Moreno."

Finally, there is a slight chance that your boat hasn't arrived yet at the harbor (and therefore your Guide is a "no show" at the airport). In this case, the boat would have radio-contacted Baltra (or San Cristóbal) with a message to wait at the airport, proceed to the harbor, or at the worst, proceed to a hotel.

GETTING TO PUERTO AYORA

As of this writing, there are signs by each of the departing zones at Baltra Airport; one reads "Santa Cruz" and the other "Puerto Ayora." Since Puerto Ayora is on Santa Cruz Island, and with crowds of people filing onto buses by the "Santa Cruz" sign, those going to Puerto Ayora may start to get a bit anxious. Not to worry; the "Santa Cruz" sign refers to the Cruise Ship SANTA CRUZ.

The procedure is that the buses first transport those that are meeting their boats in Baltra Harbor, about a 10 minute drive. These same buses will then return and pick up those going to Puerto Ayora. Be prepared for a slow journey; all together it will take about 3 hours. First, from the airport you take a half hour bus ride to the southern tip of Baltra Island. The sign says that the fare is S/200. Don't panic; it's not $200, but 200 sucres (or 10 cents). Pay as you board. During the ride, you will get more of a feeling for the arid, desolate environment of Baltra Island. When the bus reaches the narrow Itabaca Channel which separates the Islands of Baltra and Santa Cruz, you cross via passenger ferry (about a 10 minute ride after a 20 minute wait) where another bus is waiting to take you to Puerto Ayora. Before boarding the ferry, you pay a combination fare (for the ferry and bus) which comes to about 2000 sucres (approximately $1).

Surprisingly, your tickets for the ferry and the Santa Cruz bus have numerical seat assignments on them. Also, the ticket is for a specific bus. Match the number on the ticket with the number displayed on the bus. The buses are numbered because there are several Day Tours that depart from Puerto Ayora (via bus). The passengers are dropped off at, you guessed it, the same place where the ferry drops you off. These buses are waiting for the Day Tour boats to return, and you don't want to get on them.

The bus ride (about 1 hour — a good deal less once the paved road is completed) to Puerto Ayora will be an interesting introduction to the climate of the Galápagos Islands. You start and finish at sea level, traversing the typically-moist central Highlands (see the section on Climate in Chapter II).

Once you arrive in Puerto Ayora, your boat will probably be anchored in Academy Bay; the dock is just a block or so from where you get off the bus. If all else fails, and no one seems to know anything about the boat, ask the bus driver to take you to the Hotel Galápagos. You can spend the night there, and they can radio-contact the boat and sort everything out for you.

GETTING TO PUERTO BAQUERIZO MORENO

The San Cristóbal Airport is actually on the outskirts of Puerto Baquerizo Moreno. If you're not going to the boat, you are scheduled (or will want) to spend the night at the Grand Hotel. There will be a bus marked SAN (the name of the airline, which has an ownership affiliation with the hotel) that will take you there.

LIFE AT SEA

Once on-board the boat, your vacation shifts into a higher gear. First off, you will be assigned your quarters. If for some reason you arrive before some of the other passengers, you may have your choice of cabins. Don't make an obsession of going from cabin to cabin, and certainly don't get into a quarrel over the selection, but if you have the opportunity, look the cabins over. Some may have a private bathroom (possibly with shower), somewhat better sleeping arrangements and/or storage facilities, etc. A few boats have cabins on the upper deck, which have a nicer view. Ask the Guide for a recommendation.

Unpacking — Once you've been assigned (or chosen) your cabin, get unpacked. The cabins are much smaller than even the smallest hotel room (including those in Tokyo), so you have to really organize your stuff. Stow things away in a compartmental fashion, so you can easily find them. If there's not a lot of storage room, you may want to leave some clothes in the pack or suitcase (which usually goes under the bottom bed or bunk). Keep your snorkel gear and suntan lotion topside (in your mesh gear bag; see Chapter VI), near the aft deck. Have your photographic equipment together and ready to go. Keep a plastic bag handy for dirty clothes. Don't leave your things lying about, thinking that you'll tidy up after a bit. "After a bit" may be after dark; some boats have no cabin lights, and besides, your cabin "mate" might be asleep. You might want to be asleep too, only to be stymied by a bunk full of junk. Also, the boat may be under way, and trying to unpack on a moving boat is not my idea of fun. Keep a flashlight where you can easily find it.

Chow Time — Lunch is the next order of business. There are few things in life as enjoyable as your first meal on-board a yacht that will soon be departing on an adventure-filled journey. Savor the moment and everything that comes with it!

A few words about table manners at sea. Unless you're on a comfortable-sized yacht, the dining room may be a bit cozy. There also may not be a designated waiter on-board. If there is, fine; if not, be prepared to help set and clear the table.

The Beverage Tab — While the policy varies from boat to boat, passengers are usually required to pay for what they drink. An "honor system" tab is set up on a clipboard that's usually kept by the refrigerator or cold box; on Cruise Ships, a barman keeps a formal tab. Each person is listed on the tab sheet, followed by columns designating the various beverage categories, such as mineral water (the only "safe" water on-board), cola, and beer. Often that's all the choices there are, although most boats offer wine and cocktails. You settle the bar bill at the end of your tour. This is an easy-enough arrangement before and after meals, but people also want something to drink with their food. And (on the yachts) they're already seated, crowded around the table before they realize that they'd like a beer or soda. So someone has to ask everyone else what they want to drink, get the bottles out, open them up, mark down each person's beverage on the tab sheet, and then serve the drinks. It's a real job. And I've seen some people not offer to take their turn at this, not once in a whole week. As if no one takes notice! Be extra considerate of your shipmates. Respecting someone else's "space" becomes very important when you're living in close quarters.

The Head — The marine toilet is another minor inconvenience. Only the Cruise Ships and some of the fancier yachts have automatic flush toilets; typically the deed is done by working a pump handle back and forth. A fill-valve is manually opened and closed to allow water into the bowl. And no toilet paper down the toilet; separate waste buckets are provided, even on the Cruise Ships.

Electricity — If you have any appliances that need recharging (such as a video power pack), you may have to get tuned in to the boat's generator cycle. Different boats have different power generating systems. On several of the yachts, they run the diesel-driven electrical generators when the engines are off — typically from the middle of the afternoon until 10:00 p.m. At this time, 110VAC power is available. The rest of the day, everything on the boat runs off 12VDC. There will even be two sets of lights, each operating on a different voltage.

Now that's one system; there are many others. It's important that you have the captain tell you about the operating system on your boat, including the location of the appropriate outlets (some are 12VDC outlets, and they look the same). Even the Cruise Ships have nuances. The GALAPAGOS EXPLORER, for example, has 220VAC outlets in the cabins. If you need 110VAC, you have to ask the purser (the operations and financial officer) for a transformer.

What To Wear — On the small yachts, most people wear their bathing suits or shorts all day, including at meals. The Cruise Ships are more formal, and they ask that short pants not be worn during dinner; the crew all wear their dress whites during and after dinner, and several "cruise-oriented" passengers wear jackets and ties. That's not my image of the Galápagos, but there you have it. Regardless of the boat, you will need to wear a sweatshirt or light jacket in the evenings, when it gets a little chilly (especially during the dry season, from about June-December).

Most of the yachts do have a dress rule — you can't wear shoes on-board, not even tennis shoes. Thongs and sandals are okay. The idea here is that they don't want you leaving little sand deposits all over their boat.

Orientation — Getting to know the rules is facilitated by the Guide; on Day 1, an orientation session is held. At this time the Guide will go through the various procedures on-board the particular boat. The Rules of the *Galápagos National Park* will also be explained to you. Remember, the Guide is a representative of the Park and is required to tell you the Rules and to enforce them. Most of them take this function quite seriously, which is commendable.

On a Cruise Ship, you will be assigned to a group at this time (based primarily on language). Each group will have its own Licensed Guide to conduct the island tours. Maximum group size is 20 passengers, per the National Park regulations. Your group will have a name, usually that of one of the animal species, such as "Boobies" or "Cormorants." When announcements are made, they may say, "Boobies will depart at 10:00 and Cormorants at 10:30." Just remember if you're a Booby or a Cormorant.

During or after the orientation, the boat will be under way. You will soon be arriving at and visiting your first Galápagos Island.

A DAY AT SEA
The Morning Schedule

Your day at sea begins at sunrise (about 6 a.m. throughout the year). Actually, I'm usually out of bed and on-board, camera in hand, by 5:30. I like to catch the first light whenever I can. While waiting for the sun to do its thing and for the coffee water to boil (there are no espresso machines or good coffee beans on-board any boat), I go through the ritual of cleaning lenses and sorting film. I also try to take some time and read up on the island to be visited, getting an idea of the wildlife to be seen, their characteristics, and the kinds of shots I may want to take. For study purposes, I would suggest using this book and/or the Jackson **GUIDE**.

You'll notice that the boat isn't where it was yesterday evening. In order to maximize your touring possibilities, the vast majority of the boats travel between islands at night. So you'll be gently woken from your sleep almost every night by the sound of the engine(s) starting up. For me, it's quite comforting to hear the engines in the background as I drift back to sleep. The actual sailing time varies quite a bit and depends on the speed capacity of the boat as well as the inter-island distance. The central islands are fairly close together, so the boat will usually depart about 4 a.m. to arrive before sunrise. The outer islands are further apart (sometimes 30-40 miles), and the departure time might be as early as midnight.

Soon after the sun rises, most of the passengers do the same. If you're a photographer, you'll want to take advantage of the early light and get on the island as soon as possible. However, unless you're on a photography trip or perhaps a birding tour, this may not happen. Some people like to sleep in, and the crew doesn't really push things. You're only going to one Visitor Site in the morning, and it's actually easier for the crew to have you gone for one large block of time, say from 8:00 til 11:30, then to have you go ashore, come back for breakfast, and then go back for swimming and snorkeling. What you can do is make the other passengers aware that the lighting is better early in the day, and if they can get through breakfast by 7:15, they can get some better shots. Also, if there's a Cruise Ship anchored nearby, you definitely want to get ashore and on the trail before they disembark their large contingent of passengers. So there's some flexibility in the morning schedule, and it depends a lot on the situation as well as the makeup of your shipmates.

On a Cruise Ship, these subtle flexibilities do not exist. By necessity (for handling up to 90 passengers), there are fixed times for all activities. These times are posted and announced each evening prior to the social functions. A public address system (heard everywhere on-board and even piped into your cabin) is used to announce pending activities.

Breakfast typically consists of eggs (prepared various ways on various days) or pancakes, fruit, juice, toast, and instant coffee or tea. The Cruise Ships have a buffet-style breakfast with several selections, much in the style of many hotels.

Once breakfast is over, the Guide will announce the departure time for visiting the island. On the Cruise Ships, the departure times will be announced on the P.A. system. Put on your suntan lotion (don't forget to oil your feet), and gather up your gear. I usually just take my camera equipment (with first aid cream and a few bandages in the camera bag) and a pair of binoculars. Ask the Guide if snorkeling is on the schedule. If the answer is even "maybe," have your mesh gear bag containing your snorkeling gear ready to go. Remember to wear a hat.

Note: You may not take any food or drink (except for water) to any island. The fear is that of introduced organisms. For the same reason, you may not use the island as a bathroom.

Many people take drinking water (a bottle of mineral water in their plastic container or canteen) with them, but unless I'm on an all day hike (to the rim of the Alcedo Volcano, for example), I tend not to get thirsty.

Wet Landings vs. Dry Landings — From the previous evening's briefing, you will know whether there's going to be a "wet landing" or "dry landing." The term "wet landing" seems to cause a degree of apprehension in some visitors prior to their tour. In my opinion, a dry landing is actually more cause for concern than a wet landing; a brief explanation is in order.

A wet landing is actually a beach landing. The *panga* cannot make it all the way to shore without damaging the propeller and fouling the engine. So you will have to step out into a foot or so of water. Actually, you swing your feet out over the side and then step into the water. Reverse the procedure when you get back in; sit down facing outwards and swing your feet in. Understandably, you don't wear your shoes during a wet landing. You're told to carry them, but I tie the laces together (with a bow or slipknot) and toss them onto my shoulder, thus freeing my hands for steadying myself if need be.

A dry landing is made up against a natural dock of lava rocks, and you wear your shoes. These landings are a bit tricky because the *panga* is moving with the wave action, and the rock you step onto often is slippery and has a small flat portion. It's important that you watch what you're doing and listen to the Guide, who will offer you a hand as you disembark. When accepting the Guide's hand, grasp the wrist and the Guide will grasp yours. This "wristlock" is much stronger than a handshake grip. Once on shore, continue to place your feet carefully along the first few feet of rocks, which are often quite slippery (depending on the tide level).

While the *pangas* are quite sturdy, they do have a balance point. Once again, listen to the Guide and when disembarking, don't stand up until the passenger in front of you is about to step out. Passenger loading and unloading should be done on an alternate side basis — first the left and then the right.

You want your hands free when getting in and out of the *panga*, so your bags should either be daypacks or fanny packs. Toss your snorkeling gear bag in before you enter; when disembarking, have someone hand it to you after you have both feet on land. Camera gear should be in a water-resistant case or bag. If you have your camera out, like I always do, keep it covered with a plastic bag. Those of you seated towards the bow will get a lot of spray action. You'll actually get more than that, probably a good splash or two, if the *panga* is going against the current. It's also important that you wear your camera (and/or binoculars), with the neckstrap around you; waves and other passengers have a way of knocking you off-balance.

Note: Your landing craft may be met by a reception committee of sea lions. All this presents no problem and actually adds to the entertainment value of the tour, with one notable exception — a bull sea lion. Sometimes the bulls are not real happy about letting tourists into their territory, and they'll stand there barking at the *panga*. There is some chance that the landing will have to be aborted in favor of the next beach. Listen to your Guide.

The Morning Tour — Once you land, your island tour will take about 1-2 hours. Put your shoes on if you had a wet landing. I wear socks as well; they prevent blisters and sunburn. If you brought your snorkel gear, set it down on a rock, well above the high tide line. Check with your Guide, and make sure the location is okay. Remember that you must stay on the trail. Don't get too far ahead if the Guide is looking after some stragglers. On several of the islands, you will be walking over lava rocks for a good portion of the tour. Some of them are not well-anchored, and will give way under you. Get the balance point of your feet figured out, and you'll be fine, literally skipping over the rocks.

Keep your eyes moving. Look up and check-out the bird activity. Have your camera around your neck, the battery "On," the shutter advanced, and the exposure set. Take an average reading on the side of the road, and then set the exposure to Automatic (see Chapter VII, PHOTOGRAPHING THE GALAPAGOS ISLANDS).

Your Guide knows where the wildlife is, so stay close. When you get a photographic opportunity, be courteous to, and mindful of, the others in your group. Be careful not to step in front of someone about to take a picture. Sometimes if the best photo angles are occupied, you'll just have to wait your turn. You actually help everyone, and get some excellent photos, by stooping down to take your shots. The perspective and composition are usually improved from this low vantage point.

After your tour, there may be swimming and snorkeling time (usually about an hour — the Guide will tell you). It helps if you wear an underwater watch, so you know when to return to shore. Don't wander off by yourself. If you're snorkeling, the best views are close to the rocks. You'll return to the boat about noon; the cook will usually have some *hors d'oeuvres* waiting for you.

Note: If you are boarding the *panga* wet-landing-style, take off your shoes and rinse them in the water. If you are boarding dry-landing-style, you will be reminded to take off your shoes once you're on the yacht. Aside from keeping the yacht and *panga* clean, rinsing your shoes helps to prevent the accidental transmission of indigenous and (even worse) introduced plant seeds to another island.

Back on the boat, lunch will be ready, and you'll be ready for lunch. The main course will consist of anything from fresh fish to meat. There will be lots of vegetables with fresh fruit for dessert. If you're on a Cruise Ship, lunch will be buffet-style, and you can either eat in the dining room or outside on the sun deck.

The Afternoon Schedule — After lunch, the Guide will announce the next departure time — usually around 3:00. By now, many of the passengers are ready for a *siesta*. As you visit your cabin, you'll be pleasantly surprised to find your bed made and the waste buckets emptied. Incidentally, if you have any clothes to be dried, this is an ideal time. There are several clotheslines on the yachts, usually up by the radar and radio antennae.

I like to rest topside, maybe catching some rays and sleep at the same time. Also some good photos. The boat will be under way shortly, heading to the next island or to another Visitor Site on the same island you saw in the morning. Every once in a while, I open my eyes and look around — for dolphins! You never know when they're going to show up, riding the bow wave for a few miles before going back to their other business matters. I've been the first to spot them on several occasions, something I'm rather proud of. And, you bet, I have my camera on-deck with me.

I also use this time to read up on the next Visitor Site. If you're on a Cruise Ship, there may be a Galápagos video being shown. In due time the Guide or Big Brother (or Sister) on the P.A. system will announce that the departure time is nearing. Once again, get yourself and your stuff ready.

The Afternoon Tour — In some ways this will be a repeat performance of the morning show. In other ways, it will be a whole new show, with different plants, different animals, different landscape, and maybe a different landing. Different lighting too. I don't mind a late afternoon departure, because it means I can stay on the island later. The Guides must have you off the island by 6:00 p.m., but some passengers like to get back early to have a "cold one." If you're a photographer, try to convince the others of the great shots that can be taken by one and all as the sun gets lower in the sky. Afternoons are also great for sea birds, because there's more of them around, having returned or returning from their off-shore fishing activities.

Eventually it will be back to the boat time. Guess what's waiting for you? You got it — dinner! It's a rough life at sea, and it gets rougher as the days go by.

The Evening Schedule — Dinner is a little heavier version of lunch. On a Cruise Ship, it's a sit down, formal affair, with a Captain's Table, waiters, and wine lists. After the evening meal, there is a debriefing session during which the following day's schedule is announced and explained. Some of the Guides do a good job of sketching out the Visitor Sites and a list of the important features (see Photo #7). Take this time to ask any questions you may have.

After the debriefing session, the social functions usually begin. If you're on a yacht, this will include cards, music, swapping lies, and downing a few. On the Cruise Ships, there is live entertainment and a dance floor. On some tours with Tour Leaders (remember them), there are evening workshops, and this is when you can really learn about the Galápagos. It adds another dimension to the trip.

After 9:30, people will begin to drift off — literally. It's been a long day, and the ocean sun has a way of getting to you. Tomorrow is another big one, and it's time to hit the sack. You'll soon wake up to that comforting sound of the engines starting. I'm a pretty light sleeper, and there are nights when, after the ship is under way, I'll go up on-deck. It's a beautiful sight to watch the bioluminescent particles drifting by; it seems like the whole ocean is lit up. There are times when I'll visit the bridge, stand next to the captain, and watch the radar equipment continuously form outlines of the surrounding islands. After a while, I'll go back to my cabin and will soon be back asleep.

TIPPING THE CREW

Before the islands are introduced, let's skip ahead to the end of the cruise, when it is customary to tip the crew for a job well-done. It may be customary, but there's no set procedure for it. There are, however, some basic ways of going about this awkward business; you can tip each crew member or give an overall "crew tip" to either the captain or Guide for distribution. You also have the choice of giving your own tip directly to the crew or putting the gratuity in a tip box. A lot depends on the situation, which we'll try to sort out.

First off, the total crew tip ranges from $50-$75 per passenger per week. This range is an estimate, and is subject to the service you feel that you received. This is exactly the same concept as a restaurant, except the time span is a lot longer and the service is more extensive. Out of this estimated total, a little less than half (depending on the total number of crew members) goes to the Guide. This, after all, is the person you have had the most contact with. The remainder of the tip is split among the rest of the crew. On a yacht, this includes the sailor(s), cook, and possibly an engineer (who maintains the engine and equipment). On some yachts, the captain is an employee and shares in the gratuities; on other yachts, the captain is an owner. It's up to you to determine the situation.

Having taken it this far, it sort of makes sense to tip the Guide personally. From there, it depends on the boat, how well you know the crew, and how much small change you have ($5 bills or lots of 1000 sucre notes). Traveler's checks are welcome and accepted. Simply sign the bottom and print your passport number on the back. Do not insert the date or the name of the recipient; this will facilitate cashing the traveler's check by the "end user." If all you have is a $20 bill or 10,000 and 5000 sucre notes, it may be easier to put the money in an envelope or tip box (on Cruise Ships) or to assemble the crew and put the money down (on a small yacht). In general, it's not the best to hand the money to a crew member and ask that person to distribute the tips. One of two things happen in this situation; either the designated tipper stiffs one (or more) of the crew members, or one (or more) of the crew members think that they've been short-changed. In addition, on a Cruise Ship you may want to tip certain individuals, such as a particular waiter, etc.

INTRODUCING THE GALAPAGOS ISLANDS

> . . . By far the most remarkable feature in the natural history of this archipelago . . . is, that the different islands to a considerable extent are inhabited by a different set of beings. I never dreamed that islands, about fifty or sixty miles apart, and most of them in sight of each other, formed of precisely the same rocks, placed under a quite similar climate, rising to a nearly equal height, would have been differently tenanted. . . .
>
> *Charles Darwin, 1845*

The islands are different, each with its own population of wildlife. And the population on a given island will vary with the seasons as well as from year to year, depending on climatic conditions. These are natural cycles, an important part of the Galápagos learning experience. Keep this in mind as you visit each island. It may be very disappointing to find that most of the blue-footed boobies have abandoned their nesting site on a particular island 3 months earlier than usual. While this may have deprived you of an opportunity to observe and photograph them, their early departure is a vital part of natural history. You may witness sea lion pups that have been orphaned by their families and left to die; it's an extremely sad sight to behold, but this too is part of nature. You'll get lots of great photos and will see wildlife found nowhere else in the world. But most of all, you'll experience the living laboratory of evolution at work — the Galápagos Islands.

Note: Most of the Galápagos (about 97 percent), including a few islands entirely, is "off-limits" to the public. The *Galápagos National Park Service*, in conjunction with the *Charles Darwin Research Station*, has established over forty official Visitor Sites. These are areas where, accompanied by a Licensed Guide, tourists may enter. The Visitor Sites are typically delimited by a series of trail markers. The following sections will introduce the reader to most of the Visitor Sites. It should be noted that from time to time, owing to necessity, certain areas are closed off and new Sites are opened. I see this happening with greater frequency in the future, in part because of the ecological impact of tourism on some of the central islands. At the same time, with more frequent flights to San Cristóbal Island, there will be pressure to open up more Visitor Sites in the Southern Islands.

During the following sections, frequent references are made to the Map of the Visitor Sites; you will find the map at the end of this book.

THE CENTRAL ISLANDS

Many of these islands are commonly visited during a 1 week Galápagos tour. The island of Pinzon and the islets of North Plaza and Daphne Minor are off-limits to visitors.

BARTOLOME (BARTHOLOMEW)

The small island of Bartolomé is located off the eastern shore of James Island, across what is called Sullivan Bay (see the Map). Actually, Sullivan Bay is a Visitor Site on James Island (see below) as well as a body of water. Your two-part (sometimes three-part) excursion begins with a dry landing, followed by a strenuous 30-40 minute hike to the summit of a once-active volcano. I classify this as strenuous only because it is a steep climb; the footing is fairly easy, however (although loose and sandy), with a wooden stairway covering most of the distance. Also, there are no tricky rocks to traverse. The stairs are for your convenience as well as to prevent erosion; do not walk to the side of them. This is one of the most popular visits in all the Galápagos because of the beautiful panoramic views offered at the top (see Photo #30).

The view is educational as well as inspiring. The volcanic features include lava formations as well as spatter cones and cinder cones (see the section on Formation in Chapter II). Your Guide may refer to them as pyroclastic cones, which is a general term used to describe formations of solid material (as opposed to liquid lava) ejected from the volacano.

Speaking of cones, you will see Pinnacle Rock, a most striking example of a tuff cone (a vertical rock formation of hardened ash). There are also good examples of pioneering plants, including some beautiful stands of lava cactus.

After your descent to sea level, you will get back in the *panga* and take a short ride over to the "trail of two beaches" (on the left side of Photo #30). This will be a wet landing. Leave your snorkel gear at the north beach before taking the trail through the mangroves to the south beach. Here, one often sees mating sea turtles and white-tipped sharks close to shore. After retracing your steps back north, you will be rewarded with some excellent swimming and snorkeling. Occasionally, penguins are spotted in this area.

Unique Photo Opportunities: Pinnacle Rock is quite striking and the most-photographed landmark in the islands (see Photo #31). You'll have all kinds of angles and distances to choose from, including close-ups from the *panga*. The view from the summit offers the best panoramic view of the islands; this is the best opportunity to take a shot of each other (and perhaps have a fellow passenger take a shot of both or all of you), posing in the foreground.

The volcanic features are also fascinating subjects. With several spatter cones grouped together, Bartolomé is your basic moonscape and offers excellent photographic opportunities of the unique geological formations. Finally, unless you visit the western islands, this may be your best opportunity for a penguin photo. Even if it's not the best composition, you might want to take a couple of shots just for documentation.

DAPHNE MAJOR

The Daphne twins, Major and Minor, are islets located north of Santa Cruz and west of Baltra. Daphne Minor is closed to the public. Erosion problems and other ecological considerations (as well as related research) have kept Daphne Major closed as well. Recently, the *Galápagos National Park Service* has reopened Daphne Major, but boats are presently limited to one visit per month. Unless the blue-footed boobies are known to be nesting in the interior craters and the currents are relatively calm (making the dry landing safe), your captain will recommend against visiting the island.

Unique Photo Opportunities: Yachts often sail between Daphne Major and Minor, offering good views and excellent shooting opportunities of these partially-eroded tuff formations. If you are fortunate enough to land on Daphne Major, excellent shots of blue-footed boobies and possibly red-billed tropic-birds await you.

JAMES (SANTIAGO)

James is a large, somewhat barren island northwest of Santa Cruz with a mostly-volcanic landscape. The once well-represented vegetation has been severely altered by the feral goat population, at one time estimated at upwards of 100,000 (started by only four introduced animals in the early 1800s). Due to an extensive, joined effort by the *Galápagos National Park Service* and the *Charles Darwin Research Station*, the goat population has been significantly reduced in recent years to around 60,000. Several of the visiting yachts have been known to sail away with "a side of goat," and it is common to refer to all good on-board meat dishes as *"chivo de Santiago"* — goat from James Island.

The Visitor Sites on James are as follows:

Buccaneer Cove — Located on the northwest corner of the island, this area was a haven for pirates during the 1600s and 1700s. This is typically a cruise-by point due to the sometimes unsafe (wet) landing conditions (when the sea is active) and the lack of unique wildlife. Also, the large fenced-in vegetation area (used as protection from the goats) doesn't make it the most popular of Visitor Sites.

James Bay — Located on the west side of James Island, the wet landing on the dark sands of Puerto Egas, James Bay leads to one of the more rewarding visits in the Galápagos — a swim in the Fur Seal Grotto. First, though, a trail leads inland to the remains of a salt mining operation, one of several largely-unsuccessful attempts to commercialize the Galápagos. Some groups will make the 1 hour round trip to the Sugarloaf Volcano (about 1000 ft elevation). But it is the Fur Seal Grotto that produces the most pleasure for visitors. Here one can swim with both fur seals and sea lions in a series of rocky pools. For many, this is the only opportunity to see the fur seal, once thought to be on the verge of extinction (see Photo #60).

In addition to the fur seals, James Bay offers the best opportunity for tide-pooling in the Galápagos. Your Guide will point out sponges, nudibranchs & tiny (nodilittorinoid) snails, barnacles, hermit crabs, and several fish species (including the endemic four-eyed blenny). Be careful in this area, though, as the wet rocks are usually covered with very slippery algae.

Espumilla Beach — After a wet landing on a large beach, a walk through a mangrove forest leads to a lagoon usually inhabited by a group of flamingos as well as pintail ducks and common stilts. This is a nesting site as well as a feeding area for the flamingos. Sea turtles dig their nests at the edge of the mangroves, and care must be taken not to walk on these large depressed areas in the dark-hued sand. There is often time for swimming and snorkeling at the end of the tour.

Sullivan Bay — Located at the eastern coast of James Island, across from Bartolomé, Sullivan Bay offers a rare look at a recently-formed lava field. The eruptions are thought to have taken place around 1890, which is recent enough in geological terms. A dry landing is usually made, but if the seas aren't calm, a wet landing at the beach area may be necessary. Visitors get to swim and snorkel.

Unique Photo Opportunities: The clear, often sunlit water of the Fur Seal Grotto gives those with underwater cameras the best opportunity to get some great aquabatic shots of both fur seals and sea lions. In addition, James Bay usually provides the visitor with a chance to photograph the Galápagos hawk and the yellow-crowned night heron, often at close range. There are also excellent wide-angle opportunities of naturally-sculptured tuff formations. At Sullivan Bay, it's all wide-angle photography, with great opportunities for texture shots of the smooth, rope-like *pahoehoe* lava flows.

MOSQUERA

Mosquera is a tiny islet located between Baltra and Seymour Islands (see the Map). It is basically a long, narrow beach with a large population of sea lions. Due to its proximity to the Baltra Airport, Mosquera is a favored Visitor Site for many of the yachts on the first or last day of the tour. Needless to say, this is a wet landing site; swimming and snorkeling are part of the activities.

You will note that Mosquera is flat, seemingly not related to the other volcanically-formed islands. Actually, as with several of the islands in the Galápagos (including Baltra, the Plazas, and Santa Fe), this area has been geologically uplifted. An uplift is a land mass formed by lava flowing through a subsurface geological fissure (a fault), gradually lifting the mass through and past the ocean surface. In the Galápagos, the uplifted islands have been over a million years in the making; marine fossils are still evident in many of these locations (see the section on Urvina Bay, Isabela Island in this chapter).

Unique Photo Opportunities: This is one of the best locations for sea lion shots.

SOUTH PLAZA

The Plazas are a pair of islets situated just off the east coast of Santa Cruz. Only South Plaza is a Visitor Site and is another example of a geological uplift. In this case, the southern portion of this narrow islet (only a couple hundred yards wide) has considerably more uplift to it, forming cliffs with spectacular views.

The tour begins with a dry landing. There is often a sea lion guarding the natural dock; let the Guide take care of the situation (which is often achieved with little more than a clapping of the hands). The trail leading to the cliffs goes through a combined Coastal and Dry Vegetation Zone with prickly pear cactus and extensive patches of salt-tolerant sesuvium. The sesuvium is usually seen as distinctive red mats, although it turns green when rainfall is abundant.

The prickly pear (*opuntia*) cactus is the food base of the land iguana, also found in this area. Over the last few years, the generally large population of land iguanas on South Plaza has been depleted by the 1982-83 *El Niño* weather phenomenon, during which a high percentage of the cacti were destroyed by root rot (caused by the excessive rainfall). The cacti were never able to recover, due to a long-term drought, and in turn many of the land iguanas were starved off and their numbers reduced. The effects are still seen, with fewer and skinnier land iguanas in the area, but according to the Darwin Station, it is only expected to stabilize the population, not to threaten it.

The walk along the sea cliffs is a very pleasant experience, as swallow-tailed gulls, shearwaters, and red-billed tropicbirds are making seemingly-endless back and forth flights in preparation for landing in their nests, located in the crevices found along the overhanging ledges.

Towards the end of the cliffside walk, you will encounter a bachelor sea lion colony, a battle-scarred collection of old bulls in various stages of recuperation or in total retirement.

Owing to its proximity to Puerto Ayora, South Plaza is a very popular Visitor Site, and many of the Day Trip boats come here on a frequent basis. I would go so far as to say that this is an over-visited area, with already-noticeable effects, such as a decrease in the wildlife population densities as well as trail erosion.

Caution: Swimming and snorkeling opportunities are sometimes offered here. While some Guides would view this statement as over-cautious at best, the sea lion bulls here can be very aggressive, and I know several incidents where tourists have been bit. Be very careful!

Unique Photo Opportunities: Standing near the cliffs and panning your camera across the skies, you should be able to get some spectacular gliding shots of red-billed tropicbirds and swallow-tailed gulls as they fight the off-shore winds to land safely in their nesting areas. Don't stand too near the edge, though, for there is potential danger here; the records show that there have been a couple of tragic falls. The swirling winds increase the danger potential. Actually there are a few recessed areas where the dropoff is very gradual, and I find them to be safe and convenient shooting locations. It's where I took one of my favorite in-motion shots of a tropicbird (see Photo #28). Just make sure your hat is on good and tight, so the wind doesn't get it.

This is the only bachelor sea lion colony you will see, and these veterans, complete with their battle scars, are worthy subjects. There are also good wide-angle lens opportunities with the red sesuvium in the foreground and your anchored boat in the background (see Photo #8).

RABIDA (JERVIS)

Often termed the geographic center of the Galápagos, the islet of Rábida is located just south of James Island (see the Map). The tour begins with a wet landing on a dark red beach, the coloring of which is volcanic in origin. A short walk leads to a salt water lagoon, where flamingos are sometimes seen; this is a feeding area for them, and not a nesting site, thus accounting for their only occasional presence. The salt bush at the far side of the lagoon are a nesting area for the brown pelican, providing a rare look at pelican family life.

Rábida is said to have the most diversified volcanic rocks of all the islands. The interior of the islet is a sloping hillside covered with palo santo trees.

The tour often ends with a swimming and snorkeling opportunity; actually, this is my favorite snorkeling site in the islands, offering a tremendous diversity of near-shore and pelagic fishes.

Unique Photo Opportunities: The dark red coloring of the beach is most picturesque and makes a great background for sea lion shots (see Photo #12). The flamingo lagoon may offer another opportunity for some beautiful pictures. This will probably be the only pelican nesting area you will see, and these always-interesting birds may oblige you with some unique poses (see Photo #58). If you have an underwater camera, definitely bring it with you for the snorkeling session.

SANTA CRUZ (INDEFATIGABLE)

Centrally located, the island of Santa Cruz is also the center of Galápagos tourism. About half of the island's 12,000 residents live in or around the town of Puerto Ayora, many of them part of the infrastructure required to support the tourist trade. Puerto Ayora is also the home of the *Charles Darwin Research Station*, an important Visitor Site as well as the operations center for Galápagos wildlife conservation and preservation programs. These programs are carried out by the *Galápagos National Park Service*, also located in Puerto Ayora.

There are several Visitor Sites on Santa Cruz besides the Darwin Station, including Las Baches Beach, Conway Bay, the Highlands, Tortuga Bay, and Whale Bay. The Highlands itself offers a number of tours, including *Los Gemelos* (the twin pit craters) and the Tortoise Reserve.

Puerto Ayora — As pointed out, Puerto Ayora (population approx. 6000) is the economic center of the Galápagos Islands. All the tour boats visit Puerto Ayora for at least 1 day, anchoring in Academy Bay (named after the famous scientific expedition of 1905-06 by the *California Academy of Sciences* and their boat, the ACADEMY). After a visit to the Darwin Station (see below), tourists are allowed some free time in town to do some shopping as well as restaurant-and-bar-hopping. Occasionally, trips are made to the Highlands, making stops at some of the Visitor Sites located in this lush, fertile area (see below).

There are several gift and souvenir shops in Puerto Ayora, with the T-shirt being the prime commodity. There are several generic designs, with the best prices (about $6) coming from the low profile shops on the fringes of town. The fancier stores in town command some high prices, but keep in mind that you can't find good Galápagos shirts on the mainland.

This is also a good opportunity to purchase any toiletry items you may have run out of. Don't forget those snacks you've been thinking about — a box of cookies, some candy, etc. Or maybe a bottle of rum. You can take care of most of your list at any of the general stores in town.

If you need to exchange currency, please note that there are no official *cambios* in the Galápagos. While several shops post *cambio* signs, they are providing this service at significantly higher-than-mainland rates. The best exchange rate can usually be had at the Bodega Blanca (located next to the Hotel Galápagos), one of the few places in the islands to cash a traveler's check.

Should your camera be dead, batteries can be purchased at Banon Maria, a general store located next to the *INGALA* and *CETUR* offices. Should your camera really be dead, there is a repair facility called Photomechanik, operated by Carl Heinzberger who claims to be able to work on most major brands on a 24 hour emergency repair basis.

Note: Before concluding that your camera needs to be repaired, always replace the batteries, even if the ones in the camera are fairly new. Especially batteries bought in South America, which are known to have a very short lifetime. Which is another reason to bring along some spares.

If you get hungry, there are several good (but not great) eating spots in Puerto Ayora. There is the Four Lanterns (located on Pelican Bay), an outdoor pizzeria which also offers *crepes* and sandwiches. Their *espresso* is very good, especially after you've been at sea for an extended period of time without good coffee. For Chinese food, Ecuadorian-style with lots of fish, there is the Chifa Asia, located near the main dock. There are outdoor tables, and even if you're not very hungry, this is a good beer stop before heading back to the boat.

Speaking of beer, there are several "stops" you may want to consider. The first, and my favorite, is the Hotel Galápagos, located right next to the Darwin Station. This is the classiest place in town, with the best view in town, and the best-stocked bar in the islands. For after-hours, serious-conversation-time, head on over to La Garrapata, an outdoor pub and cafe located in the heart of scenic, downtown Puerto Ayora. And if your feet get twitchy and demand to dance, next door to La Garrapata is the town's hot disco, La Panga, where the landings are said to always be wet.

For those that wish to extend their stay in the Galápagos, Santa Cruz is the place is visit and Puerto Ayora is the right place to stay. While there are several accommodations, ranging from $2/night pensions, I heartily recommend the Hotel Galápagos. This is the kind of rustic hotel you envision when you visit an out of the way location. A double room, located in a separate cabin, goes for about $70. The ocean views are wonderful. The Hotel Delfin has a similar rate, and a nice location as well (on the other side of the bay, or *"otra lado"* as the locals say); rooms are subject to availability, and first priority is given to their Day Cruise Program (see the section on Day Trip Yachts in Chapter IV). For extended stays at a pleasant location (also at a pleasant price — double rooms for about $20-$30/night), consider the Lobo Del Mar or the Sol Y Mar, both comfortable, ocean-view hotels.

Unique Photo Opportunities: If you visit the Hotel Galápagos, a walk around the grounds will provide some great opportunities to photograph the large marine iguanas that patrol this area. If your Guide takes you to the "other side," a tidal lagoon has a few resident stilts, lava gulls, and herons; this may be your best chance at getting some close-ups of these beautiful birds. While your boat is anchored in Academy Bay, you might find the uniquely-shaped houses up on the cliffside (*el barranco*) to be interesting subjects. Many of the residents are interesting as well; ask your Guide to tell you who lives where and some of the local history.

Charles Darwin Research Station — Every Galápagos tour visits the *Charles Darwin Research Station*, which was established in 1961 to solve the problems of wildlife conservation in the archipelago. Aside from the development of operations to ensure the survival of endangered plant and animal species, the Darwin Station has coordinated several conservation-oriented educational programs for Ecuadorian students. In addition, a Visitor Center is actively managed. For many tourists, this is the only opportunity to see giant tortoises — certainly the closest-range opportunity. There are three tortoise pens housing animals of uncertain island ancestry; since their race cannot be determined, they are not useful for breeding purposes. Thus, visitors are allowed to touch these animals, the only exception in the National Park to the "hands off" rule.
   The Tortoise Rearing Center is also visited. National Park Wardens have collected tortoise eggs from various islands where they have been preyed on and threatened to the point of extinction by several species of introduced mammals. The eggs are then incubated, and the hatchlings are raised for several years, until they are able to withstand the predatory efforts of the mammals that man has introduced to the Galápagos. Since 1970, several hundred tortoises have been repatriated to their native islands. The Hood (Española) Island subspecies is the most notable success. In the early 1960s, this race had been reduced to just three males and eleven females. As a result of the coordinated efforts of the Darwin Station and the *Galápagos National Park Service*, over 200 Hood Island tortoises have been repatriated.
   Other parts of this unique tour include a Nature Trail, which winds through the Darwin Station and Park Service grounds. Along this trail are numbered posts alongside typical examples of the vegetation. The numbers correspond to a special brochure available at the Information Center. Your Guide will also take you to the Van Straelen Exhibit Hall, where the Galápagos natural history story is told in pictures and words. After the tour, there are occasional lectures on island conservation. As the speaker will point out, the Darwin Station has no fixed income and depends on contributions to carry out its conservation and education programs. Your donation would be well received at this time. See the section on Growth, Tourism, and Conservation in Chapter II for complete information on contributing to this worthy cause.

Groups can now be taken to the once "off-limits" pen of Lonesome George, the last-surviving member of the Pinta Island subspecies. The origin of his name is sadly evident. There is an excellent chance, however, that George, estimated to be about 50-60 years old (still young by tortoise standards) may not be bonesome forever. The Darwin Station has paired George with a couple of females from a different, but closely-related (Wolf Volcano, Isabela Island) subspecies, and he is said to be showing an "active interest." For all the gossip and complete details regarding the love life of Lonesome George, ask your Guide!

After your tour, you may want to stop at the two souvenir kiosks (one is operated by the Darwin Station and the other by the Park service — proceeds go directly to and help support these organizations). Several items are for sale, including books, T-shirts, etc.

Unique Photo Opportunities: For most visitors, this is the only opportunity for pictures of the giant tortoises. Take advantage of it! On sunny days, there is usually a bit of glare coming off the carapace (shell), and the use of a polarizing filter may be necessary.

The Highlands — Several tours visit the Highlands of Santa Cruz. As your bus or van leaves Puerto Ayora, the scenery will continuously change as you ascend through all seven Vegetation Zones of the Galápagos. If your journey is during the garúa season (approximately June-December), whatever sunlight there was down below has long since disappeared by the time you reach the top. Often, the "mist" feels more like rainfall, and a jacket is advised (as well as protective bags for your photographic equipment). See the section on Climate in Chapter II.

A favorite stop is *Los Gemelos* (The Twins), a pair of large pit craters (or sinkholes) formed by a collapse of the ground located over a subsurface fissure (fault). Another point of attraction is a trail leading to an area where there are usually several vermillion flycatchers.

Speaking of birds, the Highlands offer several unique habitats (due to the change in altitude and the consequent change in vegetation) to land birds, including tree finches, warbler finches, vegetarian finches, dark-billed cuckoos, yellow warblers, and Galápagos flycatchers. The large black birds you see on the side of the road are the introduced smooth-billed anis (introduced to rid cattle of ticks, which turned out to be a bit of a fiasco, as they seem to eat everything else but ticks). The wide birds often seen perching on the cattle are, logically enough, cattle egrets.

Visits are often made to *Los Túneles*, where you can don a miner's lantern (for a fee), descend into and walk through the largest known lava tunnels in the Galápagos.

The **Tortoise Reserve** provides those with a sense of adventure an all-day Highlands tour of giant tortoises in the wild. Since most groups only have a few hours to spend in the Highlands, giant tortoises can also be viewed in the wild on private farms. The best of these opportunities adjoins the Tortoise Reserve and is called *Rancho Mariposa*. Here you can see a small herd of tortoises. Have your Guide arrange the tour is advance. Perhaps you can convince your Guide that this would be a good lunch stop as well, for owners Steve Divine and

Jenny Montenegro operate a by-appointment-only restaurant, serving a lunch with selections of chicken, fish, and home-grown beef and vegetables.

Another family-owned eating spot in the Highlands is the Restaurant Narwhal. This is another "by-appointment-only" restaurant (for groups — not individuals), and reservations have to be made at least a day in advance (by radio transmitter — ask your Guide). Owners Oswaldo and Ruth Donoso will greet you with a "welcome drink" followed by a complete dinner. Oswaldo, who has spent several years in California, will tell you all about the people of Galápagos (the "Galápagueños" as they call themselves). A third restaurant called the Altair, owned by Anita Salcedo, is also recommended.

By now you're wondering how all these cattle ranches, as well as the other farms, can legally exist in a National Park. Remember that when the Galápagos National Park was formed in 1959, it excluded about 3 percent of the land area, basically those zones that were already inhabited. This includes eight towns (on four islands) and their surrounding agricultural areas, with a total population of around 12,000 residents.

Unique Photo Opportunities: The lush Highlands are a fully-saturated green during the garúa season. With a rising fog, a surreal background presents several interesting photographic possibilities. This may be your only chance to get a shot of the bright red male vermillion flycatcher, and at *Rancho Mariposa*, you will probably get the opportunity of photographing several tortoises in a colorful duckweed-covered pond (see Photo #25).

Las Baches — Located on the north shore of Santa Cruz, close to the Baltra Airport, Las Baches is a swimming beach that serves as a Visitor Site on your first or last touring day. There's not much to see while snorkeling. One of the few remnants of the U.S. World War II presence in the Galápagos, a floating pier, can be seen here.

Caleta Tortuga Negra (Black Turtle Cove) — This wonderful Visitor Site is located on the northern portion of Santa Cruz Island near Las Baches (see the Map). The tour consists of a *panga* ride through a series of mangrove-surrounded coves and inlets. Here one often views several pairs of mating marine turtles (especially between September-February), white-tipped sharks, spotted eagle rays, and beautiful yellow cow-nosed rays. In order to avoid disturbing the wildlife, the outboard motor on the *panga* is turned off and passengers are urged to be very quiet. This visit is frequently at the beginning or towards the end of tours originating at Baltra Airport.

Note: The National Park has deemed this site to be sensitive to the impact of tourism and (as of this writing) allows only boats with a capacity of 12 (or less) passengers to visit.

Unique Photo Opportunities: This will be your best opportunity for photos of marine turtles and white-tipped sharks; make sure your polarizer is on the camera (see Chapter VII).

Conway Bay — Situated on the northwestern shore of Santa Cruz close to the islet of Eden (see the Map), Conway Bay is an excellent location for viewing sea lions. The visit will most likely be a private one for your group, for most boats do not include this Visitor Site in their tour of the islands.

Tortuga Bay — Considered by many to be the most beautiful beach in the Galápagos, Tortuga Bay is a half hour walk from Puerto Ayora and is a favorite weekend spot of the locals.

Whale Bay (Bahía Ballena) — Located on the western coast of Santa Cruz (see the Map), Whale Bay is not landed at as much as it is pointed out from the boat as a navigational and historical landmark (going back to the days of the pirates and whalers).

SEYMOUR

This islet is located just north of Baltra and is also called North Seymour (with Baltra occasionally, but rarely, referred to as South Seymour). This is another geological uplift (see the section above on the Islet of Mosquera). After a sometimes-tricky dry landing, your 1 hour land tour will begin by negotiating a few feet of slippery rocks, past an area where you are likely to encounter some swallow-tailed gulls and, of course, a few sea lions. Soon you'll arrive at one of the major nesting areas of the blue-footed booby. The "nests" include the trail itself; watch where you step. Their breeding cycle does vary, however, and is influenced by several factors, including the overall feeding conditions. You may catch them at any phase of this cycle, and they may in fact have already departed (leaving a few juveniles behind to fend for themselves).

During the first quarter of the year, there is usually a strong northern swell, resulting in good-sized breakers off Seymour. As you walk along the beach, there is a good chance of spotting "body-surfing" sea lions. If they're out there riding the waves, this is a great spot to "hang out for a few minutes and cheer them on."

Regardless of the time of year, the star attractions of the tour will be the largest colony of magnificent frigatebirds in the Galápagos. Remember, the word "magnificent" here is a noun, not an adjective, and is part of the species name (distinguishing these birds from the other species in the archipelago, the great frigatebird).

Seymour is another popular destination for the Day Trip boats, and I would say that there is the same potential problem of over-visitation here as there is on South Plaza (see above).

Unique Photo Opportunities: Aside from Española (Hood) Island, this may be your best opportunity for blue-footed booby photos. If the birds have mostly vacated the nesting area, save your "blue foot" film for Española. Also, unless you visit Tower (Genovesa), this may be your only chance of getting some shots of the inflated pouch of the male frigatebird. If the sea lions are body-surfing, it's definitely worth a few shots (although, due to the distance, this is one of the rare times that you need the power of a 300mm telephoto lens to do justice to the subject matter). If you've got a video camera with you, this is an ideal scene to capture.

SOMBRERO CHINO (CHINESE HAT)

Located just off the southeast tip of James Island, Sombrero Chino owes its name to its shape. Perhaps more than any Visitor Site, this islet conveys the volcanic origin of the Galápagos. After a wet landing, the beach soon gives way to an almost primeval landscape of volcanic rubble, including sharp outcroppings, cracked lava formations, and lava tubes. The lava fields encountered here are very fragile and will break beneath your feet; one must be very careful to stay on the trail.

Through it all, Sombrero Chino conveys a strong feeling that you've come to a very special place in the world. The title of Tui de Roy's book, **GALAPAGOS: ISLANDS LOST IN TIME**, takes on its full meaning here (see the Literature section).

After your land visit, there is usually a snorkeling session across the way off James Island. This is another of my favorite snorkeling sites; if you have the opportunity, get in the water here!

Note: The National Park has deemd this site to be sensitive to the impact of tourism and (as of this writing) allows only boats with a capacity of 12 (or less) passengers to visit.

Unique Photo Opportunities: There are several excellent wide-angle opportunities for landscape photos, especially late in the afternoon. These shots can be quite dramatic, showing the lava formations in the foreground, with the Chinese hat itself in the distance. While attempting such a shot, I was fortunate enough to catch some sea lions at rest in a lava tube (see Photo #14). This is also one of the few places where you can usually manage to see a pair of oystercatchers if the tide is right.

For those snorkeling here, this is one of the best areas for excellent underwater photos. Under the category of "absurd, silly shots," as you sail away from Sombrero Chino, you can wait for just the right moment to frame the Chinese hat perfectly on the head of your cabin mate. As you sail further away, the boat may (depending on the seas and boat size) approach one of the many surrounding islets (actually and collectively called the Bainbridge Rocks). The particular islet referred to here has a lagoon in its crater, and several flamingoes can usually be seen. For this view, you will have to get to the highest point on the boat that is permitted (the Guide will direct you). Both wide-angle and telephoto shots are recommended.

SOUTHERN ISLANDS

Most 1 week Galápagos tours visit all of the southern islands, which are significantly further apart than the central islands. Thus, unless you're on a Cruise Ship or an extremely fast yacht, almost all inter-island travel in these waters is done at night.

ESPANOLA (HOOD) — The southernmost island in the archipelago, Española, is the gateway into and out of the Galápagos for some of the sea birds, (which will leave the islands either after the breeding season and/or often in times of food shortage). Thus, you will find blue-footed boobies here while their nests further north (on Seymour Island, for example) have been abandoned. The remote location relative to the other islands has resulted in a high degree of species differentiation, such as the brightly colored marine iguanas; some species (easier thought of as subspecies) are actually endemic to Española, such as the Hood mockingbird and the Española lava lizard. The waved albatross is endemic to Española as well as to the Galápagos.

There are two Visitor Sites on Española, Gardner Bay and Punta Suárez. If I had the option, I would prefer to visit Punta Suarez in the afternoon, during and after the return flights of the sea birds (from their fishing trips).

Gardner Bay — Situated on the northeastern portion of Española, Gardner Bay is a swimming and snorkeling site, with a beach that faces the islet of Gardner-near-Española. You'll have a wet landing amidst a large colony of sea lions. The Visitor Site at Gardner Bay is basically a beach, and there is no trail per se; it is considered an open area. Many visitors stay in one location, admiring and photographing the sea lions at close range. This seems to be the logical thing to do, especially since (and regrettably) many of the Guides sit on the sand and either read a book or talk with other Guides. What happens, though, is that you could miss seeing a Galápagos hawk at close range or a pair of American oystercatchers, the Galápagos doves, 3 species of Darwin's finches, the endemic Hood mockingbird, yellow warblers, lava lizards, and marine iguanas. Do as you wish, but be aware of the possibilities.

Gardner Bay is an excellent place to check-out your snorkeling equipment (especially for those who flew in to San Cristóbal, as this will be your first full day). Once your check-out is complete, however, the really good snorkeling is off Tortuga Rock (the islet in the distance that, oddly enough, looks like a tortuga).

Punta Suárez — Forming the western tip of Española, Punta Suárez offers the tourist a great abundance of wildlife, especially sea birds, and is my favorite Visitor Site. The wet landing is a bit tricky, and the *panga* may encounter some chop (depending on the current), on its long journey through the shallow harbor to and from the safe anchorage. Pay particular attention to protecting your camera equipment from the spray.

After your landing, it will be difficult to concentrate on the Guide's introductory comments, due to all the natural distractions. Aside from the sea lions, you will be approached by the endemic Hood mockingbird, and (especially in the afternoon) red-billed tropicbirds will be winging their way back and forth. The marine iguanas on Española are among the largest in the Galápagos and are brightly colored throughout the year; on other islands, these would be called "seasonal breeding colors." The lava lizards are also above-average size, and the female's red throat coloring is pronounced.

Once on the trail you will soon approach a series of tall rock formations on which a colony of masked boobies is generally found. After you continue on, nesting blue-footed boobies will most likely be everywhere on and just off the trail. These are the type of scenes you envisioned when your decision was made to visit the Galápagos Islands.

What comes next is even more dramatic, for you will soon approach an open area that forms the home (typically from March through December) to the

#40

#41

The waved albatross is a strikingly beautiful bird (#40). The overgrown, down-covered juveniles are the ultimate Baby Huey look-alikes (#41), adding a touch of humor to the feeding scene (#42).

#42

#43

#44

#45

The boobies are well-represented in the islands, with 3 resident species — blue-footed (#43), red-footed (#44), and masked boobies. In Photo #45, the somewhat vestigial nesting behavior of the photogenic masked booby is seen, whereby twigs and other materials are offered to the mate. Aside from the color of their feet, it is their courtship dance for which blue-footed boobies are so well known, part of which involves lifting the feet in sequence (#46).

#46

E. Heron

#47

The Galápagos Islands are home to Creatures great and small. Included in the latter category are the Sally Lightfoot crab (#47), green sea urchin (#48), pencil sea urchin (#49), and the leopard ray (#50).

#48

#49

#50

#51

#52

#53

The diverse Galápagos plants are well represented by drought-tolerant species, such as palo santo trees (#51), lava cactus (#52), and prickly pear cactus (#53).

#54

#55

Sea birds, shore birds, land birds; all are fascinating to observe and photograph. Seen here are the yellow-crowned night heron (the dark plumage resembling judicial robes — #54), the scavenging Hood mockingbird (breaking open an abandoned booby egg — #55), and the graceful common stilt (#56).

#56

#57

The classic shot of the flightless cormorant exiting the water and spreading its atrophied wings to dry the feathers (#57). During courtship, pelicans often intertwine their necks and bills in an amusing fashion (#58).

#58

#59

The sun is setting over Kicker Rock (#59) and your Galápagos adventure as a fur seal sadly notes your departure time is approaching (#60).

#60

entire world population (estimated at over 10,000 couples) of waved albatrosses — large, strikingly beautiful birds. You really don't want to leave this area, but you will have to move on, walking along the high cliffs of the southern shore, where the skies are full of sea birds. Finally, before you head back, you will come to a spectacular blowhole, loudly roaring and spouting forth a foamy spray almost 100 ft in the air.

Your tour will take about 2 hours (less if visiting from a Cruise Ship); you'll wish you could stay longer.

Unique Photo Opportunities: This is the place to let loose with the film, so make sure you have plenty in the camera bag when you go ashore. This is an ideal area for video as well. You'll have wonderful opportunities to photograph nesting blue-footed boobies at close range, possibly (depending on the season) even getting a few shots of their dance performance (see Photo #46). Then there's the dramatic poses of the masked boobies, their white body plumage beautifully set off against the grey rocky cliffs. This will be your best chance at photographing masked boobies (see Photo #45). Occasionally, the blue-foots and the masked boobies abandon their eggs, which are then preyed upon by the scavenging Hood mockingbirds, their long, thin bills being well suited for this purpose. This scene is worthy of documentation (see Photo #55). The brightest colors are the Christmas red and green of the marine iguanas, often jumping out at you (the colors — not the iguanas); these shots turn out especially brilliant on an overcast day or when taken late in the afternoon (see Photos #32-33).

If the waved albatrosses are in town (typically April-December), you will go through a lot more film, including shots of them feeding their overgrown, down-covered youngsters and their ritualized courtship displays (perfect for video). When you reach the cliff walk, you can start panning the camera, as the red-billed tropicbirds will be everywhere in the sky. Sometimes the lighting is just right to accent their long streaming tail feathers (see Photos #26-27). Then there's the blowhole, great for posing in front of.

Those are the sure shots. You might also be fortunate enough to get some pictures of a Galápagos hawk and/or perhaps a yellow-crowned night heron; both are frequently seen on Española.

FLOREANA (CHARLES)

Located directly south of Santa Cruz and west of Española, Floreana is also somewhat isolated, being a 4-5 hour cruise from either of its neighbors. The combination of nutrient-rich soil and an adequate water supply make Floreana an island of abundant plant life. This fact was not lost on the centuries of settlers who chose to live and farm on Floreana, giving the island a rich human history (some would call it infamous — see the History section of Chapter II).

There are three official Visitor Sites on Floreana — Punta Cormorán, the Devil's Crown, and Post Office Bay — as well as one unofficial site, the Wittmer Residence on Black Beach.

Punta Cormorán — Forming the northern tip of Floreana, Punta Cormorán is one of the most interesting Visitor Sites in the islands, with an emphasis on plant life and shore birds. Your first lesson will be in geology, however, as the tour begins with a wet landing on a beach with "green sand." Olive green that is, for these are olivine crystals, volcanically-derived silicates of magnesium and iron.

The trail soon leads to a brackish lagoon, where there are usually a few flamingos at the far end, often too far for good photos. The lagoon is also home to white-cheeked pintail ducks and common stilts (and occasionally other shore birds, including western sandpipers and semipalmated plovers, sanderlings, and phalaropes). Surrounding the lagoon are several of the steep, palo-santo-covered hills that dot Floreana; the stark, grey color and the twisty, usually barren branches give an eerie feeling to this island, whose history is mysterious enough.

The tour continues across the neck of the point to a beach on the other side. Along the way, your Guide will point out a rich variety of plants, including the beach morning glory, cutleaf daisy, lantana, leather leaf, palo verde, and scalesia. The native form of the lantana is being threatened by an introduced variety, brought to the islands in 1938 as an ornamental for a family garden and has now spread over several thousand acres.

The beach at the far end is composed of fine, white sand particles; appropriately enough, it is referred to as "Flour Beach." Some of the Guides say that this beach was "formed" of finely-digested and excreted material by the pencil sea urchin (I would have guessed "parrotfish"), but according to the local scientific community, there doesn't seem to be any truth to this nonetheless interesting story. What is true is that you can often see sting rays feeding right off the shoreline. You can see them float in and out with the wave action. If your feet are in the water, shuffle rather than lifting them; you do not want to step on a sting ray!

Unique Photo Opportunities: You'll want to get at least one documentation shot of the green beach formed of olivine crystals. There are several good photo opportunities at the lagoon, including the shore birds, wide-angle surreal vistas of the palo santo trees (see Photo #51), and the cracked lagoon bottom, visible during dry seasons (see Photo #29). This is also one of the best opportunities to take some pictures of the plant life; if you have a macro lens, this is the ideal time for it. If you decide to take some sting ray photos, you'll need a polarizer to cut out the reflection of the water. Also, the beach will provide your best chance of seeing and photographing a few ghost crabs as they peek out of their burrows; you have to be as fast as the ghosts to get this shot. For the birders in the audience, be on the lookout for the Galápagos flycatcher and the dark-billed cuckoo on the walk to and from Flour Beach.

Devil's Crown — The Devil's Crown, located just off Punta Cormorán, is said to offer the best snorkeling in the Galápagos (although it tends to be overcrowded at times and is not my favorite site). In fact, the only way to see the Crown is by water; it is termed a Marine Visitor Site, and no landings are allowed. Sometimes referred to as Onslow Island, this is an almost completely submerged volcano, and erosion has transformed the cone into a series of jagged peaks; as a result, this site really does look like a devil's crown.

You will typically get to snorkel at Devil's Crown right after visiting Punta Cormorán. The *panga* will take you over to the site and will remain in the area while you snorkel. This is a necessary safety factor, as the currents here can be very strong. Listen to and heed your Guide's advice and cautions! There are hammerhead sharks that frequent the area just outside Devil's Crown. They are not dangerous, and it is considered safe to swim in the same area, but it is always advisable to avoid them and certainly not to approach.

Unique Photo Opportunities: Snorkeling in the inside of the crown should provide an excellent opportunity to put your underwater camera through its paces. There is some coral here and many of the colorful fish that you would expect to find around such formations. Be careful not to touch or step on the coral. Unless you're a pretty good free diver, the waters on the outside are too deep for good photography.

Post Office Bay — Located at the northern end of Floreana, just to the west of Punta Cormorán (see the Map), Post Office Bay is not the most scenic of the Galápagos Visitor Sites, but certainly one of the most famous (see the section on History in Chapter II). For here is where the Post Office Barrel was placed and put into use in the late 18th century by English whaling vessels; soon the American whalers were using this "post office" as well. The idea was for the crew of the outbound ships to deposit any mail for home in the barrel; inbound whalers would then pick up any mail that was destined for their part of the world. You are invited to do the same — leave a post card or two and pick up any mail from your home area, which you can then post when you get back. This system is typically at least as fast as the regulation postal service, which says a lot about both distribution systems.

Your visit to Post Office Bay will begin with a wet landing. After the trip to the Barrel Post Office, several tours take a short walk to look at the remains of a Norwegian commercial fish drying and canning operation that was started in 1926 and abandoned after a couple of years. A lava tube that extends to the sea is also visited.

You may have some swimming time after your tour; there isn't much in the way of snorkeling here.

Unique Photo Opportunities: You have to get at least one shot of the Barrel Post Office.

Black Beach — By special arrangement, small groups may visit the Wittmer Pension (some Day Trip programs arrange to spend the night there) and meet its famous residents (see the History section in Chapter II). The trip begins with a dry landing at a cement pier and a short walk through the small settlement of Puerto Velasco Ibarra (consisting of mostly administrative buildings).

If you've read your history, this is a visit you won't want to miss. Discuss this possibility with your Tour Operator before the trip and with your Guide at the beginning of your cruise (so that the necessary requests and plans can be made). The Wittmer Pension is the "administration headquarters" of the Post Office Barrel, as well as the official Post Office for the community, and one of the Wittmers will cancel-stamp your post cards with one or more of the various seals and emblems (there are currently four) of this famous and unusual Post

Office. Other items for sale include Floreana T-shirts and signed copies of the book, **FLOREANA**, by Margret Wittmer (see the Literature section).

Recently, the Wittmer family have begun to offer guided tours of their original settlement in the highlands of Floreana; the tour requires about 2 hours and has a fixed price per group. Aside from providing a unique look at an important part of Galápagos history, the Floreana highlands is the only place that the medium tree finch is found.

Unique Photo Opportunities: As of this writing, Margret Wittmer is still occasionally meeting the public and will sometimes consent to pose for a photo. In fact, the word is that she has agreed to participate in a movie about the history of Floreana (no doubt featuring her role in the history).

SAN CRISTOBAL (CHATHAM)

San Cristóbal is the easternmost island in the archipelago. The principal town of Puerto Baquerizo Moreno is the capital of the Galápagos province; the administration offices and a major Ecuadorian Navy facility are located here, as well as one of the two major airports linking the Galápagos to the mainland.

There are also several Visitor Sites on and around San Cristóbal, including El Junco Lake, Frigatebird Hill, Kicker Rock, Lobos Islet, Punta Pitt, and Sapho Cove.

Puerto Baquerizo Moreno — Located just off the southwestern tip of San Cristóbal, Puerto Baquerizo Moreno is the second largest town in the Galápagos, with a population of 3000. With the recent opening of the major airport (which now has almost as many flights per week as Baltra), it is hoped that local tourism will expand. Indeed, the town would like to take some of the tourist dollars away from Puerto Ayora. But this won't be easy; this is a workingman's town and isn't really oriented (or visually appealing) to many tourists. Most visitors that spend the night here bypass the town altogether, going from the airport to the Grand Hotel, located on an isolated beach on the other side of town. Even the name, Puerto Baquerizo Moreno, is a bit difficult for most tourists. And the name of the town's port, Wreck Bay, is somehow not as cheerful-sounding as Academy Bay.

But the final page of this story has yet to be written. Puerto Baquerizo Moreno has a lot going for it. SAN AIRLINES (working closely with their affiliate, SAETA) is winning over customers, many of them Tour Operators, from TAME (and their affiliate, ECUATORIANA); the conversion is based more on service than price (although both are excellent). As more Tour Operators change their base of operations from Puerto Ayora to Puerto Baquerizo Moreno, the town will also change. Already there are some tourist-oriented restaurants and shops along the main street. Also, with Puerto Baquerizo Moreno being the capital of the Galápagos, the purse strings are controlled here, even if Puerto Ayora is still the economic center. This factor has to do with budgets, where certain improvements are made, facilities built, etc.

Unique Photo Opportunities: You can get some excellent sunset shots from the beach at the Grand Hotel.

El Junco Lake — Located in the highlands, this is the only sizable fresh water lake in the Galápagos. This Visitor Site is reached by bus or van, and is about a half hour drive from Puerto Baquerizo Moreno. Along the way, you will pass through several Vegetation Zones and the farming community of El Progreso; the settlement has a rather notorious history, dating back to the 1880s, related to the cruel treatment of the workers by its founder, Manuel Cobos (see the History section in Chapter II).

The cavity of the lake is the caldera of an extinct volcano. El Junco is fed by rain water, and the volume varies with the season; it may not be advisable to visit this site during the rainy season (January-April) because of possible muddy conditions. Incidentally, the name El Junco is not associated with pollution or Chinese boats, but is Spanish for "sedge," which is found along the edges of the lake.

Unique Photo Opportunities: In general, the orientation is the misty view and the birds. You may want a documentation shot of the infamous (at least in Galápagos history) settlement of El Progreso.

Frigatebird Hill — Located just outside Puerto Baquerizo Moreno, Frigatebird Hill is only one of two Visitor Sites (Seymour is the other) where one can see nesting colonies of both species of Frigatebirds (the "great" and "magnificent"). The tour is usually capped off with a stop and swim at the beach, Playa Mann.

Kicker Rock (León Dormido) — Located about an hour and a half to the northeast of Puerto Baquerizo Moreno, Kicker Rock is a remnant of a vertical tuff cone formation, abruptly rising almost 500 ft from the ocean (see Photo #9). Erosion has split the rock and given it its characteristic shape, which some see as a shoe, the origin of the name Kicker Rock. Others see it as a sleeping sea lion, or *León Dormido* in Spanish.

Although not an official Visitor Site (there is no landing area), Kicker Rock is cruised around by most tour boats that are based out of San Cristóbal. It is also cruised through, as the two large walls are separated by enough distance to allow the yachts to sail between them. Cruise Ship passengers get to do this via *panga*. Due to its proximity to the San Cristóbal Airport, Kicker Rock is visited on either the first or the last day of most tours. Aside from the beauty of the formation itself, one can usually see several blue-footed boobies, masked boobies, and frigatebirds on the cliffs as well as sea lions along the shore.

Unique Photo Opportunities: This is a great opportunity for wide-angle shots of these unusual formations from several perspectives, including shooting straight up as you sail between the rocks. Some of the best sunset shots are taken from the boat with Kicker Rock in silhouette (see Photo #59).

Lobos — Situated less than an hour's ride from Puerto Baquerizo Moreno, Lobos Islet is a seasonal nesting location for the blue-footed booby. There is no annual schedule for their presence, however. This, combined with the rough, rocky terrain, make Lobos one of my least favorite Visitor Sites. If you feel that you might have difficulty with the walk, skip this land tour.

Punta Pitt — Forming the northeast point of San Cristóbal, Punta Pitt is a new Visitor Site, opened in 1989. This area is a tuff formation that serves as a nesting site for many sea birds, including blue-footed, masked, and red-footed boobies, frigatebirds, swallow-tailed gulls, and storm petrels. Punta Pitt is considered by many to be a first class Visitor Site. It is hoped that many of the boats that sail from San Cristóbal will take the time to stop here (rather than at some of the less-worthwhile areas that are closer to the airport). Your tour at Punta Pitt begins with a wet landing; the seas can be a bit rough here at times, so protect your camera equipment.

Unique Photo Opportunities: This is the only location, except of course for Tower (Genovesa) Island, to see and photograph red-footed boobies. There are several good birding photo opportunities on Punta Pitt.

Sapho Cove (Puerto Grande) — Sapho Cove is located on the west coast, near Kicker Rock (see the Map). This well-protected cove has been used as a safe anchorage by sailing ships for hundreds of years. Today it is used by local fisherman to refit their boats and as a swimming area for tourists. There is a wet landing on the beach.

SANTA FE (BARRINGTON)

The island of Santa Fe is located in the southeastern portion of the archipelago, between the towns of Puerto Ayora (on Santa Cruz) and Puerto Baquerizo Moreno (on San Cristóbal). It's about a 2 hour cruise from Puerto Ayora and about 3 hours from Puerto Baquerizo Moreno. Santa Fe is another volcanic uplift (see the description of Mosquera in the Central Island section).

Your tour begins with a wet landing (on the northeastern portion of the island) at a beach known for ornery sea lion bulls. The trail has recently been redone by the Park Service, making it much easier to traverse. The main attraction here is the opportunity to find and observe one of the few remaining land iguanas of the species (*Conolophus pallidus*) endemic to Santa Fe Island. Some of these land iguanas can be 5 ft. long and have a beautiful golden-yellow color that shows off the scales to advantage, almost like a knight's mail (see Photo #36). Also, the spines along its back are very pronounced. In the same area, you'll also see a forest of giant prickly pear cactus. The height is an adaptive mechanism to protect them from the land iguanas and giant tortoises (now extinct on Santa Fe).

After your tour, swimming and snorkeling often follow. Be cautious about the somewhat-aggressive sea lion bulls (that are known to frequent this area) in the water.

Unique Photo Opportunities: The yellow coloring makes the endemic Santa Fe species of land iguana the most photogenic; avail yourself of this opportunity. You will also want a documentation shot of the giant prickly pear cactus trees (see Photo #53). Have a person stand in front for a size comparison. Also, there are some great panoramic views, including your boat in the harbor.

THE NORTHERN ISLANDS

The majority of the boats do not visit the northern portion of the archipelago during a 1 week tour; notable exceptions include the Cruise Ships and some of the better yachts. Almost all 10 day and 2 week cruises visit Tower (Genovesa), the only northern island with Visitor Sites. Marchena Island is a Marine Diving Site only, and Pinta is "off-limits."

TOWER (GENOVESA)

Located in the northeast portion of the Galápagos (less than half a degree north of the equator), Tower is an outpost for many sea birds (as Española is in the south). Perhaps this is why they are my two favorite islands to visit. The visit, however, is not an easy one for the captain and crew. First, it is a tiring 8-10 hour all-night sail from Puerto Ayora, Santa Cruz Island. Second, the entrance to Darwin Bay is extremely narrow as well as shallow (being part of the outer rim of a volcanic crater) and must be negotiated during daylight hours, preferably at high tide.

Interestingly, there are no land reptiles on Tower, only very small marine iguanas. This is attributed to the direction of the ocean currents, which evidently wouldn't have carried the terrestrial animals here.

Note: The Island has two Visitor Sites (see below), although the National Park has deemed Prince Philip's Steps to be sensitive to the impact of tourism and (as of this writing) allows only boats with a capacity of 12 (or less) passengers to visit; thus, the larger boats (including the Cruise Ships) only visit Darwin Bay.

Darwin Bay — As mentioned above, the anchorage at Darwin Bay, located on the southern portion of the island (see the Map) is actually the caldera of an extinct, partially-eroded volcano, with the surrounding cliffs forming the inner portion of the rim. While the origin of the name Tower is not known, one can imagine it had something to do with these towering cliffs. The tour will be a long, fairly-easy walk, but it is usually hot and dry here, so you may want to carry some water.

After a wet landing on a coral beach, the trail begins and goes past a few tide pools where several swallow-tailed and lava gulls are seen. Often they nest along the trail, and the Guide will warn you to be careful as you walk. Soon you enter a forest of salt bush, where adjacent colonies of great frigatebirds and red-footed boobies are seen nesting. The trail continues onto higher ground, and you reach an area where you can look down at a second colony of red-footed boobies nesting in mangrove trees. By the time the trail ends you are on a cliffside, with a commanding view of the bay as well as the sea birds flying back and forth in front of you.

Unique Photo Opportunities: You'll have some excellent opportunities at photographing the endemic swallow-tailed gull; make sure you focus tightly on the red eye-ring. The red-footed boobies also make wonderful subjects, especially shots of them landing, with their red feet up in the air in front of them, their own version of air brakes. There usually tends to be bright sun on this part of the tour, thus washing out the beautiful facial coloring of the red-foots, so I prefer to get close-ups on the other Visitor Site, Prince Philip's Steps.

Prince Philip's Steps — This tour begins with a fantastic *panga* ride along the base of the cliffs. During the ride, you can look directly up and see one red-billed tropicbird after the other trying to make a precise landing in their nest (usually a crevice on an overhanging ledge). Squadrons of frigatebirds are seen flying back and forth in their endless piratical pursuits. Red-footed boobies are perched on branches of palo santo trees which seem to grow out of the cliffs. And you haven't even landed yet.

Your *panga* ride continues until you reach the landing area, located near the eastern tip of Darwin Bay (see the Map). As the *panga* slows to land, you may notice a few fur seals in the water or resting on the shore. A dry landing is made at the base of a steep rock staircase named Prince Philip's Steps in honor of His Majesty's royal visit in the 1960s. Although the climb is steep and the footing may be a bit loose, it is not too difficult, and the tour is worth it. Although the climb is steep, the National Park has recently constructed a handrail, making the ascent quite manageable. You'll be at the top within a minute; go ahead and time it!

Once at the top, a trail enters an open area where nesting masked boobies and great frigatebirds are found. As the wooded area begins, a few short-eared owls are occasionally seen. Their presence and numbers generally depend on the abundance of storm petrels (on which they prey). I have been here when the petrels (and thus the owls) were virtually absent. The wooded area gradually becomes a forest of dwarf palo santo trees in which a colony of red-footed boobies is perched. Eventually the woods give way to an open lava field near the western coast. The storm petrels are usually seen here in great numbers. Although the petrels appear to be aimlessly swarming, if you let your eye follow a single individual, you will note that it is merely trying to find its way back home (which turns out to be a small crevice or part of a lava tube). If you look very carefully (with the aid of binoculars) you should be able to spot a short-eared owl lurking on the lava field in search of its next fill-up of petrel!

Unique Photo Opportunities: Have a couple of rolls of film handy and your telephoto lens on during the *panga* ride; the sea birds flying overhead offer seemingly-endless shooting opportunities. The palo santo forest is the best place for red-footed booby photos, including close ups of their feet and face. The facial colors are incredibly beautiful and intricately complex; slow film is in order as one of these shots will most probably be a blowup!

THE WESTERN ISLANDS

Very few of the boats visit the western islands of Fernandina and Isabela during a 1 week tour. The Cruise Ships and some of the yachts do travel to Tagus Cove, Isabela and Punta Espinosa, Fernandina as part of their weekly itinerary. However, for an extensive trip along the entire length of Isabela, including an optional climb to the rim of one of the volcanoes, a 2 week Galápagos Island tour is required. And highly recommended!

The western islands have a pristine, untouched quality that you won't find in the other regions of the Galápagos. This is most evident as you sail along the western coast of Isabela and through the narrow Bolívar Channel separating the island from Fernandina. These islands are still volcanically active, and fumaroles of steam and gas venting from the distant volcanoes can be seen from the boat. The fact that you only meet perhaps one other boat during your entire visit to the western islands only adds to the unique sense of adventure that is felt in this part of the archipelago.

Throughout Isabela, giant tortoises are occasionally seen near the coastline (as well as on the rim of the Alcedo Volcano). There is also considerable upwelling here, and the marine life is thus abundant — including whales! Going on-deck at night and viewing the southern sky as well as the numerous large bioluminescent particles in the water (that remain "on" for several seconds) is quite the experience. A trip to the western islands definitely rounds out and completes a tour of the Galápagos.

FERNANDINA (NARBOROUGH)

Fernandina is less than a million years old and is the youngest of the Galápagos Islands. Volcanically it is also the most active, with eruptions still occurring every few years, most recently in 1991. In 1968, the crater floor (4 miles by 3 miles across) collapsed about 1000 ft, a geological event of "most significant" status in Galápagos recorded history. This event was accompanied by hundreds of earthquakes, and fumes of ashes were gas-propelled 15 miles into the air.

There is only one Visitor Site on Fernandina — Punta Espinosa.

Punta Espinosa — Punta Espinosa is a wonderful Visitor Site. Located on the northeast portion of Fernandina, across the channel from Tagus Cove, Isabela, it is a narrow point of land, more like lava and sand, extending out from the base of the Fernandina Volcano. Your tour begins with a dry landing, and you may spot a few penguins from the *panga* on one of the rocky islets that dot this part of the coast. Due to several geologic uplifts, the dock is at landing level only during high tides, and other landing sites are used at lower tides. Once ashore, you proceed to the tip of the point across a sandy area which serves as a nesting site for the marine iguana (seasonally, during the first half of the year). The nests can be spotted as holes in the sand, and care must be taken not to step on them, or on the numerous creatures themselves. Indeed, Fernandina has the largest colony of marine iguanas in the Galápagos.

As you near the tip of the point, you will pass a large colony of sea lions. There are several territories encompassing both sides of the point, and the loud barks of several resident bulls blend with the hard pounding of the surf to add a dimension of sound to the experience. Starting in this area, and continuing out to the tip, are the flightless cormorants, nesting on the open rocks just above the high tide line. Occasionally, an adult will come out of the water bearing a piece of seaweed for the nest.

After walking the point for about a half hour, you retrace your steps almost to the landing area and continue on to a second trail which winds its way through a lava field. The recent volcanic activity is obvious from all the fissures, so watch your step. In fact, the land here is very fragile, and care must be taken to stay on the trail. While the lava flow has obliterated much of the vegetation on Fernandina, several pioneering plants can be observed, including clumps of lava cactus.

Unique Photo Opportunities: The sea lions are most photogenic when silhouetted against the high waves. I was able to spot two bulls standing at the edge of their territories and barking "not one step further" warnings at each other (see Photo #18). This is one of the few locations to photograph the flightless cormorant. The classic shot is taken after they exit the water as their atrophied wings are spread to dry the feathers (see Photo #57).

ISABELA (ALBEMARLE)

With over 1800 square miles (more than half the land surface area in the archipelago), and about 80 miles in length, the seahorse-shaped Isabela is the largest island in the Galápagos. This wasn't always the case, as originally there were six islands, each with an active volcano. The extensive lava flows from the six volcanoes (Alcedo, Cerro Azul, Darwin, Ecuador, Sierra Negra, and Wolf) joined together and formed what is today Isabela. Five of the six volcanoes (all but Ecuador) are still active. The Wolf Volcano is the highest point at 5600 ft.

There are several Visitor Sites on Isabela, including Punta Albemarle, Elizabeth Bay, Punta García, Punta Moreno, Tagus Cove, Punta Tortuga, Urvina Bay, and the town of Villamil. Two of the volcanoes, Alcedo and Sierra Negra, are also Visitor Sites. There are also a few special 3-day trips to the Cerro Azul Volcano, but this area is not discussed.

Punta Albemarle — Located at the northern tip of Isabela (forming the horns or raised ears of the seahorse), Punta Albemarle was used as a radar base by the U.S. during World War II. As one sails past, the abandoned water tanks can be viewed through a pair of binoculars. Often that's all that will be seen as very few boats land here, due in part to the rough surf.

Elizabeth Bay — Elizabeth Bay is situated on the west coast, about a third of the way up, at the narrow Perry Isthmus (6 miles wide). This is a Marine Visitor Site; landings are not permitted. The tour is a *panga* ride that begins with a visit to a few rocky islets where a small colony of penguins is usually found. The penguins prefer the cooler waters of the western portion of the archipelago, and it is only here that they breed. Flightless cormorants and giant marine iguanas are also seen. The largest marine iguanas in the Galápagos are found on Isabela, due to the upwelling activity which produces plentiful marine iguana food — algae.

The tour continues as the *panga* enters a narrow cove, lined with large red mangrove trees. Here, marine turtles, rays, and shore birds can be seen.

Unique Photo Opportunities: This is one of the best areas for penguin photos. There is limited lighting around the rocky caves where they are seen, and since most penguins are spotted early or late in the day, high speed (ASA 400) film is recommended. The backgrounds are beautiful, with the Alcedo Volcano to the north, the Sierra Negra Volcano to the south, and Fernandina across the water.

Punta García — Punta García is located on the eastern coast, across the Isabela Channel from James Island. Except for early in the morning, the dry landing is not an easy one. Sometimes not a very dry one either. All things considered, this is not my favorite Visitor Site, but it is the only opportunity to visit Isabela (and to see flightless cormorants) without sailing around to the western shore.

Unique Photo Opportunities: Aside from the lava flows, the subject here is the flightless cormorant (see the section above on Punta Espinosa, Fernandina Island). Take extra care in protecting your camera and photographic equipment on the usually-rough *panga* ride.

Punta Moreno — Situated on the southwest portion of Isabela, Punta Moreno is often the first western island Visitor Site for boats approaching from the south. The tour begins with a *panga* ride along the beautiful rocky shores where penguins and shore birds, including great blue herons, are usually spotted. The *panga* the enters a grove of mangroves, where oysters can be seen at the base of the trees. After a dry landing, a difficult trek begins that traverses the sharpest lava rocks in the islands. This is another tour to skip if you're not up for a rough hike. Also, this is a harsh, dry climate, and you may want to pack some water.

While the terrain is rough, this is a recommended tour. The environment is enigmatic; the driest lava fields you will ever see are interspersed with lagoons and small ponds containing abundant wildlife, including a few pintail ducks and flamingos. There are several clumps of lava cactus and other pioneering plants here, but a species of scalesia is also seen, as is the carpenter bee, one of the few insect pollinators in the Galápagos. There is verification at every vantage point that the advanced forms were here first and were partially displaced by subsequent eruptions of the Sierra Negra Volcano.

Unique Photo Opportunities: The *panga* ride offers the opportunity of several dramatic seascapes, especially early in the morning. In fact, this is one of the best sunrise areas I've seen in the Galápagos. The scalesia here make beautiful subjects, in particular when the bright green is shown in contrast to the stark, black lava.

Tagus Cove — Tagus Cove is located on the west coast, about two- thirds of the way up Isabela, across the narrow Channel from Fernandina. As soon as your boat enters this protected cove, you can (as they say) "see the writing on the wall." For here indeed are written the names of many ships, dating back to the 1800s. After a dry landing, you can view the graffiti from a closer distance, where it doesn't look any prettier. Fortunately the majority of the Guides prevent any further occurrences of this type of pollution.

The land tour is a bit strenuous in that a steep climb is involved; some people with difficulty walking may want to remain on the boat. This is also another of those dry areas, and a sip of packed water may be refreshing after the uphill climb. The tour begins at a trail leading to a salt water lagoon of unknown origin (because, oddly enough, it's higher than sea level). The trail slopes up the base of the Darwin Volcano, providing a great view of the fragile lava fields, the volcanic formations, and the ocean as well.

Unique Photo Opportunities: As you sail through the Bolívar Channel between Fernandina and Isabela, be on the lookout for whales and whale footprints (see the section on Whales in Chapter III). Several whales travel alone through this passage. The salt water lagoon, sometimes referred to as Darwin Lake, is optically interesting in that the water level looks at times higher (which it is) and at other times lower than sea level. You may be able to capture both effects on film.

The view from the plateau at the end of the trail can provide some dramatic shots with the rugged volcanic landscape in the foreground and the ocean in the distance.

Punta Tortuga — Located just north of Tagus Cove on the west coast of Isabela, Punta Tortuga is a bathing beach surrounded by mangroves. This is one of the few sites where the mangrove finch (one of the two tool-using finches) can be found in the Galápagos.

Urvina Bay — Urvina Bay is situated on the west coast of Isabela at the base of the Alcedo Volcano. In 1954, almost 4 miles of its coastal seabed, marine life and all, were dramatically and suddenly uplifted about 15 ft. This event is associated with an eruption of the Alcedo Volcano. The coastline was driven three-quarters of a mile further out to sea, forever exposing giant coral heads and stranding marine organisms on what was now the shore. The marine remnants and coral skeletons, some of them waist high, are visited after a wet landing on the beach. The landing can be a bit rough, so protect your photographic equipment.

Urvina Bay is also a nesting site for the brown pelican and flightless cormorant. Giant marine iguanas are also seen in this area along the coast, which you will visit prior to the uplifted marine relics.

Note: Your Guide will remind you that it is illegal to touch or take any of the marine remnants, including the deteriorating coral formations. Remember, if everyone took a little piece, in a short time there wouldn't be much left.

Unique Photo Opportunities: Aside from documenting this unusual geologic event, there are several surreal scenes of the uplifted marine skeletons that you will want to put on film.

Villamil — The town of Villamil is located on the southeastern coast of Isabela. Villamil was founded in 1897 by Antonio Gil as the center of a lime-producing operation (achieved by burning coral). During the same time period, a second town called Santo Tomás was located a few miles inland. Santo Tomás, named for the volcano next door (now generally called Sierra Negra), was formed as a small-scale sulfur operation, mined from the crater. A coffee plantation was also established. The combined population of the two towns is about 1000 people.

Adjacent to Villamil are several lagoons where flamingos and common stilts are usually seen; these are nesting areas from November-April, but the birds also feed here for a good portion of the year. There are also some very beautiful beaches that, along with the lagoons, are said to be among the most significant migratory bird viewing areas in the Galápagos.

There are visitor accommodations in Villamil, often used by tourists preparing to take the trip up the Sierra Negra Volcano (see below).

Unique Photo Opportunities: This is an excellent opportunity to photograph the common stilt, a most graceful and elegant bird; sometimes a few branches in the foreground can help capture these qualities (see Photo #56). Actually, I have found the lagoons here to be the most opportune as well as dramatic area in the islands to capture many of the shore birds on film, including flamingos, whimbrels, and occasional migrants.

Sierra Negra Volcano — Located in the southern portion of Isabela, the Sierra Negra Volcano is below the Perry Isthmus and above the Cerro Azul Volcano. Sierra Negra is considered to be the oldest and largest volcano on Isabela, with its caldera measuring about 5 miles by 6 miles across. A 1-2 day trip to the rim of Sierra Negra is available as an option to some of the 2 week Galápagos tours.

A 2 day Sierra Negra trip is recommended for maximum enjoyment. The tour begins at Villamil where a rented vehicle takes the group to Santo Tomás. From here, the 3-5 hour trip to the caldera can be made on foot or by horseback. The tour continues around the rim of the caldera until the Volcán Chico area is reached, a series of craters with fumaroles (columns of volcanic steam and gas) rising into the air. This area last erupted in 1979, but that event was not as dramatic as the month-long eruption of 1963. The site of vast sulfur deposits (vented from the fumarole of the "Sulfur Volcano," as it is called) is also visited.

Camping is permitted at the caldera rim so long as all trash is carried back down. Campfires are not allowed; gasoline or kerosene stoves must be rented and brought along. The caldera itself may not be entered.

Note: Two notes of caution. The first is the weather, which can often be overcast and misty (during the *garúa* season, from June-December) or actually be raining (January-April). Thus, the recommended time of the year to visit the Sierra Negra Volcano is from April-June. Rain gear is always advised. The second caution is related to the foggy weather, which often causes visitors to get separated and sometimes lost. It is very important to stay together.

Unique Photo Opportunities: The scenery of the highlands, the fumaroles, and misty environment combine to present many photographic opportunities — often spectacular and quite beautiful, sometimes surreal, probably dramatic, always unique, and quite often all the above.

Alcedo Volcano — The Alcedo Volcano is centrally located and just north of the Perry Isthmus. Aside from Sierra Negra, Alcedo is the oldest and largest of the volcanoes on Isabela, with the caldera measuring about 4 miles by 5 miles across. There are several steaming fumaroles, often used by hikers as a landmark, with the largest of these steam and gas vents called "the Geyser."

Two week Galápagos tours sometimes offer a 1-2 day trip to the rim of the Alcedo Volcano. Few of the Tour Operators recommend or offer the 1 day trip, due to the physical exertion required (to get back to the boat before nightfall) and the lack of quality visiting time. Thus, most Alcedo trips camp overnight on the rim of the volcano.

The Alcedo excursions are logistically very difficult. To begin with, it is the most difficult trek in the Galápagos. It is a long 6 mile climb (4-6 hours each way), part of it over steep, rugged terrain. So you have to be physically fit. And have a strong back if you are spending the night, because you'll have to pack 25-35 pounds up the volcano. Unlike the hike to Sierra Negra, there is no nearby town to rent horses or hire porters to carry the camping equipment, food, and water (one-half gallon per person per day minimum). In addition, most Tour Operators require passengers to supply their own sleeping bags, backpacks, water bottle, and flashlight. Eating and cooking utensils, food, and tents are typically provided.

To complicate things further, it's best if all the passengers go on the trek. Those that stay behind must remain on the boat for the duration of the hike; they cannot even take a walk on the beach (because the legally-required Guide is elsewhere, climbing the side of a volcano). The result is that the Tour Operator can have problems putting the trip together, because while some of the prospective passengers may be avid hikers, some are not, and the rest aren't sure. Also, the hike cannot be arranged on an impromptu basis, as the captain must secure a camping permit in advance of the trip.

The Alcedo Volcano climb begins early in the day (around 5:30 a.m.) with a wet landing at Shipton Cove on the east coast of Isabela. The approach trail is fairly easy, a gradual incline over smooth pumice (porous lava — basically road construction material). The final ascent, however, is very steep, the terrain is very uneven, and the unmarked "trail" is overgrown with shrubs. The last few hundred feet can take over an hour to negotiate. The rim is reached early in the afternoon, before the severe heat of the day. Those on a 1 day trip will stop for a light lunch, continue around the rim for a bit, and then head back down. For those staying the night, camp is made before proceeding (without most of the weight).

And now for the good news. The views up here are beautiful. The fumaroles are also very impressive. Also, this area is home to the largest population of giant tortoises (over 4000) in the Galápagos. And they are in the wild, not in holding pens. During the rainy season (January-June), they can be seen wallowing in mud pools. There are several Galápagos hawks in the area as well as vermillion flycatchers. Those of you that camp on the rim will savor the experience of this location, the edge of a still-active volcano, a special place on earth where few people have set foot. The fact that you worked hard to get there will not escape your senses.

The following day brings a sunrise you don't want to miss and a more extensive hike along the rim before the descent back to the beach and, finally, the boat.

Note: As your Guide will point out, no campfires are permitted. All trash has to be carried back down and taken to the boat. Also, no fruits or vegetables are allowed on shore, as the seeds represent potential introduced plants. Finally, evenings and nights will be wet, so pack appropriately.

Unique Photo Opportunities: I can think of no better way of describing the photographic opportunities that await the visitor to the Alcedo Volcano than to refer the reader to the opening pages of Tui de Roy's inspiring book, **GALAPAGOS: ISLANDS LOST IN TIME**. Softly-lit tortoises immersed in pools of mud and rain with several fumaroles in the distance, a hawk spreading its talons to land while a storm builds over the caldera, one photo after the other perfectly captures the images of Alcedo. You and I can do our best and capture our own images as we see them. It's mostly a matter of being there with a camera in hand and a positive-thinking eye.

THE OUTER ISLANDS

The outer islands of Darwin (Culpepper) and Wolf (Wenman) are, as they say, off the scale; they are located way to the northwest, separated from the other islands by about 100 miles. There are no Visitor Sites on Darwin and Wolf, although diving trips may occasionally visit their waters.

LITERATURE

This section is divided into categories of essential ("must"), recommended, and background (or reference) reading. Some of these publications are becoming a little easier to find in the U.S., especially in travel-oriented bookstores, but there is still a reasonably good chance that your local, friendly bookshop will have to place a special order for you.

Once in Quito, you will want to visit **Libri Mundi** (located at Juan León Mera 851), without a doubt, the best bookstore in Ecuador; they have a comprehensive selection of Galápagos literature. While **Libri Mundi** has a smaller branch in the arcade mall of the Hotel Colón, the main store is just a few blocks away from the major hotels.

Many of these books are also available through **Galápagos Travel**, the publisher of the book you are reading; call (800) 969-9014 to confirm availability, price and delivery, and/or to place an order.

MUST READING

I consider the following books and published material to be "must reading" for those wanting to learn as much as possible about the Galápagos prior to, during, and after touring the islands. Many of these books will allow you to more fully comprehend what the Naturalist Guide (and/or Tour Leader) is pointing out, and you will thus be able to ask more advanced questions. You will also be able to identify more species and behavioral characteristics on your own. Finally, you'll be free to tune out some of the tour lecture (to the extent that you are familiar with the material being discussed) and concentrate on picture taking.

A FIELD GUIDE TO THE FISHES OF GALAPAGOS, 3rd Edition. Godfrey Merlin, 1988. Quito, Ecuador: Libri Mundi. An indispensable identification guide; the color illustrations are superb. Available in Quito and the Galápagos. *There is usually a race for this book after a Galápagos snorkeling session "to see what we saw."*

FISHES OF THE PACIFIC COAST, Gar Goodson, 1988. Stanford, CA: Stanford University Press. This guidebook will familiarize you with the fishes of the Pacific coast including the Galápagos Islands. Each species is shown in full color along with a thorough guide to identification and description of behavioral traits. The book also illustrates the differences between a juvenile, adult, and breeding stage of the same fish. *Inexpensive and very informative; use it together with the Merlin book (see above).*

GALAPAGOS: A NATURAL HISTORY GUIDE, M.H. Jackson, 1992. Calgary: University of Calgary Press. This is, without a doubt, the most comprehensive natural history guide to the Galápagos Islands, including well-written chapters on evolution & ecology, plant life, reptiles, sea birds, land birds, native mammals, intertidal & marine life, and conservation. In addition, the first 3 chapters give the reader an environmental, historical, and scientific background to the Galápagos. Both a General Index and Species Index are provided as well as a complete checklist of plants and animals. *Of all the books, this is the most important. Buy this book as soon as you can and take it with you!*

THE ORIGIN, Irving Stone, 1980. New York: Doubleday & Co. A fascinating biography of Charles Darwin, the most famous and significant evolutionary biologist we have known. But many of us do not know much about Darwin himself or the extent of his accomplishments. Also, why did it take Darwin almost 25 years to publish *Origin of Species*? And why didn't he ever take a second voyage? Irving Stone answers these questions and many more in a well-researched narrative account that traces Darwin's life and achivements, including his prolific writings. Stone also captures Darwin's moods, his constant battle with illness, his family life, and his friendships/professional relationships with the leading scientists of 19th century England. *A captivating book that is difficult to put down. If you start off reading it on the plane ride to the Galápagos, it will be your constant cruise companion.*

PLANTS OF THE GALAPAGOS ISLANDS, Eileen Schofield, 1984. New York: Universe Books. This handy pocket-sized book is the best field guide to the flora of the Galápagos Islands. Illustrated by the author, this book will help you identify the unique and unusual plants of the Galápagos Islands.

MY FATHER'S ISLAND: A GALAPAGOS QUEST, Johanna Angermeyer, 1989. New York: Viking Penguin. A beautifully written book, **My Father's Island**, is a true story about the author and the summers of her early adolescence, which were spent in the Galápagos. It is in the rustic setting of these enchanted isles that Johanna begins the search for her identity and her past. For it was here that her father Hans somehow died in the 1940s. Hans was one of four Angermeyer brothers who sailed for the Galápagos in 1935, leaving the politics of Germany behind them. As Johanna matures, she learns more of the bittersweet details. Under the tutelage of her aunts and uncles, she also learns the details of island life in a beautiful yet arid and often harsh environment. The book is especially relevant for the traveler, as the offspring of the Angermeyer family now rank among the best captains of the touring yachts that sail the waters of the Galápagos archipelago. *Great to read while you're touring the islands.*

SPANISH AT A GLANCE: PHRASE BOOK & DICTIONARY FOR TRAVELERS, 1984. Hauppauge, NY: Barron's Educational Series. This is everything you need to learn the basics of Spanish. You get a pocket-sized situation phrase book/dictionary and a cassette tape (to get the sound of the language). The comprehensive 200 page phrase book is broken up into several sections including Most Frequently Used Expressions, Slang, Colloquialisms, Passport and Customs, Hotel Services, Getting Around Town, Eating Out, Meeting People, Shopping, Driving a Car, Telling Time, Weather, etc. The examples are very useful and easy to learn. *Take this book with you, and keep it within reach.*

RECOMMENDED READING

A CENTURY AFTER DARWIN'S DEATH, Dieter and Mary Plage, January, 1988. *National Geographic*, Vol. 173, pp. 123-145. A good photographic and written essay, which serves an excellent introduction to the Galápagos. Back issues of **National Geographic** are available at most libraries. *Read this article as soon as you can!*

ECUADOR & THE GALAPAGOS ISLANDS: A TRAVEL SURVIVAL KIT, Rob Rachowiecki, 1992. Berkeley: Lonely Planet Publications. A good, readable guide to Ecuador, including hotels, restaurants, shopping and touring in all regions of the country; there are complete sections on Quito and Guayaquil. The information on the Galápagos is of the summary variety.

THE ENCHANTED ISLANDS: THE GALAPAGOS DISCOVERED, John Hickman, 1985. Dover, New Hampshire: Tanager Books. An excellent human history of the Galápagos, from the Incas, through the whaling and buccaneer era, the days of Darwin, and up to modern day tourism, including issues of conservation.

FLOREANA, Margret Wittmer, 1989. Shropshire, England: Anthony Nelson Ltd. Margret Wittmer has written her own firsthand version of the mysterious deaths and disappearances that took place on Floreana Island during the 1930s (see **The Gálapagos Affair** below). **Floreana,** (translated from the German **Postlagernd Floreana**, published in 1959), also chronicles Margret Wittmer's 60 years on Floreana Island. The book is available throughout Ecuador and the Galápagos. *Those that visit the Wittmer Cafe and Pension on Floreana may have the opportunity of getting the book autographed by Mrs. Wittmer and/or a member of the family.*

THE GALAPAGOS MARINE RESOURCES RESERVE, *Oceanus*, Volume 30, Number 2, Summer 1987. MA: Woods Hole Oceanographic Institution. An informative collection of articles on subjects ranging from diving, the development of tourism, and the effects of the 1982-82 El Niño, to sperm whale behavior, fishes of the Galápagos, and a historical perspective of marine biological research in the islands.

MARINE LIFE OF THE GALAPAGOS, Pierre Constant, 1992. Paris: Calao Life Experience. This 248 page book (with 216 color photos) is the only comprehensive field guide to the marine life of the islands. There are descriptions, photos, and lists of fishes (grouped by family), sharks, rays, whales, and invertebrates (grouped by phylum and class), and it is extensively cross-referenced. While the book documents all the marine fauna, the information is a bit fragmented and not very polished in its presentation. Perhaps future editions will be more "together." *Essential for the avid snorkeler and all divers.*

PORTRAITS OF GALAPAGOS, Tui De Roy and Mark Jones, 1990. Quito, Ecuador: The Roving Tortoise. The latest work by Tui De Roy, author of the classic, **Galápagos: Islands Lost in Time** (see the Background and Reference Material section below). A collection of beautiful photos of the islands' fascinating wildlife including an intimate description of each photograph.

SOUTH AMERICAN HANDBOOK, Edited by John Brooks, 1993. New York: Prentice Hall. An absolute giant of a book in terms of both scope and detail. There are sections on every country in South America, Central America, the Bahamas, and West Indies in addition to Cuba, Haiti, Dominican Republic, and others. I have never seen type set so small and pages as thin. This isn't a book that you fall in love with; it is, however, very good reference material. *Take a copy of the section on Ecuador (and a magnifying glass) with you.*

SPANISH IN 10 MINUTES A DAY, Kristine Kershul, 1988. Menlo Park, CA: Lane Publishing. Part of a **Sunset Series,** this is a great book for those with no Spanish whatsoever. As the title suggests, a brief (yet consistent) daily session will quickly give you a feel for the language, the confidence to make the effort and say a few words, and the motivation to continue learning. *Recommended for beginners.*

SUBTIDAL GALAPAGOS, James Cribb, 1986. Ontario: Camden House Publishing Ltd. Distributed by Firefly Books, Scarborough, Ontario, Canada. A diving oddysey of the Galápagos, written and photograhed in the first person. A coffeetable variety book, with many excellent color plates. *Recommended for divers.*

VOYAGE OF THE BEAGLE, Charles Darwin, 1845. London: John Murray. Garden city, NY: Doubleday. Chapter XVII, GALAPAGOS ARCHIPELAGO, is truly fascinating while lounging on the boat, whereas it may seem a bit dull if read before you leave. *Take a copy of this chapter with you!*

BACKGROUND AND REFERENCE MATERIAL

Several of the following books are listed as "out of print." They may still be available through your local library and/or "used book/book search" dealers.

THE COLLINS FIELD GUIDE TO THE BIRDS OF GALAPAGOS, Michael Harris, 1974. London: Collins Sons & Co. This compact book is the only field guide to the Galápagos avifauna — complete with color plates. *As of 1993, this book was out of print.*

DARWIN'S ISLANDS: A NATURAL HISTORY OF THE GALAPAGOS, Ian Thonton, 1971. New York: Natural History Press. An important work and for many years the only natural history guide to the Galápagos.

ECOLOGY AND EVOLUTION IN DARWIN'S FINCHES, Peter Grant, 1986. Princeton, NJ: Princeton University Press. Peter Grant and his students have conducted extensive research studies on the Darwin's finches, including the actual mechanics of natural selection. There are 16 chapters in all, dealing with general characteristics, patterns of morphological variation, adaptation, and speciation. Generalizations are also made to evolutionary dynamics of other species. *This is the definite text on the Darwin's finches. Recommended for birders, ornithologists, and anyone seriously interested in evolutionary theory.*

THE ENCANTADAS, Herman Melville, 1854. First published as a serial in Harper's Monthly, this tale of the Galápagos subsequently appeared in its entirety as part of a collection of Melville short stories called **The Piazza Tales**, published in 1856 by Dix and Edwards, London. Melville spent several years on New England whaling ships, and the rich narrative expressed here (as well as in **Moby Dick**) was acquired firsthand. Never one to hold back an opinion, Melville vividly describes the harsh environment of the Galápagos in terms of a hell on earth, complete with fiery eruptions, demonic animals, and islands that are little more than heaps of ashes.

EVER SINCE DARWIN, Stephen Jay Gould, 1977. New York: W.W. Norton. One of several excellent books by the great evolutionary biologist, Steven Jay Gould; each book is a thematic compilation of his monthly essays in *Natural History* magazine.

FLORA OF THE GALAPAGOS ISLANDS, Ira L. Wiggins, and Duncan M. Porter, 1971. Palo Alto, CA: Stanford University Press. The complete reference guide to the Galápagos plant life.

EXPLORING TROPICAL ISLES AND SEAS: AN INTRODUCTION FOR THE TRAVELER AND AMATEUR NATURALIST, Frederic Martini, 1984. Englewood Cliffs, NJ: Prentice-Hall, Inc. Stimulating descriptions on several relevant topics, including the life on an island, the tropical environment and marine reptiles and mammals. The chapter on marine fishes is fascinating, beginning with a description of "what exactly a fish is" and then functionally classifying groups of fishes as Generalists, Speeders, Maneuverers, Wrigglers, Commandos, Grazers, and Advertisers. *Highly recommended and, unfortunately, out of print.*

THE GALAPAGOS AFFAIR, John Treherne, 1983. New York: Random House. During the 1930s the Island of Floreana was the scene of a real-life Agatha Christie mystery (unsolved to this very day) that could easily carry the title of "Death in Paradise." John Treherne offers a complete and fascinating account of this who-done-it. *Unfortunately, this book is out of print, but is available at many libraries.*

GALAPAGOS: A TERRESTRIAL AND MARINE PHENOMENON, Paul Humann, 1988. Quito, Ecuador: Libri Mundi. Distributed in the U.S. By Publishers Group West, Emeryville, CA. Paul Humann has been leading dive trips to the islands for many years; this is the best collection of underwater photographs (194 full color plates) of the Galápagos archipelago. *Highly recommended and, once again, out of print.*

GALAPAGOS FISHES: A COMPREHENSIVE GUIDE TO THEIR IDENTIFICATION, Jack S. Grove and Robert S. Lavenberg, 1990. Palo Alto, CA: Stanford University Press. Reviewed by 75 ichthyologists (and over 10 years in the making), this book, containing over 2300 drawings, as of this writing, was still "in press."

GALAPAGOS: ISLANDS LOST IN TIME, Tui De Roy, 1980. New York: Viking Press. Tui has spent almost all her life in the Galápagos; her love for these islands and the countless days she has spent observing and documenting its wilderness and wildlife is shared with the reader in an inspiring manner. This book, conveying the feel of the Galápagos like no other, is a collection of what is generally considered to be the most beautiful photographs ever taken of the islands accompanied by a sensitively-written text. Unfortunately the publisher has decided to take this book out of print despite its excellence and populatiry among Galápagos travelers.

GALAPAGOS: ISLANDS OF BIRDS, Bryan Nelson, 1968. New York: William Morrow. An in-depth look at the behavior patterns of the Galápagos sea birds. Byron Nelson and his wife actually camped out on Española (Hood) and Tower (Genovesa) Islands for a year, when (prior to tourism) it was still possible for an author to do so.

GALAPAGOS: WORLD'S END, William Beebe, 1924. New York: Dover Publications. Beebe, a renowned biologist and explorer, led a scientific expedition to the archipelago sponsored by the *New York Zoological Society*; his book paints a romantic account of this voyage. Without sacrificing technical accuracy, this book was (during its day) a blend of popular science and adventure travel at its best. It quickly became a best seller, inspiring many to follow in Beebe's footsteps. *Good background reading!*

KEY ENVIRONMENTS: GALAPAGOS, Edited by Roger Perry, 1984. Oxford, England: Pergamon Press. A comprehensive summary of the scientific knowledge of the flora and fauna of the Galápagos archipelago. There are 19 chapters, each written by a scientist who has conducted important research in areas of specialization, including geology, oceanography, terrestrial plants, inshore fish, giant tortoises, sea birds, land birds, iguanas, and sea lions.

ON THE ORIGIN OF SPECIES, Charles Darwin, 1859. London: John Murray. Garden city, NY: Doubleday. A classic; the ideas set forth in this work remain today as one of the major breakthroughs in scientific thought, and led the way for over 150 years of biological research.

GENERAL INDEX

TOUR OPERATIONS INDEX

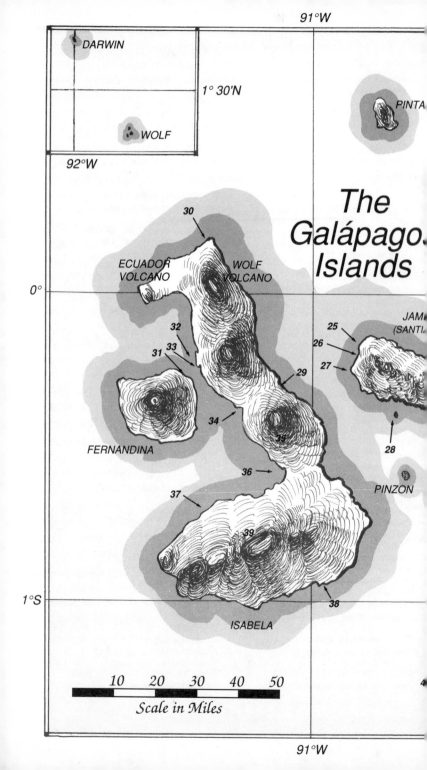

The Galápago.
Islands

90°W

Visitor Sites

1. Gardner Bay
2. Punta Suárez
3. Lobos Is.
4. Frigatebird Hill
5. El Junco Lake
6. Kicker Rock
7. Sapho Cove
8. Punta Pitt
9. Santa Fe Is.
10. S. Plaza Is.
11. Tortuga Bay
12. Whale Bay
13. Conway Bay
14. Las Baches
15. Caleta Tortuga Negra
16. Daphne Major Is.
17. Seymour Is.
18. Mosquera Is.
19. Baltra Is.
20. Darwin Bay
21. Prince Philip's Steps
22. Sombrero Chino Is.

23. Bartolomé Is.
24. Sullivan Bay
25. Buccaneer Cove
26. Espumilla Beach
27. James Bay
28. Rábida Is.
29. Punta García
30. Punta Albemarle
31. Punta Espinosa
32. Punta Tortuga
33. Tagus Cove
34. Urvina Bay
35. Alcedo Volcano
36. Elizabeth Bay
37. Punta Moreno
38. Villamil
39. Sierra Negra Volcano
40. Black Beach
41. Post Office Bay
42. Punta Cormorán
43. Devil's Crown

MARCHENA

TOWER
(GENOVESA)

20
21

$\mathcal{N}$

16
17
18
15
4
19

10

9

NTA CRUZ

SANTA FE

6
7
8
3

SAN
CRISTOBAL

43

FLOREANA

1

2

ESPANOLA
(HOOD)

0°

1°S

90°W

Puerto Ayora, Santa Cruz Island

1. Natl. Park Information Ctr.
2. Natl. Park Dock
3. Darwin Research Station
4. Hotel Galápagos
5. Cemetary
6. Residencia Angermeyer
7. Pizzeria
8. Pension Gloria
9. Boat Works
10. Quasar Nautica
11. Four Lanterns Restaurant
12. SAN Airlines
13. Hotel Solymar
14. La Garrapata Restaurant
15. La Panga Disco Bar
16. Church
17. Hotel Lobo Del Mar
18. Police
19. TAME Airlines
20. La Chifa Restaurant
21. Naval Base
22. Waterfront Park
23. Main Dock
24. Post Office
25. First Aid
26. INGALA
27. Pharmacy
28. Telegraph Office
29. Tortuga Bay
30. Puerto Ayora
31. Bella Vista
32. Los Túneles
33. Santa Rosa
34. Whale Bay
35. Conway Bay
36. Los Gemelos
37. Las Baches
38. Caleta Tortuga Negra
39. Daphnes Islets
40. Seymour Is.
41. Mosquera Is.
42. Baltra Is.
43. Itabaca Channel
44. Gordon Rocks
45. Plaza Islets